D1031725

THE
UNIVERSITY OF WINNIPEG
PORTAGE & BALMORAL
WINNIPEG, MAN.   R3B 2E9
CANADA

DRAMA
in the
People's Republic
of
CHINA

PN
2874
D7
1937

DISCARDED

DRAMA
in the
People's Republic
of
CHINA

EDITED BY

Constantine Tung

AND

Colin Mackerras

STATE UNIVERSITY OF NEW YORK PRESS

Published by
State University of New York Press, Albany

© 1987   State University of New York

All rights reserved

Printed in the United States of America

No part of this book may be used or reproduced
in any manner whatsoever without written permission
except in the case of brief quotations embodied in
critical articles and reviews.

For information, address State University of New York
Press, State University Plaza, Albany, N.Y., 12246

Library of Congress Cataloging-in-Publication Data

Drama in the People's Republic of China.

   Selected papers presented at the International
Colloquium on Contemporary Chinese Drama and Theater,
held at the State University of New York at Buffalo,
Oct. 15-19, 1984.
   Includes index.
   1. Theater—China—History—20th century—
Congresses. 2. Chinese drama—20th century—History
and criticism—Congresses. 3. Theater—Political
aspects—China—Congresses. 4. Theater and society—
China—Congresses. I. Tung, Constantine, 1933-
II. Mackerras, Colin. III. International Colloquium
on Contemporary Chinese Drama and Theater (1984 :
State University of New York at Buffalo

PN2874.D7 1987   792'.0951   86-5932
ISBN 0-88706-389-6
ISBN 0-88706-390-X (pbk.)

10 9 8 7 6 5 4 3 2 1

Table of Contents

Preface and Acknowledgements

During the week of October 15-19, 1984, a conference, the International Colloquium on Contemporary Chinese Drama and Theater, was held at the State University of New York at Buffalo (UB). The Colloquium was the first of its kind ever to be held in the West or in China, and it resulted from our realization that drama, a dynamic but frequently ideologically and politically controversial art form in China, had not been given deserved critical attention. In October 1985, a year after the Colloquium at UB, a conference on modern Chinese dramatic literature was held in Beijing and hailed in the Chinese press as the first in China since the birth of modern Chinese drama in the 1910s.

The International Colloquium at UB was attended by scholars and specialists from Australia, Austria, Brazil, Canada, China, England, the Federal Republic of Germany, Norway and the United States. This volume of collected essays is a direct result of the week-long gathering. Unfortunately we were unable to include all the papers presented at the Colloquium in this volume as the limited space available inevitably narrowed the scope of choice. Bernd Eberstein, Barbara Kaulbach, Kenneth Rea, Chung-wen Shih, Tian Fen, Rudolf Wagner, Elizabeth Wichmann, Norman Wilkinson, and Terezinha N. M. Zaratin all made significant contributions to the success of the Colloquium with their stimulating and insightful papers.

Roger DesForges, Anna K. France, Esther Harriet, C. T. Hsia, Genevieve James, Krystyna Madajewicz, Robert Newman, David Richards, and Yan Haiping chaired panels, served as discussants, and/or took part in discussions. Their participation enhanced the liveliness of the Colloquium and furthered our understanding of contemporary Chinese drama. Furthermore, Chen Gang, Gao Xingjian and Su Shuyang, our colleagues from China, who were unable to attend, also sent their papers. We missed their presence but deeply appreciated their support and contributions.

Our sincere thanks go first to Michael Metzger, then chairman of UB's Department of Modern Languages and Literatures, who, from the very first hour of planning, gave us his unreserved support, without which the conference could never have gotten off the ground. Robert Fitzpatrick and Shirley Stout of UB's Research Administration, Susan B. Burger, Cele Cook, Saul Elkin, Richard Loew, Manuel Lopez, Nina Luban, Arlene Murawski, Gerald O'Grady, Laurence Schneider, Phyllis Sigel and Marilyn Thompson lent their time and their expertise, which assured a smooth progression from the planning stages to the final arrangements.

We acknowledge with gratitude a grant to the Colloquium from the National Endowment for the Humanities, a federal agency which supports the study of such fields as literature, languages, history and philosophy, whose support also made the publication of this volume possible. The Chancellor's Office of International Programs of the State University of New York in Albany, UB's Office of Research and Graduate Studies, and the Speakers Bureau of UB's Student Association all provided financial support to this unprecedented undertaking. The appearance of this volume is to be credited also to William D. Eastman, director of the State University of New York Press, for his interest in, support of and patience with this undertaking.

INTRODUCTION

Tradition and Experience of the Drama of the People's Republic of China

CONSTANTINE TUNG

No country believes more deeply in the power of drama or takes greater pains about what is in a play than does the People's Republic of China, and no drama in any country and in history has been so frequently and so directly involved and used in ideological feuds, political purges, mass campaigns and high-level power struggles as has that of the People's Republic of China. Martin Esslin states that "all drama is . . . a political event; it either asserts or undermines the code of conduct of a given society."[1] He further explains that "there are always social implications in any dramatic situation and in the solution of any dramatic conflict simply because all human situations, all human behavior patterns, have social — and therefore also political — implications."[2] But did Mr. Esslin ever encounter such direct ties between drama and politics as are found in China today?

The traditions of contemporary Chinese drama is deeply rooted in the history of the Chinese Communist Revolution in which drama activities were intimately integrated with political and military action. In the summer of 1930, when the Political Department (*Zhengzhi bu*) was established in the Red Army and an Art Bureau (*Yishi gu*) was attached to it in order to strengthen propaganda activities in the Jiangxi Soviet, theater, as a most important subgroup in the Art Bureau, was for the first time formally recognized to be a useful tool to advance the communist revolutionary cause. When the Red Army Military Academy (*Gongnong hong-jun xuexiao*) was founded in the winter of the same year, drama had its own department within the Academy. Such high ranking leaders as Wu Xiuquan, Cai Chang, He Shuheng and Xu Teli had participated in acting on stage, and prominent military leaders such as Lo Ruiqing, Liu Bocheng and Huang Zhen, not only took part in performances but also wrote plays.[3]

1

After Mao Zedong's famous "Talks at the Yan'an Forum on Literature and Art" in May 1942, the Communist Party's literary policy became definite, and drama was entrusted with vital roles in the war. In the "Resolution on the Execution of the Party's Literary and Art Policies," issued by the Propaganda Department of the Chinese Communist Party Central on November 7, 1949, the Party directed that among all literary and art forms, drama and news communications were to be developed first. The Party recognized that spoken drama and song-plays (*geju*), if they were appropriate in form, easy to stage, and if they reflected the people's will and sentiments, were the most effective weapons to mobilize and educate the masses to fight persistently in the war and to increase productivity. Therefore, the Communist Party's Propaganda Department directed that drama activities should be universally promoted in the army units and in all regions under their control.[4] At the same time the Propaganda Department criticized the practice at many revolutionary bases of staging full-length spoken dramas that were irrelevant to the war and traditional plays that advocated feudal orders. Thus the Propaganda Department demanded that these performances should either be halted or the contents of the plays ought to be revised.[5]

The 1943 Resolution's critical attitude toward full-length spoken drama which was unrelated to war foreshadowed the lasting conflict between the utilitarian stand of the Party on arts and the aesthetic and professional views held by the playwrights and performers in the subsequent decades. One veteran writer admitted that in drama the period between 1940 and 1941 was a time in which artistic quality was stressed. In the Lu Xun Art Institute (*Lu Xun yishu xueyuan*), members were convinced that raising artistic quality and popularization were incompatible, and they considered that their "foremost and the only mission" was to improve the artistic quality of a work of art. In the Institute's Drama Department, faculty and students alike placed more emphasis on theatrical techniques and were interested in staging full-length and foreign plays. Following the lead of the Lu Xun Art Institute, many district drama troupes also began to stage "big plays." There were individual theater companies which adhered to the mass-line, but they were unable to reverse the situation.[6] Consequently, the Party Central decided to intervene, and decreed that the main responsibility of the drama workers was to direct mass theaters and mass drama activities in the army units and local districts.[7]

In spite of problems and difficulties, drama activities spread throughout the communist controlled areas. In the border region of Hebei-Shanxi alone, by the end of 1943, there were 1381 village drama groups, and over 1,000 in the central Hebei Province.[8] To develop such a widely spread theatrical network, the Party paid special attention to the development of amateur drama activities because theatrical activities of this kind were suitable to the rural condition of China, which was at this time in a prolonged and large-scale war with Japan. Drama activities in villages were scheduled to coordinate with changes of the farming seasons. A village theater group performed mainly for the audiences from the village and its expenses were taken care of by the villagers, based on the values of their farm products. The Party knew well that the level of expenses of a village drama group could often affect the attitude of villagers toward drama activities. In playwriting, short pieces were encouraged and popular,[9] and contemporary themes were emphasized for obvious reasons. According to a survey of 56 *yangge* plays performed during the time of the Chinese lunar New Year, 1944, there were 26 plays on farm productivity, 17 on army-people relationships, 10 on self-defense against the enemy and on sabotage-prevention, 2 on fighting behind enemy lines, and only one on rent and interest reduction.[10] These statistics reveal the directness of the relationship of this drama to the political and military actions of the Communist Revolution during the Sino-Japanese war.

The war against Japan ended with the beginning of the civil war between the Communists and the KMT. As the war went on drama troupes became more directly involved in the war. In the Communist First Field Army, for instance, its Fighting Drama Society (*zhandou jushe*) was divided into small groups of six which went down to various army units to give simple performances. In the areas where land reforms were going on, the performers were all sent down to assist land reforms. The Literary and Art Work Group (*Wenyi gongzuotuan*) of the Second Field Army, of which Deng Xiaoping was the political commissar, was directed to send its members to be directors or political agitators of the battle units of the Second Field Army. When the Second Field Army entered the Dabie Mountains in central China in 1947, these drama performers were dispersed to take part in land reform campaigns. In 1947–48, as the war with the KMT reached a critical point, all members of the performing arts groups were armed to join in the battle and at the same time gave performances to the soldiers and guerrilla fighters "with guns lying beside them." Many of them were killed in action.[11]

The direct and very personal experiences of the drama workers in using drama as a revolutionary weapon closely integrated with political and military action strengthened their utilitarian concept of drama. A drama born and nurtured in revolution and wars fostered an almost unshakable belief in the power and effectiveness of drama in propaganda, agitation and ideological indoctrination. Ironically, the other side of the belief in the power of the drama is an excessive sensitivity to and suspicion of even the slightest deviations from the norm expressed in a play. The Party wanted sure control of this effective weapon, drama.

When the People's Republic of China was founded in October 1949, not only the Communist Party, but also the dramatists, were confronting a new situation that challenged their experience; they had entered a new cultural milieu dominated by the cities. In matters of culture and art, cities like Beijing and Shanghai were far more sophisticated and advanced than villages and Yan'an. Under these circumstances, rifts occurred between the Party and the playwright. For the playwright, there was the conflict between his instincts and professional desire to be an artist and his awareness of being a revolutionary whose foremost task is political. Politics demands popularization of art for utilitarian purposes, but an artist dreams of creative autonomy and aesthetic excellence which in reality must be free from imposed political requirements. What Mao Zedong tried to tramp out at the Yan'an Forum on Literature and Art in 1942 has remained the center of conflict between the Party and the artist in post-1949 China. In other words, it is the Party's demand that art serve extrinsic functions versus the artist's concern for art's intrinsic values.

The Party, in the post-revolutionary time, still attempted to maintain the long revolutionary tradition in which drama's foremost mission is to serve the worker-peasant-soldier masses.[12] In his report made in July 1955, Tian Han, the then chairman of the Chinese Dramatists Association, claimed that since 1953, the Ministry of Culture had mobilized state-owned and semi-private theater troupes to perform in the countryside, mines, factories and railroad construction sites. In 1953 alone, the state-owned theater troupes gave more than 41,000 performances to an audience of over 45,070,000. Of the total performances, 5,200 were staged in the factories and mines with an audience of 7,910,000; more than 2,500 performances were given in the countryside to an audience of 4,140,000. For the armed forces the number of performances exceeded 5,600 audiences comprised of 7,360,000 soldiers.

In 1954 more theatrical performances were staged for the worker-peasant-soldier audiences. More than 57,000 performances, an astonishing increase of 36% over 1953, were given by state-owned theaters to audiences numbering 62,130,000, 37% more than in 1953. Of these, over 9,300 performances (78% more than the 1953 figure) were staged in mines and factories for 13,850,000 workers (an increase of 75% from 1953); over 3,100 performances were given in the rural areas (an increase of 24% from 1953) to 5,240,000 peasants (26% more than the 1953 figure), and for the armed forces, more than 7,200 performances (a

28% increase from 1953) were presented to 9,210,000 soldiers (an increase of 25% from 1953).[13]

These figures illustrate clearly the strong emphasis on theatrical activities of a mass-oriented mission with particular attention focused on workers and soldiers. The drama continued its service to the political needs of the nation.

During the Cultural Revolution decade from 1966 to 1976, the belief in the power of theatrical art as an effective weapon in political struggles was reinforced by the fact that the Cultural Revolution leaders, notably the Gang of Four and their associates, were largely ideologists, literary critics and, like Jiang Qing herself, theatrical performers. Ironically, it was this group of "literary" people that virtually destroyed the Chinese theater; their obsessive concern about the power of theater led them to seek absolute control of that "powerful" weapon. At the same time, great efforts were made by the Cultural Revolutionists to pouplarize their "model plays," the plays that had achieved the "perfect" ideological reliability, by means of "transplanting" them into other local and regional theatrical forms and by developing amateur drama groups. The promotion of amateur theater groups was "not entertainment for entertainment's sake. Amateur theater groups are used . . . to propagate Marxism, Leninism, and Mao Zedong thought to the people, to carry out the educational goals on the ideological and political battlefront, to coordinate closely with actual struggles and to serve the great revolutionary movements." For the Cultural Revolutionists, the promotion of such amateur theater groups in every corner of the country was "a necessity for the control of the idealogical and cultural battlefield, . . . and for strengthening the proletarian dictatorship."[14] The use of and the belief in drama as a political weapon thus reached an extreme during the Cultural Revolution years.

The Party's demand that drama serve politics was in practice interpreted, in the pre-1976 years, to mean that drama must serve a particular Party policy at a given time. The playwright was expected to write plays that represented the Party's policies on major political, social, international and economic issues. Furthermore, he was expected to provide solutions. As early as 1949, the very year of the founding of the People's Republic, veteran dramatist Guang Weiran lamented that "playwrights have frequently felt frustrated by not being able to follow the policies (*zhui zhengce*) and to catch up with issues and problems (*gan wenti*) . . . Some playwrights had finally grasped the essence of a certain policy for a certain unique problem, and had constructed a theme (for their plays), . . . but when they completed their plays, they discovered that the Party's policy had changed and the plays they had laboriously written were no longer useful."[15]

In a jointly written essay published in 1979, Gu Zhuoyu, Hu Shuhe and Chen Gang, all scholars and critics, examined the Party's drama policies of the previous thirty years. In their opinion, one damaging result of the Party's drama policy was the "practice of irresponsible exaggeration" (*fukuafeng*) which occurred at the time when Mao launched his ill-fated Grat Leap Forward in 1958.[16] The Great Leap Forward was not confined to industries and agriculture; it involved playwriting and other literary and art activities as well. Playwrights were made to pledge quotas for writing plays as their contributions to the Great Leap Forward. Tian Han, one of the most productive playwrights of China since the 1920s, vowed to write fifteen plays for the Leap, but failed to finish even one.[17] Gu, Hu and Chen agreed that in terms of quantity, the number of plays written during the Great Leap Forward year was "unprecedentedly large," but in terms of quality, extremely few plays were good.[18]

Whether or not he was able to fulfill his pledged quota for writing plays, the playwright had other worries. Cui Dezhi, a prominent and well-respected playwright, recounts his personal agony in playwriting:

> I have been writing plays for thirty years. It seems that I have never understood how to travel on the path of literary creativity. Literary creativity is meant to intersect with life, but later I did not dare to let this happen, because all who had done so were in trouble. In 1956, I tried to permit creativity to intersect with life once again and wrote two little plays. "The Guilty Ones of the Time" (*Shijiande Zuiren*) and "Obstacles to Love" (*Aide buozhe*) . . . But during the 1964 Rectification Campaign . . . I was singled out for accusation that lasted for more than one month. Since then, I have not dared to touch upon problems and contradictions of real life, and became a real member of the "praising the virtues clique" (*gedepai*). I dared to write about only those subjects that had been already decided in the works of Marx, Lenin and Chairman Mao . . . And I wouldn't dare to touch what would really reflect the minds and feelings of the people.[19]

Cui Dezhi's words disclose the condition of the Chinese playwright in those years. They present a painful picture of how a play was written and reveal the meaning of a contemporary Chinese play in terms of its relations with the reality the playwright sees and what the Party requires him to see.

One major conflict between the Party and the dramatist is that of the dramatist's professionalism versus the Party's extra-professional or non-professional demands on the dramatist. The dramatist's professionalism seeks aesthetic excellence, but the Party, on the other hand, demands the political service of the drama, a demand that requires the popularization of art. The problem of quality versus popularization was ideologically solved in Mao's Yan'an Talks in 1942, and no one has dared to challenge it. Deviation from Mao's Talks emerged not in words but in practice. The deviation from Mao's teaching by theater groups from small towns and rural areas shows a more striking example of professionalism in conflict with non-professional restraints.

Constant ideological indoctrination does not seem to have reformed the minds of many in the small town and rural theater troupes who longed to give performances in big cities. They wanted to stage classical dramas which they believed to be of high artistic quality. Among the "after-work" (yeyu) amateur theater members, many dreamed of becoming professionals in the theater. The Party, on the other hand, launched rectification campaigns one after another, trying to correct this professionalistic deviation.[20] It is unfair to claim, however, that the Party leadership had no interest in and made no efforts to improve artistic standards in theater. Its efforts toward artistic improvement in theater, however, were frequently frustrated and interrupted by ceaseless political and idealogical campaigns.

In March 1953 the Ministry of Culture called a conference on art education in which a general direction for improving theater training was laid out. In Shanghai, the Shanghai Drama School (*Shanghai xiju zhuanke xuexiao*) was upgraded to the East China Branch of the Central Drama Institute (*Zhongyang xiju xueyuan huadong fenyuan*). In winter 1953 Russian drama instructors were invited to teach in Beijing and Shanghai, and the Stanislavsky system was systematically introduced into China's theaters. During the Hundred Flowers Campaign in 1956, efforts were made to improve the living standard of the teachers in the drama institutes, and in December of the same year, the East China Branch of the Central Drama Institute was further upgraded to be the Shanghai Drama Institute. There were indeed good reasons to believe that better days were just around the corner for China's theaters. But the political wind shifted abruptly to a different direction.

In spring 1957 the Party launched the Anti-Rightist Campaign against the outspoken intellectuals whose strong criticism of the Party and the regime during the short-lived Hundred Flowers Campaign had shocked Mao. "Quite a few students and faculty members (in the Shanghai Drama Institute) were wrongly accused as 'rightists',"[21] for instance. The screw continued to tighten on the artists. In the fall of 1958, the Party issued "The Directive Concerning Educational Tasks" (*Guanyu jiaoyu gongzuode zhishi*) in coordination with the Great Leap Forward, and instituted a new policy of uniting education with productivity. Students and teachers in the Shanghai Drama Institute, recalled Su Kun, the Institute's deputy president, were sent down to nearby people's communes to receive "revolutionary" education for two full years. According to Su Kun, "during this period, teachers and students (of the Shanghai Drama Institute) wrote and staged a sizeable number of plays. Due to the fact that these plays were written to meet the political assignments for the Great Leap Forward, few plays were worthy of preservation even though these plays were effective as propaganda at that time."[22] But more disruptions occurred. In the winter of 1959, a surge of criticism against the so-called revisionist literary thought seriously demoralized teachers and students of the Drama Institute as many of them became targets of the criticism.[23]

By the latter part of 1960, the political pendulum began to swing back, the disruptive political interference with literature and theater receded. The disaster caused by the Great Leap Forward had forced Mao to yield at the 1959 Lushan Plenum; the nation under Liu Shaoqi's leadership was making adjustments and correcting the past errors. In the spring of 1961, the Ministry of Culture took measures to normalize training in the drama institutes, and once more, things looked rosy. But, again, the thaw was brief, and the rosy expectations paled.

A little over a year later, in September 1962, at the 10th Plenum of the Central Committee of the 8th Congress of the Chinese Communist Party, Mao Zedong attempted to regain the power he had lost three years ago, and gave a hysterical battlecry: "Never forget class struggle!" Thus, under the banner of "never forget class struggle," the political pendulum swung again toward violence. In drama institutes, courses on drama theory were cancelled; all Western dramas and Chinese plays written during and after the May 4th era were eliminated from teaching as well as from the stage. At the same time, efforts to promote drama on contemporary themes were launched.

The first results of the emphasis on drama on contemporary themes were displayed in the 1963 East China Spoken Drama Learning Festival (*Huadongqu huaju guanmo yanchuhui*), held in Shanghai from December 25, 1963 to January 22, 1964. At the Festival thirteen full-length plays and seven one-act plays, all written in 1963, were staged by nineteen spoken drama companies from various provinces, cities, and units of the armed forces in the East China region.[24] Some of the plays, such as *The Song of the Dragon River* (*Longjiang song*), were later transformed into model plays during the Cultural Revolut. The 1963 Spoken Drama Learning Festival was the initial display of the force in drama of the group whose members, including Mao's wife Jiang Quing, were later to be knwon as the Cultural Revolutionists.

The struggle for control of the theater in the early 1960s was a vital part of the ideological and political counter-offensive by Mao at the 10th Plenum of the 8th Central Committee of the Chinese Communist Party in September 1962. In 1962 Jiang Qing, instructed by Mao, personally examined over 1,300 Beijing operas and suggested a ban on many of them which were deemed ideologically unfit. In July, the same year, after seeing the performance of *Hai Rui's Dismissal from Office*, Jiang Qing insisted that this play be banned. At the time of the 10th Plenum, Jiang Qing again called the attention of the Ministry of Culture to ideological problems in the theater. But the Ministry of Culture did not heed Jiang Qing's complaints. On March 17, 1963, the Communist Party's Department of Propaganda issued a directive to have all the "ghost" plays banned.[25] Thus, the 1963 East China Spoken Drama Learning Festival seems to have signified the beginning of actual control of Jiang Qing's group over theater. It is no wonder that the *People's Daily* 1967 New Year Day's editorial claimed that the 1963 drama "reform" was "really the beginning of the Great Proletarian Cultural Revolution."[26]

While the radical Cultural Revolutionists were attempting to seize control of the theater, the moderates also were trying to preserve the little freedom they had gained since the latter part of 1960. In the spring of 1962, they gathered at the All China Forum on the Writing of Spoken Drama, Opera and Children's Plays (*Quanguo huaju, geju, ertongju chuangzuo zuotanhui*), held in Guangzhuo (Canton). In the Forum, one of the most cultured, cosmopolitan and colorful leaders of the nation, General Chen Yi, was invited to speak. In his speech Chen Yi criticized the Party's discrimination against the intellectuals.[27] Said Chen Yi with some humor: ". . . the capitalist class is still smarter (than we). It doesn't take care of meals, jobs or anything of the scientists and intellectuals, but it doesn't impose thought-reform on them either. . . . Today I want to say some nonsensical things! In matters of theater, movies and business management, we are simply not as good as those capitalists! . . . It is not as simple as imprinting class labels on everything."[28] Chen Yi's criticism of "imprinting class labels on everything" was a direct confutation to Mao's cry, "never forget class struggle." Chen Yi, who had read plays and poetry by many Western writers, especially by the French writers, gave an open-minded and liberal talk at the Forum, showing his support of creative freedom.

Chen Yi first pointed out the serious harmfulness of the Party's approach in dealing with literary problems. "It is so serious," said Chen Yi, "that people won't dare to write; it is so serious that people won't speak, and it is so serious that people can only praise. This is not a good omen. . . . It is very dangerous!" "In our society," Chen continued, "everyone should be positive, everyone should smile, be happy and worriless. We should all be able to say what we know, and to contribute all our abilities and talents. . . . Our society ought to be like this. But it is really not a society as such."[29] Telling the truth was what Chen Yi believed to be a writer's duty, and therefore, he criticized two aspects in current China that had prevented a writer from telling the truth: One being the restrictions on and suppression of a writer's individuality, and the other, the prohibition on writing tragedies. Chen Yi, instead of going to the very source of restriction and oppression of the writer's individuality, challenged only the individuals who abused power and asked: "Who gives you the power to strike (daji) this one today and that one tomorrow, and to draw conclusions recklessly one after another? . . . Did the Party Central give you the power or did the Department of Propaganda?"[30] The very personal way of using the "you" in Chen's speech seems to have implied that Chen's accusation was directed toward some individual or individuals in the Party and that a power struggle was going on and theater was to be the battle ground of the power struggle.

One practice oppressive of a playwright's individuality has been collective writing of a play. Collectivism in creative writing has been a unique phenomenon in post-1949 drama, a phenomenon which again demonstrates the Party's particular concern with and close scrutiny of the socio-political influence of drama. Collective writing of a play exercises a mutual check on an individual's private views and unconscious revelations which may be unacceptable to the Party, and at the same time, collective playwriting also means collective responsibility. (There have also been many cases where a drama leader, wanting to share the glory of being a playwright, has insisted that his name be added to the authorship credit). Chen Yi ridicules this collectivism and advocates individuality and individual views in a play. He stated that if a writer "allows his work to be revised by others at will, the writer is a weakling, . . . and he cannot be a writer."[31]

In his belief that literature should express what a writer really thinks and what is true, Chen Yi tackled a taboo of the socialist realist literature: tragedy. Speaking bluntly, Chen Yi said:

> Today we have replaced the old happy "endingism" with a new happy "endingism", . . . We don't want to write tragedies because it is said that there is no tragedy in our new society. What I see is that many of our comrades are creating tragedies everyday and performing tragedies everyday. Why can't we write tragedies then? The effect of a tragedy is often greater than a comedy. . . [It gives us] the painful joy, a joy that is higher than the ordinary joy."[32]

Chen Yi drew upon Aristotle for his theory of tragedy. Knowing the practical mentality of many Party leaders, functionaries and some drama leaders, Chen Yi approached the problem of writing tragedy in a realistic manner. Said he:

> If we eliminate the defeat aspect of the Long March, then it is no longer the Long March! What educational significance could there be if this ten-thousand mile Long March is fundamentally distorted? We have always covered the eyes of the people and not wanted to clear the people's vision for fear they would see our shortcomings and defects.[39]

Chen Yi concentrated his criticism of the Party leadership on literature. He felt that the Party leadership had caused unwarranted interference in literary creativities and pointed out that many writers had been wrongly accused and punished in many rectification campaigns. Finally he asked the Party leadership not to make writing assignments for the playwrights on specific political or social issues.[34] Chen Yi's stand for creative autonomy, a playwright's individuality, and the artistic quality of a play contradicted the revolutionary tradition of drama which had, by now, been placed increasingly under the control of the group which urged drastic changes for drama and for the entire nation.

General Chen Yi's speech was representative of the moderate view in the Party leadership, and significantly the same speech was republished in *Wenyi Bao* (Literary Gazette), July and August 1979, at the peak of the post-Mao liberalization of 1978-1979. Few Party leaders have ever been as outspokenly critical of current Chinese literary conditions as General Chen Yi. Having intended to be a writer himself, General Chen Yi understood the writer's dilemma and hardships under such circumstances. Chen Yi's 1962 Talk in Guangzhou is still the most enlightened and liberal talk on drama ever expressed in China since 1949, but in 1962 his strong support of freedom for the playwrights was not able to create a decisive influence upon the literary and drama conditions, which were inevitably determined by the political power struggles erupting in Beijing and Shanghai. In Shanghai, the radical group's sure control over drama was soon demonstrated at the East China Spoken Drama Learning Festival.

Less than five months after the curtain had fallen to conclude the 1963 East China Spoken Drama Learning Festival in Shanghai in January 1964, on June 5, an even more important drama activity, the Learning Festival of the Beijing Opera on Contemporary Themes (Jingju xiandaixi guanmo yanchu dahui) was convened in Beijing. The Festival lasted nearly two months, till the end of July, twice as long as the East China Spoken Drama Learning Festival. Twenty-nine Beijing opera companies from eighteen provinces, cities and minority autonomous regions participated in the Festival, with over 5,000 "learners" (*guanmozhe*) from many areas. Thirty-five new Beijing operas on contemporary themes were staged, including *Sparks Among the Reeds* (*Ludang huozhong*), which later became the well-known model play *Shajiabnag*. *The Azalea Mountain* (*Dujuanshan*), *The Red Lantern* (*Hongdeng ji*), *Taking Tiger Mountains by Strategy* (*Zhiqu weihushan*), *The Red Guard of Lake Hong* (*Honghu chiweidui*), *The Red Detachment of Women* (*Hongse niangzijun*), *You Should Never Forget* (*Qianwan buyao wangji*), and *Jie Zhenguo*. Several of these plays were later revised and became the famous "model plays" (yangbanxi) of the Cultural Revolution.

From the point of view of the radical drama revolutionaries, the Beijing opera was the last stronghold of conservatism, and the Festival was considered a great victory for them. They had transformed the conservative and feudal Beijing opera into a revolutionary one that was able to perform operas on contemporary themes. Speeches made by such high officials as Peng Zhen, then mayor of Beijing, and Lu Dingyi, then head of the Propaganda Department, and editorials of the *People's Daily* and the *Red Flag* (*Hongqi*) on this occasion [35] already heralded what the leaders of the Cultural Revolution, which officially began in 1966, would say, write and practice.

At the same time, educators in the drama institutes were forced to shift their drama training to the teaching of class struggles. Faculty and students, again, were sent down to the countryside to receive "socialist education." From the 1957 anti-rightist movement to the commencement of the Great Cultural Revolution in 1966, drama took what Su Kun described as a long "crooked path."[36]

The outbreak of the Cultural Revolution resulted from complex political and ideological factors in the ruling Communist Party, and again, drama stood in the very frontline of the struggle. Violent criticism of the historical play *Hai Rui's Dismissal from Office* by Wu Han, the vice mayor of Beijing and a scholar of Ming history, began the decade-long chaos. In contemporary Chinese politics, power struggles have often been disguised and justified in ideological "debates" which in turn have often taken the form of literary polemics. Thus, writers and playwrights were frequently the first targets and victims of a political purge. The Cultural Revolution was no exception. As the Cultural Revolution progressed, political control increasingly shifted into the hands of a group dominated by men of letters (supported by Mao, of course), at the head of whom were the "infamous" Gang of Four. With the exception of Wang Hongwen, the other three of the Gang were closely associated with the theater and literary circles. On the ideological front, drama was the most trusted weapon of the Cultural Revolutionists.

During the ten years of the Cultural Revolution, no other works in literature and theater were better known than the "revolutionary model plays" (*geming yangbanxi*),[37] all in the form of modernized Beijing opera. In terms of the very polished use of language and bold yet imaginative theatrical innovations in acting, singing, stage scenes and music, these revolutionary model Beijing operas are good theatrical pieces and will have lasting influence in Chinese theater. They will not replace the traditional Beijing opera, but they have distinguished themselves as a new theater. Jiang Qing and her associates caused devastating damage to the theater not with their model plays nor with their drama theories (as no theory is perfectly good or completely wrong); they did it by banning all other dramas deemed ideologically counter-revolutionary and by ruthless persecution of writers, playwrights and theater professionals.

The death of Mao Zedong on September 9, 1976 and the fall of the Gang of Four a month later on October 6 gave a sense of liberation to the nation. In the first two years of the post-Mao era, the playwrights were still very cautious and uncertain. They still had the "lingering fear in their hearts" (*xin you yuji*). Plays produced in these years followed the tradition of praising the leaders, only now the Party's new chairman was Hua Guofeng. Suddenly in 1978, the creative sparks of the playwrights were ignited. The playwrights were encouraged by the new Constitution proclaimed in early 1978 in which the people were promised the so-called "four big freedoms," including the freedom of expression. The Third Plenum of the Central Committee of the Eleventh Congress of the Chinese Communist Party, held from December 18 to 22, 1978, further strengthened the people's confidence in the continued liberal trend by formally reversing the verdict that denounced the 1976 Tiananmen Incident as anti-revolutionary and by criticizing Mao's error in starting the Cultural Revolution. The normalization of U.S.-China relations (on January 1, 1979) which was simultaneously announced in mid-December 1978 by Premier Hua Guofeng and President Carter, was also a morale booster to many liberal writers and intellectuals in China.

Among the first plays that had attempted to break the *kuangkuang* (restrictions and taboos) was Zong Fuxian's *When All Sounds are Hushed,* (*Yu Wushengchu*) published and staged in 1978.[38] Quiet, gentle, born to a well-educated family, but himself an educated worker, Zong Fuxian in his play created a hero who participated in the Tiananmen demonstration against the Gang of Four before the Party did so in the Third Plenum of the Central Committee in late 1978. To many Chinese it was unthinkable that a playwright would dare to openly reverse a political verdict without the Party Central's sanction. Perhaps Zong, being a young playwright, was less experienced in treacherous politicadl intrigues and cared less about political dangers. Cui Dezhi, the veteran playwright who had been criticized, accused, purged and frightened in many ideo-political campaigns, wrote another play in 1979. The play, *The Spring Flower*, (*Baochunhua*), published in the April 1979 issue of *Juben*, created for the first time in post-1949 China a heroine who was not of proletarian origin, and who later became the bride of the son of a deputy secretary of the Party committee of a factory. Another taboo, the class barrier, was torn down. These and many other playwrights have shown their individualistic courage in their quests and explorations into the "forbidden areas" (*jinqu*) with their plays.

On the other hand, there were attempts made by the authorities and conservatives[39] to mend the fence against individualistic expression that might be socially provocative and overt criticisms that aimed too high and too close to the source of the authority. The cases of Bai Hua's play *Unrequited Love*, (*Kulian*, 1979) which was made into a movie, and Sha Yexin's *If I were for Real*, (*Jiaru wo shi zhende*, 1979) are all well-known to the world. Then in 1983–1984 there was the "anti-spiritual pollution" campaign against "bourgeois" decadence. The politics behind these and other literary cases is not a major concern here, but indications seem to reveal that while the conservative-dogmatists were trying to restore the Maoist line and were intolerant of novel ideas, the "modernizationists," led by Deng Xiaoping, Hu Yoabang and Zhao Ziyang, needed political and social stability and diminution of the conservative-dogmatist opposition. Thus for some time, it seems, there has been a joint effort of the two opposing factions to place lids on the writer's freedom of expression.

In spite of the on-and-off Party policies toward writers and playwrights, the overall trend since the end of the Cultural Revolution has been a gradual broadening of freedom of creativity. By the end of December 1984, the pragmatic "modernizationists" won another round against the conservative-dogmatists. At the Fourth Congress of the Chinese Writers Association, convened on December 29, 1984, the two arch-conservatives, Hu Qiaomu and Deng Liqun, the latter of whom was held responsible for pushing the anti-spiritual pollution campaign too far, were not present.[40] The two sent their congratulations by phone and telegrams, but their congratulations were received with total silence by the attending writers.[41] Zhou Yang, the one-time literary "czar" who had executed the Maoist literary line faithfully before his own downfall during the Cultural Revolution, also sent his blessing by phone from the hospital, and his blessing was answered with "prolonged and warm applause of the entire body of the delegates,"[42] because Zhou Yang had stood up for the writers during the recent anti-spiritual pollution campaign which caused his removal from the position of deputy head of the Party's Department of Propaganda. At the Congress, the Party's own blessing was delivered by a younger member of the Party Central Secretariat, Hu Qili, a rising star in the Modernizationist camp. In his speech at the opening session, Hu Qili criticized the leftist interference in literary creativity and stressed the importance of literary freedom, and he advised that "writers should think with their own heads."[43]

The Fourth Congress of the Writers Association, with its endorsement of the moderate Modernizationist group in the Party, does not necessarily assure a brighter future for the writers. Struggles between the pragmatic and reform-minded Modernizationists and the conservative-dogmatists will certainly continue, but a measurable trust in the Party's sincerity and optimism for better conditions for literary creativity in the future were evident in literary journals and papers.

For years, Chinese leaders have stressed the importance of a drama on contemporary themes because such a drama can respond to the propaganda needs of the Party. The playwrights have responded to the Party's call for plays on contemporary themes, but they have nevertheless been cautious about how to represent reality and the Party's policy without provoking the Party's censorship. A particularly revealing phenomenon is the playwright's way of handling dramatic conflict. It is the level of the dramatic conflict that reflects the playwright's very careful and conscious effort to deal with contemporary themes. To the Party leaders, a large number of audiences, and many critics, realism in literature and in drama is no more than a facsimile of real life, and the level of dramatic conflict in a play is always translated as the level of reflection or criticism of political reality. The level of dramatic conflict is determined by the positions of antagonistic positive and negative characters.

During the Cultural Revolution, particularly in its last years, as power struggle accelerated, the level of conflict in a play was increasingly manipulated for and determined by precise political considerations. The political manipulation of dramatic conflict was best exemplified in a series of meetings in February and March 1976. These meetings were called by the leaders of the Cultural Revolutionists, and were attended by responsible personalities of the theater and the Ministry of Culture. The purpose of the meetings was to make plans on writing plays aimed at their political foes, the so-called capitalist-roaders, in the Central Government and in the Party central. The plan demanded that the dramatic villain, thus the conflict, be raised to "the provincial level, to the ministerial level of the Central Government." In the original script of their last movie, *Counter-Attack* (*Fanji*), the villain, a capitalist-roader, was a deputy Party secretary in a university, but it was decided in the meetings that the villain should be a first secretary of a provincial Party committee, and be changed from a reformable to an irreformable (*buken huigaide*) villain. It was also planned that this film must be ready for showing on October 1, the PRC's national day. Apparently the movie did not meet the deadline, and on October 6, the members of the Gang of Four were all arrested.[44]

The case of the movie *Counter-Attack* demonstrates the political basis of dramatic conflict in a Chinese play. This practice definitely influences and determines the interpretation of dramatic conflict or situation by Chinese leaders and by the society at large, and the Chinese playwright is certainly aware of this. This awareness has affected the playwright's arrangement of conflicts in his plays. He must be careful about whether the conflict is one within the people, thus non-antagonistic according to Mao, or one between the people and the class enemy, thus antagonistic. He would be in trouble if he created an antagonistic conflict between the people and a Party cadre in his play. Above all, the level of conflict must be controlled so that the conflict cannot be construed as a criticism of the higher authority of the Party. One way of controlling the dramatic conflict is by assigning the proper position to the negative character in relation to the positive character in the play. The negative character should never be the most powerful man in the dramatic structure of the political hierarchy, which always realistically duplicates the real. A negative character's mistakes and crime can only be corrected and dealt with by a more powerful positive character in that political system. Thus one always finds the negative character a deputy secretary, and the positive character the first secretary of the Party, in Chinese plays on contemporary themes.

The demand for correct representation of contemporary life in drama causes undue anxiety on the part of the playwright who is required to write about the "important and big subject" (*zhongda ticai*) which is almost without exception political. Some playwrights turn to writing plays on historical themes, thinking, often wrongly, that such thematic distance would permit ambiguity and flexibility in their works. The rise of plays on historical themes in the People's Republic of China was a post-Anti-Rightist Campaign phenomenon, as many plays on contemporary themes such as Yang Lüfang's *Kookoo Birds Sing Again* (*Buguniao youjiale*, 1957), Hai Mo's *The Pan-pipe is Played Horizontally* (*Dongxiao hengchui*, 1956), and Zhao Xun's *Homecoming* (*huanxiang ji*, 1956) were criticized and their authors purged during the anti-rightist movement.[45] To many playwrights, writing historical plays appeared safer. Among the best known plays on historical themes are Tian Han's *Guan Hanqing* (1958–1961) and *Xie Yaohuan* (1961) Cao Yu's

Galls and Swords (*Danjian pian*, 1961), Guo Moruo's *Cai Wenji* (1969) and *Empress Wu* (*Wu Zeitian*, 1960–1962), and, above all, Wu Han's *Hai Rui's Dismissal from Office* (*Hai Rui Baguan*, 1961).

Allegorical interpretation has a long tradition in Chinese criticism. The distance of the time of the event in a historical play from the present does not prevent an interpretation in the contemporary context, and, indeed, a playwright's treatment of dramatic characters, plot and language in his play on a historical theme does often betray his stand and view on analogous current political and social issues. Furthermore, the playwright's intention to be ambiguous and indirect is often compromised by the level of conflict in his play. In all of the aforementioned plays on historical themes, emperors, empresses and high officials are either heroes, heroines or villains. Any unsympathetical treatment of the character who represents the highest authority of the state in a play is inevitably understood as an allegorical attack on the present. Thus, criticisms of *Hai Rui's Dismissal from Office* ignited the Cultural Revolution, and *Guan Hanqing* and *Xie Yaohuan* were banned, the playwrights Wu Han and Tian Han fell as victims of the Cultural Revolution, accused, jailed, tortured until they died.[46]

Drama has flourished since the end of the Cultural Revolution. Joining with the general trend of literature, drama has also moved back to the tradition of critical realism born during the May Fourth era more than half a century ago. Of course, the playwright is still aware of the limits imposed on him, but he has much broader freedom to choose a subject for his play and to experiment with new drama forms. There have been incidents of criticism or accusation of plays for their questionable political stands, but the Party authorities have become more tolerant, and criticism of such plays as Sha Yexin's *If I Were for Real*, Bai Hua's *The Golden Lance of King Wu and the Sword of King Yue* (*Wu Wang jin'ge Yue Wang jian*, 1983), Bai Fengxi's *When the Bright Moon Shines* (*Mingye chuzhao ren*, 1981), and even Bai Hua's *Unrequitted Love* did not develop into political campaigns. More often, the Party seems to have refrained from direct intervention in literary polemics when such polemics are not too political. Even more significantly, opinions that are different from and in opposition to the Party's view, as in the case of Sha Yexin's play, have been permitted to be aired publicly. The Party under the leadership of the Modernizationists has moved toward tolerance and moderation in literature and ideology.

The last confrontation, however, between playwrights and the Party leadership, and between the open-minded group and the conservative faction within the Party was over a play *WM* (*We*) or *WM* (*Women*) (The WM are the initials in the Chinese pinyin system for the Chinese pronunciation of *Women* which means "we" in English) in the summer and fall of 1985. *WM* (*We*) dramatizes the cynicism, frustrations, sorrows, struggles for a better life, loves and longings of seven young men and women through the years from 1978 to 1984. The realistic depiction apparently displeased the conservative wing in the Party leadership, who abruptly and without explanation ordered cancellation of the planned performance of the play. The stage director, Wang Gui, was fired from his position as director of the Spoken-drama Troupe of the Air Force's Department of Political Affairs and stripped of all his Party functions.

The playwright, Wang Peigong, and his colleagues fought back. Supportive articles appeared in journals and newspapers, and the *Juben*, the official drama monthly of the Chinese Dramatists Association, published the play in its September 1985 issue, an obvious and rare defiance of the conservative leadership in the Party and an indication of support from the more liberal group of the Party's leadership, which made the publication of the play in *Juben* less risky. Meanwhile in Shanghai, Sha Yexin, author of the controversial play *If I Were For Real* and newly appointed director of the Shanghai People's Art Theater, had learned about the play and subsequently premiered the play, under the directorship of Wang Gui, in Shanghai on October 4. Encouraged by the Shanghai move, the newly formed Chinese Dramatic Literature Association (*Zhongguo xiju wenxue xuehui*) in Beijing, truly a playwrights' own organization, formed a theater group, drawing its members from and with the support of several major theater groups in the capital, and staged *WM* (*We*) beginning on October 20, with each of the performances sold-out. But on November 13 the performance was again suddenly stopped. Two days later, on the 15th, the Chinese Dramatic Literature Association announced that the play would resume its performance shortly because, it was said, they had the support of even more powerful leaders in the Party. The fate of the play is still undecided, awaiting the outcome of inner-Party squabbles.

The *WM* (*We*) affair shows the lingering tradition of the Party's high-handed control over the theater, but this tradition has met resistance both from within the Party and from the playwrights, a phenomenon which would have been unthinkable during the Mao era. Nevertheless, the *WM* (*We*) incident shows that drama, more than fiction, poetry, dance and music, continues to stir up ideological and political fears among the Party leaders who appreciate the capacity of the theater to wield subversive power.

No longer required to write "important and big matters," the playwright has shown greater interest in ordinary people's ordinary life as the subject of his playwriting. Love, a taboo before 1976, is a favorite dramatic subject for both the playwright and the audience. Intellectuals, college professors, medical doctors, scientists and engineers, who were previously labelled as bourgeois, have now appeared on the stage as heroes and heroines.

One far-reaching policy enacted by the Modernizationists is to expand China's contact with the outside world, and the Chinese drama and theater have benefitted by the new international contact. Chinese playwrights and theater professionals have begun to search eagerly for models and inspiration from Western theaters. Ibsen's *Peer Gynt*, Brecht's *Galileo*, Miller's *Death of a Salesman*, Sartre's *Dirty Hands*, Albee's *The Zoo Story*, and O'Neill's *Anna Christie*, to name just a few, have been staged in China by Chinese directors. Foreign experts such as Miller directed his *Salesman*, and George White directed O'Neill's play in China. Theater troupes from England, France, Germany and other countries have given performances in China, and Western drama scholars and specialists have been invited to lecture and to conduct workshops in Chinese drama schools. Chinese stage directors, on the other hand, have also developed a strong interest in non-realistic theatricality and in staging non-realistic plays, because such plays and histrionics are often introspective probes into areas beyond the reach of the kind of realism that monopolized the Chinese stage for three decades. Among the experimenting stage directors, Hu Weimin of the Shanghai Youth Spoken Drama Company and Chen Yong, a female director of the China Youth Art Theater in Beijing, have been successful with their non-traditional stage directing.

The playwrights, too, have been encouraged by the new air of cosmopolitanism, and have written plays with innovative forms and new themes. Playwrights of the post-1976 generation such as Gao Xingjian, Ma Zhongjun, Sun Huizhu and Sha Yexin are most adventurous and their works have already created new trends in China's dramatic literature.

While the playwrights and stage directors are experimenting with theatrical ideas from the West or of their own, they are also looking retrospectively into traditional Chinese theaters as sources and inspirations for their creativity. The brisk interest in heightening the aesthetic quality and dramaturgy in theater and dramatic literature is a clear implication of the emergence of an ever-enhancing consciousness of theatrical professionalism. The days when theater was required to coordinate and to propagate revolutionary tasks, to boost the troops' morale, and to participate in political campaigns are gone. "Literature and art serve politics" has been broadened and altered to "serve the people" or to "serve society." A playwright can now devote his time and thinking to his art rather than to concern about Party lines.

But the revolutionary tradition in which drama is considered as a weapon or a tool is still alive. There are playwrights who are enthusiastic about the four modernizations and the new economic reforms. They have written plays lauding the progress and criticizing problems of modernization, and they have written plays that portray the prosperous life in the Special Economic Zone (*jingji tequ*) in Shenzhen. Many of these plays, however, were written in a hurry. The playwright has enough enthusiasm but is unable to digest the material he collected in his notebook and the impressions he had during his recent excursion, "going deep into life" (*shenru shenghuo*). As literature of reportage, these plays provide precise records and direct reflections of the life, problems and sentiments of the subject, as does a newspaper. It is a transmission of information in the form of drama. These plays are informative and journalistic, but often fall short as art.

As China is steadily gaining political stability and economic prosperity, and as Chinese dramatists have begun to enjoy more freedom to create and to be more informed, it is reasonable to be optimistic about the future of Chinese drama and theater. Through the utilitarian-revolutionary tradition, together with the traditional Chinese intellectual's concern for the nation, society and people, and the playwright's eager search for artistic excellence, the Chinese playwrights and their plays will continue to play vital roles in China, the playwrights are both artists and "muckrakers." The studies in this volume represent a first collective recognition, by scholars and specialists in the West, of the vitality and significance of this drama which deserves continued interest and attention.

Notes

1. Martin Esslin, *An Anatomy of Drama* (New York: Hill and Wang, 1981), p. 29.

2. Ibid., p. 103.

3. Zhao Pinsan, "Guanyu Zhongyang Geming Genjudi Huaju Gongzuo Huiyi" (Drama Activities in the Central Revolutionary Base: A Recollection), *Zhongguo Huaju Yundong; Wushinian Shiliao Ji, 1907*-1957, ed. by Tian Han, et al (Beijing: Zhongguo Xiju Chubanshe, 1957) pp. 184–193.

4. "Zhonggong Zhongyang Xuanchuanbu Guanyu Zhixing Dandgde Wenyi Zhengcede Jueding" (Resolution of the Department of Propaganda of the Chinese Communist Party Central on the Execution of the Party's Literary and Art Policy), *Zhogguo Xiandai Wenxue Cankao Ziliao* (Hereafter CKZL), ed. by Beijing Normal University, the Chinese Department. (Beijing: Gaodeng Jaioyu Chubanshe, 1959) II, pp. 27–28.

5. Ibid.

6. He Qifang, "Guanyu Yishu Qunzhonghua Wenti (Problems Concerning Massification of Literature and Art), CKZL, II, pp. 82–83.

7. CKZL II, p. 28.

8. Zhou Yang, "Tan Wenyi Wenti" (On Literary and Art Problems), CKZL, II, p. 57.

9. Ibid., p. 58–59.

10. Zhou Yang, "Biaoxian Xinde Qunzhong Shidai — Kanle Chunjie Yangge Yihou" (To Represent the New Mass Age: After Seeing the Yangge at the Spring Festival), CKZL, II, pp. 59–60.

11. Liu Nianqu and Wu Qing, *Zai Renminde Wutaishang* (On the People's Stage), (Shanghai: Shi Ju Wen Chubanshe, 1949), pp. 679–72.

12. Tian Han, "Women Zenyang Genghaode Wei Diyige Wunian Jihua Fuwu" (How Shall We Serve Better for the First Five-Year Plan), *Xiju Bao*, (August 1955), p. 6.

13. Ibid.

14. "Jianchi Nongcun Yeyu Wenyi Huodongde Zhengque Fangxiang" (To Persist on the Correct Direction of Amateur Literary-Art Activities in Villages) *Renmin Ribao* (June 11, 1972), p. 4.

15. Guang Weiran, "Xiju Chuangzuo Congshu Diyiji Zongxu" (General Preface to the First Volume of the Drama Series), *Shengli Lieche*, (Beijing: Sanlian Shudian, 1950), pp. 6–7.

16. Gu Zhuoyu, Hu Shuhe and Chen Gang, "Geming Xianshi Zhuyide Shengli: Shilun Jianguo Yilai Huaju Chuangzuode Chengjiu" (The Victory of Revolutionary Realism: A Preliminary Discussion on the Accomplishments of the Dramatic Literature Since the Founding of the PRC), *Wenxue Pinglun* (April 1979), No. 4, p. 23.

17. *Life* (June 2, 1967 and July 14, 1967). There was an interview with Ma Sicong (Ma Sitson), a violinist and president of the Central Music Conservatory in Beinjing, who escaped from China in 1967. His story about Tian Han is on p. 72 of the July 14 issue.

18. Gu, Hu and Chen, p. 23.

19. Cui Dezhi, "Yongyu Ganyu Shenghuo; Nuli Tigao Zhiliang" (Be Brave to Intersect with Life; Be Diligent in Improving Quality), *Renmin Xiju* (November 1979), No. 11, p. 3.

20. Zhongguo Xijujia Xiehui, *Zai Geminghua Daolushang Qianjinde Hao Jutuan* (The Good Drama Troupes Marching On the Revolutionary Path), (Beijing: Zhongguo Xiju Chubanshe, 1966), passim.

21. Su Kun, "Huigu, Zongjie, Zhanwang" (Retrospection, Conclusion, and Anticipation), *Xiju Yishu* (November 1982) No. 4, pp. 3–12.

22. Ibid., p. 6.

23. Ibid., pp. 5–6.

24. Ke Quingshi, "Dali Fazhan he Fanrong Shehuizhuyi Xiju; Genghaode Wei Shehuizhuyide Jingji jichu Fuwu" (Diligently Develop and Prosper Socialist Drama; To Serve Even Better the Socialist Economic Foundation), *Yijiuliusan Nian Huadongqu Huaju Guanmo Yanchu Wenji*, (Shanghai: Shanghai Wenhua Chubanshe, 1965) p. 2.

25. *Jiang Qing Tongzhi Lun Wenyi* (Comrade Jiang Qing on Literature and Art), May 1965, N.P., pp. 209–210. *Wu Han he Hai Rui Beguan* (Wu Han and Hai Rui's Dismissal from Office), (Beijing: Renmin Chubanshe, 1979), p. 5.

26. *Renmin Ribao* (People's Daily), (January 1, 1967), p. 1.

27. The Chinese expression, "zhishifenzi" is invariably translated into English as "intellectual." In fact, "zhishifenzi" has a much broader meaning in Chinese than "intellectual" in English. In Chinese, anyone who has a senior high school or a college education is a "zhishifenzi" which means a man with knowledge (zhishi) or an educated man.

28. Chen Yi, "Zai Quanguo Huaju, Geju, Ertongju Zuotanhuishangde Jianghua" (Talk at the All-Nation Forum on Spoken Drama, Opera and Children's Drama Creativity). *Wenyi Bao* (July 1979), p. 5. Chen's entire speech was published in *Wenyi Bao* (July 1979) pp. 2–16, and (August 1979), pp. 40–48.

29. Ibid., p. 6.

30. Ibid.

31. Ibid., p. 10.

32. Ibid., p. 16.

33. Ibid.

34. Ibid. (August 1979), pp. 40–48.

35. Several of the speeches and editorials were collected in *Wenhua Zhanxianshangde Yige Da Geming* (A Great Revolution on the Cultural Front) (Beijing: Renmin Chubanshe, 1964).

36. Su Kun. See note 21.

37. The nine model plays are: *Zhiqu Weihushan* (Taking Tiger Mountain by Strategy), *Hongdeng Ji* (The Red Lantern), *Shajiabang, Hai Gang* (On the Docks), *Longjiang Song* (Song of the Dragon River), *Hongse Niangzijun* (The Red Detachment of Women), *Qixi Baihutuan* (A Surprise Attack on the White Tiger Regiment), *Pingyuan Zuozhan* (Fighting on the Plain), and *Dujuan Shan* (The Azalea Mountain).

38. *Yu Wushengchu* has two English versions, one, *When All Sounds Are Hushed*, was published in *Chinese Literature* (April 1979), and the other, *In a Land of Silence*, was published in *Twentieth-century Chinese Drama: An Anthology* (Bloomington: Indiana University Press, 1983). The original Chinese was published in *Renmin Xiju* (December 1978).

39. The Maoists and the Cultural Revolutionists have often been called the radical left. But in the dialectical sense and with consideration of the innovative reforms and the changes carried out by the "Modernizationists" under the leadership of Deng Xiaoping, Zhao Ziyang and Hu Yaobang, the Maoists and the Cultural Revolutionists, who resisted the reforms and changes with dogmatic and provincial stubborness, have made themselves truly conservative. I am not the only one, nor am I the first to denote the Maoists and the Cultural Revolutionists as conservative. In a report by David R. Francis, "China's Economy Growing Like Topsy; Could Triple Soviets' by Year 2000" in *American Banker* (Thursday, March 14, 1985, p. 16), the author, quoting Professor Abram T. Bergson, a Harvard economics Professor, describes the Chinese leaders as innovative and the Russians as conservative. To me, the Maoists and the Cultural Revolutionists are radical in means and method, but conservative in ideal and ideology.

40. *Renmin Ribao*, (December 30, 1984), p. 1.

41. *Zhongyang Ribao* (The Central Daily), International edition, (February 24, 1985), p. 2.

42. *Renmin Ribao*, op. cit.

43. Hu Qili, "Zai Zhongguo Zuojia Xiehui Disici Huiyuan Daibiao Dahuishangde Zhuci" (Congratulatory Speech on the Fourth Congress of the Chinese Writers Association), *Renmin Ribao* (December 30, 1984), p. 1.

44. Wenhuabu, Pipanzu, "Sirenbang Guchui 'Xie yu Zouzipai zuo Douzhengde Zuopingde Fandong Shizhi" (The Reactionary Nature of the Gang of Four's Instigation of 'Writing Literary Works to Struggle Against the Capitalist-Roaders'", *Renmin Ribao* (November 28, 1976), p. 2.

45. See Chapter 12 in *Zhogguo Dangdai Wenxueshi Chugao* (A Preliminary Draft of History of Contemporary Chinese Literature), by Guo Zhigang, et. al. (Beijing: Renmin Wenxue Chubanshe, 1981), Vol. II.

46. For Tian Han's and Wu Han's last days in the Cultural Revolution, see Tian Ye (Tian Han's daughter), "Ku Baba" (Crying for my Papa), in *Juben* (April 1979) pp. 47–50; and Wu Zhang (Wu Han's son), "Xingcunzhede Huiyi" (Remembrance of a Fortunate Survivor) in *Wu Han he Hai Rui Baquan* (Beijing: Renmin Chubanshe, 1979) pp. 103–113.

Glossary

Aide buozhe	爱的波折
Bai Fengxi	白峰溪
Bai Hua	白桦
Baochunhua	报春花
Buguniao you jiaole	布谷鸟又叫了
buken huigaide	不肯悔改的
Cai Chang	蔡畅
Cai Wenji	蔡文姬
Cao Yu	曹禺
Chen Gang	陈刚
Chen Yi	陈毅
Chen Yong	陈颙
Cui Dezhi	崔德志
daji	打击
Danjian pian	胆剑篇
Deng Xiaoping	邓小平
Deng Liqun	邓力群
Dongxiao hengchui	洞箫横吹
Dujuanshan	杜鹃山
Fanji	反击
fukuafeng	浮夸风
gan wenti	赶问题
Gao Xingjian	高行健
gedepai	歌德派

geju	歌剧
geming yangbanxi	革命样板戏
Gongnong hongjun xuexiao	工农红军学校
Gu Zhuoyu	顾卓宇
guanyu jiaoyu gongzuo zhishi	关于教育工作指示
Guan Hanqing	关汉卿
guanmozhe	观摩者
Guang Weiran	光未然
Guo Moruo	郭沫若
Hai Mo	海默
Hai Rui Baguan	海瑞罢官
He Shuheng	何叔衡
Hongdeng ji	红灯记
Honghu chiweidui	洪湖赤卫队
Hongqi	红旗
Hongse niangzijun	红色娘子军
Hu Qili	胡启立
Hu Qiaomu	胡乔木
Hu Shuhe	胡叔和
Hu Weimin	胡伟民
Hu Yaobang	胡耀邦
Huadongqu huaju guanmo yanchuhui	华东区话剧观摩演出会
Hua Guofeng	华国峰
Huanxiang ji	还乡记
Huang Zhen	黄镇
Jiang Qing	江青
Jiaru wo shi zhende	假如我是真的
Jie Zhenquo	节镇国
jinqu	禁区
jinqji tequ	经济特区
Jingju xiandaixi guanmo yanchu dahui	京剧现代戏观摩演出会

Juben 剧本

Kulian 苦恋

kuangkuang 框框

Liu Bocheng 刘伯诚

Liu Shaoqi 刘少奇

Longjiang song 龙江颂

Ludang huozhong 芦荡火种

Lu Xun yishu xueyuan 鲁迅艺术学院

Luo Ruiqing 罗瑞卿

Ma Sicong 马思聪

Ma Zhongjun 马中骏

Minqyue chuzhao ren 明月初照人

Qianwan buyan wangji 千万不要忘记

Quanguo Huaju, Geju, Ertongju Chuangzuo Zuotanhui 全国话剧 歌剧 儿童剧创作座谈会

Shajiabang 沙家浜

Sha Yexin 沙叶新

Shanghai Xiju Zhuanke Xuexiao 上海戏剧专科学校

shenru shenghuo 深入生活

Shijiande zuiren 时间的罪人

Su Kun 苏堃

Sun Huizhu 孙惠柱

Tian Han 田汉

Wang Gui 王贵

Wang Peigong 王培公

Wenyi Bao 文艺报

Wenyi Gongzuotuan 文艺工作团

WM (Women) WM(我们)

Wu Han 吴晗

Wu wang jin'ge Yue wang jian 吴王金戈越王剑

Wu Xiuquan 伍修权

Wu Zetian 武则天

Xie Yaohuan 谢瑶环

xinyou yuji 心有余悸

Xu Teli 徐特立

yangbanxi 样板戏

yangqe 秧歌

Yang Lüfang 杨履方

yeyu 业余

Yu Wushengchu 于无声处

Yishu Gu 艺术股

Zhandou Jushe 战斗剧社

Zhao Xun 赵寻

Zhao Ziyang 赵紫阳

Zhengzhi Bu 政治部

Zhiqu weihushan 智取威虎山

zhongda ticai 重大题材

Zhongshen dashi 终身大事

Zhongguo Xiju Wenxue Xuehui 中国戏剧文学学会

Zhongyang Xiju Xueyuan Huadong
Fenyuan 中央戏剧学院华东分院

Zhou Yang 周扬

zhui zhengce 追政策

Part One

Drama on Historical Themes

1. Hai Rui Dismissed From Office *and China's Opposition Movement, 1958–1959*

LIN CHEN

According to legend, the Egyptian god Osiris was hacked into fourteen pieces by his spiteful brother, Seth, who then buried the remains in different places. The goddess Isis tracked down the fragments and reassembled her husband, thus performing one of the first acts of resurrection. In many aspects, the task I will attempt here in this article is similar to that of Isis. The "pieces" we seek to locate and identify are the seemingly disjointed and unrelated passages buried in China's historical anecdotes, literary criticisms and stage play scripts. The Osiris I attempt to piece together and resurrect is China's incipient "opposition movement," which took shape during the Great Leap Forward (1958–59). It is now possible to trace the opposition by Deng Xiaoping and his followers to the leftist line advocated by Mao Zedong and his followers back to 1958–59 by the use of materials recently available. A re-examination of the great debate during this period between the Maoist faction and its pragmatic opponents may help clarify the major policy shift of the post-Mao regime in China led by Deng. Since the Liu-Deng faction, which had assumed power in the aftermath (1959–65) of the Great Leap Forward, was again under Maoist attack beginning with the Cultural Revolution (1966–76), a study of the initial opposition movement[1] should also help elucidate our understanding of the structure of intraparty rivalry and the historical linkages between latent political opposition and regime change. This study is primarily focused on a stage play by Wu Han, one of the most vocal critics of Mao and among the most articulate spokesmen of the "opposition." Variously entitled as "Hai Rui Dismissed from Office" (*Hai Rui Baguan,*) "Hai Rui Curses the Emperor, (*Hai Rui ma huangdi*) etc., Wu's work first appeared as historical anecdotes in popular magazines and journals.[2] Subsequently, it was adapted as an opera or play script and was revised seven times.[3] The play was finally staged in various cities all over China and its unexpectedly enthusiastic reception stunned Mao and his followers. As a vehi-

30

cle of political communication, *Hai Rui Baguan* achieved its intended purpose in enlisting public opposition to Mao's program after the great policy debate at the Lushan Plenum (August 2-16, 1959). Even when Mao stepped down from power in the post-Leap period (1959-65) it was continually used as an instrument to discredit the leftist line and at the same time to mobilize political support for an alternative policy package promoted by the pragmatists headed by Liu and Deng. For these reasons, when Mao and his followers were again ready to try to seize power from the pragmatists in November 1965, *Hai Rui Baguan* became the first target of their attack. For some time, both Liu and Deng disappeared from the political scene. After the death of Mao in 1976, however, the downfall of the Gang of Four, of which Yao Wenyuan was a member,[4] followed within a month. The reinstatement of Deng Xiaoping, a close friend of Wu Han, once again shows the persistent relevance of *Hai Rui Baguan*.

In the following, I begin with a brief description of the plot and an analysis of the purposes of the play. Next, I discuss the peculiar political circumstances under which the work was written and the reasons why they call for a particular mode of analysis or methodology. While the main task is to trace the origin and the process of the opposition movement, I also seek to unravel the implications of the specific policy options in a larger context. In the conclusion, I try to examine the stage play as a cultural symbol for remolding political reality. To trace how the Maoists reacted to the factional conflict in relation to the different social and economic interests, I hope that it may enhance our understanding of the relationships among the different political groups today.

Hai Rui Baguan — *The Plot*

"Hui Rui Dismissed From Office" is a short story first written by Wu Han in 1959. Based on well-known anecdotes which depict the reign of Emperor Wanli (1573-1620), it was initially published in the form of newspaper and magazine articles. However, after being adapted as a play, it was staged in various Chinese metropolitan centers and localities.

The curtain rises on a scene that depicts the last years of Emperor Wanli. Reminiscent of all the periods of a declining dynasty in Chinese history, this was a time of nationwide economic hardship and intolerable misery. Flood, drought and other national calamities brought about a deterioration of general living conditions. Unprecedentedly heavy tax and corvee duties were simultaneously imposed upon the peasants as a result of many ambitious and large-scale public projects undertaken by an insensitive and capricious tyrant. Under these circumstances it became impossible for the small independent farmers to hold on to their own farms. Many of them realized they had to desert their lands. A few ingenious ones could manage to sell them to the large estate proprietors at only low prices. As the gentry bought a larger number of farms for almost nothing, many smaller plots were annexed and amalgamated outright by the big landlords through semi-legal or illegitimate means. A growing concentration of lands in the hands of the ruling class was thus brought about while the self-cultivating farmers were reduced to destitution as tenant farmers or day laborers.

As a rule, economic deterioration in Chinese history was often accompanied by widespread social unrest. The play therefore shifts to a scene of political confrontation between the Emperor and one of his top court officials, Hai Rui, the hero of the play. We should remember that it is a classical Chinese political tradition that the foremost role and duty of a scholar-official is to speak out for, and defend the welfare of, the people, even against the Emperor. Hence Hai, a conscientious and duty-bound court official as presented in the play, suggests to the Emperor the necessity of a swift change of policy: as it is evident that the main source of widespread popular discontent stemmed from the government's unpopular land policy, the annexed plots should be immediately returned to their rightful owners—the small independent farmers.

The drama reaches a climax at the moment of direct encounter between a self-righteous despot and a popular hero. Hai's open criticism of the prevailing policy and his undaunted spirit win him wide support. However, to the disappointment of all, the final scene concludes with Hai's ouster from his official post. It is not altogether impossible that the Emperor might have misunderstood his motive. Or he might simply have been outmaneuvered by other court officials. But whatever the case, with this tragic anti-climax the curtain falls.

The Purposes of the Play—Political Campaign Commercial?

"Historical plays are the best tool for educating the poeple[5]." They should meet the demands of the time[6]." For they are written not for the dead, but the living."[7] "Since all people attend stage plays, whether men or women, old or young, the more learned or the less educated, they have the function of social education[8]." The effects go far beyond those of a book[9]."

As *Hai Rui Baguan* was written at the same time as the author made the above comments, they may probably be taken as annotations to the purposes of the play. As the author said, it was written to meet the demands of the times. It was intended to be an educational tool.

But what was wrong with the times? Were not the authors writing for the living? Was there any compelling reason for so serious a scholar as Wu Han to use his time playing with this seemingly amateurish kind of work? And, moreover, where was the unsurmountable difficulty, or rather, inevitable peril or risk which called for such extreme forethought and precautions? These questions may, at first, appear puzzling and inexplicable. However, once we come to suspect and realize that the nature of the author's work is essentially political they all become intelligible and sensible. Much could go wrong, particularly when we recall that this was the time of the Great Leap Forward. There might be just as many reasonable demands from the people, about which discreet writers chose to be silent. Although there were many who suffered, they did not express their miseries to the authorities because they were afraid or lacked proper "education." Unless there was some need to serve the living and to meet the demands of the times, there appeared no reason for a serious scholar to take on so difficult and dangerous a task.[10]

As Leo Strauss has succinctly stated,

> "Persecution . . . gives rise to a peculiar kind of writing, and therewith to a peculiar type of literature, in which the truth about all crucial things is presented exclusively between the lines . . ." "It had all the advantages of public communication without its greatest disadvantage — capital punishment for the author[11]."

Since *Hai Rui Baguan* was written under the circumstances of possible persecution, one suspects that it is a work of political protest. In order to look for its most crucial messages, as suggested by Professor Strauss, we shall try to "read between the lines" by taking special notice of strange mistakes, omissions and even fabrications in the play. By examining these points closely, we can find the most important messages in the play. And by reading the present into the past we can see how Wu protested on behalf of the people.

Themes of the Play

1. The Restoration of the Private Plots (tuitian)

> "During those scores of years, social conditions had greatly changed. The Emperor appropriated the land of the peasants on a large scale. . . . The land-owning farmers became destitute tenants." "As the lands were annexed

and concentrated, corvee duties became increasingly heavy and livelihood difficult. The peasants labored all the year around for their masters . . . yet there was no liberty nor monetary pay[12].

In this exposition of the background of the play there are three vital points. The first is the author's admitted emphasis on the origination of injustices by the landlords through the appropriation of the peasants' private plots[13]. The second is the introduction of the issue of monetary pay. And the third is the exaggeration of the issue of "liberty" (*ziyou*). The author could not have been unaware of the political consequences of stressing the first point. Furthermore, it was common knowledge that neither monetary reward nor "liberty" had ever become a political issue in Hai Rui's time (1515–1587). It is therefore reasonable to suspect that these emphases and exaggerations, in disregard of historical facts and his long-held academic position of historicism,[14] were deliberate. Since they might be borrowed to reflect the demands of the times, their meanings can be understood only by putting them into the contemporary political context.

First, we may see, in the theme of the restoration of private plots, a protest against the land policy of the Mao administration. Because the further collectivization in 1958 lands previously held by the people had, in effect, reduced the wealthy and the moderately wealthy peasants to destitute tenants, they were the first to oppose the commune system. When the general standard of living deteriorated as a result of the failure of the poeple's communes, the bourgeois elements also voiced their discontent. Finally, as dissatisfaction grew, even Party members became skeptical of the commune system.[15]

Although there were different reasons for the discontent of these three groups, they all demanded the re-institution of the family as the basic unit of production. On August 29, 1959, an article in *People's Daily* admitted that there were many critics of the communes, who were saying that "it was set up too early" or that "its management was a mess." They complained that there had been a lack of prudent planning and that the Great Leap Forward had become a great leap backward because production had not increased but declined. They said that, "The people's commune is not as good as the advanced cultural cooperative (*gaoji nongye huzhu hezuoshe*); the advanced cooperative is not as good as the elementary cooperative (*chujishe*); the elementary cooperative is not as good as the mutual-aid team (*huzhuzu*), and the mutual-aid team is not as good as 'going it alone' (*dan'gan*)."[16] So their slogan was "The smaller the unit of production the better," and "The greater the number of private plots into which the collective farms are divided the better." What they demanded was re-institution of the pre-1958 system of production based on private ownership. They wanted to possess, and to re-assume their right to make use of, what they had produced. Since these issues involve almost every aspect of the individual's life and the discontent with the 1958 change was widespread, it is not unlikely that it was this prevailing discontent, rather than historical and factual accuracy, which was on the mind of the author. Because his primary objective was to criticize the commune system introduced during Mao's Great Leap Forward, he was willing to use, exaggerate or even to fabricate in spite of the historical record, the evils resulting from the amalgamation of the lands in Ming times. In giving expression to the widespread opposition to the leftist policy, he probably thought that his play was a "reflection of the times to serve the living."

Secondly, there is the issue of monetary pay. This can be easily understood as a criticism of the change, made during the Great Leap Forward, from the pre-1958 reward system. After 1958, pay differentials and monetary wages were abolisehd in order to hasten the proces toward complete economic equality in the whole of society. However, on closer examination, the play can also be seen as an objection to the newly introduced system of production and distribution, because the two are intricately related and intertwined. Those who opposed the Great Leap Forward concluded that one of the main causes for production decline was the lack of incentives resulting from the change to the new system. To arrest the downward trend and to boost production, there had to be a return to the previous policy, which had rewarded on the basis of contribution, giving more to those who worked harder.[17] Only such a return, it was argued, could again revive the farmer's love and attachment to his land and work. Thus the problem of material incentive leads immediately to the question of private property. Against the principle "to each according to his need," they demanded to re-introduce the principle "to each according to his labor." In short, they wanted to abolish the post-Leap distribution system.

Third, as for the issue of liberty, this is perhaps the strangest idea in the alleged historical context. Being a specialist of Ming history, Wu could not have been unaware of the obvious absurdity of injecting this modern, in fact, western, idea of liberty (*ziyou*) into a traditional period of Chinese history. The fact that he did so therefore should indicate how important it was to him. With this in mind, we can readily see that the issue of liberty was most useful for the author to advance the opposition's argument in an ongoing political debate. It could be used to support the demand to change the systems of production and distribution, and also to oppose political intervention, central control and regimentation in favor of instituting a different way of life.

For instance, those who suffered from the programs introduced by the Great Leap Forward were opposed to the commune and collective labor. Since everybody knew that no one could say so openly, some requested in the name of liberty that the family be resurrected as the production unit by "going it alone." Although no one would risk his own life and safety to oppose the idea of collectivization publicly, it was nevertheless difficult for the Maoists to prosecute those who, in the name of liberty, implicitly expressed their wish to use and consume what they had produced.

When the Great Leap program began, many families had been broken because members of the family were assigned to different places to work. Furthermore, in enlisting the female labor force to boost production and taking advantage of the situation to re-structure Chinese society, the Party had in effect tried to do away with the family, and had sest up public mess halls in the communes. Under such circumstances, many who opposed the change complained that "there was not enough food" and asked "why the Party should have intervened in everything." They also found fault with the way the public mess halls were managed. They said that it amounted to the abolition of the "ten freedoms" (*shida ziyou*). So, under the slogan "Let every family cook so that every chimney makes smoke" (*jiajia qihuo, huhu maoyan*), they wanted to resume the family way of life in the collectivized farms. Under the slogan "Break up the groups and leave them alone as individuals" (*mandiren buchengqun*), they opposed collective production in favor of individual cultivation. In the market, liberty or freedom was used to demand liberalization (*ziyouhua*), *laissez faire* (greater lattitude for the local authorities and freedom from central control and interference), or a competitive economic system (*ziyuojingji*), based on the principle of "self accountability by the production unit" (*zifuyingkui*) free from central planning. At this point, one could hear the cry for liberty even in the army, the bureaucracy and the higher educational institutions. Since the Party always exercised its power in disregard of the particularistic professional values of these institutions, the professionally minded people wanted to free themselves from its intervention.[18] Therefore, in making these demands for private kitchens, family life, "going it alone," private ownership, free economy and professionalism, what these people wanted was a complete change in the social, economic and political system. What they demanded was a reversal of the policies, practices, and processes introduced since the Great Leap Forward.

It was perhaps in this sense that it appeared to Wu that the play was giving expression to the demands of the people. However, from the perspective of those who were in favor of the Great Leap Forward, the meaning of the messages might have been quite different. Since those who opposed the Great Leap Forward were from many different social and economic groups, and since their demands included changes in production, distribution and way of life, the play could be considered as a political platform of an oposition.[19] Even though Wu was writing primarily on behalf of the people to appeal to Mao himself for a change or halt of his oppressive and unpopular policies, yet since that range of the demand was so comprehensive and its nature so fundamental, it became a devastating attack on the revolutionary left.

2. The Dismissal of Hai Rui (baguan)

> "Be audacious to think, to speak and to
> act. This has been in vogue since the
> Great Leap Forward. I also attempted to
> write plays in the same spirit."[20]

The second theme in the play is the dismissal of Hai Rui. In the first four drafts of the play we noticed that the author had as his only theme the return of the private plots (*tuitian*)[21], but, beginning with the fifth draft, one can see a new theme: this dismissal of Hai Rui (*baguan*). As presented in the play, Hai was an upright official with great concern for the interests of the people. He fought the oppressive policies of the gentry and the whole ruling class; and he also opposed the amalgamation of the private plots in disregard of the livelihood of the peasants. Unfortunately, his efforts to restore the private plots met the united opposition of the official-gentry class, because such measures were against their interests. As a result, Hai was dismissed from office. Since this theme of the unjust dismissal of an upright official was added at the time when Marshal Peng Dehuai was removed from his post as the Minister of Defense, Wu was probably adapting his former draft in a demand that the regime reverse its unjust verdict.

There is some evidence to support this interpretation. A change in title suggests the new theme. The only article which Wu published before August 2, 1959 was the one entitled "Hai Rui Curses the Emperor,"[22] which appeared in *The People's Daily* on June 16, 1959. In this article what Wu stressed was the courage of Hai Rui in sending remonstrative memorials to the emperor. He made no mention of Hai's military power. But drafts which followed the Lushan Plenum (August 2-16, 1959), when Peng was dismissed, were entitled "The Dismissal of Hai Rui."[23] In an article entitled "On Hai Rui" written on September 17, 1959, only one month after the Lushan Plenum, the author took pains to explain his hero's military power. "He has the right to command the army under his jurisdiction, so he has great power."[24] On another occasion he made a particular point indicating that "he (Yu Qian, read Hai Rui) had once held a post in the Defense Ministry."[25] Furthermore, Hai, as presented in the play, was fighting against the ruling class's arbitrary appropriation of the people's land. Though he had failed in his courageous struggle against the ruler and his subordinates, Hai was loved and respected by the people and had the support of a few of his friends and some of the intellectuals. This description is also appropriate to Peng's case; at the Lushan meeting, he fought the ruling class led by Mao, and criticized the shortcomings of the commune and the Great Leap Forward.[26] His downfall aroused much dissatisfaction among bureaucrats' Party cadres, and intellectuals who supported his views and also gave rise to widespread discussion and sympathy among the people. Moreover, an article appearing in the *People's Daily* on August 16, 1967 pointed out that Marshall Peng had once compared himself with Hai Rui while he was advancing his criticisms at Lushan against Mao's economic and social policies. In another article, which appeared on the same day, Liu Shaoqi allegedly invoked or alluded to the spirit of Hai Rui[27]. After Peng had been dismissed, Liu was reported to have said, "In the Lushan Plenum we made a mistake."[28] The many changes made in the play at the time when Marshall Peng was removed, reinforced by additional reports of Peng's comparing himself with Hai Rui, strongly suggest that the new theme in the play was a protest against his dismissal. Although the play tacitly appealed to the people to demand the reinstatement of Marshal Peng, it also advised them to learn several lessons from his example. First, the author implies that the people may legitimately oppose the oppressive measures of the landlords and the ruling class. As Wu said,[29] the greatest landlord was, in Hai Rui's time, the Emperor. But in the present, the greatest landowner was the state or Chairman Mao, who had been mainly responsible for further amalgamation of the peasants' lands. Since the supporters of Mao are the equivalent of the officials and the gentry class, the people should oppose them as Hai Rui had done.

Second, the people should demand the reversal of the unjust verdicts on all upright officials. Like Hai Rui, Marshal Peng had shown great courage in appealing on behalf of the people. He had criticized Mao for the shortcomings of collectivization and the Great Leap Forward, but he considered himself a loyal official because his policy was based on the long-range interest of the state.[30] From this perspective, Mao's decision to dismiss Marshal Peng and many others[31] who shared his view was most unjust and unfortunate for the nation. It was therefore imperative for the scholar to perform the task of the loyal opposition.

Third, those who were disgraced should not be discouraged. Instead, they should emulate Hai Rui and work for their eventual return or rein-

University of Winnipeg, 515 Portage Ave., Winnipeg, Manitoba, Canada R3B 2E9

statement. Hai Rui's downfall is shown as temporary. As a good official, he had the support of friends, intellectuals and the people, and eventually his good name was restored after political conditions had changed. Perhaps the author hoped that, in a like manner, all good officials could also win if they were determined to "rise again." As he said, "since the Great Leap Forward, the change had already taken place." But, in order to bring a swift change, all the people must follow up the "new mode." He wanted them to think fearlessly, to be audacious in speech and action —this is the example of Hai Rui and also the message of the play. All people in all kinds of work should emulate Hai's spirit. It is obviously for this reason that the author could claim that his seemingly amateurish work in writing a play "was also courageously attempted."

3. The Eradication of the Scoundrels (chuba)

"In the first four drafts, I emphasized the theme of the restoration of the private plots. . . . But under the circumstances, I found it was impossible and did not solve the problems of the peasants. From the point of view of historical developments, these kinds of political measures are incrementalist. In writing a historical play today, what is the meaning in promoting this kind of incrementalism? After considering this matter time and again, I finally changed the main theme to 'the eradication of the scoundrel' and made the theme of private supplementary. This is a great change."[32]

In 1961 Wu wrote these words in a separate article which he later attached to the play proper as its preface. At a time when the play was still entitled "The Dismissal of Hai Rui," the author pointed out that the theme of the play was neither the restoration of the private plots, which he had stressed previously, nor Hai's dismissal, which he did not even mention, but rather the eradication of the scoundrels. The question for us now is why he even bothered to use the theme of "private plots" in the first place? Why did he need to point out the main theme of the play more than a year after the failure of the Great Leap Forward? The author took pains to point out that "this is a great change." Where is this change, and why did the main theme of the play need to be changed so often? Since the play is essentially political, I attempt again to set the change of themes in the play against those in the larger political context. For this purpose I divide the development of the play into three periods.

a. Advocating reform (June-September 1959)—Though Wu said that the restoration of the private plots was a kind of incremental reformist measure (*gailiangzhuyi*), there is reason to believe that this was exactly what he had been advocating when he wrote the first four drafts of the play. During this period, there was no indication that he intended to instigate the people to demand a basic policy change by the regime. Rather, the primary aim of the play seemed to be an appeal to the "Emperor", or the highest political leader, to consider the general deterioration of social and economic life since the introduction of the people's commune and the Great Leap Forward. As Wu suggested, Hai Rui's policy, or his advice to the Emperor, was based on the long-term interests of the state. So, despite his criticisms, he was still loyal to the Emperor and he, like all members of the "opposition," was still working for the good of the ruling class. The difference was that Hai's policy was aimed at the long-term interests of the state, whereas the Communist Party was in favor of a more immediate result. The same can probably be said of the role Wu played himself. Despite his criticisms, he remained loyal to the Supreme Leader, and his work was thus a positive contribution to the Party. Although the restoration of the private plots was only a modest reform, he probably thought that the overall situation would change if he could mobilize sufficient support in favor of an immediate cessation of the collectivization program. As later developments show, his effort was already too late. But, not intending to give up at this point, he adapted the play as a work of more vigorous political protest, because rapid developments in the larger social context had already made the play obsolete in its original form.

b. Period of protest (September 1959-November 13, 1960) — Between September 1959, about the time when Marshall Peng was dismissed, and November 1960, when the play was again published in a revised version, two important revisions were made. One is in the title of the play which was changed from *Hai Rui* to *Hai Rui's Dismissal from Office*. The other is the addition of the theme of the eradication of the scoundrels; the execution of the scoundrels (*chuba*) being added to the story. These revisions both appeared in the final draft and there was no doubt some relation between them.

Let us recall again for a moment the situation following the Great Leap Forward. The removal of the "good officials" showed that the faction in power had no intention of changing its policy. At the same time, the downfall of Marshal Peng and his associates signaled danger for those who shared his views. So the author protested for Peng lest, subconsciously perhaps, the same fate would befall him. However, to Mao and his followers, Wu's appeal was no less than a mobilization of support. Indiscriminate and harsh sentences had been dealt out to many people and even petty offenders against the law during the Three-Antis Campaign (1951–1952) and the Anti-Rightist Movement (1957–58), so the demand to reopen cases in the hope of redressing grievances (*fan'an*) was very popular after the Great Leap failure. But even if Chairman Mao had by then undergone a change of heart, it would have been too great risk for him to reinstate Peng, because the military might lend the dissidents its support. It was therefore natural for Wu to feel at this time that his plea remained unheard, and the demand of the opposition had made no impact.

   c. Call for a change of leadership (November 1960–August 8, 1961) — Probably because the appeal for the reversal of the verdict (*pingfan*) was to no avail, or because Wu belatedly realized that a fundamental change was needed, he finally called for a change in the top leadership. In the "Preface" which he added to the play in August 1961, he said it was useless to advocate the incremental measure of reform through the restoration of the private plots because it could not solve the problems of the times. Therefore in the final draft of the play, the emphasis was on the eradication of the scoundrels. It is evident that by "the scoundrels" he was referring to the Maoists, the Party ideologues or the ruling group — the contemporaneous counterparts to the landlords, officials and the gentry of the historical past. The scoundrels sentenced to execution in Scene 9 were Xu Ying and Wang Mingyou. Since the notorious Xu Ying was the son of Xu Jie, the landlord (read Chairman Mao), what Wu implied was probably that some of of Mao's most ardent followers should be executed. At the time when Wu made these revisions few pehaps realized who the "most ardent followers" were. These became obvious at the beginning of the Cultural Revolution. The most savage critics of Wu include Yao Wenyuan (allegedly Mao's son-in-law), Jiang Qing (Mme. Mao), Guan Feng, Lin Jie, and Qi Benyu, who were supported by Marshall Lin Biao and Luo Ruiqing, the chief beneficiaries of Marshall Peng's downfall.

   It is still difficult to estimate the enormous discontent following the Three-Antis Campaign and the Anti-Rightist Campaign. It is equally difficult to assess the impact of massive social disruption and economic dislocation during the Great Leap Forward and the establishment of the communes. When Wu made these changes it was natural that Mao and his supporters might have felt that Wu's call was actually aimed at inciting all those who had lost or been victimized in these campaigns and mass movements. Those in the military, the bureaucracy, industry, higher educational institutions and the departments of culture and propaganda who expected to suffer similarly, if the Great Leap Forward policy ran it course, were probably among those most likely to answer the call and rise against the revolutionary left then in power. Thus from giving positive advice to the top leadership for reform, to protesting against the dismissal of Marshall Peng, from an appeal for the interests of the people to a call for the elimination of the ruling class, the author's position had changed greatly as his hopes for the improvement of the regime vanished. It is perhaps for this reason that Wu said that the change of emphasis in the play was a "great change" which was made only "after considering the matter time and again". It may be true, as he admitted, that he still hesitated to bring a violent scene into the play, yet it seems clear that possibilities of bloodshed had been carefully considered. As he said, "it would be better if no man were killed. But up till now this question is still undetermined. What we can do now is probably to listen more to others' opinions. For the moment we shall wait."

Conclusion

These changes in the play perhaps can be taken as an indication of what the author expected the people to learn. But they may also have been made in view of the changes in the larger political context. In either case, one thing seems certain. *Hai Rui baguan*, as a historical play, did fulfill some of its expectations. It did have something "to teach" in its messages to follow the example of Hai Rui. It had also "met the demand of the times" in giving expression to the outcries for "liberty, monetary payment and the restoration of the private plots". In support of the good officials and the demands of the people, it had "served the living."

Wu's messages were obviously all extremely dangerous. But there is a uniquely political institution in China as a civilization. From ancient times, there has been a courageous tradition of criticism by Chinese historians in venturing admonition and advice to the Emperor in times of ill-government.[33] In a country of mass illiteracy and unchecked imperial power it has been the intellectuals, particularly the historians, who have assumed the role of guardian of the public interest. Now, after his disappointment in Mao's persistently refusing reforms, and having realized the increased pressures upon officials, friends and intellectuals, Wu might well have thought that the duty of criticizing and advising the Emperor had been thrust upon him.[34] For this historical task the cost is always one's own life. Yet to a renowned historian such as Wu there was no alternative.

If a historical play is a reflection of reality, in a variety of ways it is also the creator of history. As cultural symbol, the play first defines reality in a particular way through which the people may come to understand the meanings of the social and political order. At the same time, it has also provided some criteria by which they may come to evaluate the propriety of many of the Maoist regime's policies. The former function of symbols is what C. W. Morris called "the designative" while the latter is called by Abraham Kaplan "the appraisive" or the "prescriptive".[35] In both ways the play, as political weapon, affected Mao's government adversely while it popularized and strengthened the opposition.

After the initiation of the Three Red Flags[36], the government had repeatedly propagated them as programs designed to lead China toward the goal of rapid modernization through simultaneous social transformation. Opposed to such views, Marshal Peng led Mao's opponents in condemning the social transformation and economic modernization through communization. At Lushan, he complained that there was a lack of prudent planning and that the Great Leap Forward was started *taizaole* (meaning "a mess" although it can mean "too early" if you are extremely careful in your tone). One month later, after the downfall of Marshal Peng, Wu, who was a family friend of Deng Xiaoping's and had tutored his children, implied that such programs were oppressive measures by the ruling class directly opposed to the people's interests. He compared the amalgamation of the land of the peasants for the purpose of increasing production to the illegitimate appropriation of land by the gentry-official class for their own benefit. He also drew implicit parallels between the leftists' efforts to mobilize all human forces to achieve immediate results in industry and agriculture and the most exacting immediate results in industry and agriculture and the most exacting corvee duties of the most decadent reigns in Chinese history. It is true that the story of Hai Rui is obviously only an allegory, and that the past is used to satirize the present (*yigu fengjin*), but the fact is that, when the present is compared to the past, the play is making a definition of the situation in its accusation of the contemporary political situation. Wu's judgment of the regime's policy might be based on temporary failures which the supreme leader, in leading China toward a socialist pattern of modernization, had deemed a necessary cost which the people must pay. However, Wu's challenge was fundamentally opposed to Mao's view in that he offered to evaluate Mao's policy in terms of how well it could serve the interests of the people on whose behalf Wu spoke.

As a traditional scholar, Wu may have been accustomed to judge all political realities in humanitarian and Confucian perspectives. But when these views were propagated publicly, they could stir up adverse feelings and even actions against the party in power. By 1965 Mao's regime had been in power for sixteen years, yet it had failed to eliminate all the remnant and latent values associated with Confucianism and bourgeois thinking. Moreover, as the regime became stabilized, many particularistic institutional values and norms had developed within the various sectors of the modern state.

Thus, once the failure of the Great Leap policy became inevitable, two problems re-emerged and appeared large and threatening. One was the remnants of the Nationlist regime supported by upper class and bourgeois elements, and the other was social differentiation developed through increasing functional specialization and new emphasis on expert knowledge. When the forces associated with the Nationlist regime took advantage of the new problems, the opposition became suspect because it appeared to be preparing the way for a comeback of the old socioeconomic system. On the one hand, there were the peasants and the small merchants, on the other, there were the professionals. Disappointed by their new hopes in the communes, it was natural for the peasants to become nostalgic for the system of private plots. Frustrated by the strict control of the state, the business-minded demanded the reinstitution of free markets. Furthermore, there were many other groups which resisted interference by the Party. The bureaucracy, industry, the professional military corps,[37] and the higher educational institutions[38] all longed to be free from intervention from the Party ideologues who would invariably come to impose values incompatible with their respective functional requirements. These groups, both old and new, became the backbone of the opposition. They blocked the program of the Maoists and resisted rapid and total change. Such resistance perhaps can be most vividly shown by what had happened in the communes and the military before the current crisis.

Following the initial failure of the commune system in 1959, the leftists admitted[39] that there were many peasants who erected marks in collective farms to subdivide their private possessions. Some devoted their time and energy to plough their own private plots (*ziliudi*). Not only did many private family-owned businesses reappear in the market, but they competed with the state cooperatives for profits.

The military was not greatly concerned with the abuses and the ill-management of the communes. Yet it was obviously unhappy. As the Party insisted that the PLA participate in agricultural production and study Mao's thought the army diverted much of the time and energy of its personnel for training in the use of modern equipment and weaponry.[40] The bitter experience of the PLA during the Korean War (1950–53) was still fresh in the memories of the top military leaders. They must have realized how much they still had to rely on Soviet supplies in times of national emergency. Thus, the time demanded of the military either for production or for learning Mao's thought was a serious cost against their prior concern for professionalism. Moreover, Mao's foreign policy of self-reliance also conflicted with the expectations of the military leaders for uninterrupted Soviety military supplies. Because of his Peng's special responsiblity and the difficulty for him to argue for the "special interests" of the military at the Lushan Plenum, Peng found it convenient to couch his plea for professionalism in his general criticisms of

Mao's decision to dismiss the spokesman and the leader of all of them. Hence Mao's decision to dismiss Peng is understandable in view of the possible consequences of his insubordination and his enormous influence within the military. At the same time, as it must have appeared to Wu Han, there was no sign of an immediate change of policy, therefore no promise of improvement of livelihood. The people, especially the upper or middle peasants, became more disappointed and impatient.

Under these circumstances, the play served to clarify the main issues and unify all the forces of opposition in support of Peng's reinstatement (*pingfan*). It made the various latent, private emotions of dissatisfaction public. It not only mobilized the prevailing mood of opposition into a coherent and "legitimate" social fact, but, by its definition of the situation in a particular way, it led the people to believe that the policy offered by the opposition was a better alternative. In offering to evaluate Mao's policy in terms of how well it could serve the present interests of the people, it questioned not only the wisdom of Mao as leader but also the validity of the revolutionary left ideology. It perpetuated the deviant practices and encouraged the forces of dissidence against which the Maoist leadership could hardly maintain itself. It corrupted the mind of the people, especially the young, by advocating self-interest, individualism, liberty and a bourgeois way of life. According to Mao, this would undermine the selfless, obedient and devoted behavior[41] on which China's rapid modernization program must eventually depend. Since *Hai Rui baguan* has exacerbated and created many problems for the regime, it is not surprising that as soon as he had weathered the worst storm, Mao decided in November 1965 to launch a massive cultural movement comparable to what had occurred in the social and economic field during 1958. He did so because the critical years following the Great Leap Forward and the establishment of the communes had shown that China's most formidable obstacle to modernization still persisted in the field of culture. So, it was imperative for Mao to initiate a cultural revolution to lay the foundation for China's further attempt to modernize itself.

The Cultural Revolution (1966–76) is now referred to by Mao's opponents as the "lost decade." After Deng's political comeback in 1977, China's policy has made an almost complete reversal of the Great Leap policy which Mao attempted to reactivate during the Cultural Revolution. By reintroducing free markets, material incentives, and quality education, by opening up the domestic market for foreign investment while dismantling the communes, the policy of the new leadership made another swing. Many of the writers, professionals, intellectuals and officials such as Peng Zhen and Fan Jin, formerly Mayor and Deputy Mayor of Beijing, were again rehabilitated.[42] At the same time, the supporters of Mao, such as the Gang of Four and the disparaged military commanders who once held sway during the Cultural Revolution, were made to step down from positions of power. It was during the tumultuous period of revolution that Wu Han died. His wife and daughter were also persecuted to death.[43] According to figures given by a Chinese source, the number of people who were imprisoned, and implicated in trumped-up charges resulting from *Hai Rui Dismissed from Office* ran to "tens of thousands" (*chengqian shangwan*). It was perhaps because of this powerful influence that the play exerted that Chester Leo Smith called *Hui Rui Dismissed from Office* "the greatest drama of the twentieth century." However, one is left with the most puzzling question: what was Wu's real motive?[44] Was he "a man who held his own against communism"?[45] Or was he "allied with and working for much more powerful men?"[46] Or, was he simply an unyielding honest historian true to his professed standard of historicism and professionalism?

In view of the many obvious mistakes, distortions and outright fabrications which were made through the many drafts of the play, I am not certain that he can be called a true historian bent on preserving intellectual honesty and professionalism. But to quibble over such trifling questions is probably to miss the point, because his stature as a true historian, or rather a "Grand Historian"[47] in the classical Chinese tradition, lies precisely in his determination to look beyond private interests, whether of individual, a faction, an interest group, a political party, communism or some other ideology. After all, what more can one ask of a man who had offered his own life and family[48] in defense of the public interest? Perhaps Kwok was right when he concluded that Wu "fulfills in the present a charge cherished and practices in the long, past of China — the right of the scholar to remonstrate.[49] For, the social meaning of human behavior cannot simply be imputed by the analyst by the use of one's own preconceived values, notions, models or theories.[50] As Max Weber taught, the only guide is "empathy". Through this perspective, it is most instructive to read the articles published recently by Wu's own kind, such as Xia Nai, Hou Wailu and Zhang Youren, a group of highly respected historians commemorating the death of Wu Han. One article by Zhang Youran was entitled "Loyal Heart of Martyr, True Qualities of the Historian: Profoundly Cherishing the Memory of Professor Wu Han".[51] Indeed, there is no other description more befitting than the phrase "true qualities of the historian." To appreciate this, we must try to understand it in the cultural context of Chinese society and in the history in which he lived. Professor Wu, who had never intended to write history in a play, has proved beyond any doubt that he lived up to the ideals of the historian, the scholar, the man he himself understood best by the name of Hai Rui. In the study of *Hai Rui baguan* we have at least learned that the informal and invisible built-in mechanism which served to check imperial power based on Confucian tradition has worked every time throughout Chinese histroy, be it imperial, republican or communist.

Notes

1.   In this article, I have chosen the term "movement" rather than "party" or faction" to describe China's opposition activity under Communist rule. Max Weber defined a "party" as "A spontaneous society of propaganda and agitation seeking to acquire power. . . . for the realization either of objective aims or of personal advantage, or of both." Consequently, the general orientation of the political party, whether in its personal or impersonal aspect is that of *Machtstreben* (Striving for power). See Robert Michels, *First Lectures in Political Sociology*, trans. Alfred de Grazia, University of Minnesota Press, 1949, p. 134. However, Formisano was of the opinion that "the basic idea of party often loaded with cultural connotations, serves to organize political phenomena which may not fit a party mold." p. 473. Although Schurmann differentiated "faction" from "opinion group" (See Franz Schurmann, *Ideology and Organized in Communist China*, 1968, pp. 55–56, 126, 164), the term "faction" obviously does not fit with the subject of our discussion.

2.   For example, *Wucai jiao, Dahongpao, Xiaohongpao*, "Hai Rui Pulling a Riverboat on the Bank" (Hai Rui beiqian), "Hai Rui Sends a Memorial to the Throne" (Hai Rui shangshu), "Hai Rui huichao" (Hai Rui Returns to the Court), "Hai Rui Curses the Emperor" (Hai Rui ma huangdi), *RMRB* June 16, 1959; "On Hai Rui" (Lun Hai Rum), *RMRB* September 21, 1959; "The story of Hai Rui" (Hai Rui de gushi), etc. The last three were written by Wu Han before he wrote *Hai Rui Baguan* (hereafter *HRBG*) in 1961.

3.   Wu Han, *HRBG*, 1961, p. iii; "Historical Plays Revisited" (Zai Tan lishiju), *Wehui Bao*, May 3, 1961. *Shengsi pai* or *Sannu qiangban* and "Hai Rui sends a memorial to the throne", had already been staged for some time when Wu Han attempted his script on *HRBG*. The last one was played by Zhou Xinfang (Qi Lintung) in celebration of the tenth anniversary of the establishment of the communist regime in 1959 while Wu Han's own *HRBG* was played by Ma Lianliang and Qiu Shengrong in February 1961.

4.   Yao was arrested on October 7, 1976. See Fox Butterfield, "China's Leftists are Now Called 'Capitalist-Roaders,'" *New York Times*, October 20, 1976.

5. Wu Han, "On Historical Plays" (Tan Lishi ju), *Wenhui Bao*, February 25, 1961.

6. Wu Han, "Historical Play Revisited."

7. Wu Han, "some Problems on Historicism" (Guanyu lishizhuyi de yixie wenti), *Beijing Wanbao*, February 18, 1961.

8. "(Xijubao) Report on an Interview on May 18, 1961 with Wu Han on his Historical Play *HRBG*," *Xijubao*, November 9, 1961.

9. Wu Han, "Historical Play Revisited".

10. For the much repeated and reproduced story on Hai Rui, see *Sheng-si pai, Wucai jiao, Dahonogpao*, "Hai Rui Pulling a Riverboat on the Bank", "Hai Rui Sends a Memorial to the Throne", "Hai Rui Curses the Emperor", "On Hai Rui"; and "The Story of Hai Rui". The information given in the "Preface" and "Introduction" of *HRBG*, (1961, p. iii.) are most valuabale. In the "Preface" Wu indicated that he was doing research on Hai Rui in 1959 and that it was at the end of that year (after the Lushan Plenum) that several of his friends working in the theatre sought him out to adapt the story as a stageplay. At the end, he indicated that the seventh draft was completed on November 13, 1960 and the final revision was completed by August 8, 1961.

11. Leo Strauss, *Persecution and the Art of Writing* (The Free Press, 1982), p. 25.

12. Wu Han, "Hai Rui," *Chuntianji* (Beijing, 1961), p. 230.

13. Wu Han, *HRBG*, p. iii.

14. Wu Han, "On Controversy" (Shuo zhenglun), *Xuexi ji*, 1962, p. 150. See also Arif Dirlik, "The Problem of Class Viewpoint Versus Historicism in Chinese Historiography," *Modern China*, 3:4, October 1977, pp. 465–488; Cliff Edmunds, "Politics and Historiography after the Great Leap; the Case of Chien Potsan," F. Gilbert Chan and Harlan W. Jenks, eds., *Maoism and Revisionism in China: 1949–79*.

15. Wang Jinwu, et al., "The Anti-Rightist Campaign at Present Is a Series of Deep and Violent Class Struggles in Our Socialist Construction of the State (Muqian fan you qing xhuyi douzheng xi woguo shehui zhuyi jianshe shiji yizu shenkede jieji douzheng)," *Jilin daxue renwenkexue xuebao*, No. 4, 1959.

16. For an explanation of these terms of economic organization and structural change during 1958, see Cheng Chu-yuan, *Communist China's Economy 1949–1962*. (Seton Hall University Press, 1963).

17. "How Did the Peasant Discuss 'To Each According to His Work'" (Nongmin zenyang yilun anlaofenpei), *Honqqi* No. 1–12, 1959, pp. 34–36.

18. David A. Charles, "The Dismissal of Marshal Peng Te-huai, *"China Quarterly*, No. 8, October-December, 1961.

19. However, one must try to resist the temptation to over-interpret the opposition as one which was aimed from the very beginning only to oppose the Communist regime or Communism. More will be said in the conclusion.

20. Wu Han, *HRBG*, p. vii.

21. Yang Qinding, "Cong *Hai Rui Baquan* zhi gege banben de bijiao kan tade fandonbenzhi," *RMRB* April 16, 1966.

22. Wu Han, "Hai Rui curses the Emperor".

23. Yang Qinding. op. cit.

24. Wu Han, "On Hail Rui," *Denqxiaji* (Beijing, 1961) p. 148.

25. Ibid. p. 151. What was occupying the mind of the author can be seen in his article on "Yu qian", where he explicitly indicated that he once held the post of "Defense Minister".

26. See David A. Charles, "The Dismissal of Marshall Peng Te-huai," pp. 63-76; *The Case of Peng Te-huai, 1959-1968*, (Hongkong: Union Research Institute 1968).

27. "Looking at Zhou Yang's Wolf Ambition from Hai Rui Plays," (Cong Hai Rui xi *Wucaijiao* kan Zhou Yang de langziyexin), *RMRB*, August 16, 1967.

28. For the Maoist allegation see, "Peng Dehuai and his backstage boss cannot escape the responsibility of these heinous crimes!" (Peng Dehuai jiqi houtai zuizenantao), *RMRB*, August 16, 1967.

29. Wu Han, "On Hail Rui," pp. 229-231.

30. Ibid. p. 237.

31. David A. Charles, "The Dismissal of Marshal Peng Te-huai," pp. 63-76.

32. Wu Han, *HRBG*, p. iii.

33. Wu Han, "Some Problems on the Study of History," (Xuexi lishi zhishi de jige wenti), *Xuexi ji*, p. 253.

34. See Wang Yunwu, ed., *Wenwenshan wenji* (Shanghai: Shangwu, 1937), p. 76.

35. Harrold Lasswell and Abraham Kaplan, *Power and Society*, (New Haven: Yale University Press, 1950).

36. "The Three Red Flags" refers to the initiation of the general line of socialist revolution ,the Great Leap Forward, and the establishment of the people's com-

mune by Mao in 1958. The red flag is a flag of revolution. To call these programs "red flags" it was perhaps implied that all true Communists follow their red flags, the Chinese people should support the offensive against the old society to achieve a social revolution of reconstruction as intended by Mao's new programs in 1958.

37. John Gittings, *Role of the Chinese Army*, (London, Oxford University Press, 1967), p. 177–241.

38. Lin Chen, "The Politics of China's Education, Patterns of Continuity and Change, 1949–73," *Asian Forum* October 1973, pp. 21–23.

39. Wang Jinwu, et. al., op. cit.

40. John Gittings, op. cit.

41. Harry Schwartz, "Modernization and the Maoist Vision — Some Reflections on Chinese Communist Goals," in *China Under Mao*, ed. by Roderick MacFarquhar, (Cambridge: MIT Press, 1966), pp. 3–19.

42. "New position for three-family village gangster: Fan Jin was promoted as Chairman of Beijing Municipal Political Consultative Conference," *Shijie ribao* (World News Daily), New York, March 24, 1985, p. 20.

43. Wu Han died on October 11, 1969. His wife Yuanzhen died in March 1976. Their daughter committed suicide in September 1976. See Han Jian, "Wu Han de Beiju" (The tragedy of Wu Han), *Lianhe Bao*, March 1, 1979.

44. This was the question raised by Risher and many other authors. See Tom Fisher, "The play's the thing: Wu Han and Hai Rui revisited," *The Australian Journal of Chinese Affairs*, No. 7, 1972, p. 26, and clive Ansley, *The Heresy of Wu Han* (University of Toronto, 1971), p. 84. However Pusey appeared to be of the opinion that Wu "was a man who had held his own against communism and the thought of Mao Tse-tung." See James Reeves Pusey, *Wu Han: Attacking the Present Through the Past*, (Harvard University Press, 1969) p. 68.

45. James Reeves Pusey, p. 68.

46. Clive Ansley, p. 84.

47. According to Xia Mian, Wu was known as "the Grand Historian" (*Taishigong*) by his schoolmates during his college days. Xia Mian, "The Comrade Wu Han I Know" (Wu suo zhihdao de Wu Han tongzhi), *Shehui kexue zhanxian* No. 2 (1980), p. 24–29. See what is in fact an incomplete catalog of the most memorable and heroic lives of scholar-officials in Chinese history in *Zhengqi ge* (Song of the Upright Spirit) by Wen Tianxiang (1236–1283) of the Song dynasty. The phrases such as "In Qi there was the chronicle by the Grand Historian Qian and in Jin there was the pen of the invincible Dong Hu" (Zai Qi taishi Qian, zai Jin Donghu bi) are familiar passages to many traditional school children, who are always required to memorize them. Knowing that to write true to historical facts in the chronicle that Cui Shu, the new King, usurped the throne by killing his Majesty would incur Cui's wrath and thereby risk his own life, the

Grand Historian of Qi wrote down exactly these words. Hence he was put to death by Cui Shu. Nevertheless, when similar circumstances arose, Dong Hu, the official historian, was not a little less undaunted by the precedent. He was also put to death by a new emperor because he recorded faithfully to historical facts that "Zhao Dun, the new king under whom Dong came to serve, usurped the throne by killing his Majesty of Jin". See Wang Yunwu, ed., *Wenwenshan wenji* p. 76.

48. Han Jian, "The Tragedy of Wu Han," op. cit.

49. See the Introduction by D. W. Y. Kwok in C. C. Huang's translation of *Hai Rui Dismissed from Office*, (University of Hawaii, 1972) p. 23.

50. However, for a different view, see Richard C. Thornton, "The Structure of Communist Politics," *World Politics*, No. 4, July 1972, p. 517.

51. Zhang Youren, "Lieshi danxin, shijia bense: shenqie huainian Wu Han Jiaoshou," *Shehui Kexue Zhanxian*, No. 2 (1980) pp. 30–34.

Glossary

Baguan	罢官
Beijing ribao	北京日报
Beijing wanbao	北京晚报
chengqian shangwan	成千上万
chuba	除霸
chujishe	初级社
Dahongpao	大红袍
da'gan	单干
Fan Jin	范缝
fan'an	翻案
fanduipai	反对派
gailianzhuyi	改良主义
gaoji hezuoshe	高级合作社
gaoji nongye huzhu hezuoshe	高级农业互助合作社
Guan Feng	关锋
Hai Rui baguan	海瑞罢官
Hai Rui beiqian	海瑞背纤

Hai Rui huichao	海瑞回朝
Hai Rui ma huangdi	海瑞罵皇帝
Hai Rui shangshu	海瑞上疏
huzhuzu	互助組
jiajia qihuo, huhu maoyan	家家起火，户户冒烟
Liu Mianzhi	刘勉之
lieshi danxin	烈士丹心
lishizhuyi	历史主义
Lin Jie	林杰
Lin Biao	林彪
Lushan	庐山
mandiren buchengqun	满地人，不成群
Peng Zhen	彭真
pingfan	平反
Qi Benyu	戚本禹
Qiu Shengrong	裘盛戎
Renmin ribao	人民日报
Sannü qiangban	三世抢板
Shengsi pai	生死牌
shijia bense	史家本色
shida ziyou	十大自由
taizaole	太糟了
Taishigong	太史公
tuitian	退田
Wanli	万历
Wang Mingyou	王明友
Wu Han	吴晗
Wucai jiao	五彩轿
Xia Nai	夏鼐
Xiaohongpao	小红袍
Xu Jie	徐阶
Xu Ying	徐瑛

Yuan Zhen　　　　　　袁真

yigu fengjin　　　　　以古讽今

Zhang Youren　　　　张友仁

Zhou Xinfang　　　　周信芳

zifuyingkui　　　　　自负盈亏

ziliudi　　　　　　　自留地

ziyou　　　　　　　　自由

ziyou jingji　　　　自由经济

ziyouhua　　　　　　自由化

2. *Images of Women in the Dramas of Guo Moruo: The Case of* Empress Wu

BRUCE GORDON DOAR

Allow me to mention another woman,

Since she said she was Wu Zetian re-incarnate.

If, with any certainty, I can trace Wu's ghost,

There are three points where the two converge:
   ambition, lust and cruelty.

As for her statecraft and her love of people and state,

There is nothing in that claim!

I have no need to spell it out:

comrades know to whom I refer,

Yesterday, she disrupted the court of law,

Today she must endure its sentence.

Perhaps she (and others beside) still dream of Qianling,

But there the only attendant is the autumn wind.

Gong Liu, 1982[1] (Qianling was the shared grave of Empress Wu
and Emperor Gaozong, located in Qianxian, Shaanxi Province.)

The Fengxian Grotto at the Longmen Caves in Henan Province is
dominated by a massive grey limestone image of Amitabha Buddha. This
Buddha displays the cranial bump and the distended ear-lobes which are
the auspicious signs whereby a Great Man or Universal Monarch can be
recognized. An inscription on the plinth of the sculpture records that Wu
Zhao in A.D. 672 gave twenty thousand strings of cash from her
cosmetics purse towards financing this image, which was completed three
years later.[2] This was an early indication of Wu Zhao's intention later to

rary—and historical/mythological settings, began to be depicted on the Chinese stage.[8] The tradition of the classical Chinese theaters, which continues to now, is, in the main, one of dramas with historical settings and with singing performances as their major focus. Its presentation has been described as "imagistic", and its characterization as formalistic, because of the delegation of *dramatis personae* to role categories. These generalized assertions cannot obscure the face that drama was regarded as being pertinent and relevant to contemporary life: historical garb served to highlight the continuity of a dramatic problem or dramatized situation being presented, as much as it provided visual delight.

Traditional satire—within a theatrical tradition largely consisting of what we would anachronistically call "historical dramas" —is a deep structure which needs to be understood to make sense of the 20th century developments, including the debate on the relationship between history and historical dramas in the 1950s and 1960s. Traditional satire is a vast and, as yet, largely unexplored area of study. In 1952 the eminent dramatic theorist Zhao Jingshen told a group of comic actors that comedy and satire were intrinsic aspects of Chinese theater from the earliest times. Zhao defined satire as "laughter with significane." Linking satire with the traditional Chinese theater's other salient feature, the use of historical settings, Zhao Jingshen expressed the view that while the technique of satirising the present through the mirror of the past might be the tradition, it was not appropriate to the post-1949 period: "I believe in the principle of making the past serve the present, but there are those who could maliciously distort this assertion to mean 'use the past to satirize the present'."[9] A tendency to interpret historical dramas as *pièces à clef* is inherent in the Chinese theatrical tradition. At the beginning of the 20th century a new political discourse began to challenge traditional political morality. In this process, nearing completion by the 1950s, political ideology began to win territory from ethics, since the areas of social concern were largely shared. These brief remarks on satire indicate the historically determined dimensions of the debate on historical drama in the post-1949 context, in which Guo Moruo continued to write for the stage. Historical settings in plays often served as a vehicle for satire. While the demand for theatrical realism, or more correctly verisimilitude, emerging in the late-19th century, saw a development (mainly in *huaju*) away from historical settings, mainstream theater continued the earlier tradition. Guo Moruo was a leading practitioner of the historical mirror in his *huaju* works. Guo Moruo's most successful pre-1949 drama *Qu Yuan*[10] dealt with the personal political struggle of the Warring Kingdoms poet. Qu Yuan lived durring the years of final collapse of the Zhou Dynasty, when the kingdom of Chu fell victim to the depredations of the warlike kingdom of Qin. In the wartime Chongqing of 1942, the choice of setting and subject was appreciated by audiences.

To distinguish "historical dramas" written after 194r9 from the "entire" tradition of Chinese theater, the newly written historical dramas were termed *xin lishiju* (literally, "new historical dramas"). Most of China's prominent *huaju* dramatists—such as Cao Yu, Tian Han, Qian Xingcun (A Ying), Lao She and Guo Moruo—contributed to the genre. These plays were themselves also contributions to a debate on historical drama in which many prominent historians, including Wu Han[11], became involved. In 1959 a conference was held in Beijing to discuss a new drama about Wu Zetian, a *yueju* (Shaoxig Opera) called *Zetian Huangdi*. A number of eminent historians attended that conference, including Wu Han, Jian Bozan, Shang Yue, and Lü Zhenyu. Debate about the new genre was also taken up in the pages of China's leading theatrical journal *Xiju bao*. The discussion of the relationship between history and historical dramas had developed continually through the 1950s and 1960s. The Cultural Revolution serves as one endpoint to the debate. Guo Moruo, a veteran writer of historical drama, wrote two plays in this environment: *Cai Wenji* (1959) and *Wu Zeitan* (1960, 1962). Both were recreations of the lives of two women prominent in Chinese history. Guo Moruo regarded Cai Wenji (dates uncertain; daughter of the Later Han dynasty writer Cai Yi (132–192) as China's greatest poet in the epic lyric genre after Qu Yuan (c.340–278 B.C.)[12]; Wu Zetian, of course, had the distinction of being China's only female emperor. Both were remarkable. At the 1959 conference, Wu Han criticized the play *Zetian Huangdi* for stressing the Zetian's failures rather than her accomplishments. Guo Moruo's play certainly redressed the balance.

The debate had two major aspects. On the one hand, it addressed the obvious question of the satiric mode and the relationship of this to the injunction to writers to "make the past serve the present". On the other hand, it examined the relationship between the soft-core history of the dramatist and the hard-core history of the historian. What was permissible, and what was not? Considered from a certain perspective, this bifurcation of the debate into literary and historical aspects is more apparent than real. The texts of history and non-historical texts are often interchangeable. The debate on historical drama, furthermore, was always more relevant to history than to drama. It was founded on a premise which opposed a conception of the noble purpose of history with a conception of the anecdotal and trivial intention behind the writing of unorthodox history, a distinction which is by no means clear-cut and which tends to fray around the edges.

In the debate the question of language was rarely a central issue and ideology was discussed frequently as though language had no bearing upon it. Mao Dun attempted to introduce liguistic concerns into the debate. In *Guanyu lishi he lishiju* (Concerning History and Historical Drama)[13], he wrote that the question of language was the fundamental issue in the discussion. He said that the debate had come to focus on three issues: the technique of making the past serve the present, the unity of historical and artistic truths, and the role of the "people" in history. Language is an essential aspect of all three issues; if a playwright ignored language then the result would be a flat and mechanical drama which failed in its intention to make the past serve the present. Furthermore, only the judicious use of language would delineate clearly past and present, and keep the two sufficiently distinct to obviate a constantly implied satire of present day society. The greatest danger, according to Mao Dun, was a playwright's injudicious and careless use of language, whereby the past was transformed into the present:

> Forgive me for speaking bluntly, but from my reading of many versions of *Woxin changdan* (A Bed of Brushwood and the Taste of Gall), I find that roughly fifty percent of the text shows an interpretation of the principle of having the past serve the present which insists in forging connections between subject matter and the reality of China today: this inevitably means that the work may turn into a reflection of reality, which, in fact, slanders our reality. The actions and character of a ruling clique in a slave society existing over 2,400 years ago, no matter how enlightened, could be seen ultimately to reflect the realities of a socialist construction under the leadership of our Communist Party. Surely this is a form of self-vilification? This is simultaneously a transformation of the present into the past, and a serious departure from the viewpoint of historical materialism.[14]

Mao Dun here deplores the establishment of a satirically volatile and slippery dialectic between the dramatized historical situation and present political realities. This artistic—and ideological—problem was the obverse of that faced by Bertolt Brecht in the GDR in the early 1950s. Brecht was keen to reassert the dialectical function in socity of his epic theater, which at the time he felt to be in danger of becoming museum theater.[15] Yet a dialectical treatment of historical themes was second-nature to the Chinese theatrical tradition: in the pervasively ideological atmosphere of post-1949 China the concern of many was to endow the theater with more non-dialectical qualities. Many playwrights were concerned to make their work more observational and preserved in history, rather than being part of a dangerous hall of mirrors.

In a postscript to his work, Mao Dun revised his ealier views. He upheld the power of myth and the notion that historical dramas should impart "an education in patriotism". Yet he initiated no discussion of the relationship between history and myth. He simply acknowledged his earlier failure to distinguish between history and mythology, which resulted in his assertion that nearly all traditional Chinese dramas were historical dramas. He asserted that mythology can be as "valid" as history, because it is a creation of "the people". He had reached an impasse. The question of what constitutes a literary-historical fact had been so revised in the course of this debate, that historical dramas created in this context could acquire endless referents as their themes became activated on all fronts and became overladen with extra-literary considerations. Yet dramatists writing in this environment were aware of the statements they were making and the interpretations which would be applied to their work.

This was the environment in which *Wu Zetian* appeared, although this play, like *Cai Wenji*, was the result of two decades of interest in ancient literary heroines, including these two. Guo's Empress Wu was a classic example of "verdict reversal" (*fan'an*) or "transvaluation of values". Wu Han, the historian and playwright friend of Guo Moruo, put it quite bluntly:

Wu Zetian (624–705) was a remarkable person in our nation's history, a person who, in her time, played out a progressive role. However, because of the mischief-making of feudal teachings regarding the Rites, she became an object of abuse for a good many "upright gentlemen" who set themselves up as moral custodians. As a result, her reputation suffered. Comrade Guo Muruo's new five-act historical work *Wu Zetian* reverses the judgement of history regarding her, for which I applaud and defend him.[16]

Wu Zetian is one of the Guo Moruo's more neatly crafted dramas. The action has two main foci. Events are compressed into five years (679–684), a time which in fact predates Wu Zhao's usurpation of the throne and her assumption of the title *Zetian Huangdi*. Central to the initial train of events depicted in the play is a minor conspiracy against Wu Zetian, fomented by the arch-villain Pei Yan, and involving her natural son, the Crown Prince Xian, a slave girl at the court named Shangguan Wan'er, and a young orphaned eunuch called Zhao Daosheng. This conspiracy, its discovery by Empress Wu, and the punishment of the conspirators occupy the first two acts. The self-containment of the first two acts is so neat that suspense is almost terminated at the conclusion of Act II. The second half of the drama depicts an empire-world controversy, in which the high officials Xu Jingye (who does not make an actual appearance in the play), Pei Yan and the poet-official Luo Binwang are implicated for individual and opportunistic reasons. Empress Wu uncovers this plot through those at court loyal to her and her policies. The two halves of the play parallel, rather than complement, each other.

The weak Emperor Gaozong appears only in the first two acts of the play. He is aged fifty-three when the action commences in A.D. 679. Wu

Zhao is already Empress Consort and responsible for the daily administration of the Empire. She has acquired a total ascendancy over her
husband, who is often incapacitated by dizzy spells and content to have
her make decisions regarding state matters in his stead. Towards the
close of Act II, his terminal ililness has nearly run its entire course. Guo's
characterization of Emperor Gaozong conforms with the archetype of
"the weak-willed husband" (Li Zhi, 1527–1602). Guo Moruo finds little
sympathy for the Emperor, often pitied by orthodox historians for living
under constant threat from his wife. On this score, in notes attached to
the play Guo re-interpreted an incident recorded by Sima Guang
(1019–1086) in his *Zizhi tongjian*, in which Empress Wu attempted to
prevent the Emperor receiving medical treatment for his migraine by
bloodletting. Sima Guant cited this as evidence that she did not wish to
see her husband recover. The Emperor, however, insisted on the treatment, and in thirty days was dead. Empress Wu could not win on this
score, either, because she was also charged with administering poison.
Guo asks, with unwittingly reflexive rhetoric, "How can a historian living several hundred years after the event know the psychology which
forms a person's ideas?" Regarding Gaozong's death he asks: "Might this
not have been because the needle was not sterilized, so that when blood
was being drawn from the head, tetanus germs were introduced into the
bloodstream?" Guo points out that Empress Wu would have ample opportunity in the course of twenty years to kill Emperor Gaozong.

"From the standpoint of feudal morality" emperor Gaozong should
have been condemned, Guo asserts, because Empress Wu had been a
concubine of *cairen* rank belonging to his father, Emperor Taizong.
Moreover Gaozong and Wu Zhao parented a child during the mandatory
three-year mourning period prescribed for a father or husband. For that
time Wu Zhao had remained a nun in the seculsion of the Ganye Convent. In 654 the title of concubine of *zhaoyi* rank was conferred on her
and in the following year she became Empress Consort (*huanghou*).
After this, in Guo's interpretation, Emperor Gaozong entered into "improper liaisons" with Empress Wu's older sister, Lady Hanguo, and Lady
Hanguo's daughter, Lady Weiguo. "The depravity of feudal monarchs
was rather alarming", Guo comments. Yet for Guo Moruo, Emperor
Gaozong has redeeming features, if only by default: "If there had been
no Emperor Gaozong, there would have been no Empress Wu." The
Emperor's faith in Wu Zhao's competence enabled her to wield power for
twenty years while he malingered.

The Zhanghuai Crown Prince, Prince Xian, is the twenty-eight-year-
old heir-apparent when the play opens. He becomes involved in the
palace conspiracy which occupies the first half of the play, in the
mistaken belief that Empress Wu is going to have him killed. Although

he is the natural son of Empress Wu and Emperor Gaozong, he regards his real birth mother as Lady Hanguo, Wu Zetian's elder sister. By tradition the Crown Prince was the son of Lady Hanguo, but Guo argues that the Prince was born to Wu Zhao when she was a nun in the Ganye Convent, where she secretly conceived both him and his older brother. They were born in the same year (652) in the home of Lady Hanguo, in whose care they were entrusted. Emperor Gaozong compounded the confusion by concealing his son's true birthday, because it testified to his improper behavior.

When in Act II, Scene I, Empress Wu brings the disreputable physician Ming Chongyan to see the Crown Prince, the doctor's gratuitous prognostication of a short life for the prince convinces him he will be the Empress's next victim. So he decides to strike first and begins to amass a cache of weapons in his palace. When his conspiracy is discovered by the Empress, he denounces her for killing Zhangsun Wuji, one of the founders of the dynasty; Shangguan Yi, formerly, the West Terrace; Lady Hanguo, Empress Wu's own sister and the woman he believes to be his real mother; and her own brother. "Sooner or later you will kill me", he charges. Confronting him, the Empress is unforgiving, although later in the play she acknowledges that he was acting at the bequest of the powerful clans and not in accordance with the dictates of his own conscience. She demotes him to the rank of commoner and sends him into exile; later she maintains that his enforced exile was to acquaint him with social conditions in the south and the hardships of the people there. ("The experience would have made him a more fit successor to the throne.") In the second half of the play he will serve as a rallying point for the rebel cause of Pei Yan, but only as a symbol because Pei Yan has him murdered. Orthodox historians, such as Sima Guang, believed the Empress was responsible for his death.

Shangguan Wan'er (664–710) was a poetess, who played a pivotal role in events during her lifetime. She was the granddaughter of the eminent scholar-official Shangguan Yi (c. 616–664), who had been executed for drafting a memorial to Emperor Gaozong which accused Empress Wu of sorcery. Shangguan Wan'er's grandfather and father, Shangguan Tingzhi, were both executed and the entire family was enslaved. Thus Shangguan Wan'er and her mother Zheng Shisan Niang entered the palace at Luoyang as slaves. Guo's play opens when Shangguan Wan'er is fourteen, shortly after she entered the service of the Crown Prince as an attendant, a move which had been recommended by Pei Yan. In the Eastern Palace of the Crown Prince, she is drawn into the conspiracy he is hatching, both because of a desire to avenge her family and because of her love for the prince. When Empress Wu exposes her plotting, she treats Shangguan Wan'er with compassion, in contrast with the punishment she metes out to her own son. Empress Wu admires her forthright nature and literary abilities. Later she becomes Wu Zetian's private secretary, responsible for drafting edicts and other state documents, as well as her constant companion. She exhibits all the hallmarks of the Carlylean poet as hero, so favoured by Guo in his dramas. Like Empress Wu, the historical Shangguan Wan'er has a dubious reputation. She continued to be a central figure in events at court, even after Wu Zetian passed from the scene. Zheng Shisan Niang is included in the play largely to advance the action, particularly in its second half, when she is party to the conspiracy of Pei Yan. Later she defects to Empress Wu and acts as her double agent, facilitating her entrapment of the conspirators.

Luo Binwang (c. 640–?) is a major character in the play, and was, of course, a renowned literary figure of his day. His inclusion in the play serves to highlight the relationship between political authority and writers. His vacillating attitudes enable him to be drawn into the conspiracy. Pei Yan promises him that after the success of their rebellion, Luo will be made Grand Secretary, but Pei Yan intends to double-cross him. After learning of the uprising and Luo's drafting of *Wei Xu Jingue tao Wu Zhao xi* (Declaration of War Against Wu Zhao On Behalf of Xu Jingye) on behalf of the rebels, Empress Wu gives explicit instructions that he is not to be harmed. She prizes his literary talents. The historical Luo Binwang disappeared from the records after the failure of Xu Jingye's uprising. Some sources say he died in obscurity; others that he became a monk. Guo adopted the latter theory, elaborating upon it so that his exile as a monk enforced by Empress Wu is a form of re-education in Hangzhou.

Pei Yan, the *flaneur* (*wulai zhi tu*) of Wang Fuzhi's phrase[17], becomes the major negative character (*fanmian renwu*) of the play. He first appears as the Chamberlain of the Yellow Portal, but later has risen significantly to the post of prime minister. He is a study in ambition, wishing to become emperor and intent on deposing his co-rebel Xu Jingye at a later stage. He fulfills the archetype of the usurper, and in Act III, Scene 2 lady Zheng likens him to various usurpers in history such as Wang Mang, who set up the short-lived Xin Dynasty (A.D. 8–23); Sima Zhao (211–265), a general who destroyed the Wei Dynasty; and Yuwen Huaji (?–619), who killed Emperor Yang in 618 and proclaimed himself emperor. Zheng quotes her daughter's observation that "those who hatch conspiracies against good people cannot be good themselves."

A trap for Pei Yan is laid in Act IV, Scene 2, the final and most dramatically memorable scene of the play. Shangguan Wan'er visits Pei Yan in the former study of Crown Prince Xian. She tells him the rebels in the south led by Xu Jingye have been crushed. Twenty important rebel leaders have been decapitated, including Xu Jingye and Luo Binwang. Crown Prince Xian has been murdered. Pei Yan, believing that Shangguan Wan'er still harbours a desire to avenge her father and not realizing that her visit is at the bidding of Empress Wu, suggests that a lethal dose of arsenic be administered to the Empress. At this point, a double of the Crown Prince enters, accompanied by two demons from the netherworld. Pei Yan is terrified by the "apparition", which Shangguan Wan'er feigns to be unable to see. He confesses to her that he was responsible for making Crown Prince Xian hatch the conspiracy against Wu, and for arranging the murder of the Crown Prince so that it would reflect on Empress Wu. This confession, extracted under terror, finally seals Pei Yan's fate. The Empress enters and orders his execution.

While these various characters from the *dramatis personae* of Guo's play all, in some measure, differ from their counterparts in orthodox history, the shifts are all necessary not simply to allow for the exigencies of plot, but to accommodate the massive *fan'an* Guo performs on behalf of his heroine Wu Zetian.

Wu Zetian long exercised a powerful influence on the imagination of Chinese historians. As can be seen from the historical notes attached to Guo Moruo's *Wu Zetian*, the historical data about her are wildly contradictory. The complexity of her character is brought out by her biographers writing in English: Lin Yutang, C. P. Fitzgerald, and R. W. L. Guisso.[18] Lin Yutang, writing in a semi-novelistic fashion, in his *Lady Wu: A True Story*, based his account on orthodox historical sources, but has chosen to overlook incidents recorded there which rebound to her credit. C.P. Fitzgerald is the first biographer writing in English who attempted a more balanced appraisal of Empress Wu's achievements and failures. Denis Twitchett, Howard J. Wechsler, and Richard W.L. Guisso in their contributions on Empress Wu to *The Cambridge History of China* update the portraits of Wu Zetian available in English, drawing as they do on recent Japanese research.

Denis Twitchett and Howard Wechsler state the problem facing historians treating Wu Zetian:

> Everything concerning this remarkable woman is surrounded by doubts, for she stood for everything to which the ideals of the Confucian scholar-official class was opposed — feminine interference in public affairs, government by arbitrary personal whim, the deliberate exploitation of factionalism ruthless personal vendettas, political manipulation in complete disregard of ethics and principles. From the very first the historical record of her reign had been hostile, biased and curiously fragmentary and incomplete.[19]

We have already quoted the verdict of the authors of *Jiu Tang shu*. The authors of *Xin Tang shu* (New Tang History), Ouyang Xiu

(1007–1072) et. al., were similarly harsh in their judgment of Wu Zetian, likening her to Empress Lü, who usurped power in the Han Dynasty after the death of her husband, Emperor Gaozu. One of the most balanced discussions of Empress Wu by a traditional historian is contained in the analistic account of her reign in *Shigang pingyao*[20] by the Ming radical philosopher Li Zhi (1527–1602). Li Zhi does not hold Wu Zetian culpable for taking over the day-to-day running of the state from her ineffectual husband, whom he described as "a typical wife-fearing husband." He makes the marginal comment that she was a "sagely ruler" (*shengzhu*) when he notes her decision to promote the honorable official Xu Yougong. Li Zhi also applauded Empress Wu's decision to hold recruitment examinations as "unexpectedly good". Moreover, he found the decision of Empress Wu to take male lovers, such as Xue Huaiyi and the Zhang Brothers, perfectly understandable. It was analogous to the actions of emperors in taking concubines. As he stated simply, Xue Huaiyi "was a concubine of Emperor of Zetian". Li Zhi wrote:

> Lady Wu's crimes were many, and cannot be lightly dismissed. But what was the basis of the charge that she was lascivious and heeded the advice of favorites? Why is it leveled at her? Since she regarded herself as the Emperor, she was therefore unwilling to act as a woman. The likes of Zhang Changzong and Zhang Yizhi, were, for her, women. If a woman does not choose to act as a woman, how can men act as men? For, if they had been men, then they would not have had "lotus looks" to win her favor.[21]

As Li Zhi saw it, Empress Wu simply reversed sexual roles and behaved no differently from a male in her position. Li Zhi reserved his harshest comments for the flatterers and the vicious officials who wielded power under her.

Wu Zetian was certainly remarkable. From the various modern historians it is clear that she was able to turn the contradictory aspects of her personality to political advantage with a consummate skill. She was ruthless in the pursuit of power, but her cruelty was never characterized by the thoroughness attributed to the rule of Qin Shi Huang. Moreover, she had the extraordinary knack from all accounts of unpredictably acting with compassion.

It is understandable that she was depicted frequently to traditional Chinese fiction and drama. One of her most famous appearances was in the 19th century novel by Li Ruzhen (1763–1830) entitled *Jinghua yuan*. The novel proposes a discourse in which the natural order is out of harmony with the presence of a female on the throne, but while Empress Wu fulfills the image of a usurper, the overall portrayal of her is "positive". We see her, for example, in Chapter 7 dispensing justice with compassion, and in Chapter 40 she initiates an era of clemency when her 70th

birthday celebrations are about to take place. By Chapter 59 of the novel
it is clear that the sexes are set on collision courses: while women prepare
themselves for examinations and participation in the political order, their
entry into political life under the aegis of Empress Wu is doomed not to
occur because of the revenge of men preparing uprisings aimed at over-
throwing their dispossessor, Empress Wu. Her star is now waning. Li
Ruzhen asserts that there is no evil which Wu Zetian's paramours, the
Zhang brothers, do not perpetrate, but he does not elaborate. The novel
concludes with the birthday celebrations of Empress Wu, rather than her
defeat. Various incidents in this novel inspired Peking Operas and other
Chinese dramas.

While *Jinghua yuan* does not depict Empress Wu as a "nymphomaniac" as has been asserted,[22] there is a large body of pornographic
literature, much of it homo-erotic, concerning the sexual exploits of Empress Wu and the males she gathered into her following. This subsequent
literature did perpetuate the myth of Empress Wu as a nymphomaniac,
possibly because the unusual existence of a "seraglio of males", in the
shape of the *Kongheful* (Stork Institute) fired the imaginations of later
pornographers.

Wu Zetian continued to be a subject for novelists and playwrights in
the 20th century. One of the better plays was *Wu Zetian* by Song Zhidi
(1937). Guo Moruo saw a performance of this work in Shanghai in 1937.
Song Zhidi believed that Wu Zetian's reputation had suffered at the
hands of historians, because, as he writes in his preface to the the
published text, unlike Qin Shi Huang she was never given a separate
treatment in the histories, so that all of her achievements were attributed
to the Tang Dynasty. Song Zhidi said that her reforms represented a
revolution against the oppression of women in traditional feudal society.
He wrote that, when conceiving his play, he sought to focus on one major aspect: that resistance and struggle of a woman in a traditional feudal
society, that is "one dominated by the male mind". He admits to a
fascination with the sexual mythology surrounding Wu Zetian. As a
child he used to hear his drunken grandfather cursing: "Wu Zetian,
women, thieves and prostitutes!":

> In my mind this Wu Zetian character long remained a hateful impression.
> Often I unconsciously compared women in society regarded as bad to Wu
> Zetian, while at the same time I mentally envisaged her lascivious life,
> which I secretly loathed yet greatly admired.[24]

He writes that after Wu Zetian assumed power, she wrought an extreme vengeance on the male sex. He writes that, since this behaviour
commenced when Wu Zetian was in her sixties and seventies that he

suspects it cannot be regarded as the demands of sex: "Encounters in her childhood could have nurtured a psychological make-up which embodied opposition to the male sex. Because her father died when she was young, she was dependent on her mother and was often humiliated by uncles. When she entered the palace, she was forced to become a nun, and these circumstances may have laid the basis for her later usurpation of the Imperial throne."[25]

Looking back with hindsight in 1960, Guo Moruo was not impressed with Song Zhidi's play. He wrote that "Song Zhidi reversed the verdict on Wu Zetian's behalf, but in treating the relations between the sexes, he was clearly influenced by Oscar Wilde's *Salome* and he portrayed his Wu Zetian as a libertine with males."[26] Guo also noted that Song was cavalier with his use of historical materials, although Song Zhidi had readily acknowledged this.

Guo Moruo never saw the Shaozing Opera *Zetian huangdi*, but he read the script and pronounced it to be influenced by Song's drama. Both plays had traced Wu Zetian's career from the time she was a young nun in the Ganye Buddhist convent through until her old age. The time span was considerable. Guo compressed the major events of Wu's life as he saw them into five years, tracing her career from 679 to 685. (Empress Wu did not assume the title Zetian Huangdi until 690). He said that in carrying out this compression, he sought to adhere to "the three unities".[27]

In his play Guo Morou also set out to refute the often repeated charge that Wu Zetian was licentious in her sexual behaviour. In an essay attached to the published version of the play, Guo Moruo advances a number of tenuous arguments to prove his case. Firstly, Guo Moruo contends that Wu Zetian was seventy-six when the Zhang brothers — Zhang Changsong and Zhang Yizhi — became her paramours. Moreover, he argues that she would have been sixty-two when her career as a libertine with the perfume dealer Xue Huaiyi commenced. Guo Moruo uses an idiosyncratic dating, which makes Wu Zetian five years older than most other dating systems establish. Furthermore, biology hardly precludes a sixty-year-old woman from taking a younger lover. For example, at age sixty Catherine the Great commented to Potemkin that with her twenty-two year-old lover Plato Zubov, she came back to life "like a fly in spring."[28] This would have met with the approval of the usual Wu Zetian of the histories. Another piece of "evidence" Guo Moruo uses to refute the charge that Wu Zetian was licentious was her banishment of her nephew Helan Minzhi for "outraging public opinion" in his sexual behaviour, which included rape and incest: hardly convincing evidence that Wu Zestian was opposed to licentiousness![29]

Guo Moruo in 1960 was not prepared to make Wu Zetian a showcase for libertarian sexual attitudes as Song Zhidi had done in the 1930s. Guo maintained that that earlier dramas had stressed Wu Zetian's "failures" rather than her achievements, which was the task he then set himself. Guo's play is essentially a poetic rhapsody for the achievements of Wu Zetian's rule and in it, Wu Zetian becomes an image of political authority.

Guo Moruo wrote that in his play he touched on the major achievements of Wu Zetian's reign, although it was necessary that he brought many events forward to compress them into the time frame he used. Guo Moruo stresses that Wu Zetian's period of rule was an age of consolidation, which built on the foundations established in the Zhenguan period (713–741) of Emperor Xuanzong. For Guo Moruo, her reign was marked by political stability, being an age with few peasant rebellions. She encouraged agriculture and sericulture, and extended taxation and corvee relief to farmers. He further argues that she was instrumental in promoting the egalitarian *juntian* system of land ownership, although the evidence which Guo cites for this is flimsy.[30]

While Guo Moruo concedes that it is impossible for a feudal monarch "to stand on the side of the people," Wu Zetian comes close to doing so in Guo's dramatization. The prosperity of the nation vindicates the policies of Wu Zetian. Drawing on statistics recorded in *Zizhi tong jian*, he has Wu Zetian tell her Yellow Portal Chamberlain Pei Yan in Act I:

> "I too am aware that the people of the Empire do not oppose me. Consider that when Emperor Taizong met his maker, there were only slightly more than three million households in the country. Now, after I assisted the government of His present Majesty for more than twenty years, there are six million households. Can it be said that I have performed badly?"[31]

The encouragement of farming and sericulture was one of the wise policies of Empress Wu that ensured she had "lower level support." In 674, before the play commences, Empress Wu made twelve proposals which Guo says indicate her political program. He quotes these from "Biographies of Empresses" in *Xin Tangshu*: (1) encourage agriculture and sericulture, lighten taxes and corvee; (2) exempt the area around the Capital from taxes; (3) cease warfare, ethically transform the Empire; (4) prohibitg excessive spending on palace buildings; (5) practice economies in labour performed for the state; (6) open up the channels of communication between subject and ruler; (7) stifle slanders; (8) all from the ranks of prince and duke down must make a study of *Laozi*; (9) even while a father lives, three years of mourning must be observed for mothers (as for fathers); (10) officials from the previous reign period must retain their titles; (11) officials from the capital, of the eighth rank and above, must be given salary increases; (12) officials of long service, and who are talented, if they fill lowly ranks, must have the impediments to their promotion removed.[32]

In Guo's play, these policies are in force before its commencement. Luo Binwang tells Pei Yan in a speech in Act I.

"Her twelve point proposal of five or six years ago is known throughout the empire. Included are proposals which stipulate that children observe three years mourning for a mother, even if the father is still alive, and another that able people of low rank should be promoted. To ingratiate herself with farms, artisans, women and officials of humble origin, she didn't hesitate to invert the hierarchy and confound observed social ranking.[33]

In this speech, we are introduced to the opposition to Empress Wu's "open government". Opposition to Wu Zetian, Guo Moruo insists, came from ambitious officials who had motives no more lofty than usurping power for themselves. Pei Yan is one of these officials, while Luo Binwang 'is a weak-willed *literatus* who is drawn into the plot against Wu Zetian, which forms the central action of the drama. In reply to Luo Binwang's speech, Pei Yan says:

"The most intolerable thing about her is the cavalier manner in which she makes official appointments. Emperor Taizong instituted a system of six hundred and forty three official posts. He stipulated for posterity that 'the likes of craftsmen and merchants were not to receive official appointments, nor were they permitted to stand together with officials or the nobility, nor sit with them to eat.' To promote her clique, Empress Wu violated Emperor Taizon's will and testament. On the pretext of making appointments based on ability, she allows anyone at all to make recommendations for office, and even permits people to recommend themselves. Family reputation and record of service are completely ignored. For the past twenty years, the followers of Empress Wu have monopolized almost all official posts both inside and outside court."[34]

Thus, opposition to Wu Zetian comes from the dispossessed and the threatened, who are also the old forces of privilege.

In another controversial play of the early 1960s about Wu Zetain—Tian Han's *Xie Yaohuan* (1961)[35]—poor peasants rather than high officials are the dispossessed, because they suffer expropriation of their land. This situation has not arisen becuase of the policies of Empress Wu, but rather because of the refusal by vicious officals who surrounded the empress to have them implemented. They include her relative Wu Sansi and the head of her "secret police" Lai Junchen. Tian Han's play was based on what was originally a *wanwanqiang* drama entitled *Nü xun'an* (The Female Inspector-General).[36] The title was a reference to Xie Yaohuan, a female official in the *Shangyiyuan*, who brought to Wu Zetian's attention an injustice in Jiangnan in which peasants were driven off their land and forced into rebellion. Empress Wu appoints Xie Yaohuan military governor in the Jiangnan region to placate the rebels and redress the in-justice. Tian Han's play was later labelled a "poisonous weed," and was described as a direct attack on Mao Zedong and his land reform policies. Despite the later charges of Cultural Revolution theoreticians, Tian Han's image of Wu Zetian is that of a benign and enlightened rules, as is Guo Moruo's.

In Guo Moruo's play, Wu Zetian's authority is almost secular in its sanctioning. Guo stresses her delight in her humble origins, as the daughter of a poor timber merchant. What Shils describes as the inherent sacredness of sovereign power[37] is played down in Guo's interpretation. According to some historians Empress Wu relied on the Buddhist Church for her power, and she repaid this support with lavish gifts. Indeed, later in her reign she propagated the belief that she was Maitreya incarnate. Guo's Empress, however, is peculiarly secular. Her faith in Buddhism is little referred to. Guo notes her movement away from the Taoism favoured by Emperor Taizong and reflected in her twelve-point proposal, in a conversation between Wu Zetian and her dying husband, Emperor Gaozong, towards the close of Act II.[38] Earlier in his philosophical development Guo Moruo might have regarded dynamism as still consonant with Taoism.[39] But Guo in 1960 had moved away from this position. In this play, he chose to divorce her patronage of Bud-dhism from any sacred underpinnings. Her commissioning of the many images of Buddhas and Boddhisattvas is simply interpreted as her patronage of the arts. The Longmen shrines appear in the play almost as a secular tourist venue. In Scene 1 of Act III the young monk Zhao Daosheng tells Zheng Shisan Niang, Shangguan Wan'er's mother: "The Buddhas in the grottoes are really worth a visit! There are more than a hundred thousand figures and all very life-like." In the final scenes of the play, Wu Zetian herself tells Zhao Daosheng (Priest Dinghui) to take Luo Binwang and Jiang Qi to the Fengxian Monastery and "see they en-joy the sights around Longmen."[40]

In Guo's play Wu Zetian draws the spiritual sanction for her authority from her mastery of ethical precedents drawn from history. Yet the historical Wu Zetian gave at least equal weight to a judicious selection of certain traditional religious signs of monarchy—the significant actions and symbolic forms which indicate perceived structures of power and the cosmos. Her accompaniment of Emperor Gaozong on the pilgrimage for the Fengshan sacrifice is a notable example. Such acts both justify and articulate a ruler's possession and wielding of power. The historical Em-press Wu sought to change their significance through the attempt to replace and re-align the ideological structures which gave such actions meaning with her synthesis of apocryphal Confucianism, Taoisty mysticism, and Buddhist millenarianism. In Guo Moruo's play she limits herself to adages and sayings from various orthodox Confucian works in her admonition to those about her. Clifford Geertz's remark about Elizabeth I is peculiarly relevant to Guo's Empress:

> The center of the center, Elizabeth not only accepted its transformation of her into a moral idea, she actively cooperated in it. It was out of this — her willingness to stand proxy, not for God, but for the virtues he ordained, and especially for the Protestant version of them — that her charism grew.[41]

The virtues which Guo's Wu Zetian distills are compassion, understanding, patience and forbearance: her femininity is totally enshrined in these ethical concerns, which signify her possession of authority. Her disquisitions on nurture embody a Mencian concept of the parental duties of a monarch, with a gender twist.

Two images which dominate the play and which constitute the themes running throughout it are that of *zui* (the sin or crime of rebellion against a magnanimous sovereign) and *xing* (punishment demanded by that crime or sin). So the Wu Zetian of popular mythology who was the perpetrator of crimes, in this play becomes the one who is sinned against. Guo redeems the historical Wu Zetian with a near puritanical zeal. The offenses against the family traditionally ascribed to Empress Wu are transformed similarly into the family's offenses against her. Thus, her natural son conspires against her. For this she dismisses him and acquires her family of choice — Shangguan Wan'er, a surrogate daughter. The guiding hand she extends to Shangguan Wan'er symbolizes the role she must act out for her subjects. In the Second Scene of Act II, Wu Zetian "adopts" Shangguan Wan'er after compelling the young girl to acknowledge her sins and crimes. This assertion of will is underwritten by a display of forgiveness. While stern punishment of Shangguan Wan'er is recommended by Wu Zetian's advisers, Wu resolves to keep the girl on her personal staff. She points out the young girl has shown sensitivity towards the feelings which naturally exist between a mother and son in not informing her of her son's involvement in conspiracy. Shangguan Wan'er's complicity, however, underlines filial duty rather than offends it. Furthermore, Shangguan Wan'er's superior ethical worth is underlined by her "natural" superiority: Wu Zetian declares that she "loves" the fifteen-year-old girl for the talents she possesses. "It is for the sake of this court that I have a passion for talent," Wu Zeitian declares.[42]

Thus Wu Zetian's closest personal relationship, forged through confession and forgiveness, is also a relationship of poetic geniuses. In Guo Moruo's play, it is the poetic talent of Shangguan Wan'er, which first draws the attention of both the Crown Prince and Empress Wu herself. In coupling Wu Zetian and Shangguan Wan'er as a poetic duo, Guo Moruo, on the basis of some historical evidence, has created the entity of which he is so fond in his dramas: the poetic hero in its Carlylean form. Moreover, the feminine dimension of this has many antecedents in Guo Moruo's writing.

Guo Moruo believed that the success or failure of his play hinged on this second scene of Act II. Positioned just before the interval, it had to make a deep impression on audiences. To reinforce it, Act III opens with a parallel scene, an encounter between the mother of the redeemed Shangguan Wan'er, Zheng Shisan Niang, and the young Zhao Daosheng, who had also been implicated in the plot and who is now a novice Buddhist monk. In the following exchange the two discuss the reform of Shangguan Wan'er:

Zheng: Yes. She committed a crime which deserved the death penalty, but Her Majesty the Empress did not put her to death, but kept her beside her as before.

Zhao: That shows the magnanimity of Her Majesty. Even though I murdered the doctor and Ming Chongyan she still forgave me, and allowed me to return to the correct path.

Zheng: Yet many people say that Her Majesty is cruel.

Zhao: There is no truth in that. Her Majesty is compassionate towards sheep that stray from the path, but she cannot act with compassion to the wild beasts which devour people.

Zheng: (discerning truth in these remarks) Yes, what you say is correct. One cannot be compassionate to wild animals.

Zhao: It's the wild animals who say that Her Majesty is cruel.

Zheng: You are right. (the truth of Daosheng's remarks hits home, and she becomes silent) Can I offer you a cup of tea?[43]

In this dialogue, Guo again emphasizes that the theme of *zui* relates intrinsically to authority and disobedience. The relationship between Empress Wu and Shangguan Wan'er is now viewed from the outside, and again shown to be forged through Wan'er's recognition of her guilt. The empire itself consists of those who stray from the path and can acknowledge their sin, and those who remain intractable, show no guilt, and refuse to respond to moral example tempered by compassion. A comparison of Guo Moruo's handling of the theme of guilt and Song Zhidi's handling of the theme, in the latter case closely bound up with sexuality rather than a sexual political authority, is an interesting study, but falls outside the scope of this paper. Song Zhidi attempted to come to terms within the context of guilt and authority, whereas Guo Moruo sought liberation for his image of Empress Wu as authority whose femininity was congruent with the image of the kind and caring mother.

Yet Guo Moruo felt obliged at least to acknowledge the charge that Wu Zetian was lascivious in his play. He does then in Scene 2 of Act III by portraying the charge as misogynistic Confucian propaganda in the service of political rivals. Aside from its prurient interest, the charge in orthodox literature was coupled with elaborations of her cruelty and misrule. It thus became part of an overall condemnation of women in positions of political power. Scene 2 of Act III of his play centers around an incident recorded in *Zizhi tongjian*, in which Wu Zetian is confronted with the *Tao Wu Zhao xiwen* (Declaration of War Against Wu Zhao, hereafter *Declaration*). *Declaration* was drafted by Luo Binwang on behalf of the rebellious powerful nobles led by Xu Jingye, who staged the uprising of 684 against the Empress. The action of the uprising occupies the second half of Guo Moruo's play. *Declaration* has come to be regarded as a masterpiece of classical Chinese writing, exemplifying the best features of Tang *guwen* prose. For this reason it was included in *Guwen guanzhi*,[44] whose editor added notes regarding the structure of the piece. From the aspect of the play's theatricality, the inclusion of this lengthy passage was hardly suitable. Guo Moruo gave explicit, instructions that the passage was to be read slowly and distinctly, with the punctuation read aloud for the benefit of the audience's comprehension. Nevertheless, I cannot help but concur with Wu Zetian's own comment in Guo's play about the *Declaration*: " . . . can the ordinary people understand this type of writing."[45]

Ideologically, the scene in which Wu Zetian confronts the charges in this document against her is central to the play. It forms the pivot of Guo Moruo's *fan'an* of Wu Zetian, as in a sense he puts Empress Wu on trial.

Luo Binwang's *Declaration* was not only a masterpiece of classical prose, but a masterpiece of Confucian misogyny. It tabled countless precedents for the observation that women had no place in government. Its use in the scene is a clear example of the tradition of *fan'an*, which demonstrates the ideological struggle for the possession of the word.

In Scene 2 of Act III, Wu Zetian has come into possession of the intercepted denunciation of her by the rebels. She gives it to Shangguan Wan'er, now her secretary, to read aloud:

Wan'er: "The usurping woman from the clan of Wu is refractory by nature, having been born into chill and threadbare poverty . . . "

Wu: (approvingly) Fine. A prose piece strives for a stirring opening. The beginning is good. What it says is correct as well, I am not compliant like those of noble extraction and my family knew real poverty. My father was a timber merchant, while my uncle was a farmer.[46]

But did Luo Binwang stick to the facts? Denis Twitchett and Howard Wechsler point out that she was the daughter of Wu Shihuo, a member of a locally prominent clan in Taiyuan and one of the earliest supporters of Emperor Gaozu at the time of his rebellion in Taiyuanfu. She was thus from a traditional scholar-official family and through her mother she was descended from the Yangs of the Sui Dynasty's imperial house. The reading continues:

Wan'er: In her early days she served as Emperor Taizong's maid and
            on occasion when he was changing his attire, she gained his
            favors. With the passage of time, she inveigled the Emperor
            with her lasciviousness. Concealing her intimacy with the late
            Taizong, she contrived to become the new emperor's con-
            cubine. With her entry into the palace she was in the grip of
            envy, but gave no sign she felt her beauty could be surpassed.
            From behind her sleeves, she wove a web of artful speech,
            and her vixen's charms bewitched the Emperor. . . ."
Wu: Those two sentences are well put. (nodding) He knows how to
            write.[47]

This orthodox denunciation of Wu Zetian did not date her alleged lasciviousness from her later years, but made it a hallmark of her personality and a reflection of her will to power. Much is ambiguous about this passage from Luo Binwang's piece. The character *geng* in the phrase *gengyi*, which I have rendered as "when he was changing his attire", is written with the character *geng* ("farmer") by the editor of *Guwen guanzhi*, but this would seem to make interpretation more difficult. Luo Binwang couples her seducaton of a father and then his son with a hatred of her own sex expressed in her jealousy. These actions are all portrayed as aspects of her lust for power. The denunciation continues:

Wan'er: "She trampled the rightful empress in the plumed chariot, and
            snared the emperor like a bitch in heat. A she-wolf with the
            heart of a venomous serpent, she selected her companions
            from the lascivious and depraved, and treated cruelly the
            loyal and upright. She killed her sister and butchered her
            brother. She assassinated the Emperor and poinsoned her own
            mother. Man and the gods unite in their revulsion of her,
            Heaven and Earth join in intolerance . . . "
Wu: (her smile now breaking into laughter) Ha, ha, ha, ha!
            There's simply nothing I have not done.[48]

The charges that she was behind the deposition of Empress Wang (the "rightful empress") by Emperor Gaozong, that she formed an alliance with the depraved at court (such as Li Yifu and Xu Jingzong), that she harshly treated loyal ministers such as Chu Suiliang and Changsun Wuji, that she killed her own sister (Lady Hanguo) and kin (Wu Weiliang), mother (Lady Rongguo) and, ultimately, Emperor Gaozong himself were not charges confined to the document of Luo Binwang. Guo Moruo's play, however, begins after Empress Wang has been deposed, and it depicts Changsun Wuji as an ambitious rebel, while the death of Emperor Gaozong in Act II, Scene 2 is the result of his terminal illness, not her administration of poison. No mention of the other charges is made in Guo's play.

And the charges continue:

Wan'er: "Still she harbored evil intent in her heart, as she gazed ambitiously on the state regalia . . . "
Wu: We should send those two lines to Pei Yan.
Wan'er: "She incarcerated the Emperor's beloved son in a rustic castle. She installed her own thieving kin in positions of honor and authority."[49]

With this, the catalogue of Empress Wu's sins concludes. Luo Binwang now draws parallels between her and famous exmaples of women who exerted malevolent power in history:

"Alas! There is no-one today like Huo Zimeng or the Marquis of Zhuxu. When swallows pecked at the Emperor's grandsons, it was known that the royal house of Han would soon fall. When the bodily secretions of the dragon gave rise to a queen, the Zhou court would soon topple . . . "
Wu: One moment he compares me to Empress Lü, the next with Zhao Feiyan and then with Bao Si. In short, he says that women are evil and are the harbingers of disaster — hardly a balanced view.[50]

One has to agree with Wu Zetian's assessment of this section of the document. The allusions Luo Binwang draws upon are uniformly misogynistic . Huo Zimeng and the Marquis of Zhuxu (i.e, Liu Zhang) were defenders of the Han royal house against female usurpation or subversion. Huo Zimeng (Huo Guang) helped to restore Emperor Xuandi, after a brief usupation in the Han dynasty by the depraved Prince of Changyi. The Marquis of Zhuxu, Liu Zhang, helped restore the Liu clan, after the Empress Dowager Lü, wife of the founder of the Han dynasty (Liu Bang) attempted to usurp power on behalf of her clan. Comparisons between Empress Wu and Empress Lü were common. In the verdict on Wu Zetian by Liu Xu in the *Jiu Tang shu*, quoted towards the beginning of this paper, Liu referred to the cruelty shown to the "human swine." The incident of the "human swine" was recorded in both Sima Qian's *Shiji* and in Ban Gu's *Hanshu*. They tell how the favorite of the founder of the Han dynasty, Liu Bang (who assumed the throne as Emperor Gaozu), one Lady Qi, wished to establish her son Ruyi as the heiraparent, a move which aroused the ire of his first wife Empress Lü. After the death of the Emperor, Empress Lü chopped off the hands and feet of Lady Qi, gouged out her eyes, singed her ears, and fed her a poison which rendered her mute by destroying her vocal cords. She then confined her in a privy and dubbed her "the human swine". She then summoned the heir to the throne to come to view his mother.

Lou Binwang also likens Empress Wu to Zhao Feiyan (Flying Swallow), the wife of the Han Emperor Cheng (32–7 B.C.). Zhao Feiyan and her sister had been brought into the palace as concubines, and the sexual appetites of the sisters, and of Zhao Feiyan in particular, were rumored to have resulted in Emperor Cheng's untimely death. A widow, Zhao Feiyan was said to have confined the Emperor's sons in her apartment, where she had them put to death. A contemporary folk song deplored the incident in a line: "The swallow pecked at the emperor's offspring."

The bodily fluids of the dragon, according to legend, were a treasure of the Xia dynasty transmitted to the Zhou royal household. None dared tamper with this religious heritage until towards the end of the reign of King Li, someone wished to examine this Pandora's box. The bodily fluids, their sanctity disturbed, flowed into the courtyard of the palace where they transformed into a terrapin-like creature, which began to stalk the corridors of the palace. It entered the female apartments, where a maid casting her glance on the divine beast, immaculately conceived a child. Later this daughter would become famous in history as Bao Si, the favorite of King You (r. 781–771 B.C.) of the Western Zhou dynasty, after she presented him with a son. Her caprices engaged the King's full attention. Because she was unable to laugh, the King had the beacon fires lit, which indicated the outbreak of war. All the officials in the palace assembled, in various states of undress. The ruse had the desired effect of making Bao Si laugh, but later when the beacons signalled a genuine state emergency, the nobles ignored the warning, and the Western Zhou dynasty fell to enemy armies.

Guo Moruo echoes the earlier playwright Son Zhidi in making dramatic use of Luo Binwang's *Declaration*, although Song Zhidi did not "table" the document in the manner of Guo Moruo. Recognizing some truth in the accusations of Luo, Song Zhidi's Empress did not respond to the condemnation with the cool displayed by Guo's Wu Zetian. Yet Guo's characterization of the Empress was consistent with the anecdote recording her reactions in the *Zizhi tongjian*, about which the late-Ming writer Li Zhi commented that this display of cool demonstrated that Empress Wu was a "sagely ruler" (*shengzhu*). Both playwrights, however, in their choice of this document, tapped directly into a stratigraphy of Confucian misogyny.

Guo Moruo, however, in the altered historical context of the debate on the function and socio-political role of historical dramas, used the *Declaration* and Luo Binwang's role in the play to exemplify also the relationship between political authority and the writer. When Shangguan Wan'er's reading of the *Declaration* concludes, Wu Zetian comments:

> Wu: Those two lines make a fine conclusion. It is an excellent piece of writing, with fine rhythms. Yet, it totally lacks strength. No one of its several hundred words hits home to me. Observe, is there a single sentence about the common people in the entire piece? There is an ancient saying which goes "Punish crimes to show the people." In their attack on me, nothing is said on behalf of the common people.[51]

The writer, then, has a duty both to speak on behalf of the common people, and to serve the dynasty in power, since Guo's Empress Wu says that "all changes of dynasty were caused by ministers usurping the throne."[52] While there is a possible contradiction implicit in the coupling of these two views, it might be deliberate on Guo Moruo's part.

Guo makes dramatic use of the literary skills of Luo Binwang in his play. Scene I of Act IV opens with Luo Binwang incarcerated in a cell in the West Imperial Prison, reciting his famous poem *Zai yu yong chan* (On Hearing in Prison a Cicada Chirping). The poem expresses envy of the cicada, which is free, unlike the poet. During its declamation, Shangguan Wan'er enters and comments on its excellence. She tells Luo of Empress Wu's admiration for the literary style of his *Declaration*, and relates how she and the Empress have examined his case, by collecting all his works and scrutinizing them. They found their content wanting, because of the threnodic air pervading them. While Pei Yan, after his capture, denounces Luo Binwang as an "unprincipled scribbler", Empress Wu regards him as one of the greatest poets of his age and vows to use him "for the nation's benefit." She decides against executing him and instead sends him to the beautiful resort of Hangzhou to be tonsured as a monk. She addressed him: "After your arrival there, you must repent your past crimes and compose more poems and essays for the sake of the people! (*yiyu ren de shiwen*)."[53]

Her concluding speech to Luo outlines her administration's policy on literature:

> Wu: There is an ancient saying: "The nation belongs to its people." Henceforth, the court will be more vigilant in its attention to the farming seasons, and will make better use of the land's resources. We shall

reward learning, develop trade, foster handicrafts, initiate public debate and employ the talented. The whole nation will be as one family, while the lands around will be welded into a single nation. Everyone across the land will live and work in peace. A period of great harmony will ensure that our glorious civilization will become renowned far and wide. You writers must devote your attention to such things'[54]

Writers were thus urged to be an integral part of a collective social enterprise.

Guo Moruo's presentation in the character of Empress Wu of an image of a woman in a position of comfortable authority was a departure from feminine images created by Guo Moruo in his earlier writing career. Feminist preoccupations were an aspect of his passion for "inverting tradition" (*fan'an*) and they underscore so many aspects of his work. His historiography was predicated on a primitive communism, replete with a "non-sexist" Utopia. It was the introduction of private property which destroyed this Utopia at the dawn of time. In his early polemical pieces he variously depicted China as a passive woman, as a woman raped, as a beautiful seductress, and as an ebullient socially-committed young female student. On the subject of translation (which he sometimes called *fan'an*/adaptation)[55] he wrote that Chinese intellectuals should not merely play the matchmaker (and translate), but should also acknowledge the virgin and (pro)create (original writings).[56] For the Creation Society Guo Moruo, the very act of literary creation was presided over by goddesses, not gods; goddesses are the muses of Chinese poetry. Like Lu Xun, Guo relates the Chinese creation myth, in which Nü Wa, the goddess, fulfills the Atlantean role of supporting the Heavens and separating order from chaos. "Rebirth" and "renaissance" were fundamental images for a May Fourth pantheism; goddesses are reborn in a primordial chaos created by male warlords.[57]

Guo's feminine themes are most evident in the imagery of his poetry and poetics, and in the portrayals in his dramas. Like Lu Xun, he attacked the misogyny of traditional Chinese ethics, and in this attack Ibsen provided a point of departure for both men. In 1926 Guo Moruo clearly stated his basic feminist tenets in "Xie zai *Sange panni de nuxing* houmian" (Afterward in *Three Women of Defiance*), a postface to a collection of the three dramas. This essay indicates that both Cai Wenji and Wu Zetian were prominent figures of interest at this early date:

If we look at the famous women of history and then confine discussion to China, the strengths and abilities of women such as Zhuo Wenjun, Cai Wenji, Wu Zetian and Li Qungzhao were by no means inferior to those of men: moreover, the stature they achieved made them superior to males, because they were refractory women unwilling to obey the morality centered on males. It was not the superior strength of their abilities, however, which resulted in their becoming rebels; they first became rebels and as a result the strength of their talents could develop.[58]

Through their acts of rebellion, they emerged from the position of slavery in which women in China had been held "for several thousand years". Guo argues that "the morality which is centered on the male" had succeeded over generations through the family system in casting females in the role of "apes" or "orang-utan" (*xingxing*), while men assumed the subservient "female" qualities — suspicion, jealousy, slyness, sloth, obedience and dependance, into which men had the first instance, cast women. Men had made women an object of derision. The position of women in Chinese society as Guo Moruo depicts it in this highly political piece constitutes a problem for society in its entirety, and at the same time is a problem for each and every individual in society. Guo suggests that "self-salvation" is the solution. Guo's ideas at this time echoed many other leaders of the May Fourth generation, such as Lu Xun, Chen Duxiu and Hu Shi, and he sought out female modesl from Chinese history for emulation by the contemporary age. *Three Women of Defiance* was a collection of three dramas: *Wang Zhaojun, Zhuo Wenjun* and *Tangdi zhi hua*.[59] The first two plays in the collection were written in 1923. *Wang Zhaojun* was directly influenced by Oscar Wilde's *Salome*, which Guo's close friend Tian Han had translated into Chinese. Wang Zhaojun had been a favorite heroine of traditional dramatists.[60] Guo writes that traditionally Wang Zhaojun was depicted as a victim of fate, who had been inadvertently sent by a duped emperor into exile to serve in the harem of a Hunnish chieftain. Guo transformed this unwitting victim of destiny into a rebel who went to marry the Hun chieftain in definance of Emperor Yuandi. Thus "a tragedy of destiny" became "a tragedy of personality."[61] *Zhuo Wenjun* celebrated the heroine of the same name, who broke the Confucian moral code by eloping as a widow with the romantic poet Sima Xiangru.[62] Zhuo Wenjun, like Wang Zhaojun, was herself a poet, and Guo emphasizes her talent in his play. Both plays show the influence of Ibsen, whose works Guo had read as early as 1917–18.[63] Indeed, Guo describes Zhuo's father's house from which she flees as "a crystal prison."

The third play in this early trilogy *Tangdi xhi hua* (Devoted Siblings) has its source in the *Shiji* of Sima Qian, and relates the story of the brother and sister, Nie Zheng and Nie Ying, who are rebels against the tyranny of Qin. Nie Zheng is an assassin, while Nie Ying suicides in the struggle for righteousness, her country and the common people.[64]

From the celebration of women who existed in legend, to the depiction of the image of the social rebel and the assassin, Guo Moruo's women

reflect in some measure the changing position of the Communist Party at
the various times he wrote, as well as the personal position and stance of
Guo Moruo himself, variously inspired, exiled, defiant, beleaguered, en-
circled and ultimately comfortably in power.

Similarly the debate on historical dramas never strayed far from the
position that historical dramas must serve the present. Furthermore, the
Chinese tradition of satire through the historical mirror ensured that this
PRC perception of the function of theater was underscored by a long national tradition. It was a tradition which writers could not defuse, despite
whatever promises of breaking with tradition the debate in the
1950s–1960s seemed to extend.

Guo Moruo by the 1950s was a veteran writer of historical dramas.
Since women predominate in his pre-1949 dramas, it was only natural
that he would attempt works about women which he felt matched present
concerns. Wu Zetian, as a woman in a position of supreme political
authority, might also seem a natural choice. Yet contemporary attitudes
demanded that he eschew Empress Wu's traditional image as a libertine,
and stress instead her role as a mother. But this image of a mother was
itself a desexed image of a mother, being cut loose from biology. The
mother-child, ruler-subject relationship which required filial piety on the
one hand and reciprocity on the other, accorded with the contemporary
image of authority. Traditional signs of authority were given an iconic
significance. Historically sacred signs were secularized. The play also ex-
amines the new concerns of authority: its relationship with dissent, with
the writer being a major focus for social disaffection. The peasantry are
depicted as content with the *juntian* (collectivization). This latter theme
provides an interesting contrast with the handling of the same theme in
Tian Han's *Xie Yaohuan*.

While the sex of Wu Zetian may have been merely a foil, and ultimately irrelevant to the function of Empress Wu as an image of authority, the Wu Zetian of Guo's play was frequently equated with the Jiang
Qing of history. The charge was usually refuted, and the strongest argument for a refutation was the fact that when the play was written Jiang
Qing was not significant politically. At a conference on Guo Moruo held
in Sichuan in 1979, one year after Guo's death, two speakers at the conference felt it necessary to refute the equation of Guo's Empress and Jian
Qing. Tan Luofei and Lu Wenbi stated in their paper:

> . . . as a person Jian Qing had none of the fine qualities of Wu Zetian, but
> she concentrated the evil qualities of all the evil women of history. More-
> over, she was wildly ambitious to become empress. To what end?[65]

This statement testifies to the volatility which heteronomous literary
texts invariably acquire in a politico-literary atmosphere, in which

referents richocet like the silver balls on the ends of the wires of a per-petual-wave mobile. Engles, in letters written in 1890, warned against a situation in which literary scholarship is deprived of its autonomy.[66] He stated that "the materialistic conception of history now has a host of sympathizers for whom it constitutes a pretext for not studying history." Since such men lack dialectics, "They are forever spying a cause here, an effect there." Such scholarship testifies to a reversion to literary-historical impressionism, which, he asserts, set up metaphysical polar op-positions. These Engels maintains only "exist in the real world during times of crisis." Yet the closing years of the 1950s and the early 1960s, the time of the Hundred Flowers movement, rural collectivization, and the Anti-Rightist Campaign may well have been a time of crisis in China. It was in this environment that Guo dramatized the ethical sanctions which he felt authority must establish for itself, and the relationships such authority should establish with society's estates: the peasantry, the writers, and the officials.

In the 1980s, many of Guo's themes had lost their earlier pertinence. Yet the linking of Wu Zetian and Jiang Qing in the quote above demon-strates the continuing relevance, in the late 1970s, nearly two decades after Guo's play was first staged, of Wu Zetian's repudiation of Luo Bin-wang's *Declaration* as mere misogyny.

Notes

I wish to thank a number of persons for their assistance in the preparation of this paper, which is a revised version of that presented at the Colloquium. They include C.T. Hsia of Columbia University for his many suggestions and encour-agement, Milena Dolezolova-Velingerova of the University of Toronto for her apt comments regarding the imagery of women throughout the plays of Guo Moruo, Anita Chang of Macquarie University for discussions regarding *Jinghua yuan*, and Robert Millers and Sue Dewar of the University of Sidney for discus-sions regarding the place of women in the late Roman Empire and feminist issues.

In preparing this paper, I have used the following edition of Guo Moruo's play: *Wu Zetian* (Renmin wenxue chubanshe edition/Beijing; 1979). I have abbreviated it *WZT* throughout these notes.

1. Gong Liu, *Qianling qiufeng ge* (Song of the Autumn Wind at Qianling). In *Shiyue* (October, bimonthly), 1982-3, pp. 104–105.

2. See Guo Moruo, "Guanyu Wu Hou qi ze" (Seven Items Regarding Empress Wu), in *WZI*, pp. 131–132.

3.   Guo Moruo, "Wo zenyang xie *Wu Zetian* (How Did I write *Wu Zetian*?), in *WZT*, p. 116.

4.   "Boundless admiration": "In the history of modern Chinese culture, he was, like Lu Xun, a renowned scholar of profound learning and comprehesive genius. After Lu Xun there was another glorious banner on the battlefield of Chinese culture, under the leadership of the Chinese Communist Party and the guidance of Mao Zedong thought." Deng Xiaoping, "Zai Guo Moruo tongzhi zhuidao dahui shang de daoci" (Speech in Honour of Comrade Guo Moruo at his Memorial Gathering), quoted in *Zhongguo wenxuejia cidian (Xiandaii diyi fence)*, (Hong Kong: 1979), p. 420. The respect he is accorded in China is indicated by his appellative, Guo Lao.

For an assemblage of contemptuous opinions, see Fang Dan, "Zaofan shiren Guo Moruo: ping *Li Bai yu Du Fu*" (Rebel Poet Guo Moruo: An Evaluation of his *Li Bai and Du Fu*), Part I, in *Xin guancha* (New Observations Monthly), (Hong Kong), 1:4, p. 36. Guo played Schiller to Mao Zedong's Frederick William III, according to some. Guo's poetry addressed to Chairman Mao is included in *Moruo shici* (Selected Poetry), (Beijing; 1977).

The Guo Moruo scholarship industry has emerged by and large since his death in 1978. Among the unusual interpretations of Guo Moruo's work is Fang Dan's contention that *Li Bai yu Du Fu* was autobiographical comment on the Lin Biao affair. (see Fang Dan, op. cit.). By apotheosis, I refer to "Guo Moruo Putuo jiu shaonu" (Guo Moruo Rescues A Young Girl on Putuo Mountain), a modern "legend" included in an anthology of pieces which mythologize incidents in the careers of Chinese revolutionary leaders, *Guo Moruo Putuo jiu shaonu: xin chuanqi gushi* (#2 in the Shanhai-jing series), (Hangzhou; 1983), pp. 1–8. In this story Guo Moruo convinces a young girl, who is heart-broken, not to commit suicide, during the course of a visit to Putuo Mountain in Shandong Province. This "legend" is ironical in light of the fact that when Guo's translation of *Die Leiden des jungen Werther* appeared in Chinese in 1928, many young readers of it were led to suicide, an effect which Goethe's original work had achieved also in Europe a century earlier. The modern "legend" about Guo Moruo edited by Li Qingbao, underscores Guo Moruo's role in the history of modern Chinese literature as a romantic poet and "feminist," because in the story it is by means of the persuasive force of a poem which convinces her that life is preferable to death as a victim of romantic passion. I use the term "feminist" here in its widest possible sense to indicate an advocacy in politics and culture of the emancipation of women. I agree with the position that a male can be a "feminist." I am not indicating by my use of this term any aspect of Guo Moruo's private life.

5.   Liu Xu et al, *Jiu Tang shu juan* 6, "Zetian Huanghou", (Zhonghua shuju edition, Beijing; 1975), p. 133. The referene to the "human swine" and "dragon's semen" are allusions to female usurpers of the throne, which were cited in Luo Binwang's *Tao Wu Zhao xiwen* (Declaration of War Against Wu Zhao), which was included in Guo's play. These two allusions are discussed later in the body of the paper. The "malicious gossip about a concealed nose" is an allusion to Zheng Xiu, the favorite concubine of King Xiu of the Kingdom of Chu (r. 328–299

B.C.). When the King of Wei presented a beauty to King Huai, Zheng Xiu was extremely jealous, so she told the new arrival that the king loathed the shape of her nose. The new beauty then covered her nose whenever she was in the presence of King Huai. Zheng Xiu then told King Huai that the beauty was saying that the king stank. Furious, the King ordered that her nose be sliced off.

The capriciously cruel Queen Zheng Xiu appears in Guo Moruo's drama *Qu Yuan*.

6. Boris M. Exjenbaum, "Literary Environment" (English translation by I.R. Titunik of "literaturnyj byt") in Ladislav Matejka and Krystyna Pomorska ed., *Readings in Russian Poetics: Formalist and Structuralist Views* MIT Press: 1971, p. 56.

7. Mao Dun, *Guanyu lishi he lishiju: Cong Woxin changdan de xuduo butong juben shuoqi* (Concerning History and Historical Drama: A Discussion From My Reading of A Number of Different Texts of the Drama "A Bed of Brushwood and the Taste of Gall"), (Beijing: II 1963), p. 77. Modification of this earlier view occurs in the *Houji* (Postscript), pp. 151-2. From the dateline of the book and its Postscript, it is clear the main body of the work was circulated prior to its first printing in 1962. The main body of the text has the dateline 2 December 1961; the postscript is dated 1 July 1962.

8. *Shishi-xinxi* (new dramas treating contemporary events) and *shizhuang xinxi* (new dramas with contemporary costuming) were two Jingju (Peking Opera) genres from the beginning of the 20th century. Althoug the two were very often one and the same, the terms do not correspond exactly, because while *shishi-xinxi* were performed almost invariably in modern costuming, the modern dress in a *shizhuang(xin)xi* did not necessitate the play's depicting a newsworthy current event, which always formed the basis for a *shishixinxi*. See B. Doar, *We Will Create A Music for the Falling Empire: Developments in Chinese Dramatic Criticism, 1898*-1918, (Unpublished Ph.D. thesis), University of Sydney, 1982.

9. Zhao Jingshen, "Preface", in Ren Erbei, *Youyu ji* (The Sayings of Actors), (Shanghai: 1981), p. 8.

10. Guo Moruo, *Qu Yuan*, is in English translation by Gladys Yang and Yang Hsien-yi. See Yang & Yang ed., *Selected Works of Guo Moruo: Five Historical Plays*, (Beijing: 1984). This volume contains an English translation by Bonnie McDougall and Peng Fumin of Guo's *Wu Zetian*.

11. See Tom Fisher, "'The Play's the Thing': Wu Han and Hai Rui Revisited", in *The Australian Journal of Chinese Affairs*, #7, Contemporary China Center, Canberra 1982, p. 22.

12. Guo Moruo, "Tan Cai Wenji de 'Huqie shiba pai' taolun *ji*". (Anthology of Discussion of Eighteen Beats on the *Huqie*), (Beijing: 1959), p. 1.

13. Mao Dun, op. cit., p. 118.

14. Ibid., p. 123.

15. See Anthony Tatlow, "Bertolt Brecht Today: Problems in Aesthetics and Politics", in Anthony Tatlow and Tak-Wai Wong ed., *Brecht and East Asian Theater: The Proceedings of a Conference on Brecht in East Asian Theater*, (Hong Kong: 1982).

16. Wu Han is quoted in Lin Manshu, "Ping Guo Moruo de *Wu Zetian*". (A Critique of Guo Moruo's *Wu Zetian*) in Lin Manshu, *Ping Guo Moruo de 'Li Bai yu Du Fu*, (Hong Kong: 1974).

17. Wang Fuzhi (1629–1692), *Du Tongjian bian* (Zhong hua shuju edition, Beijing: 1975), p. 729.

18. C. P. Fitzgerald, *The Empress Wu*, (Canberra; 1955); Lin Yutang, *Lady Wu: A True Story*, (London: 1957); R. W. L. Guisso, "The Reigns of the Empress Wu, Chung-tsung and Jui-tsung (684–712)," ch. 6 in *The Cambridge History of China*, (Cambridge UP: 1976), v. 3, pp. 244–5.

19. Denis Twitchett and Howard J. Wechsler, "Kao-tsung (r. 649–83) and the Empress Wu: the Inheritor and the Usurper," in *The Cambridge History of China*, (Cambridge UP: 1976), v. 3, pp. 244–5.

20. Li Zhi, *Shigang pingyao*, (Zhonghua shuju edition: Beijing: 1974), pp. 534–551.

21. Ibid., p. 548.

22. Lin Yutang, "Feminist Thought in Ancient China," in *T'ien-hsia Monthly*, 1:2, (1935), pp. 127–150.

23. R. W. L. Guisso, op. cit., p. 319 points out that the source for most later elaborations on the Stork Institute was a memorial of Zhu Jingze cited in both *Zizhi tongjian* and *Jiu Tang shu*.

24. Song Zhidi, *Wu Zetian* (Shanghai: 1937), p. 1.

25. Ibid., p. 3.

26. *WZT*, p. 109.

27. Ibid., p. 111.

28. Henri Troyat, *Catherine the Great*, (London: 1979), p. 300.

29. *WZT*, p. 110.

30. *WZT*, pp. 130–131.

31. *WZT*, p. 23.

32. *WZT*, pp. 13–114.

33. Ibid., p. 11.

34. Idem.

35. Tian Han, *Xie Yaohuan*, reprinted in *Ming Pao* monthly supplement #4, 1961.

36. Ibid., p. 1.

37. See Ben-David, J. and Clark, T.N., eds., *Culture and its Creators: Essays in Honor of Edward Shils*, (Chicago University Press: 1977).

38. *WZT*, p. 44.

39. Guo Moruo, "Lun Zhong-De wenhua shu: Zhi Zong Baihua xiong", (Letter on Chinese and German Cultures: Letter to Zong Baihua), dated 20.5.1923, in *Chunagzao zhoubao*, (Creation Weekly), (Shanghai), #5, 10 June 1923.

40. *WZT*, p. 106.

41. Clifford Geertz, "Centers, Kings and Charisma: Reflections on the Symbolics of Power,;; in Ben-David and Clark eds., op cit., p. 157.

42. *WZT*, p. 23.

43. Ibid., pp. 53–54.

44. Guo Moruo does not use the standard version of *Wei Xu Jingye tao Wu Zhao xi* (Declaration of War Against Wu Zhao on Behalf of Wu Jingye) as recorded in *Luo Binwang wenji*, and *Tangshijishi* (Notes of Tang Poetry), but rather the standard version recorded in *Guwen guanzhi*. See *Guwen guanzhi*, HK Commercial Press edition; 1961, pp. 299–302.

45. *WZT*, p. 72.

46. *WZT*, p. 69.

47. Ibid., p. 69.

48. Ibid., pp. 69–70.

49. Idem.

50. Ibid., p. 70.

51. Ibid., p. 72.

52. Ibid., p. 104.

53. Ibid., p. 106.

54. Idem.

55. See Guo Moruo's preface to his translation of the plays of J. M. Synge published under the pen-name Guo Dingtang, *Yuehan Xingu de xiju ji*, (Shanghai; 1926), p. 49.

56. Guo Moruo, "Lun shi san zha" (Three Letters on Poetry) (1921), in Peng Fang ed., *Guo Moruo tan chuangzuo* (Harbin; 1982), pp. 4–5.

57. "Guo Moruo tan *Nushen*", (Guo Moruo Discusses "The Goddesses") in Sang Pengkang ed., *Guo Moruo: "Nushen"* huijiao bian (Collected Commentary Version of "The Goddesses"), (Changsha; 1983), p. 191.

58. *Guo Moruo tan chuangzuo*, pp. 91–92.

59. *Tangdi zhi hua* has been translated into English by Peng Fumin and Bonnie McDougall under the title *Twin Flowers*. See Yang and Yang eds., *Guo Moruo: Five Historical Plays*, (Beijing; 1984), pp. 1–86.

60. The most famous of the plays abut the popular heroine was *Han gong qiu* (Autumn in the Han Palace) by the Yuan playwright Ma Zhiyuan.

61. See Guo Moruo, *Moruo Wenji*, v. 3, p. 76.

62. 179–117 B.C.

63. Guo Moruo, "Mai shu" (Book Buying), (1924), in *Baogian ji*, p. 102.

64. See footnote 59.

65. Tan Luofei and Lu Wenbi, "Lun Guo Moruo lishiju zhong guanghui de funu xingxiang" (Glorious Images of Women in the Historical Dramas of Guo Moruo" in *Guo Moruo yanjiu lun ji*, (Chengdu: 1980), p. 298.

66. See Boris Exjenbaum, op. cit.

Glossary

A Ying

Ban Gu

Bao Si

cairen

Cai Wenji

Cai Yi

Cao Yu

Chen Duxiu

Chongqing

Chu Suiliang

Crown Prince Xian

Dinghui 定慧

Empress Lü 吕后

fan'an 翻案

fanmian renwu 反面人物

fengshan 封禅

Fengxian 凤县

Ganye Convent 感业寺

Gaozong 高宗

geng 耕

gengyi 更（耕）衣

Gong Liu 公柳

Guanyu lishi he lishiju 关于历史和历史剧

Guo Moruo 郭沫若

guwen 古文

Guwen guanzhi 古文观止

Han shu 汉书

Helan Mingzhi 贺兰敏之

Hu Shi 胡适

Huaju 话剧

huanghou 皇后

Huo Zimeng 霍子孟

Jian Bozan 翦伯赞

Jiang Qi 江七

Jiang Qing 江青

Jiangnan 江南

Jinghua yuan 镜花缘

Jiu Tang shu 旧唐书

juntian 均田

Kaiyuan 开元

Konghefu 孔鹤府

Lady Hanguo 韩国夫人

Lady Qi 戚夫人

Lady Rongguo 荣国夫人
Lady Weiguo 魏国夫人
Lai Junchen 来俊臣
Li Qingzhao 李清照
Li Ruzhen 李汝珍
Li Yifu 李义府
Li Zhi 李贽
Liu Bang 刘邦
Liu Xu 刘昫
Liu Zhang 刘章
Longmen 龙门
Lu Wenbi 陆文璧
Lu Xun 鲁迅
Lü Zhenyu 吕振羽
Luo Binwang 骆宾王
Luoyang 洛阳
Mao Dun 茅盾
Mao Zedong 毛泽东
Marquis of Zhuxu 朱虚侯
Ming Chongyan 明崇俨
Nie Ying 聂嫈
Nie Zheng 聂政
Nü Wa 女娲
Nü Xunfu (xun'an) 女巡府(巡按)
Ouyang Xiu 欧阳修
Pei Yan 裴炎
Qian Ling 乾陵
Qianxian 乾县
Qian Xingcun 钱杏村
Qin Shi Huang 秦始皇
Qing 清
Qu Yuan 屈原

Ruyi 如意

Shang Yue 尚钺

Shangguan Tingzhi 上官庭芝

Shangguan Wan'er 上官婉儿

Shangguan Yi 上官仪

Shangyiyuan 尚仪院

Shengzhu 圣主

Shigang pingyao 史纲评要

Shiji 史记

shishi 时事

Sichuan 四川

Sima Guang 司马光

Sima Qian 司马迁

Sima Xiangru 司马相如

Sima Zhao 司马昭

Song Zhidi 宋之的

Taiyuanfu 太原府

Taizong 太宗

Tan Luofei 潭洛非

Tang 唐

Tangdi zhi hua 棠棣之花

Tian Han 田汉

Wang Fuzhi 王夫之

Wang Mang 王莽

Wang Zhaojun 王昭君

wanwanqiang 碗碗腔

Wei Xu Jingye tao Wu Zhao xi 为徐荆业讨武曌檄

Woxin changdan 卧薪尝胆

Wu Han 吴晗

Wu Sansi 武三思

Wu Shihuo 武士彟

Wu Weiliang 武惟良

Wu Zetian 武则天

Wu Zhao 武昭

wulai zhi tu 无赖之徒

Xian 贤

Xie Yaohuan 谢瑶环

Xie zai sange pannide nüxing houmian 写在三个叛逆的女性后面

Xiju bao 戏剧报

xin lishiju 新历史剧

Xin Tang shu 新唐书

xing 刑

xingxing 猩猩

xiqu 戏曲

Xu Jingzong 许敬宗

Xu Jingye 徐荆业

Xu Yougong 徐有功

Xuanzong 玄宗

Sue Huaiyi 薛怀义

yiyu rende shiwen 益于人的诗文

yueju (Shauxing opera) 越剧

Yuwen Huaji 宇·文化及

zai yu yong chan 在狱咏蝉

Zetian Huangdi 则天皇帝

Zhang Changzong 张昌宗

Zhang Yizhi 张易之

Zhanghuai Crown Prince 章怀太子

Zhangsun Wuji 长孙无忌

Zhao Daosheng 赵道生

Zhao Feiyan 赵飞雁

Zhao Jingshen 赵景深

zhaoyi 昭仪

Zheng Shisan Niang 郑十三娘

Zhenguan 贞观

Zhou   周

Zhou Li   周礼

Zhongzong   中宗

Zhuo Wenjun   卓文君

Zizhi tongjian   資治通鑑

zui   罪

Part Two

Drama, Ideal and Theory

3. Prescriptive Dramatic Theory
of the Cultural Revolution

ELLEN R. JUDD

The Great Proletarian Cultural Revolution began in 1965 with Yao Wenyuan's criticism of the Beijing opera, *Hai Rui Dismissed from Office (Hai Rui Baguan)* and opera remained a central issue for debate about cultural and political issues throughout the Cultural Revolution. If repudiation of the previous seventeen years was essential, in accordance with Mao Zedong's axiom that destruction must precede construction (*bupo buli*), the creation of a new proletarian culture was also a major theme of the Cultural Revolution. Jiang Qing has been quoted as having said:

> Since the time of the Paris Commune, the proletariat has not solved the problem of its own literary and artistic direction. Only in 1964, with our making of the revolutionary model operas, has this problem been solved.[1]

Beyond the creation of the increasing number of model works, the leaders of the revolution in opera also promoted the creation of a prescriptive dramatic theory closely tied to the model operas but applicable in principle to all genres of literature and art.

The goal of the Cultural Revolution in the arts was never only the creation of some good artistic works of proletarian character—it was recognized that that had happened in the past—but a qualitative break in the artistic life of the Chinese people as part of a profound and thorough cultural revolution. The model operas that were the centerpiece of the artistic revolution were models in more senses than simply as texts: Their processes of creation were models of carrying on the class struggle in the ideological realm. The work-style and practices of the opera troupes which created the model operas were models for the social organization of the new art, on the professional level. Models of social organization on the amateur level were similarly created, later, in the course of the movement to popularize the model operas. The shared formal features of the model operas became models of a new dramatic theory.

94

Writing of the ten years of revolution in Beijing opera in 1974, the top artistic writing group of the time, Chu Lan,[2] wrote that:

This is a scene of thorough revolution destroying the literature and art of the exploiting classes and establishing the literature and art of the proletariat for the first time in history. How to conquer the old Beijing opera and its influence on peoples' minds, how to create brand new revolutionary Beijing operas, how to make images of workers, peasants and soldiers firmly occupy the stage—the solution of this series of problems has no precedent which can be followed.[3]

Chu Lan then proceeded to indicate that the model operas had to be, with reference to Mao, exemplars of uniting revolutionary political content with fine artistic form. The politics received most emphasis but the artistic questions were not neglected. Toward the end of the Cultural Revolution increasing efforts were made to elaborate certain features found in the model operas into a general theory of literature and art. The key elements of this theory were briefly referred to as the "basic task" (*geben renwu*) and the "three prominences" (*san tuchu*). In full, the former stated that "the basic task of socialist literature and art is the creation of proletarian heroic types/images/characters" (*dianxing/xingxiang /renwu*), and the latter followed upon this in indicating more precisely how these proletarian heroic characters were to be portrayed: "among all the characters, give prominence to the positive characters; among the positive characters, give prominence to the heroic characters; among the heroic characters, give prominence to the main heroic character." There was a large set of additional prescriptions attached to the principle of the "three prominences." Some of these will be indicated below in the discussion of the theory itself which follows. A preliminary presentation of the course of development of the theory may aid the later analysis.

The earliest indication of this theoretical direction is to be found in Jiang Qing's programmatic address at the 1964 Beijing opera festival:[4]

We advocate revolutionary contempoary operas which reflect the real life of the past fifteen years of national contruction and which create images of contemporary heroes on our opera stage. This is the primary task (*shouyao renwu*).[5]

That address was authoritatively identified as the starting point of the revolution in Beijing opera,[6] but it was less concerned with elaborating dramatic theory than with pointing out a new practical direction for opera in the coming years. At that time, according to Jiang Qing, the key issue was that of opera texts,[7] and correspondingly the emphasis was on developing model texts of some revolutionary operas, with the development of theory accompanying those texts but appearing and become elaborated at a slower pace.

The "basic task" was more exactly stated by Jiang Qing two years later in an address to the People's Liberation Army given under Lin Biao's sponsorship:

> We must work hard to create worker/peasant/soldier heroic characters — that is the basic task of socialist literature and art. Only with this type of model (*yangtan*) and with successful experience in this area will we be persuasive, able to consolidate our hold on this front, and able to knock down the stick of the reactionaries.[8]

By the mid-1970s, when the Cultural Revolution's dramatic theory was being extensively elaborated and propagated, Lin Biao's disgrace prevented this source from being cited prominently, although there is at least one isolated mention of it (with reference to Lin Biao deleted) crediting this speech by Jiang Qing with the theoretical advance encompassed by the concept of the "basic task."[9] But in general the writings on dramatic theory were then largely concerned with repudiating and distancing themselves from Lin Biao and his views on literature and art. Nevertheless, the connection has not been missed and post-Cultural Revolution critics[10] have also cited this speech as the first clear mention of the "basic task."

The next advance in the theory was the presentation of the "three prominences" in 1968 by a close associate of Jiang Qing's, Yu Huiyong, who attributed this development to her as well.[11] In the following years a series of additional propositions were added to the "three prominences" to make it the basis of a dramatic theory rather than an isolated axiom. At the same time, its significance and scope were progressively extended. From a statement on characterization, it became a principle (*yuanze*) and then the basic principle (*genben yuanze*) of socialist literature and art.[12] By 1974 it was being promoted as the central and essential principle in a prescriptive theory of proletarian literature and art in all genres, with any deviation from or criticism of this theory defined as a departure from a proletarian class stand. The theory was presented strongly and prominently in articles by the top central writing group on art, under the pseudonym of Chu Lan, in 1974[13] and in a more controversial theoretical form by Fang Yun, the pseudonym of a writing group organized by Yu Huiyong in the Shanghai Municipal Culture Bureau.[14]

The final development of the theory, in 1976, was the prescription to create works about struggle against capitalist roaders and hero(in)es whose heroism was revealed in this particular type of class struggle. This was less a theoretical development than an application of the existing theoretical emphasis of basing characteristization on class struggle to the political situation obtaining in 1976.

The dramatic theory to be analyzed here, then, is the one whose development is outlined above, as it reached its most elaborated development in the mid-1970s, and especially in the more theoreticized version in which it was presented by Fang Yun. The focus is upon the central theoretical concepts of the "basic task" and the "three prominences," with less attention being given to the theoretically subsidiary question of portraying struggle against capitalist roaders. The more direclty political issues of the "literature and art of intrigue" (*yinmou wenyi*) have been discussed in detail by Chinese commentators.

It is important to note that this entire theoretical development took place, and was explicitly conceptualized as taking place, in the context of struggle against opposing views of literature and art. Initially this was a repudiation of the preceding seventeen years, summed up as being an era in which the stage was dominated by "emperors, ministers, talents and beauties" (*diwang, jiangxiang caizi jiaren*), in contrast to worker, peasant and soldier hero(in)es. Confucian and Soviet revisionist ideas on literature and art and criticism of the model operas were also vehemently repudiated during these years. The course of producing the model operas and the new literary theory of the Cultural Revolution was one dominated by explicit processes of conflict and the carrying on of this conflict was integral to both the works and the theory. Parallel with the creative and theoretical developments and partly integrated with them, there were also movements of criticism directed toward other works and theories. This context of conflict will be addressed here only insofar as it forms part of the theoretical developments under examination, but must be kept in mind as a major factor shaping the cultural context in which this theory emerged and become dominant.

The "Basic Task"

The concept of the "basic task" is not itself highly complex, although it does have certain unspoken assumptions which are significant, and both the source and the theoretical implications are worth exploring. The concept was presented primarily by assertion, with some reference to the authority of Mao Zedong or Jiang Qing, but without substantial argument or explanation. As Jiang Qing early indicated: "We must emphasize creating artistic images of progressive revolutionaries to give everyone education and encouragement and to lead everyone forward."[15] This inspiration was implicitly assumed to operate by emotional identification with the hero(in)es of the proletarian works of literature and art. The model operas exemplifying this approach were highly emotive and could hardly have been in sharper contrast to to the detached and reasoned type of literature and art created and advocated as proletarian by some Westesrn and Third World dramatists, such as Brecht[16] and Boal.[17] These different approaches to proletarian literature and art were not discussed during the Cultural Revolution and there was no rejection of the emotional identification with dramatic characters on either aesthetic or political grounds.[18] What was prominently at issue, given the efficacy of such identification, was what kind of character was to be presented to the public to influence it. Here the discussion focused overwhelmingly on class, although it might be argued that in practice, if not in theory, there were other factors present as well (age, gender and political status):

> The central question in creating revolutionary model operas is wholeheartedly and resourcefully portraying proletarian heroic models (*dianxing*). From an historical perspective, which class's heroic images are portrayed and which class's representative characters rule the literary and artistic stage is a concentrated reflection of political struggle within literature and art and is the the main mark of which class's political line is being served in literature and art. In making the revolution in Beijing opera, it is necessary to emphasize portraying literary and artistic images of proletarian heroic characters, to make workers, peasants and soldiers become rulers of the stage, and to restore the original face of a history turned upside down by the landlord and bourgeois classes for thousands of years. The proletariat clearly raised the basic task for socialist literature and art of creating proletarian heroic models, and this basically draws a clear boundary between our literary and artistic movement and the literacy and artistic movements of all the exploiting classes in history. The practice of the revolution in Beijing opera proves that only by doing a good job of portraying proletarian heroic models, can the realm of literature and art use Marxism-Leninism-Mao Zedong Thought to repudiate Confucianism and remake the world in the proletariat's image. Only by doing a good job of portraying proletarian heroic models can the literary and artistic stage show the revolutionary struggle of the Chinese people under the leadership of the Chinese Communist Party, praise the great victories of Chairperson Mao's revolutionary line in each revolutionary period and on every front, and encourage the masses of the people to push history forward. Only by doing a good job of portraying proletarian heroic models, can the dictatorship of the proletariat over the bourgeoisie in the realm of literature and art be realized. Insisting upon this basic task is insisting on the direction of literature and art serving the workers, peasants and soldiers. This is a question of principle upon which there can be no wavering at any time.[19]

It was precisely this strict equation of proletarian purpose with portrayal of the proletariat (and its allies) on stage which, along with the motivational efficacy of artistic characterization, lay at the root of the "basic task" and both explained and legitimated its absolute primacy. Any deviation was vulnerable to charges of serving the landlord or bourgeois classes. Consequently, there was no room for discussion or debate on this issue and writing about the "basic task" largely concerned the problem of how this related to other aspects of artistic works, such as theme and plot, and how most effectively to portray such proletarian hero(in)es. On the relationship of characterization to theme and plot, Fang Yun succinctly summarized the position: "Correct thought on policy in works of literature and art must, ultimately, be realized through the speech and actions of characters, and mainly be realized through the leading role of heroic characters in the struggle of contradictions."[20] The issue of how to create these hero(in)es effectively was extensively addressed by the "three prominences" and its associated propositions — indeed, this was the problem which gave rise to that theoretical development.

The numerous articles on or referring to the "basic task" do not deal with the question of its theoretical sources in detail, but do refer to some authorities — Engels, Mao and Jiang Qing — in a sense suggestive of source but more in a legitimating sense. Jiang Qing's pronouncements on this subject have been quoted or cited above, but the reference to the other two authorities is more complicated.

A newly proposed proletarian literary and artistic theory must necessarily consider the views of the founders of Marxism and, in the ideological climate of China during the Cultural Revolution, the classical sources of Marxism-Leninism carried a great weight in almost every sphere. This was so in literature and arts as well, despite the absence of more than isolated observations on these subjects by Marx and Engels.[21] Further, while there are a number of Marxist approaches to literature and art, they do not represent a unified theory in that area and are more concerned with social context than aesthetics. There was, therefore, considerable lattitude possible in moving from the Marxist classics toward a theory of proletarian literature and art. The chief relevant sources are letters written by Engels to various contemporary leftist writers.

On the subject of characterization, Engel's letter to Margaret Harkness is the most relevant. His comment in that letter that realism implies the creation of "typical characters under typical circumstances"[22] would have been familiary to all Chinese readers with any acquaintance with literary theory. Engels certainly viewed characterization as a very important aspect of novels and drama, but he did not elaborate a poetics or assert the absolute primacy of any particular aspect of artistic work.

More extensive and complicated reference was made to Mao's writings, some of which will be discussed in the next section of this paper. In the present context, the significant texts are his "Letter to the

Yan'an Beijing Opera Institute After Seeing *Driven Up the Liang Mountains*" and the "Talks at the Yan'an Forum on Literature and Art." The letter congratulated the creators of a modern Beijing opera on an historical theme which was first performed in Yan'an in 1944. Of the several things Mao might have said about it—it used an historical theme to express the Communist position on the war with Japan—he praised it for restoring ordinary people to a place on the stage and thereby correcting ruling class distortions of history. Mao declared this to be a major development in the reform of opera and that many more operas should be created along those lines.

The references to the "Yan'an Talks" are more complicated. In accordance with the position given Mao's works during the Cultural Revolution, the "Yan'an Talks" were cited as providing a "complete set of theory, direction and policy for proletarian literature and art,"[23] despite their very definite historical character as part of the new democratic revolution of an earlier era and despite having very little to say about specifically artistic questions. References were made to the "Yan'an Talks" in general, to the passage on the relation between art and life, and to the call to praise the proletariat and laboring people. However, Mao's version of the highest priority was broader than the "basic task": "All the dark forces harming the masses of the people must be extolled; this is the fundamental (*jiben*) task of revolutionary writers and artists."[24]

Mao's position on the arts was one of insisting upon their political character and advocating or requiring that that politcal character be one of serving the interests of the people (*renmin*) in either the new democratic or the socialist contexts. However, he did not address specifically artistic questions, either through a concern not to interfere excessively in the work of artists or through an underestimation of the implications of artistic elements, such as formal structure, for political expression in art. His own artistic practice was known to continue the use of the classical poetic form of *ci* to express revolutionary sentiment.

Criticism of Cultural Revolution poetics has returned to a comparable position, criticizing the Cultural Revolution for its rigidity on artistic questions and advocating a wider range of artistic practic in accordance with the "hundred flowers" policy and its associated six criteria for distinguishing "fragrant flowers" from "poisonous weeds."

This may well have beneficial effects for artistic activity in contemporary China, but is not a wholly satisfactory position in theoretical terms. It fails to come to terms with the political implications of artistic form. Much of the political content of an artistic work is expressed indirectly through what might appear to be purely artistic means—language and form—but which are precisely the vehicles through which any set of (necessarily political) ideas are realized, and it is this artistic transformation which gives special power and immediacy to those political concepts. The especially interesting feature of Cultural Revolution poetics is its effort to address the question of the political implications of artistic form and to construct a specifically proletarian dramatic form. The further elaboration of the "basic task" into a poetics based upon the "three prominences" must therefore be viewed as a serious political and aesthetic development and not only as an excruscence of bureaucracy or a political manoeuvre to promot Jiang Qing and her associates.

The "Three Prominences"

The theory itself revolved around two main features of drama — characterization and the relations between characters, and the presentation and development of conflict. These two were closely connected, as the characters were presented primarily through their action in dealing with contradictions and conflict.

The theory was presented as based upon the experience of creating the model operas. This mode of exposition made the theory more concrete, further utilized the "model" quality of the model operas and accorded with the emphasis on practice in Mao Zedong Thought. However, as indicated above, major portions of the theory emerged in the late 1960s before even the original eight model operas had assumed definite form. At most, it might be argued that the theory and the model operas developed together with mutual influence, but the theory cannot accurately be said to derive from the experience of creating model operas. In some cases the model operas even deviate from the theory. The dramatic theory bears close connections, however, to the more ideological and political climate in which it emerged and grew.

The pivotal feature of the theory, and one asserted as a principle (*yuanze*), was the "three prominences." Raised to the level of principle, what might otherwise have been one of a large number of contemporary political ideas about literature and art in China became instead a feature dominating over the "method" (*fangfa*) of "combining revolutionary realism and revolutionary romanticism" or the "orientations" (*fangzhen*) of "letting a hundred flowers bloom," "weeding through the old to make way for the new," and "using the past to serve the present and the foreign to serve China."[25]

This principle, together with its numerous associated propositions, constituted a clearly prescriptive dramatic — and by extension literary and artistic — theory which touched upon all aspects of dramatic work. If it did not exhaustively treat each aspect, it did give unambiguously clear instructions on how to do correctly proletarian dramatic work in terms of each question that was addressed. It was this prescriptive purpose, backed by the authority of the highest leadership and their publishing and performing networks, which was paramount, rather than any descriptive goal of analysis or criticism. Criticism was valued, also, but as a method of carrying on class struggle in the arts and of ensuring the dictatorship of the proletariat in all areas of art.

In the terms of this theory, there were five categories of character: main heroic characters, changing (*zhuanbian*) characters, heroic characters, positive characters and negative (*fanmian*) characters. The negative characters were invariably class enemies, for the most part officers of the Japanese or Nationalist armies or spies. They were few in number, as it was an essential feature of this theory that the positive and heroic characters must predominate, but their presence was important for both political and dramatic purposes. They were politically necessary because class struggle was at the core of every proletarian drama even if its main line of dramatic conflict lay in the realm of contradictions among the people. While shorter works, such as some short stories, might be able to dispense with class enemies in developing a structurally simpler plot with less scope and limited to contradictions among the people, full-length dramas and novels were expected and required to portray class struggle. Not to do so would be interpreted, in the idelogical context of the Cultural Revolution, as advocating the idea that class struggle had ended, one of the ideas most strongly repudiated as revisionist in that period. Dramatically, negative characters were very useful for the development of conflict. Although class conflict could appear as the subject matter of a play without the actual appearance of class enemies, their appearance did facilitate dramatic conflict and, given that the theory basically presumed that ideological content was primarily expressed in drama through embodiment in characters, their appearance was indispensable for approved proletarian dramas. Further, the characterization of the hero(in)es was partly effected through contrast with the negative characters and by portrayal of their intelligence, courage and resolution in combatting class enemies. The theory prescribed that the negative characters be created with the primary purpose of revealing the virtues of the hero(in)es, especially the main heroic character. The qualities of the negative characters were of no other interest or purpose in proletarian drama. In order to ensure strong dramatic conflict, the negative characters should be formidably bad, but must not distract attention from the heroic characters, to whom they must give way and whose characterization they must serve to develop. Prescriptions for the positive characters were much less detailed. These were members of the masses, and therefore positive, but not developed with detailed individuality. Attention was reserved for the heroic and the negative characters. Their chief function was to contribute to the portrayal of the main heroic character, usually by showing his/her close relationship to the masses and the respect of the masses for him/her.

Heroic characters were to be constructed along similar lines to the positive characters, with the addition of notable heroism. Again, their main purpose was to contribute to portraying the main heroic character. Both positive and heroic characters were generally portrayed without human blemishes. The Cultural Revolution's criticism of earlier artistic work for portraying "middle characters" (*zhongjian renwu*), that is, characters neither wholly good nor wholly bad, precluded the portrayal of such characters in proletarian drama.

The changing character bore some superficial resemblance to a middle character, but was distinctly different. The changing character was a positive and often heroic character who made grave mistakes because of wrong ideas but who, under the influence of the main heroic character, recognized his/her mistakes and corrected them. The internal changes of these characters were not of interest to this theory, and the purpose of portraying such characters was, as one would expect, to show the influence and unfailing correctness of the main heroic character.[26]

The main heroic character, then, carried the burden of embodying almost the enitire meaning of the drama and of doing so in a vivid and moving manner. The main heroic character was conceptualized as a concentrated representation of the greatest class in history, the proletariat, and therefore had to be portrayed in a suitable grand style. Any criticism of the main heroic characters as being overly idealized was declared an insult to the proletariat.[27]

The main heroic character's presentation of the ideas of the drama was not confined to or even mainly attained through explicit statements in dialogue, although didactic passages did occur. Rather, this happened primarily through the main heroic character's position in relation to the contradictions that structured the action of the drama. The primacy given to the main heroic character required that (s)he be involved in every contradiction in the drama and the heroism of the character implied that this involvement be that of leading the correct resolution of every conflict arising from those contradictions.[28]

The structuring of the contradictions expressed in the drama as dramatic conflict was intrinsically connected with the relationship between the various types of characters. Such a connection can, perhaps, be argued for other poetics as well, but in this case the relationship was especially explicit and specified. the predominance of the main heroic character was matched in the structure of contradictions by a similar hierarchy. Class struggle was unquestionably the main contradiction in each play and necessarily the primary sphere in which the main heroic character would be revealed.[29] This was so even in a drama centered around a contradiction among the people, as those contradictions are fundamentally conditioned by occurring in class society. Whatever the contradictions, their function in the drama was not a direct effect upon the audience but an indirect one, operating through the characters of the drama, and especially the main heroic character.[30]

Within each full-length drama there would be several lines of contradiction or dramatic conflict. In accordance with a conception of life as basically consisting of contradictions appearing, developing and being resolved, this dramatic theory required that there be a consistent structure of contradictions being revealed, intensified and actively managed so as to be resolved satisfactorily within the drama. To try to avoid the presentation of conflict or its intensification was repudiated as a theoretically unsound interpretation of both life and drama. Consequently, the development of the contradictions into peaks of dramatic conflict was emphasized as critical to the successful writing of proletarian drama.[31] The possibility of leaving contradictions unresolved at the end of dramas was precluded by the requirement of showing the hero(ine) resolving contradictions successfully.[32]

The contradictins in each drama could be divided into one main line (*zhuxian*) and one or more secondary lines (*fuxian*):

> The main line of contradiction—the main line of contradiction in a work—has a process of occurrence, development and resolution which runs through the entire play from beginning to end. Secondary lines of contradiction are less important ones in other areas. Generally speaking, the main line of contradiction in a work is the main area for the portrayal of main heroic images and realizing the work's theme. A work's secondary lines of contradiction are subordinate to the main line of contradiction, add to the main heroic character in additional respects and enrich the work's thematic content.[33]

The portrayal of the main heroic character was further related to the unbalanced nature of every contradiction:

> Chairperson Mao points out, "Of the two contradictory aspects of contradictions, one must be principal and the other secondary. The main aspect is the one playing the leading role in the contradiction. The nature of a thing is determined mainly by the main aspect of the contradiction in the dominant position."[34] Organizing the conflict of contradiction (*maodun chongtu*) with the main heroic character as the center is taking the main heroic character as the main aspect of the contradiction and giving prominence to his controlling position and leading role.[35]

Every point in the development of contradiction in the play then becomes an opportunity for portraying the qualities of the main heroic character and good dramatic practice would utilize all such opportunities.[36]

The connection between this structure of contradiction and the primacy of characterization can be found in the same general theory:

> Chairperson Mao points out, "*The basic cause of the development of things is not from outside a thing but from inside it, in the contradictoriness within things.*"[37] People's speech and actions are all controlled by a certain ideology and have deep reasons in its stand and world view. In handling the intensification of contradiction, we must strive to reveal the deep ideological conflict between characters which is realized in dramatic conflict, and take pains to go deeply into the ideological realm—only this kind of opera can have a deep ideological educative significance for the masses.[38]

All other aspects of drama—music, sets, costumes, and so on—were to be handled in such a way as to reinforce this dramatic structure and its emphasis on the main heroic character.[39] Most of these aspects—music was an exception due to its importance in Chinese drama—received little theoretical attention beyond indicating their purpose in the overall dramatic endeavor.

The ambitious and original theoretical enterprise undertaken by Cultural Revolution dramatic theory should now be apparent. Where earlier revolutionary theory or propositions on the arts in China had addressed themselves to content, genre, and a range of issues relating to the social and political context and practice of art, their theory directly concerned itself with a Marxist poetics. Its focus on characterization was an attempt to locate and theorize upon a major element of drama (and at least some other types of art) which distinguished it from non-artistic modes of communication. Confirmation for the general theoretical validity of this approach was found in the theoretical proposition that internal contradiction predominates over external factors. Rather than changing only the social and political practice of art or simply introducing proletarian content, this theory constituted an effort to proletarianize the specifically artistic elements of dramatic form.

Repudiation of the Theory

Resistance to this theory existed during the Cultural Revolution, and was occasionally articulated in a systematic way,[40] but was overwhelmed by the domination of publication and other media channels by the theory's supporters. That domination was not unlimited, as shown by the restricted spread of the theory in its most elaborated form, but did effectively prohibit open debate on either its own propositions or the status of the model operas. Consequently, the final years of the Cultural Revolution, 1974 to 1976, were a period in which all public favor seemed to go to Cultural Revolution drama and the theory connected with it, and the following few years a period of almost equally intense repudiation of it.

The terms of this repudiation are interesting both for their comments on Cultural Revolution dramatic theory and for their own perspective on the arts.

At the simplest level, this was a rejection of rigidity and the imposition of formulae for creative work. These were asserted to be stifling rather than proletarian in essence, and authority for this position was found in various texts of Mao and especially in "On the Correct Handling of Contradictions Among the People," with its advocacy of allowing a "hundred flowers to bloom" and its restriction of artistic work only by broad limits defined in social and political rather than artistic terms.

The "basic task" was criticized extensively and on numerous grounds of a generally socio-political and philosophical nature. In socio-political terms, the "basic task" was at its most vulnerable in its latest form where the heroic characters were exemplars of struggling against capitalist roaders. It was then inevitable that the theory and the works in question would be interpreted as designed to promote the prestige of Jiang Qing and her associates and followers. In the criticism this was presented in terms of bourgeois elements seeking their own self-aggrandisement and increased power.[41] In an ideological milieu in which art was seen by all as serving politics in both general and very practical senses, Cultural Revolution poetics were seen as a tool for the seizure of power by the "Gang of Four."[42] This accusation may well have a real basis, but there are also broader theoretical issues involved, some of which were touched upon in the period of repudiation. It should be kept in mind that the ideological and political climate of those years favored the portrayal of political leaders who dared to take unpopular steps in the interests of a continuing revolution and that such portrayal cannot be entirely reduced to maneuvering for direct political power.

Even without those political overtones, however, there were serious problems with the heroic characters which post-Cultural Revolution commentary was quick to identify. The crux of the problem was the nature of proletarian heroism. The Cultural Revolution heroic characters and the theorization about their portrayal was open to charges of non-proletarian glorification of individual hero(in)es separated from the masses of the ordinary people and placed above them. The focus on one single essential heroic character was criticized for its failure to portray revolutionary social and political relationships—those of the Party and the masses, the army and the masses, and so on — and for instead presenting a character whose heroism seemed derived from intrinsic personal qualities.[43] On a general theoretical level, this implied the much-repudiated view of history as created by geniuses (*tiancailun*). On a less general level, it seemed to ignore the pivotal role of the Communist Party and other revolutionary organizations and to belittle the role of the numerous ordinary members of these organizations.[44]

Further, critics pointed to the relationships of leaders and followers expressed in the "three prominences" as being hierarchical and as reducing the role of the masses to that of serving leaders, leaders whose authority was innate rather than dependent on political relationships of solidarity. This argument, then, did not deny the desirability of creating dramas with proletarian hero(in)es, but rather asserted that Cultural Revolution drama and poetics had not accomplished that and that it had actually degraded the masses.[45]

The source of these failings was in part traced to political opportunism, but the theoretical underpinnings of it received attention as well. The theory's position on characterization was identified as non-materialist in that the characters were structured in absolute terms and in relation to each other, but characterizations were not based on or derived from historical and social reality.[46] Indeed, the entire development of dramatic theory in the Cultural Revolution notably concentrated upon artistic form and the political implications of that to the neglect of other significant questions such as the relationship of "art" to "reality." Connected with this problem, there was also a theoretical criticism of the lack of character development in Cultural Revolution poetics. Only the "changing characters" develop and they do so only to demonstrate the heroic character's influence and not because of a concern with character development. Other characters are quite static. The main character is progressively revealed as heroic as contradictions intensify and are resolved, but does not actually change or develop.[47] This could be, and was, easily criticized as non-materialist in implicitly assuming the irrelevance of the external material world to heroic being by showing it only as something to be acted upon by the hero(ine).

In short, the main line of the repudiation of Cultural Revolution dramatic theory was an appeal to established tenets of Marxism-Leninism-Mao Zedong. Thought to demonstrate that the theory was not accurate or orthodox. The proclaimed breakthrough to proletarian drama was found seriously in error even in the terms of Marxism-Leninism-Mao Zedong Thought which was current during the same years that this dramatic theory flourished, at the end of the Cultural Revolution. The repudiation of it which followed occurred before the major theoretical and ideological changes of recent years and endeavored to separate the dramatic theory from Mao Zedong Thought, rejecting the former in terms of the still authoritative latter. Indeed, very early articles on this subject separated the poetics from the model operas and continued to laud the operas, although those later came under criticism (firstly being rejected as models and then being rejected more thoroughly). Recently, criticism of Cultural Revolution drama has faded as attention has turned to new work and new directions and also to a recovery of earlier work which was unavailable and denounced during the Cultural Revolution.

The post-Cultural Revolution criticism of Cultural Revolution dramatic theory was concerned with the social and political context and consequences of drama and dramatic theory. This followed the strongest line of Marxist artistic theorizing in modern China and has illuminated some of the problems of this theory. However, it missed the very issues of form which were central to the poetics itself and to its claims for theoretical advance. The propositions on form associated with the "three prominences" were repudiated as narrow formulae abstracted from class analysis and material reality.[48] While there are valid grounds for upholding that view, it is weak in that it deals with the theory on its most superficial level. The question of whether it is possible or desirable to introduce proletarian politics into art in its specifically artistic dimensions — such as form — was not addressed, nor was any alternative proletarian or socialist poetics proposed.

Critical Comments

To the outside observer, much of the criticism after the Cultural Revolution appears valid and necessary despite the intriguing and innovative nature of Cultural Revolution poetics. Certainly there was a rigidity in the theory which, together with its narrow application and impositon from above, restricted artistic development during the years in which it was dominant.

The claim of a breakthrough toward a theory of proletarian drama and of proletarian literature and art in general is questionable on more grounds than those raised, to my knowledge, during the period of criticism in the late 1970s. These additional reservations derive from an examination of those special arguments about artistic form which the critics of the theory chose not to emphasize, perhaps in part because the full development of these arguments, while tested in print in the writings of Fang Yun, were not widely spread. Nevertheless, that more complete treatment lay behind, connected and explained the widely cited propositions, such as the "three prominences" and the importance of showing the conflict in contradictions.

If the theoretical innovation of applying "On Contradiction" to dramatic structure in order to proletarianize it was ambitious, it was also done in the most simplistic manner. What was understood as the ultimate structure of the material world—a complex, permanently unbalanced hierarchy of internally related contradictions—was moved directly and explicitly into the structure of drama on a relatively superficial level. This was done despite the very general and abstract quality of Mao's "On Contradiction" and ultimate relationships, within complex and varied social and historical situations. The actual complexity which co-existed with the abstractions was lost in the transference of the general theory of "On Contradiction" to dramatic form. Further, and equally serious, there was inadequate attention given to the issue of the theoretical specificity of poetics compared with more general philosophical theory. What theoretical transformations would be needed to adapt general theory to artistic problems? The solution offered by Cultural Revolution poetics was to identify plot—the process of social contradictions—and characterization—of the main hero(in)es—as the area in which to insert the general theory of contradiction without further transformation. Indeed, the presentation of the primacy of characterization as derived from the general primacy of internal contradiction is a strictly literal argument without theoretical substance.

Further insight into the dubious quality of this application of "On Contradiction" is provided by an examination of characterization and plot development. Characters, with a few qualified exceptions, do not develop at all and are entirely one-sided, positive or negative. Contradiction is presented only between characters and not within them. The plot moves—in the poetics if not always in the models—in a smooth progression of intensification and successful resolution of conflict. The complex, spiral quality of contradiction is lost in this simple linear structure.

Perhaps most serious of all, in that it negates a major ideological purpose of this poetics, is the actual emphasis on conflict in the contradictions which structure each drama and connect this centrality with the theoretical primacy of contradiction and conflict and the political emphasis on class struggle continuing throughout the socialist epoch. However, an examination of the processes actually described and recommended, together with the examples provided by the model operas, shows the emphasis to be not on conflict but on the resolution of conflict. This is not only a consequence of the lack of unresolved conflict in either main or secondary lines of contradiction at the end of dramas struc-

tured according to this poetics. It is also because the dramatic structure
is oriented around a peak of intensification and then successful resolution of conflict. The effect of this structure is that the conflict is not central but rather serves to prepare for and underline the subsequent resolution. Strangely, such a dramatic structure is extremely vulnerable to just
that charge of portraying the end of class struggle—that being the main
type of contradiction and conflict presented—which its supporters so
strongly condemned as revisionist. And the ensuing placidity at the end
of such drama was antagonistic to that conception of the pervasively
contradictory and even conflictual nature of life which this poetics claimed
to realize artistically.

Another major problem area in this poetics concerned its portrayal of
hierarchical power relations between various types of character. This was
not a superficial question of performance effectiveness or emphasis, but
an intrinsic and essential feature of the poetics. As expressed within the
poetics, it was not a matter of differences in power but of prominence on
stage, and not a reflection of social difference but of degrees of heroism.
All the positive characters were described as proletarian or as allies of the
proletariat (peasants and soldiers) and therefore class distinctions of this
type were not at issue. The difficult problem here is the one of revolutionary leadership, for all the main heroic characters are revolutionary
leaders, albeit at a low-ranking level. Their low-ranking status permitted—in a sense—the denial of this difference and allowed these
characters to be referred to as simply exemplary proletarian hero(in)es.
This approach essentially avoided the problem by using phrasing which
denied its existence.

Part of the problem was inherent in the conception of proletarian
heroism. Proletarians were necessarily exploited and oppressed but proletarian hero(in)es were those who resisted, and especially those who
resisted strongly and effectively. In the context of an organized revolutionary movement, they were clearly the leaders, those who showed the
way and were decisive in resolving contradictions. It might well be
argued that that model operas of the Cultural Revolution sought to avoid
the difficulties of the power issue by making the heroic characters leaders
at the most basic level. And it could certainly be argued on both
theoretical and practical levels that there were unevennesses in the activism and heroism of the masses. The problem lay in the ambiguity of
both portraying this unevenness and denying its existence in substantial
terms. This ambiguity resonated with the Cultural Revolution climate of
exclusive political claims and ardent egalitarianism. Indeed, many of the
most provocative and interesting features of Cultural Revolution
dramatic theory were as closely related to the historical context of late

Cultural Revolution society as to the more abstract theoretical questions which were also involved.

Dramatic Theory of the Cultural Revolution

This political theory must be seen as a response and an initiative in the particular and intense political milieu of late Cultural Revolution China. Such an assertion implies not only attention to the probable conscious concern of the leading figures to use drama and theory about drama to promote and support their more general political goals, but also an examination of other, less consciously intended reflections and interventions. This consideration adds a further dimension to some of the theoretical problems cited above.

Primary among these was the difficult question of hierarchy. The insistence of Cultural Revolution ideology on a denial of hierarchy and its favoring of workers, peasants and soldiers was compromised by the persistence of differential power relations throughout the Cultural Revolution. This contradiction became more obvious and acute toward the end of the Cultural Revolution, the very period during which this poetics reached its peak, accompanied by a marked increase in dramatic production. The ambiguities of the Cultural Revolution in terms of power or hierarchy were expressed strongly, if presumably unintentionally, in Cultural Revolution drama and poetics. The very emphasis on the elite Beijing opera as the main forum for a breakthrough into proletarian drama revealed this contradiction. The progression of the revolution in drama and the other arts, with a primacy for a few works designated as "model" and the troupes associated with them, institutionalized hierarchy in the social practice of drama and the other arts. And within the theory of drama, this ambiguous—present but substantially denied—hierarchy was at the core of the theory, in its structure of characterization and plot.

Connected with the problem of hierarchy was another major area of difficulty—that of cadres as proletarian hero(in)es. Here again the problem was defined out of existence by an interpretation of revolutionaries as proletarian and perhaps even, as in the case of the main heroic characters, exemplary representatives of the proletariat. This might be true in many cases in terms of class origin or current class relations, but the model operas have several examples of hero(in)es who clearly have non-proletarian backgrounds, as evidenced by their ability to disguise themselves effectively as leaders on the enemy side, or by other obvious indicators of class. Even where that particular difficulty did not occur, most of the main proletarian hero(in)es had a status as Party or army cadres which did actually place them in a different position from other members of the proletariat. While it can be argued that this is simply an expression of the revolutionary quality of the proletariat, which seeks to end its oppression and confidently proceed to create a new society, the social relations of actually existing socialism indicate problems with a direct identification of cadres with proletarians because of their superior access to structures of power.

Indeed, power is central to this theory of drama. What is, above all else, portrayed in these plays is effective human power to reshape the social world. This is the reason why cadres must be the main heroic characters—only those in positions of some power can accomplish the resolution of contradiction which is at the core of every proletarian drama constructed in accordance with this theory.

Here the structure of Cultural Revolution drama and its theorization deeply connect with the revolutionary voluntarism central to the Chinese revolutionary process, especially during the Cultural Revolution. They can be seen as a concentrated expression of confidence in the human capacity to transform the world, and it is ultimately for this reason that the successful resolution of conflict dominates. If one can perhaps see allusions to certain Cultural Revolution leaders in the hero(in)es of the model operas and other contemporary works, the avoidance of portraying high or even middle-ranking leaders is also significant. Along with the difficulties of cadres as proletarian, one may see here an effort to empower wider sectors of the population, to attribute to the millions the capacity to effect historical change in significant and even spectacular ways.

Such action is difficult both to conceptualize and to practice decades after a revolution. As noted earlier by Dittmer and Chen[49] there is a link between the ambiguity of class struggle under the conditions of socialism and the stridency of its expression, in drama and elsewhere. Class enemies must be present but are hidden and hence hard to identify; and class enemies may be hard to distinguish from mistaken but essentially good members of the masses. The unmasking of class enemies, the revelation of undercover proletarian hero(in)es, and the assumption of disguise by hero(in)es temporarily entering enemy circles all indirectly touch upon this problem. They show unclear lines between the people and the enemy becoming clearly distinguished, thereby demonstrating the possibility of making such distinctions correctly—and also the necessity of doing so for the success of the revolution. In a comparatively subtle manner, this process, repeated in drama after drama, serves to further reinforce the voluntaristic revolutionary message of Cultural Revolution drama.

In manifold ways this dramatic and artistic theory was a theory for the production of works lauding and encouraging the continuation of the voluntaristic concept of revolutionary process which dominated ideological production in China in the Cultural Revolution. It was further permeated by the ambiguities of the Cultural Revolution experience with just a such a contradictory revolutionary history.

Concluding Remarks

The dramatic theory of the Cultural Revolution shows the limitations of the historical conditions under which it was produced. As with many other theories claiming to be proletarian, this claim does not literally imply creation by the proletariat, but rather for its interests, as interpreted by specialist intellectual workers. There are continuing difficulties with the conception of the proletariat, or its interests, in a post-revolutionary society. The impetus for revolution becomes mixed with a certain inertia and concern for consolidating gains already achieved. This ambiguity — or contradiction — is abundantly apparent in the predetermined pattern of conflict intensification and resolution in Cultural Revolution drama and poetics.

Both this closed quality and the heavily prescriptive nature of the theory indicate a compromise with authority which is not found in at least some proletarian dramatic theories created in pre-revolutionary conditions, the epic theatre[50] or the joker system,[51] which are more consistent in their portrayal of contradiction and less prescriptive or confident about its manner of resolution. Indeed, non-resolution of conflict has become a major convention of progressive drama.

The particular historical constraints and ideological compromises of Cultural Revolution dramatic theory partly obscure its experimental value, but that should not be wholly denied. In undertaking the revolutionary transformation of the ideological means of artistic production it shared in that revolutionary image of triumphant will which it theorized for drama. It was a major conscious effort to devise an explicit programme and method for that transformation. The question of how to revolutionize artistic form raised by this theory is — contrary to the theory — still unresolved but central to any discussion of revolutionary drama in China or elsewhere.

114 Ellen R. Judd

Notes

This paper was written during a period of research in the Department of Social Anthropology at the University of Cambridge. The author wishes to express her gratitude to the department for its facilities and to the Social Sciences and Humanities Research Council of Canada for financial support.

1. Zhexue shehui kexuebu dapipanzu, "Geming wenyi shi dang de shiye bu shi bang de shiye—ping 'si ren bang' fan geming de xiuzhengzhuyi wenyi luxian de ji you shizhi," *Hongqi*, (1977), p. 39.

2. Chu Lan was a pseudonym for a writing group in the State Council's Culture Group (*Guowuyuan wenhuazu*). The leading official statements on art appeared under this pseudonym in the late Cultural Revolution period. Yao Wenyuan reportedly wrote some of the Chu Lan articles: Colin Mackerras, "The Taming of the Shrew: Chinese Theatre and Social Change Since Mao," *Australian Journal of Chinese Affairs*, 1 (January 1979), p. 4.

3. Chu Lan, "Jingju geming shi nian," *Suzao wuchanjieji yingxiong dianxing shi shehuizhuyi wenyi de genben renwu* (Shaanxi renmin chubanshe, n.p. 1974), p. 5. Originally published: *Hongqi*, 7 (1974).

4. The claim made by her supporters that Jiang Qing was responsible for the first appearance of the concept of the "basic task" in literature and art is confirmed by the later criticism of her opponents, after the end of the Cultural Revolution: He Wenxuan and Du Shuying, "'Genben renwu' lun poxi," Hangzhou daxue zhongwenxi wenyi lilun yanjiushi, ed., *"Si ren bang" fandong wenyi sixiang pipan* (Zhejiang renmin chubanshe, Hangchou, 1978), p. 94. Originally published: *Beijing wenyi*, 1 (1978).

5. Jiang Qing, "Tan jingju geming," *Mao zhuxi de geming wenyi luxian shengli wansui* (Shaanxi renmin chubanshe, Xian, 1972), p. 2.

6. Chu Lan, op. cit., p. 4.

7. Jiang Qing, op. cit., p. 3.

8. Jiang Qing, "Lin Biao tongzhi weituo Jiang Qing tongzhi zhaokai de budui wenyi gongzuo zuotanhui jiyao," *Jiang Qing tongzhi jianghua xuanbian (1966.2-1968.9)* (Hebei renmin chubanshe, n. p., 1969), p. 9.

9. He Dong, "Xiuzhengzhuyi wenyi heixian de fanqi," *Wenyi pipan ji (er)* (Zhejiang renmin chubanshe, n. p., 1974), p. 10. Originally published: *Shanxi ribao* (11 May 1974).

10. He Wenxuan and Du Shuying, op. cit., p. 95.

11. Ibid., p. 95; Wenhuabu pipanuzu, "Ping 'san tuchu,'" *Jiefa pipan 'si ren bang' wenxuan (san)* (Sanlian shudian, Xianggang, 1977), p. 118. Originally published: *Renmin ribao* (18 May 1977); and Shanghai shi wenhuaju dapipanzu,

"'Si ren bang' de zhongshi zougou Yu Huiyong," *Guangming ribao* (25 November 1977).

12. Wenhuabu pipanzu, op. cit., p. 118–119.

13. Chu Lan, op. cit.; and Chu Lan, "Suzao wuchanjieji yingxiong dianxing shi shehuizhuyi wenyi de genben renwu, *Suzao wuchanjieji*, p. 25–32. Originally published: *Renmin ribao* (15 June 1975).

14. He Wenxuan and Du Shuying, op. cit., p. 95–96; and Shanghai shi, op cit.

15. Jiang Qing, "Tan Jingju geming," p. 4.

16. Bertholt Brecht, *The Messingkauf Dialogues* (Eyre Methuen, London, 1965).

17. Augusto Boal, *The Theatre of the Oppressed* (Pluto, London, 1979).

18. The process of emotive identification with characters having an impact on action seems to have been deeply assumed and to have required no argument or explanation. One wonders whether one may here identify the influence of Confucian ideas about the moral power of example of the upright person—on the part of these strident denouncers of Confucianism.

19. Chu Lan, "Jingju geming shi nian," p. 6–7.

20. Fang Yun, *Geming yangbanxi xuexi zhaji* (Shanghai renmin chubanshe, Shanghai, 1974).

21. Lenin was not referred to in discussions of Cultural Revolution dramatic theory, perhaps because of his clear favoring of a diversity of approaches in the arts.

22. Karl Marx and Frederick Engels, *On Literature and Art* (Progress, Moscow, 1978).

23. Fang Yun, op. cit., p. 3.

24. Mao Zedong, "Zai Yan'an wenyi zuotan hui de jianghua," *Mao Zedong lun wenyi* (Renmin wenxue chubanshe, Beijing, 1966), p. 29. This is quoted from the official version of the "Yan'an Talks," which is what was current and quoted during the Cultural Revolution. This passage is, in any event, identical with that in the earliest available text, that of 1943. Throughout this paper quotations from Mao's works will be from the official texts.

25. Fang Yun, op. cit., p. 3.

26. Ibid., p. 47–49.

27. Ibid., p. 69; Jiang Tian, "Nuli suzao wuchanjieji yingxiong dianxing," *Suzao wuchanjieji*, pp. 38–39, originally published, *Renmin ribao* (12 July 1974);

and Chu Lan, "Zhongguo geming lishide zhangli huajuan—tan geming yangbanxi de chengjiu he yiyi," Chu Lan, Jiang Tian et. al., *Chuangzuo pinglun ji* (Shanghai renmin chubanshe, Shanghai, 1974), pp. 17–18, originally published, *Hongqi*, 1 (1974).

28. Fang Yun, op. cit., p. 13, 24, 27–28.

29. Ibid., p. 1–2, 66.

30. Ibid., p. 80ff.

31. Ibid., p. 54–56.

32. It is interesting that at the very end of the Cultural Revolution a feature film appeared which ended with an episode of unresolved class conflict. *Nanwang de zhandou* (*Unforgettable Struggle*) attracted considerable attention for this innovation. It was seen as politically significant in underlining the continuation of class struggle. It was more notable as a breakthrough in the dramatic expression of contradiction within the Chinese context. The theory discussed here did not take up the questions raised by that approach, either for lack of sufficient time or because of the incompatibility of the new approach with this theory.

33. Ibid., p. 80.

34. Boldface in the original. This is a quotation from "On Contradiction": Mao Zedong, "Maodun lun," *Mao Zedong xuanji*, 1 (Renmin chubanshe, Beijing, 1966, p. 297.

35. Fang Yun, op. cit., p. 29.

36. Ibid., p. 30.

37. Boldface in the original. This is also a quotation from "On Contradiction": Mao Zedong, op. cit., p. 276.

38. Fang Yun, op. cit., p. 91.

39. Ibid.

40. He Dong, op. cit. p. 10.

41. He Wenxuan and Du Shuying, op. cit., p. 100–102; and Zhongguo huajutuan, "Jianchi weiwu bianzhengfa chedi pipan 'san tuchu,'" Hangzhou daxue, ed., op. cit., p. 165.

42. Wenhuabu pipanzu, op. cit., p. 124.

43. Zhongguo huajutuan, op. cit., p. 164.

44. Qiao Shan and Yu Qi, "'San tuchu' shi fan makesizhuyi de wenyi zhuzhang," *Jiefa pipan 'si ren bang' wenxuan (er)* (Sanlian shudian, Xianggang, 1977), p. 89, originally published, *Guangming ribao* (15 February 1977); and Zheng Zekui and Xhang Guangchang, "Yige xiuzhengzhuyi wenyi de fandong kouhao," Hangzhou daxue, ed., op. cit., p. 175.

45. Wenhuabu pipanzu, op. cit., p. 122.

46. Qiao Shan and Yi Qi, op. cit., p. 85–87; and He Wenxuan and Du Shuying, op. cit., p. 98.

47. Qiao Shan and Yi Qi, op. cit., p. 87–89.

48. Ibid., p. 83; and Yu Jun, "Dali tichang 'liangjiehe' de chuangzuo fangfa," Hangzhou daxue, ed., op. cit., p. 168, originally published, *Guangming ribao* (9 January 1978).

49. Lowell Dittmer and Chen Roxi, *Ethics and Rhetoric of the Chinese Cultural Revolution* (University of California Press, Berkeley, 1981).

50. Bertolt Brecht, op. cit.

51. Augusto Boal, op. cit.

Glossary

bupo buli	不破不立
Chu Lan	初澜
ci	词
diwang jiangxiang caizi jiaren	帝王将相才子佳人
dianxing	典型
fanmian	反面
fangfa	方法
fangzhen	方针
fuxian	副线
genben renwu	根本任务
genben yuanze	根本原则
Guowuyuan wenhuazu	国务院文化组
Hai Rui Baguan	海瑞罢官
jiben	基本
Jiang Qing	江青
Lin Biao	林彪
maodun chongtu	矛盾冲突
renmin	人民

renwu   任务

san tuchu   三突出

shouyao renwu   首要人物

tiancailun   天才论

xingxiang   形象

yangban   样板

yinmou wenyi   阴谋文艺

yuanze   原则

zhongjian renwu   中间人物

zhuxian   主线

zhuanbian   转变

4. Model Drama as Myth: A Semiotic Analysis of Taking Tiger Mountain by Strategy

KIRK A. DENTON

The world of artistic creation during the first five years of the Cultural Revolution was dominated imperiously by a single genre. The "revolutionary model drama," as it was labeled relegated other genres, literary and visual, to the depths of artistic oblivion. Those genres not jettisoned completely, such as the short story, manifest narrative structures, methods of characterization and patterns of symbolism which clearly suggest the pervading influence of the model drama. Moreover, this solitary genre produced a mere eight works, all of remarkably similar content. Eight dramas qualified as "model" and were permitted to be produced, on stage and in film, throughout China. For five years these eight dramas constituted the complete oeuvre of artistic creation and bore the burden of the prodigious propaganda of the Cultural Revolution period. In these few works, thus, can be seen an intense concentration of ideology. Indeed, it was the onerous charge of the model dramas to mythologize the Maoist ideology, to attempt to legitimatize and sustain its vision of reality.

This paper proposes to analyze one of these model dramas, *Taking Tiger Mountain by Strategy* (*Zhiqu Weihushan*, hereafter *Taking*) as a modern myth. The drama will be examined and dissected not as a literary or artistic text but as a mythic form giving shape to a certain perception of being in the world. I intend to demonstrate how, by manipulating and exploiting signs, especially those of the traditional popular culture, the model drama avails itself of communicative codes to paint a reassuring and imposing picture of the Maoist ideology.

The analysis is based on the model of modern myth described by Roland Barthes's study, "*Myth Today*".[1] Barthes's study is semiotic; that is, it has at its core the notion of the sign. The sign is the associative total of a concept (signified) and a thing which has a physical, acoustic or visual property (signifier). Barthes takes this tripartite notion of the sign and extends it to myth. Yet myth he sees as a "second-order semiological

119

system." Myth takes hold of signs which are full (meaningful) on the linguistic or visual levels of signification and deprives them of meaning by raising them to a second level at which they become empty forms for the expression of an ideology. This mythic, second level of signs is formed by the associative union of signifiers (which are the signs of the first level of signification) and a signified (which is the ideological impetus). Barthes clarifies his model with the following diagram:

	1) signifier	2) signified	
First Level	3) sign I) SIGNIFIER		II) SIGNIFIED
Mythic Level	III) SIGN		

A cover of a French magazine, *Paris-Match*, for example, displays a black man in a French army uniform; his eyes are raised and he is saluting a French flag. This is the simple meaning of the iconic sign (the sign on the first level of Barthes's model). But the photograph signifies much more than this apparent meaning. The black man, the uniform, the salute have become empty forms on a second mythic level of signification to connote that "France is a great Empire, that all her sons, without color discrimination, faithfully serve under the flag."[2] Myth here has given form to the idea of French imperiality. This dual level of signification is similar, and Barthes recognizes the debt, to Hjemslev's bifurcation of denotation and connotation.

For Barthes, the signified on the mythic level is bourgeois mentality. But this space in the model can be occupied equally well by the leftist ideology when it "accepts to wear a mask, to hide its name, to generate an innocent metalanguage and to distort itself into Nature."[3] The efficacy of myth to sustain an ideology and authenticate that ideology's view of the world lies in Barthes's first-level sign. It is this sign, at once meaningful and but a form, which lends a natural guise, an innocence and ineluctability to the mythic level of signification. As such, myth becomes a devious agent for the propagation of an ideology.

The revolutionary model drama of the late 1960s is a reformed descendant of the traditional Peking Opera. It was surely not fortuitous that the highly heterogeneous form of Peking Opera was picked up by Jiang Qing in the early sixties as the most operative vehicle for the propagation of ideology. Traditional Peking Opera is above all a performing art. And it is more than any other art form the performing art which makes use of the most varied types of sign systems to communicate to its audience. Peking Opera avails itself of gestural, musical, rythmic, terpsichorean, facial, acoustic, literary and linguistic sign systems, organically interconnected into a united whole. There is an extraordinary depth, complexity and potential vigour to the dramatic sign of the Peking Opera. As perhaps the most eclectic of all art forms, the Peking Opera possesses a multiplicity of sign systems to convey meaning; the means by which to naturalize the ideological message, in Barthes's terms, are manifold.

As all popular Chinese art forms, the Peking Opera has a clear dual nature: it is both narrative and lyrical. The drama has both spoken dialogue which furthers the action and lyric arias which elaborate the story and contain the ideologic message. This dual structure, which has characterized all of the popular Chinese literature and performing arts since the Tang *bian wen*, furnishes a well-balanced form with which to both propagate ideas and cloak those ideas in an appealing guise. It seems clear that a form such as the novel, as has been recently pointed out by Milan Kundera, strives toward complexity, ambiguity and contradiction and lends itself poorly to the promotion of political cant.[4]

What was surely not overlooked by Jiang Qing in her decision to appropriate Peking Opera for revolutionary purposes is precisely what the Peking Opera is not: it is not a written form, an immutable literary text designed for private, individual reading. The dramatic form is a public phenomena, shared communally by members of an audience. As such, it takes on ritualistic dimensions. The model dramas, thus, offered a form of public ritual to function in the process of the legitimatization of ideology.

A performance text is, moreover, by its nature accessible to revision and emendation. It is not a written medium, an unalterable text which, once published, relinquishes itself perilously to the equivocal world of the individual reader with his personal interpretations and judgments. A dramatic performance can be easily changed from day to day. Revision not only precludes the kind of individual reading experience that a written text demands, it enables the creators of the drama to experiment with and develop the language of their genre. Indeed, it was through the continued revision of the eight model dramas over the years from 1964 to 1970 that we see evolve the mythic language of the genre, its subjection to the ideology. This corruptibility of the text, moreover, allowed for hasty emendation in the case of unforeseen political changes.

The textual history of *Taking* is typical of all the model dramas. The original literary wellspring for the drama is the 1957 adventure novel *Linhai xueyuan* (*Tracks in the Snowy Forest*).[5] The novel is an episodic story about the gallant exploits of a PLA troop in ridding northeastern China of the remnants of Goumindang dominion. Though the socialist import of the novel is clear, the novel draws freely and self-consciously from the traditional culture (indeed, the very structure of the novel is reminiscent of that of *Shuihu zhuan* (*Outlaws of the Marsh*), avoids sterotypical characterization and indulges in a great amount of humour. It is above all an adventure story, designed to divert and entertain; the ideological message is secondary.

In 1958 chapters ten through twenty-one of the novel were first adapted for the Peking Opera stage under the title *Zhiqin guanfei Zuoshandiao* (*Taking the Bandit Vulture By Strategy*). In preparation for the 1964 Festival of Peking Opera on Contemporary Themes, the forum for much of her reforms of Peking Opera, Jian Qing revised and edited this 1958 script.[7] Major revision of this script was undertaken in 1966–67[8] and then again in 1969.[9] It is the 1969 script and its filmed version, the culmination of a long process of revision, which is the focus of the present analysis.

The language of mythology develops gradually throughout this process of revision. Though the novel and early drama manifest ideological messages, it is not the message but the story which is paramount. Mimesis does not succumb to the sway of ideology. By the 1969 version of the drama, however, the ideology has taken hold of every detail of the performance; mythification has occured. The revisors of the drama were guided by two broad principles of revision: a de-emphasis on story and a focusing of attention on the principal hero. As the one retreats the other advances. The story is gradually reduced to a bare thread. Characters are dropped. Action which is presented dramatically in the early texts is narrated indirectly through a character or expurgated altogether in the later versions. Story detail which seeks verisimilitude in the early texts is excised.

The effect of this streamlining of the plot is to free the characters, most notably the principal hero, from the confines of the mimetic world of the drama. In this way the principal hero becomes the focus of the ideological impetus. The role of the principal hero is exalted in all areas (literary, visual, and acoustic) of the performance. He comes to dominate the stage and the text and is made out to be the very image of the ideology.

As the Czech structuralists have made clear, the nature of drama is that everything presented on stage is semiotized; the very fact of the appearance of something of stage gives it a signifying role. In *Taking*, following Barthes's model, everything on stage signifies on two levels. Before proceeding to an analysis of the structural relationship of signs on the first level of signification and how they ultimately point to the Maoist ideology on the second, however, a brief word should be said about the incorporation of traditional signs by the socialist ideology in the 1950s and 60s.

The exploitation of signs by the traditional popular culture had begun as early as the War of Resistance in anti-Japanese propaganda. It was generally in the fifties and sixties, though, that ideology was imparted to traditional signs. S.H. Chen, in his informative article on the poetry of the Million Poem Movement of the Great Leap Forward, describes how some signs from the traditional popular culture became conventionally linked with the image of Mao Zedong. In part as a result of the broad rhyming possibilities of his name and in part from positive traditional associations, such terms as *feng* (wind), *hong*, (red) and *deng* (lantern) all come to connote Mao and his Thought. The Party, writes Chen, becomes incarnate in such images as the sun (*taiyang*) and mother (*qinniang*) which have positive values in the popular culture and which rhyme with the word for party *dang*.[10] In other media (newspapers, Mao's quotations) these kinds of signs and many more are systematically brought together to signify Mao Zedong and the Maoist ideology. They unite in a highly methodical structure to point to the ideology. In the process, the traditional sign systems of the Peking Opera are both determined and exploited.

As mentioned above, the signs which form this new system derive for the most part from the traditional popular culture. They generally follow the basic binary oppositions of the symbolic correlations of the *yin* and *yang*, the dual forces of nature in the Chinese cosmological schema. Symbols, visual signs, acoustic signs, literary metaphors and imagery which make up the mythic language of the model drama can be neatly classified into those associated with the *yang* force and those associated with the *yin* force. This bipartite division, which is a broad underpinning of Chinese culture, is fundamental to the language of the drama. It is this set of signs which forms the stuff of the first level of signification.

Signs in the drama traditionally associated with the symbolic correlations of *yang* are exploited to promote and characterize the roles of the positive characters (workers, peasants and soldiers) while signs associated with the symbolic correlations of *yin* are used to denigrate negative characters (bandits and Guomindang soldiers). This binary division of signs in the drama is absolutely systematic. Properties of *yin* are invariably attached to negative characters and those of *yang* unfailingly are attributes of the positive characters, especially of the principal hero. This pattern of signification in the drama conforms to the following *yin-yang* oppositions, which are basic to the symbolism of Chinese traditional culture:

Yang	*Yin*
external	internal
ascendant	descendant
brightness	darkness
spring	winter
sun	moon
noise	silence
day	night
heat	cold
vision	hearing
red	black
joy	fear
fire	water
lungs	intestines
life	death
male	female

The most obvious manifestation of this meticulous manipulation of signs is the opposition of light and dark in the drama. All scenes in which positive characters figure prominently take place during the day. The stage is lit up brightly, often by simulated rays of the sun (about which more will be said later). Conversely, scenes in which bandits dominate take place at night or in the shadowy confines of their bandit lair, a murky cave atop Tiger Mountain. When positive characters appear together on stage with negative characters, spot lights are cast explicitly upon the former; nowhere is the contrast between light and dark more glaringly apparent.

Without exception, bright coloured costumes and props belong solely to the realm of positive characters, while somber earthy hues define negative characters. The dominant colors of the positive characters are bright green and a nearly flourescent red. An intertext is formed here with Tang poetry, where these two colors have been conventionally lined to signify the flourishing vegetation of late spring and summer. The traditional association of growth and efflorescence is not lost in *Taking*.

Indeed, the allusion helps to link the PLA troop with nature, with life, and oppose it to death and decay. The two colors are, moreover, symbols of the elements earth and fire, the two elements in the Five Elements schema which are imbued with the *yang* force.

The color red, popular symbol of happiness and prosperity for joyous and festive occasions, is pervasive in *Taking*. Red is the color aligned with the element fire which, of the five elements, possesses the greatest amount of *yang*. Though the colour was appropriated by the Chinese communists in their incipient years from the Russian revolutionary movement, it is clear that it has been grated effortlessly upon a solic indigenous foundation. By the time of the Cultural Revolution, the designation "red" had come to signify one's political and ideological correctness, how fully and sincerely one had embraced the Thought of Mao Zedong. In the model drama red is an omnipresent sign of Mao Zedong and Maoism. Red flags are flown about the stage. A very large one forms the backdrop of the final scene of the drama, when the PLA soldiers have taken Tiger Mountain. PLA soldiers wear red armbands and red stars adorn their caps. A peasant girl dons a bright red jacket and a red flower is set off in her dark hair. Yang Zirong, the principal hero, sports a red banner diagonally across his chest and his riding crop is colored red. The bandits never appear in red of any shade. Their costumes are of colors of the earth: dark greens, dark blues and black. Black, it should be noted, is the color linked to the element water, the element directly opposed to that of fire. It is apparent that the producers of the earlier versions of the drama were less dogmatic about their application of the color red: a photo of the 1964 production reveals two bandits wearing red sashes. It would seem that in 1964 the sign "red" had less of its strict ideological signification than in 1969 when a bandit in red would be an unthinkable transgression.

The sun, as has been noted, had by the fifties come to signify the Party. In the model dramas the sun figures as a hackneyed sign for Mao Zedong and his ideology. Typical of its use in the model dramas is the following explicit example from *Baimao nü (The White-Haired Girl)*:

Today we will see the sun appear.
The sun is Mao Zedong.[11]

As a symbol from the traditional culture, the sun is charged with positive significance. It is the hegemonic symbol of *yang*, the source of all brightness and life in the universe. It is a designation for the emperor. In *Taking* the sun appears recurrently both as a literary image in the text and as a visual image on the stage. In an aria in which she longs for an end to bandit oppression, Chang Bao, the daughter of a mountain peasant, sings: "I only hope that the sun will shine over the secluded mountains."[12] The setting for Scene Five (in which the principal hero, Yang Zirong, treks through the dense forest to Tiger Mountain disguised as a bandit) is described as having "endless rays of sun penetrate into the forest."[13] Yang Zirong successfully reaches the mountain and cleverly worms his way into the bandit leader's inner circle. When alone for a moment he sings a long aria reaffirming his staunch will to defeat the bandits. He stands on a clearing atop the mountain, the bright rays of the red sun are beaming down upon him as he sings: "I will fight the bitter cold, melt the frozen snow, for in my heart I have the morning sun."[14] To add to the density of the sun imagery, the orchestra is playing "The East is Red, Rises the Sun". This is perhaps the climax of the drama. Yang Zirong, filled and warmed by the Maoist ideology, has reached a state of perfect illumination. He is as if transformed into the *yang* force itself. He is the image of the sun, the emperor. It is surely not fortuitous that Yang's surname is homophonous with the *yang* of *yin-yang* and *taiyang*.

The sun is the heavenly body symbol for the element fire. Shared properties of heat and light connect the two logically. Fire imagery is found throughout *Taking* and is strictly parallel with sun imagery and opposed to images of water. Fire comes to signify the anger and passion of the oppressed classes and their fervent desire for revenge. Oppresssion by the bandits, conversely, is consistently described in terms of snow and ice which are but frozen water. In Scene Two, Li Yongqi, an angry young peasant, sings: "Flames charge to the sky, men shout out."[15] Later in the same aria, he sings: "Brilliant flames of rage burn in my chest."[16] Chang Bao, we learn in the opening scene of the drama, has been rescued from freezing to death in a mountain valley by the PLA scouts. In Scene Three, Chang Bao "speaks bitterness" of the beginning of her family's suffering at the hands of the bandits: "Eight years ago, in a nocturnal snow storm, disaster descended upon us."[17] With fire in their hearts, runs the analogy, the peasants and soldiers will melt the snows of oppression, which transformed into water will seek the lowest ground and flow away. In Scene Five, Yang Zirong sings: "I wish I could order the flying snow to melt into spring waters."[18] Thus, under the supreme guidance of the blazing sun, Mao Zedong, the innate class hatred of the peasants and the impassioned desire for revenge of the PLA soldiers will melt away the snows of oppression. In this way fire is made to overcome water.

It is also significant in this respect that a heating stove, and by analogy the more general *topos* of the hearth, plays an important role in two of the drama's scenes. A small stove in the middle of the PLA detachment's cabin is the central prop around which all of Scene Four revolves. It stands in clear opposition to the winter scene outside. To make the opposition even more obvious than the scenery arrangement already does, the cabin door is made to fly open from the force of the winter storm. The Head Staff Officer closes it, then warms himself around the stove. All characters who enter the cabin during this scene proceed directly to the stove to warm themselves. This is no mere mimetic detail. The hearth is a sign of the center of a family's home and thus of community and fraternity. The sharing of the warmth of the fire becomes a sign of the familial unity of the PLA soldiers which will protect them against the chaos and disorder of the harsh storm outside.

One of the principal properties of fire is that it ascends. Conversely, it is the nature of water to descend. This opposition is absolutely central to the arrangement of imagery, metaphor and symbol in both the literary and visual realms of *Taking*. Symbols of ascendancy, as has been noted by Mircea Eliade, the scholar of religious symbolism, in all cultures refer in some way to enlightenment and spiritual liberation.[19] In the model drama, signs of ascendancy, without fail, delineate positive characters from negative characters, who are marked by signs of descendancy.

One example of this opposition is the posture of the two kinds of characters. While positive characters are made to stand tall and erect, negative characters invariably stoop, cower and grovel to the ground. The more immediate source of this opposition is to be found in the role system of traditional Peking Opera. It is quite apparent that the bandit characters are derived from the traditional comic *chou* role, often depicted with a hunched back; and that the PLA soldiers are akin to the *sheng* role, always straight-backed and of impeccable moral fiber. Yet, the ultimate source lies in the fundamental cosmological opposition between heaven and earth, between that which ascends toward heaven and that which falls to earth, between fire and water.

One of Jiang Qing's actor proteges who played the role of Yang Zirong in the later productions of the drama makes an interesting remark about his predecessor which leads us to believe that the directors were conscious, to a certain degree, of the moral implications of posture: "The directors (of the early productions) forced him to violate his proletarian dignity by 'bending eighty degrees' in submission to Vulture. In the raucous scenes in the bandit's lair, Vulture was positioned at stage center, proudly surrounded by his men, while Yang Zirong, then played by a man much older and less vigorous than myself, stood meekly in the corner of the stage."[20] Of course, the directors of the early drama sought not to denigrate Yang Zirong but were merely observing the exigencies imposed by the reality of the fictional situation: Yang Zirong must be made to act like a bandit if his disguise is to be maintained. An adherence to mimesis is shown little respect in the later productions.

The ascendancy/descendancy opposition is also manifest in the drama's use of animal imagery. Almost invariably the bandits are likened to quadrupeds which, by their nature, are low to the ground. Clearly the revisors were conscious of the associations of this animal imagery, for they changed one bandit's name from Tuft Cheek to *Ye-lang-hao* which means Wild Howling Wolf. Bandits, moreover, are made to physically appear as quadrupeds by hunching their backs. Some bandits are made to resemble dogs by wearing hats with ear flaps turned down, like large droopy ears. In the text, bandits are referred again and again to "jackels and wolves" (*chailang*), "wild dogs" (*fenggou*), and "Mongrels" (*sangjia quan*).

In contrast, positive characters are equated with great birds. Birds, in Daoist symbolism, represent spiritual enlightenment and the attainment of sagehood. The very first image of the *Zhuangzi* is that of the *kun* fish rising out of the mire and confusion of the sea to metamorphize into a *peng* bird and fly toward the sun. The tightness and consistency of the sign system in the drama is revealed when we learn that feathed creatures are associated with the element fire in the Five Elements symbolic correlations.

In the text are many examples of bird and flight metaphors to describe positive characters. In Scene Three, Chang Bao sings: "How I wish I could sprout wings, grab my gun, fly to the mountain ridge and kill all those jackels and wolves. . ."[21] But the most salient exmaple of bird imagery is visual. When the PLA squad is skiing its way toward Tiger Mountain for the final assault in Scene Nine, with fluttering white capes and gymnastic effects, the soldiers are made to appear like a flock of birds.

The fact that the bandit chief, Vulture, is nicknamed for a bird would seem to threaten the rigor of the opposition. The vulture, however, is a bird in Chinese culture, as in the West, which has evil connotations. In Buddhist mythology, for example, Mo Wang, the Devil King, assumes the form of a vulture in order to fly to a holy mountain to achieve enlightenment.

The sign of the tiger is an important and complex part of the drama. The tiger is traditionally the most feared of beasts in China, roaming mountain ranges and terrorizing helpless passersby. It is also a symbol of the *yin* force of nature. In the drama, the tiger becomes a sign of evil, a clear parallel to the bandits. Yang Zirong's slaying of a tiger on his way up to Tiger Mountain in Scene Five signals to the audience the power of the *yang* force to overcome *yin*. (As we recall, Yang Zirong is equated with the *yang* force). The image of Yang Zirong as the destroyer of *yin* is invigorated through intertextual allusion. The slaying of the tiger is an unmistakeable allusion to the scene in *Shuihu zhuan* in which the hero Wu Song kills a tiger. Though all of the marvelous detail of the *Shuihu* episode is lost, the stalwart image of Wu Song nonetheless lends substance to Yang Zirong's heroic stature. The allusion serves to paint Yang Zirong in a natural guise which is culturally palatable to the audience. This scene in the drama also functions as a portent of the slaying of the bandits on Tiger Mountain in the final scene of the drama. The two scenes are clearly parallel. If the dual slayings, that of the tiger and of the bandits of Tiger Mountain, are viewed as sacrifices then a rather surprizing analogy is made to the *feng* sacrifice traditionally performed by the emperor at the base and summit of Tai Shan as an appeal to Heaven for dynasitic legitimatization.[22] The two sacrificial slayings, thus, come to represent symbolic acts for the legitimatization of the new Maoist order. Credence is lent to this interpretation by the fact that the taking of Tiger Mountain occurs on the final day of *layue*, the day of the lunar calendar which was traditionally reserved for sacrifices to usher forth the new year.

The tiger vest which Yang Zirong sports throughout the last half of the drama is an allusion to Sun Wukong, the monkey hero of the novel *Journey to the West*. It will be remembered that Monkey is freed from the mountain under which he had been pinned for five hundred years. To clothe his naked body he slays a tiger and wraps its skin around his waist. The allusion charges Yang Zirong's tiger vest with images of the magical, supernatural powers of the enlightened monkey.

Soaring pine trees are another sign of ascendancy. Tall, endless pines are placed on the set of the later productions in scenes in which positive characters figure. Whereas in the earlier productions scraggly and twisted pines are used to give the set a fearful quality, only tall, straight pines are present in the later productions. The revisors of the drama were aware of the symbolic implications of their stage settings:

> The stage set now is completely different. Sturdy, towering pines form the background for Scenes One, Three, Four, Five and Nine. Especially, in Scene Five, a forest of giant cloud-touching pines pierced by shafts of sunlight and echoing with resounding songs expressibly and vigorously reflects the dashing, firm, staunch, fearless, heroic personality of Yang Zirong.[23]

The pine tree sign as an ascendant image is lent a certain force by the traditional designation of the pine as a symbol of moral rectitude.

By far the most important sign of ascendancy in the drama is the mountain. In China mountains are sacred. The five sacred mountains have been revered over the ages by all three of the Chinese teachings. More specifically, in Daoist symbolism the mountain top figures as a place of enlightenment, where one becomes a sage, where one is closest to Heaven and to the Sun, to the source of life. The mythical Penglai Mountain is the sacred residence of Daoist immortals and symbol of eternal bliss. Says Eliade in his study of natural symbols in world religions: "The summit of the Cosmic Mountain is not only the highest point on Earth, it is the navel of the Earth, the point at which creation began."[24] The mountain in *Taking* becomes more than a mere setting for the final battle. It is the divine locus of spiritual liberation, the supreme obstacle which, if ascended and overcome, will bring one spiritually close to Heaven. Tiger Mountain is enshrouded in this sacred aura. Through intertextual interplay it becomes Tai Shan, the most sacred of Chinese mountains, to which the emperor traditionally pilgrimmaged in order to make the initial sacrifices of dynastic legitimatization. When Yang Zirong stands atop the mountain in Scene Eight, the rays of the morning sun beaming red upon him, the orchestra playing "East is Red, Rises the Sun", our principal hero ceases to be a character in a fictional drama; he has become the sacred image of spiritual enlightenment and liberation that results from embracing the Thought of Mao Zedong. The defeat of the bandits in the final scene extends this image of spiritual liberation to the realm of history. It functions ritualistically as the supreme sacrifice to Heaven for the authentication of the new Maoist order.

It goes without saying that the valley is, in contrast, the locus of oppression and spiritual ignorance, where the *yin* force, symbolized by the roaming tiger and marauding bandits, reigns. Examples of this are too numerous to warrant mention.

The acoustic semiological structure of *Taking*, though it assimilates many profoundly new elements, conforms to a much greater degree than the visual and literary realms to the conventions of traditional Peking Opera. For the most part, the model drama maintains the basic two-part musical structure of the Peking Opera: the *pihuang*, or *xipi erhuang*, musical modes. These two musical modes combine with various rythmic modes, or *ban*, to form a fairly closed set of about thirty melodic forms.[25] These melodic forms, in general and not without infractions, are used for the expression of specific emotions for specific dramatic moments. Though the model dramas are slightly freer in their application of these melodic forms of dramatic moments, they generally adhere to the traditional conventions. The *erhuang* musical mode, for example, is used in the traditional opera for the expression of regret, loss or suffering; in the model dramas, it is used for the expression of class suffering or longing for the socialist utopia. The *xipi* mode, which accompanies joyful arias and arias in which information is narrated in the traditional opera, is the heroic, active and narrative mode of the model drama. The first aria of *Taking*, in which Yang Zirong sings of the pillage of a mountain village, employs the *xipi* musical mode with the *yaoban* rythmic mode. This has been called the Dramatic Aria, having the conventionalized function of forwarding the action of the drama.[26] Later in the same aria, when Yang Zirong begins to sing about the enemy, Vulture, the rythmic mode switches to *kuaiban*, (Animated Aria) which has a fast steady beat and is traditionally used to underline anger or excitement.

The sequence of these melodic forms in any particular aria also follows certain conventionalized patterns. The arias in *Taking* generally adhere to traditional patterns. Yang Zirong's aria in Scene Five, for example, begins with the standard one line of *erhuang daoban*. *Daoban* is the interjective Aria which is traditionally sung by a character from offstage to announce his imminent arrival; this is how it is used in Yang Zirong's aria. The aria continues to conform to the traditional sequence by shifting into *huilong*, the rythmic mode which is a short but turbulent piece of *melisma*; then into the *yuanban*, or Narrative Mode, in which information is narrated to a steady rythym; and finally into *kuaiban* to bring the aria to a dramatic climax.

The rules of the traditional Peking Opera percussion system are generally adhered to, if with less complexity, in the model drama. The conventional system is exploited by the revisors to set the positive characters apart from the negative characters. Gongs, thus, which are used in the traditional system to express a certain dignity and majesty, in the model dramas only accompany the appearance of positive characters. In the later productions of *Taking*, gongs which had been used to accompany Vulture's actions are replaced by instruments which have a more muffled or muted quality.[27]

It is in the area of orchestration, in the *guomen* (instrumental passages between arias) that one sees the greatest deviation from traditional musical forms. To enlarge the expressive potential of the traditional orchestra, Jiang Qing recommended the addition of Western instruments. Consequently, to the traditional orchestra were added the following instruments: piccolo, flute, oboe, clarinet, French horn, trumpet, violin, viola, cello and bass. The enlargement of the orchestra drastically alters the tone color of traditional instrumentation. The heaviness of the brass and the volume provided by the extra instrumentation gives the drama a new intensity and a wider range of expression. Western musical features and styles are also incorporated into the orchestration. Harmony, tone color, and leitmotif, elements which though not unknown in Chinese dramatic music are not fundamental to it, are blended with traditional music in *Taking*. Two highly Western tunes are heard throughout the drama as leitmotifs: one, which is robust and quick in tempo, to signify scenes in which positive characters figure and another, somber and slow, to introduce and accompany scenes in which negative characters appear. The two tunes help to further delineate the two types of characters.

Particular Chinese instruments often retain their traditional significance in the model drama. The *sona*, for example, used in the traditional opera only as the accompaniment of a great general on a grand military occasion, is used during Chang Bao's aria in Scene Nine. A mere peasant girl is thus raised to the level of a great general. In the 1958 production of the drama, the *sona* accompanies several of Vulture's entrances; in the 1964 revision, the *sona* is replaced by a reed pipe in order, say the revisors, to "change open and clear into dark and somber" (*kailang zhuanwei yinchen*).[28]

The elimination of *nianbai*, or recitative, from the model dramas is another departure from the traditional drama. The *nianbai* is a "sound pattern of controlled rythms, cadences and metrical devices contributing to the total chemistry of theater."[29] In the model dramas, *nianbai* is replaced with dialogue and speech patterns that are close to the colloquial Peking dialect. Yet, though these speech patterns resemble those of the natural language, in no way are they those heard on the streets of Peking. Spoken language in the model dramas maintains a highly stylized quality. When Mao is quoted, for example, in the first scene of the drama, the words are shouted in a sort of staccato martial recitative. Much of the dialogue and speech strikes the listener as contrived and unnatural; an unusual stress is placed on words of political and ideological import (i.e. "sun") and various speeds of delivery give the speech a strange rythmic quality. It would seem, than, that some patterns of emphasis from the original *nianbai* are retained vestigially in the new drama.

In a broad sense, acoustic signs in the drama are arranged according to one of the basic *yin-yang* oppositions: silence and noise. The *yin* force in Chinese cosmology is thought to possess the porperty of silence while that of *yang* is described as having the quality of noise. In this respect it is significant that the bandit characters, through the process of revision, are gradually stripped of all but two lines of aria in the final production; virtually all of the singing is done by positive characters. In dialogue with positive characters, bandits are rendered speechless; they mumble, falter, choke and are often quite literally unable to speak, so overpowering are the words of the positive characters. The word, especially the sung word, is a mystical, almost supernatural entity. To be silent is to remain oppressed; to speak is to transform. When Chang Bao is first found by the PLA scouts she distrusts this new brand of soldier and continues her disguise as a boy mute. She is caught in a false world of dissimulation. Yet, when the PLA troop gains her trust and she is finally able to "speak bitterness," Chang Bao's false world is shattered and the truth is victorious. To speak is the initial step toward liberation. It is the cathartic discarding of the past so as to make room for the new ideology of the present. Speaking is the revelation of truth, silence is deception and ignorance.

In this paper I have attempted to demonstrate how elements from traditional popular sign systems are exploited in *Taking* to paint the Maoist ideology in a natural guise. Throughout the revision of the drama, signs were brought together from traditional literary, dramatic, visual, and acoustic sign systems to converge on a single ideological statement: the supremacy of Mao Zedong Thought.

An ideology requires myth to promote and sustain itself; it needs myth to transform "history into nature." If the supremacy of Mao Zedong Thought is simply stated or explained in dry theoretical treatises or newspaper articles it does not appear as a natural image of reality: it is cold and unappealing. In myth, the meaningful sign on the first level of signification lends a naturalness and ineluctability to its emptied form on the mythic level. It is this dual function of the sign on the first level of Barthes's model which is the essence of myth. And it is this relationship between the two aspects of this sign which makes it appear to the myth-reader as if the forms of the myth were "naturally conjured" or gave a foundation to the ideology. *Taking* can be read as a story in which a group of soldiers plan and make an attack on a certain bandit stronghold. On the mythic level of signification, however, this reading is consumed in the ideology and is but a part of the disguise of the ideology.

According to Barthes, myth functions in the following way:

> Myth does not deny things, on the contrary, its function is to talk about them; simply, it purifies them, it makes them innocent, it gives them a natural and eternal justification . . . In passing from history to nature, myth acts economically: it abolishes the complexity of human acts, it gives them the simplicity of essences, it does away with all dialectics, with any going back beyond what is immediately visible, it organizes a world which is without contradictions, because it is without depth, a world wide open and wallowing in the evident, it establishes a blissful clarity: things appear to mean something by themselves.[30]

Taking Tiger Mountain by Strategy functions in precisely this way. It creates a world which denies the "complexities of human acts" and the dialectics of human history. It imposes a simple world of blissful clarity.

Notes

1. Roland Barthes. "Myth Today," in *Mythologies* (New York: Hill and Wang, 1973), pp. 109–59.

2. Ibid., p. 116.

3. Ibid., p. 146–47.

4. Milan Kundera. "The Novel and Europe," *New York Review of Books*, Vol. XXXI, No. 12, (July 19, 1984), p. 17.

5. Qu Bo. *Linhai xueyuan* (Hongkong: Joint Publishing, 1977) tr. by Sidney Shapiro, *Tracks in the Snowy Forest* (Peking: Foreign Languages Press).

6. No published edition, as far as I know, exists of this early version of the drama.

7. "Zhiqu Weihushan," *Juben* (Dec. 1964), pp. 1–28.

8. *Zhiqu Weihushan* (Peking: Renmin wenxue chuban she, 1968).

9. *Zhiqu Weihushan* (Peking: Renmen chuban she, 1970).

10. S.H. Chen. "Multiplicity in Uniformity: Poetry and the Great Leap Forward, *The China Quarterly*, No. 3 (July–September, 1960), pp. 1–15.

11. *Baimao nü yuepu* (Shanghai: Renmin chuban she, 1973), pp. 14445.

12. *Zhiqu Weihushan* (1970), p. 17.

13. Ibid., p. 30.

14. Ibid., p. 33.

15. Ibid., p. 11.

16. Ibid., p. 12.

17. Ibid., p. 16.

18. Ibid., p. 30.

19. Mircea Eliade. *Images and Symbols: Studies in Religious Symbolism* (New York: Sheed and Ward, 1969), pp. 40–51.

20. Roxanne Witke. *Comrade Chiang Ch'ing* (Boston: Little Brown and Co., 1977), p. 419.

21. *Zhiqu Weihushan* (1970), p. 17.

22. Georges Chavannes. *Le T'ai Chan: essai de monographie d'un culte chinois* (Paris: E. Leroux, 1910), pp. 10–20.

23. "Nuli suzao wuchanjieji yingxiong renwu de guanghui xingxiang" *Hongqi*, No. 11 (1969), p. 70.

24. Eliade. *Images and Symbols*, p. 43.

25. Rulan Chao Pian. "The Function of Rythmn in Peking Opera" in José Maceda ed., *The Music of Asia* (Manila: National Music Council of the Philipines, 1971), p. 115.

26. Ibid., p. 115.

27. Tao Xiong. "*Zhiqu Weihushan* de xiugai he jiagong," *Renmin ribao* (May 5, 1964), p. 13.

28. Ibid., p. 13.

29. A. C. Scott. "*Hung teng chi*: The Red Lantern," *Modern Drama*, Vol. 1, No. 9 (May 1966), p. 410.

30. Barthes. "Myth Today," p. 143.

Glossary

Baimao nü	白毛女
ban	板
bian wen	变文
chailang	豺狼
Chang Bao	常宝
chou	丑
dang	党
deng	灯
erhuang daoban	二黄导板
feng	风
feng	封
fenggou	疯狗
guomen	过门
hong	红
huilong	回龙

kailang zhuanwei yinchen	开朗转为阴沉
kuaiban	快板
kun	鲲
Jiang Qing	江青
layue	腊月
Linhai xueyuan	林海雪原
Mo Wang	魔王
nianbai	念白
peng	鹏
Penglai	蓬莱
pihuang	皮黄
qinniang	亲娘
sangjiaquan	丧家犬
sheng	生
Shuihu zhuan	水浒传
sona	唢呐
Tai shan	泰山
taiyang	太阳
Wu Song	武松
Sun Wukong	孙悟空
xipi erhuang	西皮二黄
Xiyou ji	西游记
yang	阳
Yang Zirong	杨子荣
yaoban	摇板
Yelanghao	野狼嗥
yin	阴
yuanban	原板
Zhiqin guanfei zuoshandiao	智擒惯匪座山雕
Zhiqu Weihushan	智取威虎山
Zhuangzi	庄子

5. Mei Lanfang, Stanislavsky and Brecht on China's Stage and Their Aesthetic Significance

WILLIAM HUIZHU SUN

From a broad international point of view the Mei Lanfang, Stanislavsky and Brecht systems are three great theatrical systems close in time and dispersed in area; but, examined more closely in a country such as China, they have exerted specific influences at different times. There are two kinds of comparisions: the former concentrates on the spatial differences, and helps to point out the characteristics of theatrical cultures in different nations; the latter concentrates on the temporal differences, and leads to the explorations of general law in theatrical development. The present paper takes the latter approach.[1]

The Mei Lanfang system represents the perfection of the Beijing Opera and can also be considered as the epitome of the Chinese traditional theater of the last several hundred years. Since the beginning of Chinese theater, in spite of the evolution of such ancient forms as the *nanxi* of the Song, or the *zaju* of the Yuan, the basic aesthetic principles have not undergone any fundamental changes, and can be characterized by spatial and temporal flexibility in scene structure, stylized dance-like and mimetic acting, lack of superficial resemblance to life, and emphasis on depicting a beautified life and in exquisite art form. The fact that the traditional theater has remained essentially the same despite all apparent changes and has attracted the people over the years is a phenomenon peculiar to China and quite a rare occurrence in the world. From the late Ming Dynasty, Chinese society began to change significantly and the theater to renew itself. Because it had become more and more aristocratic, the *kungu* became more popular. And finally, Beijing Opera, born of the declining *kunqu* and taking over elements of the *luantan*, assumed new dominance in the Chinese theatrical world.

One can say that between the time of Beijing Opera's founding father Cheng Changgeng (c. 1811–1880) and that of Tan Xinpei (1847–1917) and Mei Lanfang's teacher Wang Yaoqing (1881–1954) the Chinese national theatre art had already established its system. What is now called the Mei Lanfang system can be traced back to the same origin as the *nanxi*, the only difference being that Mei's had become more exquisite. This was the situation when Chinese theater had no contact with foreign nations.

At the turn of the century, foreign theater began to exert influence in China, and the history of the Chinese theater took on a completely new form: the spoken drama. It was a kind of realistic drama drastically different from Chinese traditional theater. This revolution cannot be mentioned in the same breath as the earlier evolution from *zaju* to *chuanqi*, from *kunqu* to Beijing Opera. Those earlier evolutions only changed the forms but not the nature of the theater.

Here two questions arise: is Chinese drama no more than the transplant of foreign drama on Chinese soil? Without foreign influence, would the dominant traditional theater have kept generating homogeneous descendants? The answers to both questions are negative. The key was that just when Beijing Opera reached its mature stage, a revolution unprecedented in 2,000 years broke out in China, shaking the social foundations of feudalism. The exquisite art of the theater, after hundreds of years of gradual refining, also came to a crossroads. At the time of great social change, many artists and audiences hoped that the traditional theater could alter its leisurely old look and begin to reflect immediate social problems and take a clear stand in current struggles. From the end of the nineteenth century, the famous *laosheng* artist, that is, exponent of an old male role, Wang Xiaonong (1858–1918), was the first to write new plays to allude to current affairs. Pan Yueqiao and others began to perform in modern or foreign costumes. They also began to abaondon the traditional tea-house-like square platform with pillars in favor of the semi-elliptical stage, and even sometimes, the revolving stage. The revolutionary Wang Zhongsheng's plays went even farther. Mei Lanfang called them "'reformist new plays', since there are no drum-and-gong scenes, they are actually spoken dramas."[2] Wang's plays were put on stage together with shows by Mei Lanfang and other famous Beijing Opera actors quite a few times, and were given major importance in the program. In such circumstances, even Mei Lanfang, the outstanding representative of the traditional theater, neglecting his refined skills in singing and dancing for some time, wrote and performed new plays in modern costumes. He created plays such as *A Piece of Flax (Yilü ma)*, *Deng Xiagu* and *Tides in the Officialdom (Huanhai chao)*, some of which were based on real contemporary people and incidents. It was a departure from the aesthetic principles of the Mei system and quite close to that of Stanislavsky. The impetus of the 1911 Revolution had made Mei realize that:

The traditional plays that we perform are all drawn from historical facts of life of ancient times (actually, not all are facts). Some of the plays are enlightening and beneficial to our audiences. But if we can directly draw on current affairs to write new plays, will they not be more involving and interesting?

However, soon after this, he gave up the attempt. Later, when considering the problem from the point of view of the aesthetic characteristics of the Beijing Opera itself, he wrote in summary:

Modern plays act out modern stories, so on stage the actors' mannerisms and gestures should be as close as possible to our mannerisms and gestures in daily life, and should not use dance-like movements as in singing-dancing plays (e.g. traditional operas). Under these circumstances, Beijing Opera actors' dancing skills learned from an early age all become useless, and they have no place to show their special abilities.[4]

Contrasting the above two quotations, one can see that Chinese theater in its development met sharp contradictions between its intrinsic characteristics and the demands of time.

Because traditional theater was so deeply rooted in Chinese culture, the above mentioned dilemma could not be solved as simply as in many other countries. Despite the assertion of total repudiation espoused by some people during the May 4th period, the traditional theater was not destroyed. While its more realistic tributary "New Plays in Modern Costumes" joined forces with the early spoken drama,[5] the traditional theater retained its distinguishing artistic features. Presently, the introduction of modern foreign theatrical forms, the antithesis of the Mei system, helped in part to make theater reflect reality, a responsibility which could have been fulfilled by Chinese traditional theater itself had it persisted in the attempt. This enabled the Chinese traditional theater to remain intact and to further refine its exquisite art quite remote from present reality. Since Mei Lanfang was no longer entangled with "new plays in modern costumes," his personal artistry reached its peak just afterwards.

Just as the birth of the Stanislavsky system was perfectly natural in Western theatrical history, so its acceptance in China was also natural in Chinese theatrical development. The Stanislavsky system may be seen to represent the tradition of modern realistic theater in the west as a whole. The influence of Western realistic drama came into China many years before Stanislavsky's actual writing was formerly introduced into China in 1937, one year after the American edition of his *An Actor Prepares* was published. Zheng Junli translated some chapters from the American edition into Chinese, even earlier than the Soviet Union had its Russian edition. (The Russian edition was published in 1938, after the death of

Stanislavsky). After Huang Zuolin and his wife Dan Ni returned from Britain in 1939, they started to teach courses on the Stanislavsky system in Chongqing.

The main reason why Stanslavsky's theory came to China so quickly and produced instant results is because there had already been quite a few Ibsenite realistic plays introduced around the time of the May 4th Movement. During that period, plays by Shakespeare, Wilde, Bernard Shaw, Tolstoy, Gorki, Chekhov and Ibsen were translated and published, especially the last four writers' plays, which laid the literary foundations for the Stanislavsky system. First of all, the needs of Chinese society made the introduction of Western realistic problem plays possible, with the result that a revolution in acting and directing was required. The conventional way of acting in the traditional theater was certainly unsuitable for the new plays. From his short expedition into modern, "new" plays, Mei Lanfang had realized this irreconcilable contradiction. That the early spoken drama, which had used conventional acting to produce modern plays, had come to a blind alley also proved this. A modern acting and directing system was very urgently needed, as opposed to the conventional one. At that time, the first modern Chinese director, Hong Shen, came back from the U.S. and brought with him a new method. Hong Shen aspired to become a Chinese Ibsen but not a Chinese Shakespeare nor a famous actor. His ideals were close to the Stanislavsky system. Hong Shen's directing methods may not belong to the Stanislavsky system, but by comparison with the traditional theater he undoubtedly helped the Chinese theater take a big step towards it. The first thing that Hong Shen did was to let actors and actresses act together, thus breaking with the tradition whereby males played female roles and vice versa. The tradition of impersonation originally came from such feudal ideas as "male and femald should not be in close contact," but it became such an exquisite art in itself that it had a special aesthetic effect, almost transhistorical. And Mei Lanfang himself was world famous for his female impersonation. This form of beauty was completely unacceptable to the Stanislavsky system, the first principle of which was realism. Hong Shen started right there and went on to establish standard rehearsal requirements. By doing so he cleared the way for the arrival of the Stanislavsky system in China. The development of the Chinese theater that followed was greatly influenced by the U.S., which, like the Soviet Union, was deeply affected by Stanislavsky's theories. The U.S. had no long theatrical tradition of its own. Stanislavsky's 1923 visit to the U.S., the migration of some of his followers there and the successful practice of the Group Theater had helped create a strong Stanislavsky school. This tradition directly and indirectly spread its influence to China. For instance, the first Chinese essay on Stanislavsky was written by Yu

Shangyuan in the U.S. in 1924.[6] The translation of the American edition of *An Actor Prepares* sent the systematic theory directly to China where it was enthusiastically received. Around that time, the success of *Thunderstorm (Leiyu), Sunrise (Ri chu), Peking Man (Beijingren),* and *Under Shanghai Eaves (Shanghai wuyanxia),* representative plays of modern Chinese drama, both benefitted from and assisted the reception of the Stanislavsky system in China.

Although the Stanislavsky system began in big cities under Guomindang control, it was supported by the cultural leaders of the Communist Party. The revolution needed modern drama that directly reflected real life. Consequently, Stanislavsky's theory, was very quickly introduced into the liberated areas. Between 1938 and 1941, Zhang Geng taught drama theory at Yan'an's Lu Xun Art Institute, including various Western theoreticians but especially Stanislavsky as orthodoxy, with Gordon Craig and Meyerhold as negative examples. So many dramatists from both the Guomindang-controlled and the liberated area of Yan'an accepted dramatic concepts based on the Stanislavsky system.

However, before 1949 the reception of the Stanislavsky system in China was only at its spontaneous and immature stage. It was in the 1950s that it really reached its heyday. It was partly because of Sino-Soviet relations at the time, and partly because of the demand of transforming Chinese theater from its wartime makeshift state to peacetime standard theater. Soviet experts were invited to give systematic lectures. Drama institutes in Beijing and Shanghai offered various kinds of refresher courses given by Soviet experts to train an army of artists and teachers well versed in the Stanislavsky system. In the meantime, a great many Soviet and East European plays were produced all over China to give artists opportunities to apply their knowledge of Stanislavsky's system. In addition, in the Beijing People's Art Theater Jiao Juyin, a Chinese expert on the Stanislavsky system, directed a series of modern Chinese classical plays, which became real models. All this played an important role in spreading the Stanislavsky system all over China. In 1956, nearly all the Chinese plays performed at the First National Drama Festival were produced in the Stanislavsky style. That was why Korea Senda, who participated in the Festival, pointed out to Tian Han that China should not neglect Brecht, the antithesis of Stanislavsky. Brecht was already being performed in Japan, and Korea Senda predicted that the Chinese theater would soon follow suit. His prediction was well founded. In China, Huang Zuolin was a Brecht enthusiast, but his view was not well understood then.

Huang Zuolin and his wife Dan Ni were the only theater artists to have taught the Stanislavsky system formally in China before 1949. Most plays he directed in his life were based on the Stanislavsky system. He was also the first to sense the need to study theorists other than Stanislavsky. Huang was the first to introduce Brecht comprehensively into China. When young, Huang had been fascinated by Pirandello and later by Brecht. These two great dramatists were philosophical rather than realistic. Huang was not only influenced by their plays. From them he learned that in world dramatic history, the kind of realistic drama represented by the Stanislavsky system was but a short episode, and a new kind of drama would eventually come into being and introduce a philosophical episode. Of Pirandello and Brecht, Huang found the latter more suitable to the needs of the Chinese revolution. He was determined to bring Brecht to China. But in the 1950s and even 1960s very few people, including his colleagues in the Shanghai People's Art Theater, really understood him. He applied Brecht's epic theater theory to his experimental plays such as *A Great Live Report of Resisting the U.S. and Assisting Korea (Kangmeiyuanchao dahuobao)* etc. Though they aroused strong reactions at the time, they were never shown again afterwards. In 1962, Huang published his *Discursive Talk on the Credo of Drama (Mantan xijuguan)*, pointing out formally for the first time the relationship between Mei Lanfang, Stanislavsky and Brecht, and calling for liberation from Stanislavsky's "four walls." This received enthusiastic international react, for example, in Japan, but not in China, where numerous political campaigns were stifling theater circles. It was not possible for them to be open-minded about drama. Another important reason was that the Stanislavsky system had already established its unshakable dominance in China. In the mid-1960s, due to political reasons, Stanislavsky's influence was waning, although still strong. Paradoxically, during the Cultural Revolution, on the one hand he was rudely repudiated, yet on the other hand some of his principles were used to remold the traditional theater to produce "model operas" which monopolized the Chinese stage.

The end of the Cultural Revolution exonerated Stanislavsky from unfounded accusations. But the ideological emancipation that followed very quickly made people aware of the limitations of his system. Many people began to pay attention to Brecht.

Judging only from the number of productions of Brecht's plays, his reception in China is still in its early stages. The 1958 production of *Mother Courage* got small audiences. The 1979 production of *Galileo*, whose directing and acting style was not entirely Brechtian but rather a mixture of Stanislavsky and Brecht, was warmly received. Even though there had been no further Brecht plays performed up to the first presentation of this paper at the colloquium in October 1984, the Brecht system and many modern theatrical concepts and techniques associated with it have struck root in people's hearts, including such commonly accepted concepts and techniques as narrative, expressionism, breaking the "4th wall," anti-illusion, externalization of inner impulses, and the alienation effect. To coincide with this author's prediction, six months after this paper was first delivered, the first Brecht Conference in the P.R.C. was held in Beijing and three of Brecht's plays, *The Caucasian Chalk Circle, The Good Woman of Setzuan* and *Schweyk in World War II* were produced as part of the conference. The credo of drama put forward by Huang Zuoling in 1962 has caught the attention of theatrical circles. Under the direct or indirect influence of the Brecht-Huang philosophy of the theater, a number of plays have been staged that are a major departure from the Stanislavsky norm, such as *Road (Lu)* and *Hot Spell Outside (Wuwai you reliu)* by Jia Hongyuan and Ma Zhongjun, *Why Am I Dead? (Wo weishenme sile)* by Xie Min, *Mayor Chen Yi (Chen Yi shizhang)* by Sha Yexin, *Blood is Always Hot (Xie, zongshi rede)* by Zong Fuxian and He Guofu and *The Old B. Hanging on the Wall (Guazai qiangshangde LaoB)*, by Sun Huizhu. The stage innovations of the last few years have been unprecedented since 1949. Technical conveniences have made stage designers and directors more susceptible to the Brecht system than playwrights, so now in China, as far as being innovative is concerned, stage designers are ahead of directors, and directors of playwrights.

With the growing influence of Brecht, dramatists are taking a new look at the Chinese traditional theater in the light of Brecht's interest in Chinese traditional theater and Huang's "Xieyi" philosophy of theater.[7] Some new plays in Shanghai Workers' Palace have made gratifying achievements in combining strong points of Brecht and the spirit of traditional theater. For example, in *Hot Spell Outside* the soul of a dead man appears, a device often used in Chinese traditional theater; but rather than expressing his personal emotions which could not be expressed when alive, the supernatural soul in this play raises a philosophical juxtaposition between hot and cold, like the one between good and evil caused by the gods in *The Good Woman of Setzuan*. The structure of *Blood is Always Hot* is similar to the Brechtian episodic structure but also derives from that of Chinese traditional plays. It functions as an explicit play in some Brechtian way while probing its heroes' feelings in a traditional Chinese way.

We can see from the facts mentioned above that for nearly a century three great theatrical systems of different aesthetic principles have exerted their influences on China's stage. Each of them has also left its special mark on the international theatrical scene. Comparatively speaking, what first caught the world's attention were tradition-based Mei system plays such as *The Sword of the Universe (Yuzhoufeng)* and *The Drunken Beauty (Guifei zui jiu)*. Though remote from contemporary life, they attracted audiences with their refined singing, gestures and stylistic beauty. Next was drama based on the Stanislavsky system. Plays like *Thunderstorm, Under Shanghai Eaves* and *Tea House (Chaguan)* moved audiences by their realistic and minute presentation of scenes from Chinese society. In recent years, new plays that assimilate aesthetic ideals from the Brecht system have won their audiences with new images, new messages, new symbols and the beauty of reason. *Hot Spell Outside, Blood Always Hot* and *The Old B. Hanging on the Wall* are but three examples. Such comparisons have again given rise to two questions. First, does the time sequence of the three systems indicate an inexorable trend? Second, will theater of a later phase replace the earlier one? Let us look for answers in the comparison of Chinese and world theater.

The answer to the first question is affirmative, because we can find similar trends in world drama and art history. From ancient Greek tragedy to Elizabethan and Louis XIV drama, plays were mostly based on well-known myths and legends and acting was stylized. All this is similar to the traditional theater of China, India and Japan. As time went on, Western drama became even closer to real life, changing its subject matter from gods to heroes and then to common men, and in the nineteenth century developed into realistic and naturalistic drama. Finally came the Stanislavsky system, which reached the pinnacle of reflecting life directly and accurately. But, in the meantime, an apparent attempt to return to some old theatrical forms appeared. Craig, Meyerhold and Brecht abandoned realistic sets and highly believable stories. Instead, they used seemingly primitive, naive and crude techniques to shock people and force them to think. Brecht adopted the free and loose structure of Shakespeare and even the Chinese traditional theater; in characterization, he opted for categorizing like the Greek tragedy and even used masks and chorus. The purpose of rejuvenating the old forms was to help modern men see the deeper meaning of life through distorted images.

In a way similar to what happened in the history of fine arts, drama also experienced a progression from unrestrained haziness to minute realism and then to deliberate metamorphosis. Theater art at its leisurely hazy stage was unable to imitate reality precisely, yet its hazy form was highly beautified, balanced, smooth and delicate. The Mei system of China could be called the paragon of this kind of theater in the world. When theater was able to imitate real life vividly, it also lost some of its beauty of stylization. Thus, when Mei Lanfang tried his hand at modern drama, he had to give up some of his beautiful singing and gestures. However, when dramatists found realism no longer satisfying and started to look for new expressions in metamorphosis, some peculiar practices came along, such as breaking away from a logical structure, a coherent plot line and consistent characterization, using unharmonic music and pictures, presenting bewildering symbols and images. From a conventional aesthetic point of view, all this may seem anathema. But through all this the dramatists are seeking a kind of theatrical beauty which can only be appreciated by active mental reasoning. Undeniably, some practitioners of the above mentioned techniques are being no more than self-indulgent, yet they have very little influence on Chinese theater. Brecht, because of his deep insight into the human condition, has won the admiration of people in the East as well as the West. Brecht has become the symbol of new theater for Chinese dramatists.

Huang Zuolin once pointed out that in the 2,500 year history of world theater, realistic drama had been a phenomenon peculiar to the last several decades. There had been no fourth wall in the previous 2,000 or so years. It was high time to break the fourth wall. He was right. The more than 2,000 years before realistic drama is the first classical phase in dramatic development, and the Mei system is its Chinese relic. Realistic drama with the "4th wall" is the second, the modern phase, and the Stanislavsky system is its representation. The new drama that has broken the "4th wall" is the third phase, that of the negation of the negation, and Brecht is its leading figure. The third phase seems to have many of the characteristics of the first phase, but actually it transcends the previous two phases as the embodiment of the most revolutionary ideals of drama. By comparison, the Mei system is the oldest, which explains why Mei himself attempted some major changes sixty years aso. The third phase represented by the Brecht system is the youngest and the most hopeful. Though it is also the most immature, its imperfection in some ways shows its potential, which should be further developed. Its significance lies in its impact rather than in itself. Among the three great systems, the aesthetic ideals of Brecht's are most concerned with the creativity of actors and audiences, closest to the modern man's understanding of the essence of beauty, and most in keeping with his aesthetic psychology. The Brecht system meets the demands of the time. This is quite obvious in China. Before the Cultural Revolution, most people were used to passively receiving propaganda. As for drama, they were satisfied with plays that gave obvious answers. So both the Mei and Stanislavsky systems were quite suitable. Since the fall of the "Gang of Four" in 1976, people have changed from passive acceptance to active thinking and learned to ask why. They have quickly become tired of plays with ready conclusions and started looking for those that would challenge their intellect. The wide reception of Brecht in China and emergence of a group of innovative Chinese dramatists, who are interested in Brecht and determined to bring about the third phase of Chinese drama, are products' of this social psychology.

So, does the arrival of the third phase mean the monopoly of the Brecht system? The answer to this question is negative. Evolution and continuity are the two sides of the shield. Generally speaking, age is not necessarily a weakness in the arts. Because it has a long history, Mei's theater has the most perfect and immortal artistic form. Karl Marx said once that ancient Greek arts, which originated in "the immature stage of society," "still give us aesthetic pleasure and are in certain respects regarded as a standard and unattainable ideal."[9] Does this not also apply to the Chinese traditional theater? Moreover, the development of Chinese theater, as compared with other nations', has its unique characteristics. China has kept its first phase drama for the longest time and refined it to the bset quality. Of course this is partly because of Chinese society's slow evolution, centralization and unification over thousands of years. Unlike Western theater, the contents and forms of which have been transformed continuously and radically with changes in social systems and cultural centers, Chinese traditional theater has never changed fundamentally. The audience of the traditional theater has formed stable aesthetic and psychological habits almost incredible to Westerners. The audience likes a happy ending, enjoys listening to the singing with eyes closed or just savoring the beauty of the gestures. In recent years, it has become quite popular for retired workers in cities and farmers during slack seasons to practice amateur singing of traditional theater arias. What is particularly worth noting is that there are also socieites for traditional theater activities among university students. This new trend shows that people are looking for comfort in traditional elegance and peace amid mass production and the rapid pace of modern times. In addition, visits of Chinese traditional theater troupes abroad have been enthusiastically welcomed. There are various reasons for Westerners' interest in Chinese traditional theater. For some, their interest is motivated by a desire to use old forms for their third-phase new drama. All this shows that the first-phase drama still has vitality, even though its regular audiences are not as big as before.

Because of the deep-rooted aesthetic habits of Chinese theater-goers, modern drama such as that of the Stanislavsky system required a long time and struggle to gain ground in China. But once it has taken root, in the 1950s and the 1960s it attracted audiences numbering hundreds of millions. A new aesthetic habit no less strong than that of traditional theater-goers was formed. This habit was so strong that the Stanislavsky system's drama was misunderstood as China's national theater. That new drama which assimilated some features of the Brecht system and Chinese traditional theater was even termed as alien, reflecting a continuing need among some for the Stanislavsky system. As a matter of fact, plays in the realistic tradition, such as *Yu wusheng chu (Where No Sounds Are Heard)*, draw large audiences because they realistically presented social problems.

From the above facts we can see that the influences of the Mei, Stanislavsky and Brecht systems in China do have a sequential order, but that rather than replacing one another, they supplement each other in a manner of shifting focuses and priorities. This is not unusual in the world, only more prominent in China. The two most important contemporary Chinese directors' experiences might be the best evidence at this point. The Stanislavsky system's Chinese representaive Jiao Juyin presided over a traditional theater school for a long time in his young days. Later he tried to bring the quintessence of the traditional theater school into the Stanislavsky system. Brecht's Chinese advocate Huang Zuoling is an expert on the Stanislavsky system and he also tries to adapt it into that of Brecht. Since it usually takes a long time for Chinese audiences to accept new forms, the Brecht system, though no longer new in the West, is still gaining acceptance only slowly. This is partly due to the fact that there is a gap between Chinese aesthetic taste and the German *Grundliheit*; and partly due to the fact that Chinese audiences' cultural habits and modes of thinking are not yet modernized enough to keep up with the new theatrical trends of Brecht and the like. But the situation now looks favorable. Since 1978, the educational and cultural level of the whole nation has been rising rapidly, and more serious thought has been given to attitudes towards theater. Furthermore, since Chinese audiences continue to love the first-phase dramas, and since the first phase and the third phase share some characteristics in form, it is advantageous for Chinese dramatists to use traditional theatrical techniques to express new ideas. Audiences find it easy to accept when, for example, a "ghost" in *Hot Spell Outside* is in the form of an ordinary man. Currently the real resistance for forward movement comes from some dramatists who have passed the first phase and adhered stubbornly to the second as the ultimate ideal. On the one hand, they cannot see the validity of the third phase, thus obstructing innnovations in drama. On the other hand, they ignore the distinguishing characteristics of the first-phase drama and try to remould it with the Stanislavsky system. All this obstructs Chinese theater from accomplishing two important missions. The first is to break away from the "four walls" of the Stanislavsky system, and to develop a kind of drama unrestructured by a superficial resemblance to life and able to reveal the essence of life in a wider and deeper way. The second is to make use of those features which traditional drama shares with that of the third phase, adapt them to the philosophy of the Brecht system, and hence develop a kind of philosophical traditional theater which both retains the unique national features of singing and dancing and reflects the spirit of our times. These two missions are unique contributions which Chinese dramatists can make to the theater.

It will take time for these two tasks to be accomplished, but the study of the three great systems and their development in China has given Chinese theater-workers great confidence. These two missions accord with the last of theatrical development. This author believes that, if more dramatists are willing to take an interest in the study of the three great systems and their development in China, the accomplishment of the two missions will become a reality in the not-too-distant future.

Notes

1. I have taken the approach of focussing on spatial differences in *San Da Xiju Tixi Shenmei Lixiang Xin Tan* (A New Exploration on Three Great Theatrical Systems' Aesthetic Ideals), *Xiju Yishu* (Theater Arts), 1982, No. 1; Selected in *Zhongguo Xin Wenyi Da Xi* (Great Anthology of New Literature and Arts in China) Theories vol. III.

2. *Mei Lanfang Wen Ji* (Selected Works of Mei Lanfang), (China Theater Press, Beijing, 1962) p. 201.

3. *Wutai Shenghuo Sishi Nian* (Forty Years on Stage), (China Theater Press, Beijing 1961) vol. II, p. 1.

4. Ibid, p. 70.

5. See Ding Luoan, *Lun Woguo Zaoqi Huaju de Xingcheng* (On the Formation of Early Spoken Drama in Our Country), *Zhongguo Huaju Xuexi Waiguo Xiju de Lishi Jingyan* (Historical Experience of Chinese Drama Learing from Froeign Drama), (China Theater Press, Shanghai, 1983).

6. Yu Shangyuan: *Mosike Yishu Juyuan* (Moscow Art Theater), *Chenbao* (Morning Newspaper) Supplement May 9, 1924.

7. Some translate "Xieyi" as Imagistic, but Huang himself uses Intrinsicalistic or Essentialistic.

8. See Ding Luonan and Sun Huizhu, *Huaju Xiandaihua he Minzuhua de Tansuo* (An Exploration of Spoken Drama's Modernization and Nationalization), *Wenxue Pinglun* (Literature Criticism) 1982, No. 4.

9. Karl Marx: *A Contribution to the Critique of Political Economy* (translated by S. W. Ryazanskaya, International Publishers, New York, 1970), p. 217.

Glossary

Beijingren	北京人
Chaguan	茶馆
Chen Yi shizhang	陈毅市长
Cheng Changgeng	程长庚
chuanqi	传奇
Dan Ni	丹尼
Deng Xiagu	邓霞姑
Guazai qiangshangde laoB	挂在墙上的老B
Guifei zui jiu	贵妃醉酒
Guomindang	国民党
He Guofu	贺国甫
Hong Shen	洪深
Huanhai chao	宦海潮
Huang Zuolin	黄佐临
Jia Hongyuan	贾鸿源
Jiao Juyin	焦菊隐
Kangmeiyuanchao dahuobao	抗美援朝大活报
Korea Senda	千田是野
Kunqu	昆曲
laosheng	老生
Leiyu	雷雨
Lu	路
luantan	乱弹
Ma Zhongjun	马中骏
Mantan xijuguan	漫谈戏剧观
Mei Lanfang	梅兰芳
nanxi	南戏

Pan Yueqiao　　潘月樵

Ri chu　　日出

Sha Yexin　　沙叶新

Shanghai wuyanxia　　上海屋檐下

Sun Huizhu　　孙惠柱

Tan Xinpei　　谭鑫培

Tian Han　　田汉

Wang Xiaonong　　汪笑侬

Wang Yaoqing　　王瑶卿

Wang Zhongsheng　　王钟声

Wo weishenme sile?　　我为什么死了?

Wuwai you reliu　　屋外有热流

Xie Min　　谢民

Xieyi　　写意

Xie, zongshi rede　　血,总是热的

Yilü ma　　一缕麻

Yu Shangyuan　　余上沅

Yu wushengchu　　于无声处

Yuzhoufeng　　宇宙锋

zaju　　杂剧

Zhang Geng　　张庚

Zheng Junli　　郑君里

Zong Fuxian　　宗福先

6. Huang Zuoling's Ideal of Drama and Bertolt Brecht

ADRIAN HSIA

When the Soviet Union started to aid the People's Republic of China at the beginning of the fifties to build up heavy industry, it did not neglect to influence the superstructure of its new ally. Among others, the Soviet Union sent to China its drama experts who widely spread the teachings on acting of Constantine Stanislavsky (1863–1938). Within three years the teachings were firmly entrenched as an infallible doctrine in the drama and film circles. It was Huang Zuoling who efficiently began to weaken the foundation of the theater of illusion and break down the fourth wall on the Chinese stage by disseminating the theory and practice of alienation of Bertolt Brecht.[1] The on-going discussion in China about the future of its drama is a direct result of the impact of Huang's *xijuguan* (which I would translate as *Theateranschauung*) which he delineated at the Canton Conference of the All-China Theatre Association in 1962. This talk laid the foundation of his ideal of drama[2] which is closely connected with the Peking Opera. Today it is generally recognized that although he was not the first one to advocate the use of techniques of the Chinese Opera in *huaju*, the spoken drama, he is the most influential one to date.[3]

On many occasions Huang Zuoling uses an image to illustrate his ideal of theater when the Tang poet Li Bai (another transcription: Li Bo) is having one of his drinking bouts, he is summoned by the emperor; Li should mount the royal horse brought along by the messenger and appear before the emperor. Thus in his drunken state Li Bai rides to the palace. The actor playing the role of the poet must achieve two things. His upper body must enact the drunkedness of the poet while his lower body should show the sober and steady trot of a good horse. We see immediately how indebted Huang's drama ideal is to the acting of the Peking opera. In other words, his concern is mainly to use acting techniques adapted from the Chinese opera to wide the scope of the spoken drama as practiced in China. As a director, Huang is primarily concerned with the aspects of the stage rather than with the structure or content of the drama.

Like many intellectuals of the May Fourth generation, Huang learned to appreciate certain aspects of the Chinese tradition through cultural contacts with the West. To be precise, it was Brecht who opened Huang's eyes to the Chinese opera. In 1935, Brecht saw the performance of the unique female impersonator in Chinese Opera, Mei Lanfang, in Moscow. Although Brecht's understanding of the Peking Opera was not without factual flaws,[4] he was very much impressed and was convinced that the acting of the Chinese opera coincided with and thus confirmed his ideas of alienation in acting. Eventually Brecht put down his thoughts on Mei Lanfang's acting in the now famous essay "Verfremdungseffekte in der chinesischen Schauspielkunst." In 1936, Huang read an English version of this essay under the title "The Fourth Wall of China. An Essay on the Effect of Disillusion in the Chinese Theater," translated by Eric Walter White.[5] He was very pleased that a European playwright praised an art form of his country so highly. Consequently, he felt inclined towards the plays and theories of Brecht. Years later, his knowledge of Brecht came to his assistance.[6]

On January 2, 1951 Huang Zuoling, then Deputy Head of the Shanghai People's Art Theater, delivered a six-hour speech on Brecht's plays and his dramatic theory to his co-workers. The purpose was to acquaint the personnel of the Theater with Brecht in order to overcome the limitations of the Ibsenian Theater then current in China so that a play of epic dimensions could be produced to support the "Resist USA, Assist Korea Campaign." The scriptwriters of the Shanghai People's Art Theater just completed the third version of an unproduceable play entitled *kangmei yuanzhao da huobao* (A Great Live Report of Resisting USA and Assisting Korea), consisting of eight unconnected acts of different American aggressions within approximately half a century. The Aristolelian Theater was too limiting for such a *da huobao*, a "great live report." A theater with epic dimensions was required. The practical need, along with the Chinese translation of the term epic, namely *shishi* literally meaning history and poem—may have dictated Huang's understanding of Brecht's Chinese Theater. Even in 1983, three decades after the marathon talk, Huang still insisted that the epic theater was "*youshi lishi, youshi shide yijing*" (it belongs both to the historical and poetic realms) and rejected the suggestion to translate Brecht's term as *xushu ju*, the "narrative theater," which would be more appropriate for Brecht's conception of *episches Theater*.[7] Anyway, Huang used the epic theater to expand the time and space of the Aristotelian theater. The *da huobao*, when it was completed, took place in four countries, and the time spanned was from 1895 to 1951. Altogether there were over fifty scenes, and more than 180 actors were involved. The scenes were held together by a narrator who recounted the events. It was apparent that Huang was very much aware of the narrative character of Brecht's theater; it was also evident that Huang was adapting Brecht's ideas for his own theatrical needs.

After the production of *Bamian hongqi yingfengpiao* (Eight Red Banners are Fluttering in the Wind) in 1958 to propagate the "Great Leap Forward" and *Mother Courage* in 1959—it was a production of the Berlin Ensemble in Chinese—Huang Zuoling was innovating again. It was 1961, one year before his historical speech "mantan xiju guan" ("On *Theateranschauung*") that he staged a Peking Opera entitled *Loaned Wife* as a spoken drama—i.e., he dispensed with the singing, but retained the plot, the costumes and above all the acting of the Peking opera. I quote Huang concerning the story and the acting:

> The story goes something like this. Old fossil Zhang is an idler. He tricks his wife into letting him have a bolt of her cloth. He tries to sell the cloth in the street, where he meets his sworn brother, Li Tianlong, whose wife has recently died. Li is in need of money in order to make the journey to Peking to take the examinations that would make him an official if he passes it, but his father-in-law refuses to give him the promised fortune until he finds himself a new wife. Zhang, in a wild fantasy, decides to lend his wife to Li, on the condition that the fortune should be shared between them equally. But the maneouvre backfired. Zhang's wife spends the night with Li at the latter's father-in-law's home. Zhang sues Li before the magistrate, who feels he would make the best of the tangle by marrying Zhang's wife to Li. So Zhang is left with neither wife nor fortune. At one point in the story, Zhang's wife is staying overnight with Li while Zhang is held up after curfew. What follows occurs in two different places, but the actors are acting on the same stage and to the same rhythm, which is contrary to the 'illusion of life within the four walls' in the Wetern theater. While Li and Zhang's wife worry about their disgrace upon the inevitable disclosure, Zhang regrets his misplaced trust in a false friend; while Zhang's wife blames Zhang for lending her out, Zhang complains to himself of his wife's seizing the opportunity; while Zhang's wife takes a fancy to Li because of his fair complexion, Zhang wakes up from a dream imaginging the sky is aglow and there must be a fire somewhere. This amusing scene is not likely to be seen in Western theater.[8]

Although the staging of *Loaned Wife* did not seem to have brought much of a response in theatre circles, it had great importance in the process of maturing the formulation of the theory of combining the spoken drama with the Peking Opera.

By now Huang Zuoling had added the acting of the Peking opera to the epic dimensions of a new Chinese national drama which he was helping to form. Although he explained his ideal of drama in terms of

Chinese painting, it was obvious that he was thinking of the acting and setting of the Peking Opera which, in some respects, are akin to Chinese painting. To these two elements Huang added a third with another play entitled *Xinchangzheng jiaoxiangqu* (The Symphonic Poem of the New Long March) in 1978. The new long march is, of course, the way to *Four Modernizations* of the post Gang of Four era. In this play the characters speak in verses which, according to Huang, creates an effect of alienation to prevent erecting a fourth wall on the stage. With the new *Symphonic Poem*, the major components of Huang's ideal of drama were complete, for in the last drama which he directed before his intended retirement in 1983, he again emphasized the importance of using verses in drama as a device to prevent the spectators identifying the stage with real life.[9]

In China, Huang is often called the Chinese Brecht. Some went even so far as to maintain he actually looked like the German playwright. Yet even if we disregard this emotional urge to identify Huang with Brecht, it is a fact that Huang is the most influential advocate of Brecht in China. And the three major components of Huang's ideal of drama do have their counterparts in the theory of the *episches Theater*. Let us compare the concepts of the Chinese director with those of the German playwright *cum* director. When Brecht used the term epic, he was not thinking of the dimensions of time and space as exemplified in the two works of Homer. What he meant was the mode of presentation, namely narration. Brecht did not need Homer's epic poems to help him to overcome the limitations of time and space imposed by the three unities. Goethe had already done so with his *Goetz von Berlichingen*, which he structured intentionally in such a way as to break all the rules of the regular drama. There is a constant change of scene and place, and the only time limit is the natural lifespan of Goetz, the protagonist of the play. Brecht did not need to turn to Homer in order to overcome the traditional Aristotelian drama. He only had to turn to Goethe and to Schiller (who considered one of his early dramas—namely *Die Rauber*—as a dramatic novel) or to Shakespeare, whom the Germans consider more or less as their own playwright after Goethe's emotional profession "Zum Shakespeare-Tag." Therefore, Brecht was thinking of a genre of narrated events when he used the term epic. Of course he would not exclude the open time and space of a homeric epic, as they do constitute the integral parts of the whole conception. The natural by-products of the Brechtian theater became the major concern of Huang's ideal of drama, which is more or less dictated by the vastness and the long history of China.

The spoken drama was introduced into China during the European eras of Realism and Naturalism. The plays of Ibsen and Hauptmann became the mainstream of orthodoxy in China. At the end of the forties and beginning of the fifties, Huang still had to contend with this particular development of the Chinese spoken drama. Huang's major concern was not the Brechtian theater *per se*, in whcih the content and form are parts of an integral whole. Instead of moving hearts Brecht wanted to move minds, and the devices and the techniques of the epic theater — including Brecht's understanding of the acting of the Peking opera — were developed to prevent emotional outbursts which tend to obscure the analyzing power of the intellect. For Brecht, the aesthetical pleasure derived from drama — among other literary genres — should ideally be an intellectual one. But Brecht's major concern was not Huang's major concern, although the latter was well aware of Brecht's intentions, as he explained the *whole* system of Brecht to his colleagues in his marathon talk in 1951. But he could not transplant Brecht's drama system wholesale to China without taking China's reality into account. The Chinese operas were a popular art form deeply rooted in the common people who demanded their own kind of aesthetic pleasure, which is self-evident when we consider the repertoire of the Chinese Opera. When European drama was introduced to China, it had to make concessions to the Chinese reality too, like the first production of a European drama in Chinese in 1907, namely *Uncle Tom's Cabin*.[10] Chinese workers who sympathized with the negro slaves were introduced into the American plot and a few arias of Peking opera were even sung. When the spoken drama became well-established in China, it also became an effective propaganda tool in the hands of the Chinese Communist Party. Using the fastest and most effective way, propaganda intends to move hearts, in this case the hearts of the populace in China. In this regard, the spoken drama also had to become a popular art form, while the Brechtian drama is intellectual and elitist. As a Chinese director, Huang Zuoling could not transplant the Brechtian theater wholesale to China. He must select and then adapt the borrowed techniques to Chinese reality. Otherwise, the result would be like that of the production of *Mother Courage* in Shanghai in 1959, which was a complete transplantation of the production of the Berlin Ensemble. It was ignored by audiences and critics alike.[11]

Being a man of practice, Huang did not leap forward, but walked step by step. First he used Brecht to widen the scope of time and space of the Chinese stage. The result of this innovation has still not been properly assessed; however, we can assume that it must have a considerable impact on the concept of drama in China. I think the epic scope of the unique drama *Teahouse* of Lao She, which has three scenes dating from 1898 to 1948, may be linked directly with the *da huobao* of Huang Zuoling, as far as the structure of the play and the scope of time are concerned.[12]

The second step of Huang was to integrate certain techniques of the Peking opera with those of the spoken drama. Besides acting, we already saw the use of the technique of showing two places on the same stage. This went beyond Brecht's understanding of the Chinese opera, as he only had the opportunity to see a few productions. Huang's explanations of Brecht's insight into Peking opera might stretch the facts a bit: for example, he said that Brecht's comment on the Chinese actor's self-observation which prevents the complete surrender of the spectator's emotions was entirely correct. However, this would not apply to the average spectator, but only to the connoisseur, if this is possible at all. When Huang introduced verses to substitute the usual dialogue, he went further than Brecht, who only used occasional songs. In this respect, Huang was either looking towards the classical drama in Europe or the Peking opera. He probably was thinking of the latter, if we take the image of the drunken poet as the quintessence of his ideal of drama into consideration.

If we compare the Brechtian drama with the ideal of Huang further, we find that Huang has become, with the passing of time, nearly exclusively preoccupied with the technical aspects of the theater, and the question of content has been pushed to the background. We also find that Huang relies much more heavily than Brecht would ever have thought possible on the Peking opera for formulating his ideal of drama. As a matter of fact, one has the impression that Brecht merely provided the impetus — namely the praise for the Peking opera and the conception of alienation — for the birth and growth of Huang's brainchild, which has very distinctive Chinese features. This would be the reason that some Brechtians were not satisfied with the plays which Huang produced. Here I shall only quote one:

> If a Chinese contribution asserted that, in learning something from Brecht as well, Chinese theater people were also learning from the Chinese Opera, no evidence was offered; and as far as I know there is none . . . even the Shanghai director Huang Zuoling . . . has yet to furnish productive results. Furthermore, it was repeatedly asserted that the Chinese audience was acquainted with the Brechtian stage design since it was so similar to that of the Opera, but I am not aware of any evidence for this assertion.[13]

This can certainly only be correct from the orthodox Brechtian perspective, which insists that Brecht must be the center of Huang's drama ideals or any other endeavors to form a new Chinese drama. But despite all lip services in China to Brecht, his theater was only instrumental in forming a national Chinese theater. Brecht's theater made the Chinese aware again of the values of the Chinese opera. In this respect, the production of a Brechtian play should be separated from the diverse experiments to find a new Chinese theater. Huang had produced a play of Brecht's (i.e. *Mother Courage* in 1959) in the purest Brechtian manner to which the Chinese audience did not respond, while the production of *Galileo Galilei* twenty years later was extremely well; and widely received. Apart from the subject matter, the "unpure" Brechtian production of *Galileo Galilei* must have been a decisive factor. The staging of *Galileo Galilei*, in fact, should be viewed as an experiment towards finding a new Chinese theater. This fact should be emphasized, both in China and abroad. For the benefit of the orthodox Brechtians, it should be stressed repeatedly that neither Huang nor any other Chinese director or playwright, at least to my knowledge, intends to transplant Brecht's theater to China without taking the cultural heritage of China into consideration. However, it should be admitted that Brecht did give an important impetus to the Chinese theater circles. His praise of the Peking opera did give some theater people new confidence to re-examine the Chinese opera and adapt certain parts of it for the needs of the new theater. This new theater should not and would not be a modernized form of the opera.

The same orthodox Brechtian characterizes the Chinese opera in the following way:

> The *fixing* of basic types which appear as figures on the stage characterized by *fixed* masks, gestures and modes of singing, the *changeless* catalogue of gestures for actions and emotions, the *wide lack* of psychological differentiation and individualization, the constantly recurring plots, finally the technical devices such as *gaudy* masks and *fantastically* colorful costumes, the almost absence of stage design and props, the *loud* and often *shrill* music. . . . reflect . . . the ideological conditions in a severely hierarchial, almost static agrarian society with a *fixed*, centuries-old view of the world.[14]

According to this undifferentiated catalog of faults—to which Brecht would object—of Chinese opera, it would seem to be a crime to attempt to adapt any elements of the opera for the Chinese stage. If we followed this line of thinking, the Chinese opera should be discarded altogether or boxed in for the museum. Then Huang's ideal of drama which emphasizes *xieyi*[15] of the Chinese culture would be quite futile. It would only produce another theater which could be described by the same negative epithets. Fortunately, the above description, which may have certain merits, cannot be taken too seriously. It can be compared with a being from some remote planet which has no theater, who sees the performance of a play on earth and radios back: the creatures on earth all suffer from schizophrenia in a varying degree, some pretend to be somebody else while others enjoy watching them do so, Ah, it is so good we keep our own schizophrenics in a sanitarium, etc.

If we followed the logic of the argument of the Brechtian above further, we should also blame the supposedly backward state of the Chinese theater on the audience who found it enjoyable for centuries. This is indeed what he asserted:

> This theater has a corresponding audience: people go to the theater with the same attitude and degree of interest with which they go to the cinema, and the audiences from the plebian stratum, to stay with this term, are in the majority although, of course, intellectuals are strongly represented.[16]

Therefore, if we followed this reasoning further, the audience and hence the Chinese people should be changed. In a Brechtian utopia we could all enjoy pure Brechtian theater. Would Brecht himself find this state acceptable?

The view quoted above describes adequately the position of a camp which uses Brecht to measure Chinese theater and audiences. An equally extreme position would be to criticize Huang's theory because he adapted non-Chinese views. As a matter of fact, such a position really exists. A critic says:

> Studying the rules of the Chinese art should not depart from Chinese rules. While it is alright to introduce foreign theories, they cannot substitute the rules of the Opera themselves, let alone modelling the Chinese art according to foreign theories . . . Now that Brecht has been introduced, it is said that Chinese Operas are Brechtian.[17]

I cannot agree with this statement more. One of the negative effects of the call for complete Westernization of the May Fourth Movement is the complete negation of things Chinese or the complete positivation of things European. But is Huang really using foreign theories to explain the Chinese opera? I would say no. Huang cannot use Brecht to explain the Chinese opera since the knowledge of the latter on the subject was very sketchy. Even Huang himself pointed out Brecht's mistake of assuming that the number of flags on the back of a general in an opera would indicate the size of his army. In fact, Huang pointed out in his treatise "A supplement to Brecht's 'Alienation Effecs in Chinese Acting'" that Brecht's plays and the Opera are two different kinds of theater.[18] Brecht did not create any plays according to the principles of the Chinese opera. Besides, Brecht's understanding of the Opera was really Brechtian, i.e., he projected his own ideas into his understanding of it. We are reminded that Brecht had an ax to grind. He was looking for confirmation of his own ideas, and he found them confirmed in far-away China. In this way, the Chinese opera served as evidence that he was right. In a similar way, Brecht used Chinese philosophers like Laozi, Mozi, and Confucius to confirm his social and political views. Similarly, Huang is using Brecht as his witness, but to a far lesser extent. In many ways, China to Brecht was comparable to *tianzhu* (i.e., India) or *xifang jile shijie* (which means Western paradise, which is synonymous to India) for the early Buddhists. But Huang is using Brecht more or less to prove that the Chinese opera is not an inferior, but superior art form. If anything is regretable, then it should be the fact that Huang needed Brecht to prove this to the Chinese. To wit, one of Huang's concluding remarks in his essay mentioned above is:

> In the final analysis, in spite of the many similarities between the traditional Chinese theater and Brecht's 'alienation effect,' they are two different distinctive forms of performing art.[19]

At this moment, we should permit ourselves to ask again if the stylized acting of the Chinese opera haws alienating effects. My answer to this question would be positive. While the Peking opera as a theatrical art also aims to arous emotions like its brethren in the West, stylized acting does produce alienating effects as it is not identical with gestures in real life. The purpose of the Brechtian alienation is, however, to prevent identification of the audiences with the characters on the stage so that the former would not be carried away, but to have time to ponder the political or social mesage embeded in a Brechtian drama. A Peking opera does not, as a rule, contain such a message, so that alienation is actually not necessary. The aim of stylized acting is therefore not alienation, but to give aesthetic pleasure. Alienation is thus only a by-product of stylized acting. However, we can certainly capitalize on a by-product, if it serves a purpose. What is the aim of alienation for Huang? He does not write plays like Brecht which demand alienation. It would seem that alienation has become an end in itself in Huang's ideal of drama. So far, this question seems to have been neglected in the discussion in China.

In trying to render an adequate translation for Huang's term of *xieyi* drama, I used the term imagistic, as Huang used Chinese painting to illustrate what he meant. I thought of images which could indicate concrete things in the real world and could also convey ideas. But Huang had other terms in mind. First, he thought of translating his drama ideal as "intrinsicalistic theater."[20] Now he prefers the term essentialism. But is essentialism *xieyi*? I strongly doubt that. In this aspect I have to agree with the critic Ma Ye who thinks that *xieyi* is not an appropriate term. Huang did not think that the word imagism would not do his ideal of drama justice, probably because images overemphasize the aesthetic side. We certainly cen use images to project ideas, but usually we associate images with something pictorial. With "essentialism," which de-emphasizes the pictorial aspect, Huang Zuoling seems to introduce a new element into his ideal of drama, namely content. Up to now, Huang was interested in the stage techniques for which images would do justice. Essentialism points to ideas. It seems to me Huang's ideal of drama has now reached a new stage. It seems that he has now added intellectual content as a component to his ideal of drama. If this were so, we would need further clarification. Since he has now retired from his directorship, he could now perhaps find time to systematize his drama ideal to show us some examples of its fourth dimension.

Notes

1.   For a more detailed description of Huang Zuoling's dissemination of Brecht's theater, see Adrian Hsia, "Bertolt Brecht in China and His Impact on Chinese Drama: A Preliminary Examination," in *Comparative Literature Studies*, Vol. 20, No. 2, Summer 1983, pp. 231–245.

2.   This talk was first published in *Renmin Ribao*, April 25, 1962 and reprinted in Zuoling, *Daoyian de hua*, Shanghai, wenzi chubanshe, 1979, pp. 173–187.

3.   Cf. Tong Daoming, "Yetan xijuguan," in: *Xijuxjie*; Nos. 5/6, 1983, p. 25 ff.

4.   Cf. Ding Yangzhong, "Brecht's Theater and Chinese Drama," in: Antony Tatlow and Tak-wai Wong (Eds.), *Brecht and East Asian Theater*, Hong Kong: Hong Kong University Press, 1982, pp. 28–43, and Huang Zuoling, "A Supplement to Brecht's 'Alienation Effects in Chinese Acting," in: Ibid., pp. 96–110.

5.   In: *Life and Letters Today*, Vol. 15, No. 16, 1936, pp. 116–123.

6.   See footnote No. 1.

7.   Huang Zuoling, "Guanyu *shengming, aiqing, ziyou* de gediao he jige renwu," in *Xijuxie* Nos. 7/8, 1983, p. 5.

8.   Huang Zuoling, "A Supplement in Brecht's 'Alienation Effects in Chinese Acting,'" op. cit., p. 101 f.

9. See Footnote No. 7.

10. Cf. Ouyang Yuqian, "Huiyi Chunliu," in: Zhongguo huaju yundong wushinian shiliaoji bianweihui, *Zhongguo huaju yundong wushinian shiliaoji*, Hong Kong: Wenhua ziliao gongyingshe, 1978, pp. 13–47.

11. Cf. Footnote No. 1.

12. A detailed analysis is highly desireable, but it is beyond the scope of the present paper.

13. Wolfgang Schlenker, "Brecht in Asia, the Chinese Contribution," in: Antony Tatlow and Tak-wai Wong (Eds.), op. cit., p. 201.

14. Ibid., p. 202.

15. It means, roughly, describing the spirit.

16. Wolfgang Schlkenker, op. cit., p. 194.

17. Ma Ye, "Xiju de shizhi shi 'xieyi' huo 'pochu shenghuo huanjue' de ma," in: *Xiju yishu*, Shanghai: No. 4, 1983, p. 25.

18. In: Antony Tatlow and Tak-wai Wog (Eds.), op. cit., pp. 96–110.

19. Ibid., p. 110.

20. Sun Huizhu and Gong Boan, "Huang Zuoling de xiju xieyi shuo," in: *Xiju yishu*, op. cit., pp. 7–8.

Glossary

Bamian hongqi yingfengpiao	八面红旗迎风飘
huaju	话剧
Huang Zuoling	黄佐临
Kangmei yuanchao da huobao	抗美援朝大活报
Lao She	老舍
Laozi	老子
Li Bai	李白
Mantan xiju guan	漫谈戏剧观
Mei Lanfang	梅兰芳
Mozi	墨子
shishi	史诗
Tianzhu	天竺

xieyi   写意、

xifang jile shijie   西方极乐世界

xijuguan   戏剧观

xushu ju   叙述剧

youshi lishi, youshi shide yijing   又是历史，又是诗的意境

Part Three

Post-1976 Theater and Drama

7. Theater Activities in Post-Cultural Revolution China

DANIEL S. P. YANG

Introduction

In the fall and winter of 1981, I conducted theater research in the six Chinese cities of Beijing, Shanghai, Suzhou, Wuxi, Hanzhou, and Wuhan. This trip was supported by the CSCPRC, the Committee on Scholarly Communications with the People's Republic of China. During this three-month trip, I visited five leading actor-training institutes,[1] and attended a total of forty-three performances of spoken drama (*huaju*), ballet, Beijing opera (*jingju*), *kunqu* opera, and the regional opera forms *yueju, yuju,* and *xiju.* I met with approximately one hundred theater artists and scholars, many of whom are prominent figures in contemporary theater and literary circles in the People's Republic. The experience was an exciting, varied, and most rewarding one.

In May of 1983, I took a long leave from University of Colorado, Boulder to become Artistic Director of the Hong Kong Repertory Theater. During my twenty-six months of residence in Hong Kong, I was able to see around forty performances from visiting theater groups from China. In February of 1984, I was invited to Guangzhou for a week's lectures and acting workshops. I didn't see any performance there, but I was able to visit theater building, attend rehearsals, and meet many key theater people in that city.

In May of 1985, I was invited to play two lead roles in the Shanghai Festival of Gem Repertoire of Kunqu. After the ten-day festival, I lectured and toured in three other cities of Nanjing, Wuxi, and Guangzhou. This one-month third visit gave me opportunities to see another twenty performances of both traditional and modern Chinese plays. In late June of the same year, the Cantonese-dialect production of *The Importance of Being Earnest*, which I had directed for the Hong Kong Rapertory Theater, was invited to give three performances in Guangzhou. This touring occasion, plus the earlier acting assignment have given me a first-hand experience of working closely with Chinese theater artists. This ar-

164

ticle is a summary of my impressions on the state of Chinese theater as a result of these visits and interactions.

Flourishing Theater Activities in 1981

During the "ten-year catastrophe," as the devastating Cultural Revolution of autumn 1966 through autumn 1976 is usually identified by people in the PRC, China's performing arts suffered considerably. Traditional Chinese theater, music, and dance were totally banned from the stage; so were Western music, dance, and drama. For a theater specialist from the Western world who is visiting China for the first time, a natural expectation is that theater activities will be scarce and of poor quality. I was happy to discover, during my first trip to China in the fall and winter of 1981, that this expectation was, in many respects, unfounded.

During my two months in Beijing and Shanghai (approximately one month in each place) in 1981, I made a nonsystematic yet quite conscious survey of the availability of theater performances to the general public in these two cities. My method consisted of frequently reading the theater listings in several local daily and evening newspapers. I found that on any given day, the newspapers would show at least twenty performances of Beijing opera, regional opera, spoken drama, musical drama, and dance-drama. Counting other stage performances, and concerts, the Chinese audiences in these two metropolitan cities had quite a large variety from which to choose. The same was true in medium-sized cities like Wuhan, Hangzhou, Suzhou, and Wuxi.

Some statistics in the 1981 issue of *Chinese Theater Annual (zhongguo xiju nianjian,* published in December 1982 in Beijing) also support my informal survey. According to the files of the Traditional Theater Research Center of the China Research Institute of the Arts, there were 2,072 traditional theater companies in China (excluding those in Taiwan) as of December 1980.[2] The city of Beijing, for instance, has sixteen traditional theater companies, including five Beijing opera companies, one *kunqu* opera company, and ten regional opera companies.[3] The city of Shanghai had twenty-six traditional theater companies: three Beijing opera, one *kunqu* opera, and twenty-two regional opera companies.[4] The exact number of spoken drama, Western opera, ballet and dance companies in either the nation as a whole or in individual major cities is not available in the *Annual,* but they must number several hundred in total.

The 1981 *Annual* also indicates that the total number of plays produced in China (excluding Taiwan) in 1980 was 2,524, of which 2,209 were traditional theater productions, 176 were spoken drama productions, 76 were Western-style opera productions, and 63 were shadow puppet or puppet productions.[5] The 1981 *Annual* states again that 275 new plays were published in PRC journals in the year 1980, of which 139 were plays in the traditional genres (86 of which were short pieces). 114 were spoken dramas in the Western tradition, and 2 were puppet plays.[6]

In comparison, the 1982 *Annual* (published in the winter of 1983) shows that the new plays published in the year 1981 had increased to 389 – 114 over the previous year, representing a 45% increase.[7] All these statistics suggest that theater in the PRC, at least in 1980, 1981, and 1982, was thriving.

Productions of Western Plays in Translation

Occasionally, typical Western theater fare such a Shakespearean classic, a contemporary Western play, an opera, a ballet, or a modern dance performance is presented on the Chinese stage. The number of such productions is increasing every year. The 1981 issue of *Chinese Theater Annual* indicates that among the 176 spoken dramas staged in 1980, twenty-two were foreign plays, including *Romeo and Juliet, Macbeth, The Merchant of Venice, La Dame aux Camelias, Sherlock Holmes, The Miser,* and *The servant of Two Masters*—all in Chinese translation.[8]

When I first visited China in 1981, I became aware of many Western plays staged, Including *The Merchant of Venice, Measure for Measure,* a Tibetan-language version of *Romeo and Juliet* (8 performances by the Shanghai Drama Institute, followed by an extensive tour), *The Tempest, Macbeth,* and Goldoni's *Mistress of the Inn.* The *Measure* production was directed by Toby Robertson of the Old Vic; it had 47 performances by the Beijing People's Art Theater—the largest and the best modern drama company in China today. Another major event was the invitation of Arthur Miller to direct his *Death of a Salesman* for the same company, which opened in Beijing in May of 1983 with much fanfare and a lot of world attention.

1983 also saw an ambitious production of Ibsen's *Peer Gynt.* It was staged by the students of Central Drama Institute in Beijing. The script was cut down form the original eight hours to around three and a half hours. Half a year's rehearsal time was spent on this extremely difficult show which received high critical acclaims.

Another unusual production was a Beijing opera version of *Othello* staged by the Experimental Beijing Opera Troupe of Beijing in May of 1983. Adapted by two teachers at the China Classical Theater Institute, the play was cut down to seven scenes plus a prelude, campared with the original five acts and fifteen scenes. There were about thirty arias, some written in the traditional modes of Beijing opera, while others were cast in the style of Shakespeare's blank verse. Othello's make-up was brown. His costume was in 16th century European style but adding the traditional Chinese pattern of sea waves. He also wore a pair of thick-soled boots as seen in the traditional Chinese theater. The costumes and make-up of other characters were also a blend of the Chinese and Elizabethan cultures. This experimental production of *Othello* was warmly received by China's audiences and theater specialists. The renowned playwright Cao Yu, who is also President of the newly founded Chinese Society for Shakespearean Study, called the performance "a daring experiment and a total success."[9] He said the play had retained both the drive and emotional appeal of Shakespeare, and the use of traditional Chinese stagecraft and music in this Shakespearean tragedy was "a successful marriage of the two performing arts."[10]

Quality of Performance

Among Western students of Chinese theater and amoung PRC theater professionals, there is a general belief that China's performing arts suffered a twenty-five-year setback as a result of the Cultural Revolution. The damage to the traditional theater is thought to be the most severe, because during the Cultural Revolution all traditional plays were banned and a great many talented artists died. But after seeing some sixty performances in eight cities in China and another forty-plus in Hong Kong, my impression is that the picture is not that grim.

Dance apparently suffered the least damage because the dancers' technique was not affected during the "ten-year catastrophe," even though they had to give up *Swan Lake* in favor of *The Red Detachment of Women*. Though the subject matter was totally different, the techniques of dancing and staging were essentially the same. I saw three dance performances in the PRC, including the highly publicized *Thunderstorm* (adapted from Cao Yu's famous play of the same title), performed by the prestigious Shanghai Ballet Theater. My impression is that while China is still behind in choreographic sophistication and technical production, the technique of lead dancers is quite good by international standards.

In the field of spoken drama, the damage of the Cultural Revolution was not very noticeable either. I saw a total of eight productions, including plays performed by the Beijing People's Art Theater, the Shanghai People's Art Theater, the Central Experimental Spoken Drama

Troupe, and the China Youth Art Theater—the four largest and best spoken drama theater companies in the nation. My impression is that physical production, in terms of scenery, lighting, and costuming, is quite respectable, but still lags behind first-rate professional theaters in the West. Acting and direction tend to be stilted and exaggerated, a common phenomenon on PRC stages as well as television and cinema. Brecht was very much in vogue at the time. Chinese actors and theater specialists often spoke of the Brechtian acting "system" as being one of the three "acting systems" in world theater—the other two being Stanislavski's system and that of Mei Lanfang (or traditional Beijing opera in general). Theater of the Absurd was also a popular subject, often discussed in theater journals and group conversations. The concepts of the Theater of Cruelty and the Poor Theater began to be mentioned in journal articles when I first visited China in 1981, I was not aware of these ideas having any influence on actual productions.

The quality of traditional theater performances was my major concern, and I was surprised (and much delighted) to find that the damage of the Cultural Revolution was not especially evident in the eighty-plus performances I saw in China and in Hong Kong in the last four years.

The traditional theater performances I saw in China ranged from gala evenings featuring superstars to informal school performances by students in training institutes. Most were performed by first-rate professional companies such as the Beijing Opera Theater of Beijing, the Shanghai Beijing Opera Theater, the Shanghai Kunqu Opera Troupe, the Shanghai Yueju Opera Theater, and others; a few were given by second-rate professionals companies in the "provinces." In all, of the eight-plus traditional theater performances I have attended, not one was a total disgrace. The only possible exception was an understandably deficient performance given by a seventy-four-year-old *kunqu* actor, Shen Chuanzhi, who had jsut recovered from a stroke. This performance occurrerd during a ten-day *kunqu* festival in Suzhou in October/November of 1981, when all the master actors and specialists of the classical *kunqu* opera were gathered under one roof to celebrate the 60th anniversary of the founding of the Kunqu chuanxisuo, a noted training school whose original sixty students were responsible for the revival of *kunqu* opera in this century. By the fall of 1981, only sixteen of these sixty original members were alive, and all over the age of seventy. On that historic occasion, half of these sixteen master actors performed, and a number of them did it beautifully.

Some of the best traditional theater performances that I observed in China and in Hong Kong were those by famous master actors who are past their prime, yet still extremely good in the limited roles which they now perform. The great Yu Zhenfei is a prominent example. Yu is considered the best actor of this century in teh *xiaosheng* (young male) roles in both *kunqu* and Beijing opera. He is now eighty-four years old and is still active. Among his other posts, he is Honorary Artisitic Director of the prestigious Shanghai Beijing Opera Theater and the Shanghai Kunqu Opera Troupe. I was lucky enough to have seen twelve performances of his — eight in China in 1981, two in Hong Kong in 1983, and another two in Shanghai in June of 1985. The roles he played demanded little physical movement, but the singing, recitation, and role interpretation were of such high calibre that one could hardly believe the artistic longevity of this master actor.

The seventy-three-year-old actor Li Wanchun is a master Beijing opera performer in the roles of *wusheng* (young warrior) and *hongsheng* (red-faced male; for example, the role of General Guan Yu of the Three Kingdom saga). Li was disgraced and forced into retirement for ten years during the Cultural Revolution, yet he still had a great following when he performed again in 1979. I saw two of his performances in Beijing in 1981, one in a young worrior role and the other in a red-faced male role; he performed complicated movement patterns and vigorous acrobatic stunts with perfection and much gusto, revelaing almost no sign of his age. The audience, understandably, reacted with the greatest enthusiasm whenever he performed on the stage. He was equally well-received when he performed in Hong Kong in the fall of 1983. Unfortunately, this great actor died of a stroke a year later.

Another amazing performance was given by the noted Beijing opera actress Tong Zhiling, considered one of the best performers of female roles since Mei Lanfang, especially in *huadan* (coquette) roles. Tong enjoyed great popularity on the stage from her late teens in the 1930s until the outbreak of the Cultural Revolution, when she suffered considerable humiliation. When I met her in Shanghai in November 1981, she was sixty-four and was no longer youthfully beautiful. But when she appeared on teh stage, her exquisite movement and gestures, superb singing, recitation, and facial expressions somehow created the highly convincing image of a character at least forty years younger than her actual age.

There are several other famous Beijing opera performers in their sixties who are active on today's stage. Some still have first-rate technique, and watching one of their performances is one of the great pleasures offered by the theater. On the other hand, I have also seen former star actors give rather disappointing performances, inspiring nostalgia rather than giving artistic satisfaction.

The great majority of consistently excellent performers on today's traditional Chinese stage are people in their forties, who were forced into semi-retirement during the Cultural Revolution but somehow still managed to maintain their technique and remember their repertoires. In a newspaper interview, the young warrior actor Li Xiaochun, son of the superstar Li Shaochun who died tragically during the Cultural Revolution, described how he and his famous father were sent to Inner Mongolia to work as shephards at the height of the Cultural Revolution. To maintain and improve their acrobatic technique, the Li's did one hundred somersaults and back flips every morning and every evening while tending sheep. This training paid off for the son. When Li Xiaochun came to the Untied States with the 149-member performing company in the summer of 1978, he delighted and impressed American audiences in the role of the Monkey King Sun Wukong—a role for which his father had been known and which requires great acrobatic feats.

Gu Zhaoqi, the best *kunqu* opera flute player in contemporary China, told me how he managed to retain his repertoire and technique during the Cultural Revolution. Since *kunqu* opera (like all other traditional forms of theater, music, and dance) was forbidden during the Cultural Revolution, he had to practice his flute at home, "silently" (without the reed), in order to keep his 200-play repertoire in memory. Occasionally he would play the flute with the reed; the fortunate thing was, he said with a laugh, that since *kunqu* is such an obscure and elitist drama, a few of the people around him (especially the Red Guards) knew what he was playing.

The persistence and ingenuity of numerous professional actors and musicians like Li Xiaochun and Gu Zhaoqi preserved a considerable portion of the traditional repertoire and technique during the ten-year catstrophe." These people in their forties, who are the best all-around performing artists in China today, will now devote the next twenty years to entertaining audiences and to training the next generation of performers. They are the people who give visiting theater specialists the strong impression that traditional theater in contemporary China is still thriving.

Theater Facilities

I visited and toured over thirty theaters in the PRC, including the leading facilities in Beijing, and Shanghai, and Guangzhou, one newly constructed theater in Wuhan, another one in Beijing scheduled to open within a year, a few regional theater facilities in the provinces, and several theaters/auditoria in training schools. There seem to be plentiful theater facilities for all kinds of performances—one official from the Ministry of Culture told me that as of winter 1981 there were around 130 theaters/suditoria in Beijing alone which could be used to stage Beijing operas.

The theaters are adequately equipped, but few of them are handsomely accommodated. In general, backstage equipment in major Chinese theaters is about twenty years behind first-rate facilities in the West. There are elevators and a revolving stage in the new theater of the Central Drama Institute in Beijing. It is considered to be one of the better designed and equipped theaters in China; its very spacious backstage can accommodate two full-stage motorized wagons in its wings. It is a typical proscenium theater with a sizable orchestra pit that can be raised to form an apron stage. However, there is no provision for the side stages and side entrances usually associated with a modern-design proscenium stage. President Jin Shan and his design staff, who showed me the theater, were very proud of the fact that everything in it, including lighting instruments, control boards, and stage machinery, was made in the PRC. Although state-of-the-art, computerized sound and lighting control facilities were absent in Chinese theaters in 1981, one of the designers told me that this was not because China lacked the capability to make such equipment. Rather, the country had other needs which put computerized software and hardware for the theater on a much lower list of priorities.

What the designer told me about theater equipment was entirely true, but I still found that people working and teaching in the field of spoken drama were somewhat behind in concept and in technique. Stanislavski was still the only system of acting taught in theater schools, although the Brechtian "system" is often experimented with and the traditional Beijing opera is always included as part of the curriculum. Shakespeare is done in a very "traditional" fashion — very much as we did in the United States in the late 1950s and early 1960s. Jerzy Grotowski, Peter Brook, Peter Shaffer, and Josef Svoboda were hardly known to most of the spoken drama specialists I met in China, not to mention the younger leading professionals in the West such as Serban, Ciulei, Nunn, Hall, Dexter, or Papp. People were surprised to hear that Shakespeare could be done in modern dress and be reinterpreted. Zhou Caiqin, daughter of the noted Beijin opera actor Zhou Xinfang and graduate of the Royal Academy of Dramatic Arts, told me in January 1983 in Hong Kong of the semester she spent in Beijing teaching acting in the Central Drama Institute. She staged a small production of *The Tempest* using students in her class. Both students and faculty were shocked when she first indicated her desire to dress the actors in rehearsal costumes.

The Audience and Admission Prices

Audience members at a typical theater performance in China represent a cross-section of society. Because most people still wear standard grey or blue clothing in the colder months, it is difficult to tell a person's occupation or station in society on the basis of appearance. Soldiers in uniform constitute a very small percentage of a typical audience. The occasional high-ranking government official is identifiable by his or her unmistakable air of authority and by the fact that such a perosn is usually invited to the stage after the performance for picture taking. Some officials, however, prefer to keep a low profile. Quite a few actors told me how their beloved, late Premiere Zhou Enlai would often walk inconspicuously into the auditorium after a show had started and sit quietly in the back row, to be detected only at the end of the performance when the house lights came on.

Chinese audience members are quite noisy, especially at Beijing opera and regional opera performances. When I attended a *xiju* opera in Wuxi, my ancestral home, the audience talked (not whispered) so loudly during a climatic scene that the aria (excellently sung by a young actress who was simultaneously executing some very difficult pantomimic movements) was completely drowned out by the 1,200 people in the auditorium who were all anxious to comment on the unusual excitement of the performance.

Although smoking is no longer permitted in the auditorium, eating sweets and cracking melon seeds are still common phenomena. Taking photographs and making audio recordings are still allowed during performances. (In comparison, these have not been permitted at Taiwan performances since 1975 or 1976.) Shouting approval and disapproval, which used to be an inseparable element of a Beijing opera performance, is now generally replaced by applause. Members of a Shanghai audience seem to retain and enjoy the shouting more than their Beijing counterparts. They show particular enthusiasm during curtain calls. Fans of a particular actor gather in front of the stage at the end of a performance as if preorganized. They sometimes discourage actors other than their favorite from taking solo bows, repeatedly calling out the name of their favorite unitl, finally, that actor or actress takes off his or her headdress and wig to reveal his or her true self. This phenomenon seems to be a new faze in shanghai; it was not seen in the past, nor is it found in other cities. In all cities, however, large crowds frequently form at the stage door following traditional theater performances. These devoted members of the audience often wait in chilly rainy evening air for an hour or more to express their appreciation to a star actor. Zhang Junqiu, a superstar in the Beijing opera theater and one of the very few remaining female impersonators, said that audience members often camp overnight outside the theater just to purchase a ticket for one of his performances.

In spoken drama and dance performances, the audience tends to be quieter than at traditional theater performances. Much less audience approval is expressed at performances in these genres as well. Hurried curtan calls are usually taken as most members of the audience quickly leave after the final curtain.

Theater tickets seem to be very accessible to the general public although one needs to have special connections to procure tickets to a performance given by a famous actor or actress, as mentioned above. Ticket prices range from roughly US $1.50 for an all-star Beijing opera performance to US $.30 for an average show in a medium-sized city. With factory wages generally between US $30 and $40 per month and monthly rent and utility costs under $4, tickets are considered quite affordable.

PRC audiences have opportunities to see free performances as well. Factories and communes near large cities often buy blocks of tickets in major theaters to give to their employees as a bonus. I attended a first-rate Beijing opera performance in Beijing at which the entire house was bought by two nearby factories for their employees. Theater troupes also make regular tours to remote corners of the nation.

Innovative Changes in the Traditional Theater

There have been some worthwile changes made in Beijing opera theater, long known for its stubborn resistance to any deviation from tradition. The Beijing opera orchestra has been much enlarged. New Instruments, often Chinese versions of Western string instruments, have been added to enrich the tonal qualities of the ensemble, especially in the formerly non-existent bass section. I saw orchestras with over thirty musicians, as opposed to the traditional eight to ten. Contemporary players of the *jinghu*, a two-string spike fiddle which serves as the principal melodic instrument, have replaced silk with steel strings to avoid breakage and slippage during performance, at a slight sacrifice of the tonal quality of this instrument. The conductor's drum, called the *danpigu* (single-skin drum), is sometimes modified with a new device allowing the tightening and loosening of the pigskin surface to change the pitch of the drum, very much like the mechanism used to adjust the pitch of a tympani. Such deviations from tradition would have been frowned upon thirty years ago, but Beijing opera professionals, including some very noted star musicians, seem to welcome these improvements quite gladly.

The use of radio-mikes by principal performers is very much in vogue in China. It is especially effective in Beijing opera, where the actor must occasionally face upstage, making projection of the voice quite difficult. Distortion, however, is a problem on low notes, which was apparent in a performance of *The Peony Pavilion* by the Northern Kunqu Opera Theater in Beijing in the fall of 1981.

The use of radio-mikes in traditional theater has apparently created some adverse side-effects. Specialists have started to worry about its impact on the voice training of younger actors. Since there is little need for vocal projection (and excessive projection through the radio-mike is discouraged), younger actors in China are spending less time in vocal training, which used to constitute a considerable portion of an actor's daily exercises.

The most impressive change in the traditional theater, I found, is in the basic concept of physical training for Beijing opera acting students. Traditionally, students in training schools woke at 5:30 every morning. They went through a two-hour period of vocal and physical exercises before breakfast, with the meal followed immediately by further intensive physical work. This 200-year-old practice had never been challenged, although some medical specialists expressed concern about the cumulative health effects of frequent and prolonged vigorous exercise undertaken by a child with either an empty or full stomach. But today, students in training schools all over mainland China don't rise until 6 a.m., after which they go through some vocal warm-ups and moderate physical exercises such as jogging and calisthenics, and then go directly to the mess hall. After breakfast they attend two liberal education classes. At 10 a.m., when the food in their stomachs has been digested, the students then go through two hours of vigorous physical training. After lunch they take a short nap and then go through more vocal and physical exercises.

This new method, according to Vice President Xun Lingxiang of the China Classical Theater Institute, was implemented in 1952 despite forceful opposition from older instructors who firmly believed in the virtues of the traditional method. Since the initiation of this change thirty years ago, statistics show that ulcers and other stomach ailments among students have decreased considerably. Furthermore, there has not been any noticeable decline of vocal and physical abilities among the actors and actresses trained under this new system.

I visited Taiwan a few days after leaving mainland China in early December of 1981. The principal of the Fu Hsing School of Traditional Theater, the largest, government-run training school for Beijing opera actors on the island, invited me to conduct a seminar discussion with key staff and instructors of that school. Fu Hsing, as well as the other three training schools in Taiwan, are still following the traditional method and schedule. When I told them about this new innovation in mainland schools, some of the instructors got quite defensive; but when I cited the statistics resulting from mainland China's thirty-year experimentation, most of the people attending this seminar agreed that there was room for reconsideration. The conclusion of that session was that the school authorities would study this issue craefully and would look into the feasibility of implementing the mainland Chinese methods.

Some Negative Phenomena in the Theater

During my four visits to China between 1981 and 1985, I became aware of some negative phenomena in contemporary Chinese theater which may seriously affect its future development. The first of such phenomena, which became very obvious in 1985, is the decrease of theater audiences, especially those for traditional dramas.

I noticed the dwindling of audiences for Beijing opera and *kunqu* opera even during my first visit in 1981. The situation for the *kunqu* opera was quite severe and most worrisome. Members of the Shanghai Kunqu Troupe, the largest and most prominent *kunqu* opera company in the nation, told me that the average attendance at their performances was only twenty to thirty percent of capacity, especially when they performed in large cities. It was difficult for that company to book theaters in Shanghai (their home base) due to those low attendance figures and the financial risk the theater management would have to take. On the other hand, the theater management could easily engage a *yueju* opera company (a theater form native to the Shanghai region) because their productions could almost guarantee full houses. With such strong competition, it was natural that theater managers hesitated to engage a *kunqu* opera troupue.

Theater companies which have records of low attendance were very worried about eventual liquidation. Two Beijing opera companies were disbanded in late 1981, one in Hangzhou and the other in Ningbo. News of this action came while I was in China in November of 1981, and I could sense the apprehension of many professional actors. It was postulated that several other Beijing opera and *kunqu* opera companies would suffer the same fate in the near future.

I personally observed very healthy attendance at most of the thirty-four performances of traditional theater which I attended in China during my 1981 visit. However, according to many actors with whom I spoke, my impression could be a deceptive one. Their argument was that most of the shows I saw were given by first-rate companies and featured famous performers; had I attended more performances by second or third-rate companies in smaller towns, my observations of attendance would have been different.

The situation of low attendance in the theater became much worse in late 1984. For some strange reasons people simply refused to go to the theater. When I made the two recent visits in 1985, I was told that almost all theatrical performances — spoken drama, opera, ballet, as well as traditional dramas — suffered a substantial decrease in attendance. Mr. Lin Zhaoming, Deputy Director of Guangdong Spoken Drama Theater, the largest and most prominent theater company in that Province, told me in June of 1985 that two of the three troupes in his Company had stopped producing plays in the last six months due to the lack of audiences. He also said that one of the local companies for spoken drama opened a new show recently but sold only seven tickets.[11] This "Great Depression" in the theater seems to be the common phenomenon all over the country now.

One of the main reasons for this depression in the theater is due to the sudden availability of color television sets for the Chinese populace, together with the flooding of imported programs from Hong Kong, Japan, and the United States. The Chinese public simply wish to stay home and watch the highly entertaining television programs free of charge. Disco music and ballroom dancing have also caught the fancy of the younger generation, who are not interested in the traditional theater in the first place. When I was rehearsing for the Kunqu Festival in Shanghai this past May, I was told that almost all theater companies in that city were renting their rehearsal halls for disco dancing in the evenings.

Another reason for this "Great Depression" is the recent directives of the government to ask all theater companies to bear responsibilities for its financial loss and gain. Since few people are buying tickets to attend a performance, most theater companies in the nation are now taking the safe route of not putting on a show unless there is absolute assurance of making a profit or breaking even. There is a common saying in the Chinese theater today: "Stage more, lose more; stage less, lose less, stage none, lose nothing." No wonder few noteworthy new productions have been staged in China recently.

The second negative phenomenon, that of the lack of incentive among the younger generation of actors, may have a much greater adverse effect on the Chinese theater. According to the present system of compensation in the PRC, people of the same age and background are paid on the same scale, regardless of talent and capability. Actors in China are paid according to eighteen ranked scales. The highest scale, that of *wenyi yiji*, "first-rank in literature and art" is RMB $336 per month, which is about

US $192. The lowest scale, the 18th rank, is around US $25 a month. A Beijing opera actor just graduated from training school is not ranked; for perhaps a year he or she gets a "practical training wage" of about US $20 per month until promotion to the 18th rank. Most actors in their forties are paid between RMB $80 and RMB $120, or between $45 and $68 in US currency. In Beijing opera and *kunqu* opera this age range embraces the finest acting talent in China. This salary is extremely low, judging by American standards, but one must remember that goods and services remain very inexpensive in China. An actor making the equivalent of US $50 per month spends US $4.50 on rent and utilities for his three-room apartment, for instance, and he does not pay any taxes, insurance, social security, or retirement.

Actors do not have to perform on the stage to draw a salary. If an actor performs only once during the year in a minor role, he gets the same salary as a more talented colleague who acts in thirty leading roles during the same period, ,as long as they are of the same rank. Promotion to a higher rank due to exceptional talent does happen, but not fast nor often enough to generate incentive among average actors. Under this system, actors with average talent tend to "take it easy." Many of them stop the rigorous daily training necessary to keep in shape; few of them devote time and energy to improving their technique and to expanding their repertoires, for such extra efforts usually do not reap significant financial benefits. This attitude is especially common among actors in their thirties, whose training in traditional performance technique suffered severely because of the Cultural Revolution and who are, therefore, technically deficient in performing the traditional repertoire. They see little hope of stardom, and many of them simply drift along without making special efforts to remedy the situation. This phenomenon, to me, is perhaps the single most worrisome element in contemporary Chinese theater which must be faced and overcome by the PRC government and Chinese theater professionals.

Starting in late 1982, the government announced a new policy to abolish this seemingly fair but unproductive system of compensation, allowing people who work harder and have more skills to earn a higher wage. Bonuses are now given to organizations, communes, stores, and factories which reap higher profits due to better management. Theater companies are now being asked to break even, which necessitates better planning, more ambitious promotion campaigns, and the scheduling of more popular shows in the season to take in more at the box office. The bonus system will help to motivate the actors who have low incentive, the pressure to earn more at the box office may also encourage commercialism which, for the most part, is absent in contemporary Chinese theater. Whether this new policy will benefit or damage the theater situation in China is yet to be seen.

Conclusion

Without a doubt the ten-year Cultural Revolution has caused great damage to Chinese theater, and it will take time to heal the wounds. Judging from what I saw in the fall and winter of 1981, the theater professdionals in China had apparently been working very hard to make up for the time lost and to repair the severe damages. At that particular period and the year following, the rescue of traditional theater before old actors die was identified as the most urgent task. The government was launching a major campaign to extract acting secrets from old performers. Retired master performers in the traditional theater were invited to transmit their special techniques and repertoires through lectures, demonstrations, dictating memoirs, and actual performances. All their performances and demonstrations were videotaped for posterity. Promising actors, both young and middle-aged, are gathered from all corners of the nation in central locales to learn as much as they canfrom these old masters. This was but one example of the many efforts to repair the damages of the Cultural Revolution.

During my first China visit in 1981, I was very happy to discover that the recovery of the Chinese theater was proceeding much faster than I had at first expected. Only five years after the Cultural Revolution, the Chinese theater was once again alive with talented performers and enthusiastic audiences. The Chinese theater scene in the fall and winter of 1981 was definitely exciting and thriving.

However, developments in the last two years have indicated some adverse signs that the earlier thriving situation was but short-lived. The severe dwindling of theater audiences and the virtual standstill of many of the theater companies are strong evidences that the Chinese theaters on the mainland are in trouble again. I only hope that this adverse situation is only temporary, that the resourceful and hard-working Chinese theater professionals, backed up by a correct, positive, and firm policy of the government, can once again come to its rescue. If they can survive the devastating onslaughts of the Cultural Revolution and make a quick recovery in five years, they should be able to do the same within a much shorter time. Hopefully, the Chinese theater scene will again be a very impressive one by the end of this decade.

Notes

An earlier article of similar nature but covering a shorter period of research, entitled "Thetaer in Post Cultural Revolution China: A Report Based on Field Research in the Fall and Winter of 1981," was published in the inaugural issue of *Asian Theater Journal*, (The University of Hawaii Press), Spring 1984, 90–103. Permission to reprint the bulk of that article has been granted by the Editor of *ATJ*.

1. Four of these institutes are the largest and most prestigious schools of their kind in the nation: The China Classical Theater Institute in Beijing, which is the only Chinese school of traditional theater at which students can earn a college degree; the Shanghai Classical Theater School; the Central Drama Institute in Beijing; and the Shanghai Drama Institute. The fifth is a regional school in Zhejiang province, the Zhejiang School of the Arts in Hangzhou.

2. *Zhongguo xiju nianjian*, 1981, pp. 277–79.

3. Five *pingju*, three Henan *bangzi*, one *yueju*, and one *quju*. *Zhongguo xiju nianjian*, 1981, p. 277.

4. Eight *huju*, six *yueju*, four *huajixi*, three *xiju*, and one *huaju*. Ibid.

5. Ibid., pp. 296–303.

6. Ibid., pp. 289–95.

7. *Zhongguo xiju nianjian*, 1982, p. 555.

8. *Zhongguo xiju nianjian*, 1981, p. 297.
9. Yang Lin, *South China Morning Post*, Hong Kong, July 24, 1983.

10. Ibid.

11. It was a minor professional company run by the People's Liberation Army. The time was April or May of 1985.

Glossary

Cao Yu 曹禺

danpigu 单皮鼓

Gu Zhaoqi 顾兆琪

hongsheng 红生

huadan 花旦

Jin Shan 金山

jinghu 京胡

jingju 京剧

huaju 话剧

kunqu 昆曲

Kunqu chuanxisuo 昆曲传习所

Li Shaochun 李少春

Li Wanchun 李万春

Li Xiaochun 李晓春

Mei Lanfang 梅兰芳

Shanghai kunqu jingying jumu zhanlan yanchu 上海昆曲精英剧目展演演出

Sheng Chuanzhi 沈传芷

Tong Zhiling 童芷苓

wenyi yiji 文艺一级

wusheng 武生

xiju 锡剧

xiaosheng 小生

Xun Lingxiang 荀令香

Yu Zhenfei 俞振飞

yuju 豫剧

yueju 越剧

Zhang Junqiu 张君秋

Zhongguo xiju nianjian 中国戏剧年鉴

Zhou Caiqin 周采芹

Zhou Enlai 周恩来

Zhou Xinfang 周信芳

8. Modernization and Contemporary Chinese Theatre: Commercialization and Professionalization

It is the clear policy of the Chinese Communist Party (CCP) that the modernization of China includes the development of a spiritual civilization. The Twelfth Party Congress of September 1982 laid special emphasis on the idea and several campaigns in 1983–1984 are related to it. By far the most important of these is that which seeks to attack and uproot "spiritual pollution" (*jingshen wuran*).

Clearly the arts in general and theatre in particular belong in the realm of spiritual civilization. Deng Xiaoping, whose *Selected Works* were published on 1 July 1983, has urged literature and art workers to "build a high-level socialist spiritual civilization" as part of modernization.[1] Commenting on this call, one drama journal has pointed out the special significance of theatre workers, simply because they are in daily contact with many millions of spectators and "what spiritual food they supply their audiences" will exert an enormous influence over "the ideological quality and level of virtue of the broad masses."[4]

When the movement against spiritual pollution began, late in the summer of 1983, many in the theatre world feared a clampdown on the very interesting experimentation which had been taking place for about a year. Deng Xiaoping had written of his objection to works of art which left an unfavorable impression with him of the Party or the socialist system,[3] and that could spell danger for plays or operas with very light or no propaganda content. Some plays and operas were indeed banned, and some popular arts magazines suspended. According to one writer, "all non-government-affiliated actors and singers in Anhui Province are now required to sit an examination in politics and culture before they are issued performing licenses."[4] In my observation, however, the tension had eased noticeably by the end of the year. During a visit to China in November and December, several residents, both Chinese and foreign,

181

told me they had been conscious of a change for the better even over the last three months of 1983. Experimentation has continued in the theatre and remains officially encouraged.

Against the background of a China interested in promoting spiritual civilization and opposing its antithesis, spiritual pollution, this paper aims to connect some social aspects of the practices of theatre troupes in China, as well as the content of several spoken plays, with modernization. It will attempt to show that the changing priorities in Chinese society and economy in the direction of higher professional standards and efficiency are applicable also to theatre troupes. The time frame is primarily 1983.

The publication of Deng Xiaoping's *Selected Works* was an important stage in the revival of the reputation of the late CCP Chairman Mao Zedong. It becomes clear in Deng's writings that he had moved successfully to change the famous resolution on Party history issued by the Sixth Plenum of the Eleventh Central Committee in June 1981[5] not to blacken Mao's revolutionary legacy but to affirm its value.[6] In a speech to literature and art workers on 30 October 1979, Deng had spoken positively about Mao's role in the development of China's arts in particular. "We must continue and persist in the directions which Comrade Mao Zedong advocated that literature and the arts should serve the broadest masses of the people and firstly the workers, peasants and soldiers." One writer describes Deng's slogan "our literature and arts belong to the people"[7] as "the core content of his thought on literature and the arts."[8] Deng reaffirmed such Maoist slogans as "let foreign things serve China" (*yang wei Zhong yong*) and "let ancient things serve modern" (*gu wei jin yong*).[9]

Commenting on the drive against spiritual pollution and the Second Plenum of the Twelfth Central Committee of October 1983, which had launched another major rectification campaign in the Party called Party Consolidation (*Zhengdang*),[10] the famous dramatist Cao Yu, also Chairman of the Union of Chinese Dramatists (*Zhongguo xijujia xiehui*), focussed attention on Mao's ideas on the arts as "the guiding thought and essential theory" for China's socialist literature and arts. He argued that Mao had raised and solved correctly a whole series of basic questions. These included "the relationship between literature and the arts and life, whom literature and the arts should serve, the world view, stand, and outlook of literature and art workers" and others.[11]

It is perfectly consistent with these observations on Mao, whose "Talks at the Yanan Forum on Literature and Art" of May 1942 had been the target of critical commentary in 1981 and 1982, that Chinese official spokesmen should deplore too much commercialization in the arts. After all, the development of the Chinese economy has been in the direction of more private initiative, less dependence on state grants, more encouragement to make profits. It can surprise nobody to find such trends among artists.

The problem of commercialization in the arts was serious enough to merit attention from Premier Zhao Ziyang in his "Report on the Work of the Government" given in the first session of the Sixth National People's Congress on 6 June 1983. "Most intellectual and artistic products circulate in the form of commodities," Zhao observed, but that was no reason at all for allowing "the decadent ideology of 'putting money above everything else' to spread unchecked in our society." He denounced those writers and artists who "treat their works and performances as a means of grabbing fame and fortune."[12]

Following up the reference to commodities, one writer stated that, of all branches of literature and the arts, "I am afraid that the contradiction between quality and circulation patterns is at its most obvious and sharpest in the world of theatre." In making a comparison between the cinema and the theatre he pointed out that the artists and others involved in the latter often feel the impact much quicker, in terms of morale and box office takings. It follows that theatre workers must be more aware of "the tendency towards commercialization" and strive to raise quality.[13]

The theme of commercialization was taken up in a commentary (*duanping*) in China's main theatre journal. It used very forceful language in applying Zhao's remarks to theatre troupes.

> Recently, the bourgeois ideology of extreme individualism and concern only with profits, anarchism and even the theatre troup style of the old society have become clearly reflected among certain people . . . Some of them have used evil means and gone everywhere to make money. Even individual "famous performers," ignoring the deterioration in their personality and art, have made their performances into commodities for sale, and have insulted both their audiences and themselves . . . In some theatre troupes, the relationships between people have actually changed into naked "money relationships," mutual use and mutual disruption, so that the friendship among comrades had been destroyed, and unity has collapsed.

The commentary's final point was that theatre workers "should place great weight on the people's expectations of us, and not forget the heavy responsibility we ourselves bear towards the people and society."[14]

The status of a commodity in Marxist terms is clearly not the issue here. But there is a clear realization that if the need to make money comes to assume a higher priority than socialist or progressive values in the theatre, then the whole nature of troupes will change, both in the human relations among the members and in the content of what they perform. Popular taste must be a factor, the demands of the masses should be met, but no troupe should pander to the audience if any members are asking for "unhealthy" items or content. Such behavior would be to ignore the actor's responsibility to society. It may become necessary to balance the size of the audience against artistic and socialist values.

"Unhealthy" content refers above all to pornography or the promotion of superstition. These are likely to follow from a mentality which places profit as the highest aim, that is, from a commercialized theatre. Pornography is broadly defined in China. Official spokesmen see it as part of the deviation of "feudalism" to label any television or cinema scene showing kissing and embracing between members of opposite sexes as "obscene."[15] But it would probably not require much flesh, especially female, to be exposed in a stage drama before the term pornographic would become applicable. The concern with pornography is perhaps not too surprising. One Western scholar observes that the emphasis on sex and violence in China's traditional popular culture is not too different from that of any other country, "and given half the chance would provide a solid foundation for the growth of a crass popular culture which is quite indigenous."[16]

Of course, nobody is yet suggesting that commercialism has become dominant in the Chinese theatre, and my experience in 1983 suggests that dramas with the most socially "pure" content can draw large audiences. But the strength of the wording in the extract quoted above suggests some alarm over the extent of commercialization in the Chinese theatre today.

Professional State-run Troupes

Over the last four years, reforms have been suggested and carried out in many areas of Chinese life, major aims being to increase production, raise professional levels or improve the standard of living of the people. One problem has been of persistent interest in the process: how to break the "iron rice bowl" (*tie fan wan*) or "great bowl of rice" (*daguo fan*). What these phrases imply is that people do not work effectively if they enjoy too much job security, if they are sure of being able to eat. The traditional idea of socialism, that no employer should be able to dismiss a worker, is here challenged.

The principal justification is that the "iron rice bowl" encourages inefficiency and slack attitudes among workers and contravenes the socialist principle "from each according to his ability, to each according to his work." The new doctrine propounds that the harder a laborer works, the more he or she produces, the more money he or she should earn.

Applied to the countryside, the principle has resulted in the production responsibility system, whereby individuals, families or other collective groups sign contracts with the commune to take on particular jobs. This has led to a greater work enthusiasm in the countryside and numerous reports, both Chinese and foreign, attest to a far greater prosperity there than when the new system was adopted in 1979.[17]

Literature and art workers in general have been formally encouraged "to stand in the front ranks of reform" in order to overcome the problem of the "great bowl of rice."[18] It manifests itself in the theatre in particular in the form of large troupes in which many people have too little or nothing to do, so that they become cases of disguised unemployment but still draw salaries. Those who work hard receive no more than those who do not. "Practice over the last thirty years has proven that there are a great many malpractices in the present system of theatre troupe organization; holding the 'iron rice bowl,' eating from the 'great bowl of rice,' and egalitarianism have enormously affected the creativity and activism of the performing profession."[19]

The problems can be exemplified in the First Troupe of the Beijing Opera Theatre of Beijing (*Beijing Jingjuyuan yituan*) under the Beijing Municipal Bureau of Culture (*Wenhua ju*). The leader of the Troupe is a famous actress, Zhao Yanxia. The Beijing Opera Theatre had 200 members before the Cultural Revolution but this had grown to 700 or so by about 1980, including 170 in the First Troupe. "Performing-art graduates were assigned to work according to state plan and few people left as jobs were virtually life-long once assigned."[20] Standards of performance fell since performers lacked incentive to work hard. Young performers felt that their opportunities were limited. The principal criterion for promotion was seniority, so in the short term they could not rise however hard they worked, but in the long run would inevitably do so no matter how inferior their performance.

The problem lay not only in the quality of the performances but their paucity. Zhao Yanxia claims that the seriousness of the situation came home to her in 1980 when she co-led the Beijing Opera Theatre on a three-month tour of the U.S. The company earned US $310,000 in three months but gave only three performances in the four months after its return to China.[21]

On 1 April 1981 the company, under Zhao's leadership, introduced a new system of allocating resources. The essence of the new system is that the Troupe members receive only 70 per cent of their salaries from the state, the remainder coming from the troupe's income. If there is a deficit, troupe members thus receive less; if there is a surplus, 30 percent of it goes to a "public accumulation fund" (*gong jijin*), 10 per cent to the theatre treasury (*yuan bu*), and the rest is given to the troupe members. "The principle of allocation is not the grade of their present salary, but how great is the contribution each one has made."[22]

The proportion of salary paid by the state differs from troupe to troupe. In the China Youth Arts Company's (*Zhongguo qingnian yishu juyuan*)[23] Comedy Troupe, a leader of which I interviewed on 19 December 1983, 80 percent of salary comes from the state. Money given in addition from box-office takings follows the principle that the main actor or actress received 5.00 *yuan* per performance, those of middle contribution 1.20 *yuan*, and those who work least 1.00 yuan. Originally, when the Troupe was set up in February 1982, the main performer was paid only 1.40 *yuan*, so the gap has widened considerably since. In one of the eight state-run troupes in the Shaoxing district of Zhejiang Province the new organizational reform was adopted, at the beginning of 1983, but with a difference. The performers still receive all their state salary but much of the takings, after all expenses have been paid, are allocated to the company according to the size and quality of their contribution.

In all troupes which adopt the new organizational method, the system of welfare must remain the same as in other companies, since they are laid down by government law. So health services, pensions, and other such provisions cannot be affected. Zhao Yanxia chose only 71 members of her original troupe of 170 for the experiment.[24] and it does not appear to have resulted in any formal dismissals. The Youth Art Company's Comedy Troupe was already small at the time of its foundation, with only some 40 members. Zhao Yanxia's troupe has been able to reduce the state subsidies it accepts very substantially as well as increase income. In addition, "the number of busy people has risen, and of idle dropped; of those who put all their energy into their work has gone up, and of those who ask for sick or other leave reduced."[25]

One feature of the new organization method in the Youth Arts Company's Comedy Troupe, which it was the first to introduce, is a system of royalty payments. Whenever the troupe chooses a play, it pays 1,000 *yuan* to the author. I was told that it had never happened before in the People's Republic for an individual company to pay a particular author for the use of his or her own play. Professional playwrights receive salaries from their own unit, while amateurs should not usually expect payment. In fact, the royalty of 1,000 *yuan* comes in one installment and so puts the recipient's income for the relevant month in the taxable range, which begins at 800 *yuan*.[26] Inevitably this limits the value of a royalty to an author, but certainly does not negate it altogether.

In Shaoxing two deputy leaders of the Municipal Bureau of Culture (*Wenhua ju fujuzhang*) told me that all state-run troupes in the five counties of the Shaoxing region now pay royalties to the author on the basis of 100 or 200 *yuan* for 1–50 performances of a script. Two points follow from this. One is that royalties are becoming fashionable even outside the reformed troupes, the other is that, at least in some places, authors can avoid the problem of income tax.

Much discussion has taken place on the advantages and disadvantages of the new reformed system, which Zhao had introduced on an experimental basis.[27] At the beginning of 1983 the Minister of Culture Zhu Muzhi came out in support of trailing the new system. He declared reorganization "the major task for cultural and theatrical institutions" for 1983. Overstaffing was the major problem in China's 3,400 state-run performing troupes,[28] which employed over 230,000 people, many of them unfit for their jobs. He was distressed at the lack of initiative among performers and he attributed the fault to the salary system. He called for reductions in state subsidies to troupes and believed this would become possible with a more general introduction of the organizational system pioneered by Zhao Yanxia.[29]

The Union of Chinese Dramatists held a forum on 4 and 22 February 1983 to discuss the new reform. It decided on strong support and its journal printed an editorial to that effect.

> In short, we must reorganize certain aspects and links in production relations, make them correspond to the development of the artistic forces of production, and push forward the splendor of the theatre arts a step. In this way we can see that this reform is a deep revolution. Consequently, CCP members and leading cadres in the theatre world should stand firmly in the front ranks of reform and be promoters of reform.[30]

The writer of this passage expected big changes to flow from the reform in the theatre world in general. This is clear from the use of Marxist terms like production relations and deep revolution. However, although the system still has strong proponents, as of the end of 1983 the impact had been rather less than sweeping. Only a small minority of troupes have adopted the new system, including a few in Beijing and Shanghai and a scattering in Hebei Province and elsewhere. In an interview with two senior officials of the Union of Chinese Dramatists on 17 December 1983 I received an impression of very lukewarm approbation. There was considerable doubt over the success of Zhao Yanxia's venture and many problems left to be solved. The system was still experimental and no decision on whether to adopt it as formal policy was in sight. A member of the Central Opera Company (*Zhongyuang geju yuan*) in Beijing told me informally that he knew of no plans to introduce the new system in his own troupe and strongly opposed it himself. An official of the Taian Cultural Bureau in Shandong echoed these opinions.

What, then, are the problems with the experimental system?

My informal contact in the Central Opera Company was worried lest the system lead to unemployment among performers. It is all very well to talk about reducing the size of troupes, but in the last resort this can be done only by throwing artists out of work or putting them into entirely unsuitable employment. The present system has its drawbacks but is better than the alternative.

The question of how one decides on allocation of money among actors looms large. To give the main actor fare more than the others is one possibility, but is bound to make a small number far richer than the great majority. The new system is bound to exacerbate inequalities and brings no real guarantee of opportunities for more than a small minority of young performers.

Another criterion for allocation of funds is to give more to those performers who attract larger audiences, and this has been adopted in some troupes. But there are dangers in making popularity a test, because such a criterion leaves the door wide open to pandering to the masses and to commercialization, including unnecessary and unjustifiable rises in the price of tickets.

The question of artistic standards arises here. The proponents of reform argue that the competition forces standards up and creates favorable conditions for new dramas.[31] However, officials of the Union of Chinese Dramatists I have interviewed both in Beijing and Shanghai are not so sure. Audiences tend to be conservative, so the need to court popularity may prevent troupes from rehearsing new items.

But quality is even more important. The Union's original editiorial of support had laid down "the precondition of rising artistic quality."[32] But there are continuing complaints of vulgar (*diji*), despicable (*xialiu*),[33] low (*dilie*) or crude (*cuzhilanzao*) items which come with the sin of commercialization.[34] There is no doubt that in the minds of officials, commercialization results in part from the new experimental system because "low" and "crude" pieces may well be popular among sections of the masses. The performer must carry out his or her responsibility to society and refuse to perform such items. This brings us to the question of spiritual pollution. Nobody is suggesting that the new system is a major producer of such evil, but if widely introduced would make controls much more difficult than at present.

At no stage did anybody propose that the new experimental system would involve relaxations of Party control or influence. In fact, the contrary is the case. "No matter how we reform, we must never depart from Party leadership,"[35] wrote one writer in a thoroughly typical statement. But the less a troupe depends on state subsidies, the more difficult it is to control. The more it depends on popularity, the less it will welcome influences or pressures from the Party.

A final point of considerable interest relates to the countryside. The rise in the standard of living there over the past few years has brought with it greatly increased demands for cultural performances, both in terms of greater choice and better quality. Well might a commentator remark that literature and art workers "must be conscious of their sacred duty and in undertaking organizational reform must first consider the 800,000,000 peasants."[36] They are, after all, four-fifths of the total population and no social solution whicih ignores them can hope to succeed.

Zhao Yanxia's new organizational reform claims to solve the problem by making idle people busy, but it may be that her cure is not the only one. Cadres of the Union of Chinese Dramatists inform me that many urban troupes wish to visit the countryside now, far more than before. The reason is that the increasing prosperity in the countryside has made rural visits worthwhile from a financial point of view. Peasants often throw small packets of money, 3 to 5 *yuan*, to actors or actresses they like. Although this practice, which is actually a form of tipping, could come under the heading of commercialization and certainly conflicts with the model of "theatrical virtue,"[37] it was told to me with strong approbation, without any hint of disfavor. The choice of performer by the peasant will not be influenced by the organizational structure of the troupe concerned. So while the new peasant prosperity and the consequent willingness of urban troupes to go to the countryside are no arguments against organizational reform, neither do they point in its favor.

Amateurs and Semi-Professionals

The increased stress on professional standards in society in general, and the theatre in particular, is reflected in the much slighter attention given to pure amateurs now than before 1978. My investigations along the lower Yangzi Valley at the end of 1983 show that most people regard the performing arts as the proper province of specialists. One official in Suzhou told me, "We had those amateur mass propaganda and art troupes during the Cultural Revolution, not now." She thus suggested that amateur art was part of Jiang Qing's frightful dross which the Sixth

Plenum had rightly thrown out in June 1981, along with the whole idea of the Cultural Revolution.[38]

Yet official policy does still favor the promotion of amateur performing arts. What has happened is that their nature and extent has changed substantially to fit the new social order.

A definite pattern emerged from my inquiries about totally spare-time performing arts in factories, institutes, communes and other places in the lower Yangzi Valley, which is probably reasonably typical of the country as a whole.

Units of more than about 500 staff in the cities or somewhat more in the countryside are likely to enjoy the services of an amateur art troupe, often still called a propaganda team. The size of such groups varies according to that of the relevant organization as well as to the enthusiasm of the staff for amateur art, but is likely to be of the order of 20 people out of 1,000 in the cities and somewhat less in the countryside. In most cases where I inquired about sex balance, women predominated more than would reflect their proportion of the relevant staff. This pattern is not universal, and far less sharp than I observed in children's shows at kindergartens and similar places, where girl performers regularly outnumber boys by a wide margin.

Organization for amateur groups comes from appropriate partly or wholly official bodies. These include culture stations (*wenhua zhan*) in the case of neighborhood apartment blocks, trade unions (*gonghui*) in the case of factories, students' associations (*xuesheng hui*) in the case of the countryside. These bodies provide the necessary finances for musical instruments, costumes and so on. All my informants were insistent that the initiative for participation in a fully spare-time art group comes from the worker, student or peasant. He or she will apply to join (*baoming*, literally announce the name). If more come forward than are needed, a selection process is made by the trade union or relevant body. In one factory I was assured that the amateur art group itself took part in the selection through its elected leader.

The policy is still "small in scale, rich in variety" (*xiaoxing duoyang*), though I found much less insistence on this slogan than during similar explorations in 1973. What the slogan means is that amateur art groups should steer clear of long and complicated items, but should focus on short, cheap ones which are easy to prepare and perform. They should spread their nets wide in terms of form and content. In practices, I found very few which departed from these principles. Song and dance items, musical pieces for national instruments, and short ballad (*quyi*) excerpts such as *kuaiban* or *xiangsheng* form the core of most groups' repertoire. In most places I was told that very few pure amateur troupes perform dramas, either local operas or spoken plays, except as excerpts. However, in the Shaoxing district where the peasants are especially fond of their own regional drama, one-act or small-scale operas are normal for pure amateurs.

Content is both modern and traditional, but usually with a heavy emphasis on the latter. Modern items accord with the actual work of the unit, so a traditional Chinese medicine factory can expect a proportion of items about that subject, and the lives of workers there. Other modern topics include the fight against spiritual pollution, and the policy of one child per couple. My informants were unanimous that the members themselves wrote or composed most of the items given.

Most amateur art groups perform only quite rarely, at festival times. It is typical for a troupe to confine its performances to four per year, one at the Spring Festival, one at National Day (1 October), one on Labor Day (1 May) and one other. The audiences are the workers, inhabitants, students or peasants in the relevant unit. More active groups sometimes combine with others in organizations outside their own to give a larger performance to a more general audience. Most factories and communes include meeting halls among their facilities and these provide appropriate stages. The combined performance of several different groups may take place in a standard theatre.

In none of the organizations which I visited in the Lower Yangzi Valley did money change hands in connection with pure amateur performances. The performers received no payment, and the audience never paid for entry. Very few amateurs aspired to become professionals, nor did many do so. Though talent scouts do still attend amateur performances, they are less active than they used to be. Nobody saw "professionalization" (*zhuanyehua*) as a problem,[39] in other words, I heard no criticism that individual workers neglect their work to attend rehearsals or give performances. All such activity takes place outside working hours.

In addition to these mass amateur troupes, which appear to me to be in decline, there is another type where the watchword is professional excellence. They are increasing in number, and larger in size than their pure amateur counterparts. They are enthusiastic and take their art very seriously. Unlike the pure amateur groups, they often focus on one form, such as Beijing Opera. In fact, they are real theatre troupes.

In 1983 China's main theatre journal published some material on semi-amateur Beijing Opera activity in Beijing, in response to which a member of a semi-amateur Beijing Opera company in Yantai City, Shandong Province, wrote asking for experiences from various groups on how they had solved their problems.[40]

One response was from the Beijing Opera Company of the Beijing Workers' Arts Troupe (Gongren yishu tuan), and can serve as an example. The company had revived in 1978, on the basis of a core of old amateur actors from before the Cultural Revolution, with no less than almost sixty members. However, enthusiasm quickly waned when the problem of finding suitable costumes reared its head. The troupe solved this question by performing small-scale items with simple costumes and small casts. They also hired or borrowed costumes from units in Beijing which collected them from the villages or private individuals, and bought some from specified factories which produced them especially cheaply. As a result, enthusiasm revived and the troupe was able to make a selection of 70, including quite a few young ones, from among 400 who applied to join. The process was an examination.

Finance for the hire of costumes and other needs comes partly by asking factories where performances are given to contribute a little, and partly by charging a small entrance fee of about 10 *fen*. This is hardly a large sum, and the charge does not come under the heading of commercialization. But the fee does show that the company departs from the regular practice of the pure amateur troupes of keeping performances free. It also shows that the tropue depends on its own work to keep itself in operation financially.

The members appear to be prepared to make considerable sacrifices for their art.

> Some troupe members live a long way away, the journey to and fro taking nearly three hours. Some have to hurry back to a night shift when rehearsals are finished, and that's very exhausting. Sometimes family contradictions can easily arise. The leadership is very concerned about this and had done all it can to help troupe members solve this problem.[41]

The content of the pieces played appears to be mainly or entirely traditional, what the Chinese term "ancient costume drama" (*guzhuangxi*). One point is clear: the troupe members are not their own composers.

The sources of the semi-amateurs are not made clear in the case of this particular troupe, other than that at least some are workers. But private sources in Beijing very close to the theatre world, including relations of Mei Lanfang, inform me that quite a few former professionals turn to amateur performance. They include those who have retired or lost their jobs through inability to withstand competition from better people, but especially those who were pushed out of the acting profession by the Cultural Revolution and have never been able to return. In Beijing as many as 50 per cent of amateurs are former professionals. In fact it is more the professionals who supply the amateurs than the other way around. This is a major new development in spare-time theatre and forms a good symbol of the rising demands on the new kind of semi-amateur.

These semi-professional troupes are still not particularly numerous in the cities. There, fully professional state-run troupes can satisfy most needs and the demands of production are constant so that there are no busy and slack seasons. In Shanghai, for example, the growth of the urban semi-professionals was only just beginning as of the end of 1983. By far the most rapid and important development among professionalized amateurs is in the countryside. The explosion in demand for entertainment of all kinds, which has resulted from the rising prosperity in the countryside, has been met in part not by full professionals but by the revival of the folk (*minjian*) troupes, performers who are also peasants, rural workers and so on. In Shanghai and Jiangsu Province these semi-professional rural troupes are known as "literature and art factories" (*wenyi gongchang*).

One writer cites the case of eighteen peasants in Hubei who gathered capital and founded a peasant troupe on their own initiative. The company quickly received numerous invitations to give performances. He goes on:

> Zhao Chuanying of Democracy Street in Huanglong zhen, Xiangyang County, Hubei, and six other women also collected capital and set up a theatre company. In some places the peasants themselves pay for teachers to come and run a theatre school. These are also places where the peasants take the initiative themselves to build a cinema/theatre. Li Taicun, Li Baofan and their households and five other peasant households in Yanggu County, Shandong Province, have collected 200,000 *yuan* of capital and, in the style of the Yanggu County's city cinema/theatre, built a performing site with 1,100 fixed wooden seats, which they have called "the seven households peasant cinema/theatre."[42]

These are but examples which show the lengths to which the peasants are prepared to go to encourage drama. What is clear from this passage is that the commune provides no financial assistance. The peasants can and do pay themselves.

Although the rural semi-amateurs continue to work as peasants or workers, the reference to "theatre schools" suggests that they are trained like professionals. They also receive remuneration for their acting and are professional in that sense also.

The specific situation in the Shaoxing district countryside was explained to me as follows. The members of the troupes are ordinary peasants for about five months of the year, during spring ploughing, summer sowing, autumn harvest etc. In the less busy seasons, which make up about seven months, they become professionals. The members are selected by advertisement, application and examination. The members themselves choose their own leadership through election, which then must be approved by the relevant local people's government.

Although these professionalized amateurs are sometimes given state subsidies, in Shaoxing as elsewhere, they depend more or less entirely on their own work. They charge 20 or 30 *fen* for tickets and with the taking pay for costumes and other necessities. The residue is distributed among the company according to the size and value of the individual's contribution. Nobody receives a fixed salary.

The content of the dramas performed is mixed. It includes modern items reflecting contemporary life, more so than in the state-operated troupes, such as operas advocating the one-child-per-couple policy; but also reformed traditional and newly arranged historical dramas.

Some of the pieces performed are composed by dramatists from the same county, some by those in Shaoxing City and some by playwrights from other parts of China; the first thing being the largest of the three groups. The members of the troupes choose themselves which dramas they will perform, but each piece requires approval from the local branch of the Brueau of Culture.

Shaoxing is a region on which I was able to find specific information through the local Bureau of Culture. It is a district unusually rich in its drama, both traditionally and at present. Yet most of the material given could apply equally to other places as well, including the method of paying the performers. Although these rural professionalized amateurs are not yet countrywide, they are currently enjoying an unprecedented and growing prosperity. An official of the Union of Chinese Dramatists told me in Beijing that there were at present over 3,000 of these rural semi-professional troupes in Anhui Province alone, nearly as many as the total number of state-run professional companies in the whole of China.

The Spoken Play in its Socio-Political Environment

This material on semi-professionals suggests that the Chinese stage is dominated by traditional Chinese forms such as regional operas, and that is completely natural. While forms which were originally foreign imports, such as the spoken play (*huaju*) or song-opera (*geju*) are doing quite well, several theatre workers and officials in China told me they believed the *huaju* had declined a little since the late 1970's.

Statistics from 1981 give some idea of the proportions in the numbers of items in the various forms. They are figures drawn from the performances given by 156 state-run professional troupes. They show 1990 spoken plays, 31 song-operas, and 1,206 operas in one of the various traditional regional forms. We can subdivide the last figure into traditional operas (over 660) and those newly arranged, the great majority being on themes drawn from the pre-1911 historical period.[43]

Yet from the point of view of dramatic development the most striking innovations of the last few years have been in the field of the spoken play. One would not expect nor want traditional operas to be innovative. The newly arranged items are not without interest from the point of view of new ideas and experiments, but among those I saw in November and December 1983, none was notable for striking out in a new direction, even though all were thoroughly enjoyable theatre.

In addition I saw four new spoken plays and, over one evening, excerpts from three old song-operas. All of the former are of interest for their theatrical content, for what they show about Chinese society today, and for their similarities and contrasts with one another. Two of them, *Shengming, aiqing, ziyou* (Life, Love, Freedom) and *Huore de xin* (Fervent Heart), are highly and directly political and revolutionary. The other two, *Fengyu guren lai* (In a Time of Stress a Friend Comes) and *Shiwuzhuang lihun an* (Fifteen Cases of Divorce) are more social in their thrust. Family problems, of varying kinds and to differing extents, form a common thread among the four.

Love, Life, Freedom deals with the revolutionary poet Yin Fu, formal name Xu Boting (1910–1931) who was among five literary members of the League of Left-Wing Writers killed by the Guomindang authorities on 7 February 1931.

The play is thus historical in the sense that it is based on real events and its main characters were actual people. The author, Luo Guoxian, strongly depends on the right of the dramatist to alter non-essential historical facts in the interests of good theatre. "A historical drama is not a shadow and translation of history," he writes, "but a flower blossoming from the soil of history."[44] This is a good summation of a complicated problem. The drama is very much centered on Yin Fu, and Luo Guoxian, among many other researches, took the trouble to visit Yin Fu's home country Xiangshan in Zhejiang, where much of the action takes place, and visit his still-living elder sister.[45] On the other hand, neither the League of Left-Wing Writers nor the others executed are mentioned.

The author and main performers[46] told me that the audience for which the play was mainly intended was young people, especially "intellectual youth in the cities." Luo wanted "to introduce a friend to them."[47] It focuses on Yin Fu's devotion to life, love and freedom, the three concepts found in a poem by the famous Hungarian poet Sador Petofi (1823–1849) which Yin Fu translated into Chinese. Yin Fu's recitations of his own poetry are a prominent feature of the play.

Woven into and part of Yin Fu's ideals in his political commitment, for which he is willing to sacrifice his life. At the beginning of the play he describes himself as "a little less than a Communist" (cha yidian Gongchan-dang), but his last words before his execution, offstage, are "long live the Communist Party" (Gongchandang wansui).

What makes the play much more interesting is Yin Fu's human relationship with the other main characters. Two women are in love with him, one from his home village, Meier, and the other, Qier, a Shanghai girl. He is in love with the former, but his mother decides he should not marry her. Yin Fu has no choice but to obey. Meier goes to Shanghai but is killed during a demonstration.

Yin Fu finds a baby on the streets whom he takes into his house "because she is Chinese" and Qier offers to bring her up.[48] A few minutes before he is killed, Yin Fu tells Qier that he loves her "for this short time."

But the most interesting relationship, one full of tension and contradictions, is with Yin Fu's elder brother Xu Zhiqing. At the beginning of the play, their mother commands Yin Fu to obey his elder brother because their father has just died. But Zhiqing is a rising star in the Guomindang,[49] and Yin Fu does not feel he can obey him. The play's main director describes the character of Xu Zhiqing as follows:

> The brotherly feeling between him and Yin Fu is very deep. He is a filial son, and is loyal to his "party and country." He and his younger brother stand in two different camps, but at the same time they have very strong family emotions. This is a special feature of this character. He is educated and loves literature.[50]

In fact, he is by no means a negative character, despite his reactionary political affilitation. He uses his influence at one point to secure Yin Fu's release from prison and at the end shows extreme distress on stage when Yin Fu is executed offstage. He has been given an ultimatum by his superior that he could not longer save his brother unless he persuaded Yin Fu to give up revolutionary activities by a specific time. The actor of Xu Zhiqing convincingly conveyed the tensions built into this role, including his genuine love for his brother, and his commitment to his own ideals, feudal and reactionary no doubt, but genuine nevertheless.

It is possible to read into this relatively positive portrayal of a person still living in Taiwan another sign of attempt at detente with the only Chinese province still under Guomindang control. However, in my view this would be a false interpretation. The whole thrust of the play lis the wickedness of Chiang Kaishek's betrayal of the revolution in 1927, and the consequent martyrdom of the central character. Xu Zhinqing's negative features are attributable to his adherence to the Guomindang and his reactionary ideology, his positive ones are connected with his relationship with Yin Fu.

Music plays an important role in this play. Especially written for the play by a local Shanghai composer, it is in nineteenth-century European style and dominated by the strings. On most occasions when one of Yin Fu's poems is recited, quiet string music is played as background. Although it struck me as somewhat sentimental in places, the music is generally effective as a dramatic tool.

Another interesting dramatic feature was the use of short documentary film extracts between acts. Most of it shot in 1927, it showed scenes of foreign troops entering Shanghai, demonstrations and their suppression and executions of revolutionaries. This helped to add to the play the atmosphere of the period in which it was set.

One reviewer wrote of *Life, Love, Freedom* that "the power of the play lies in its simplicity and directness."[51] I found it a very effective combination of political propaganda, social and historical commentary and human relationships. Considering that the author did not begin actually writing *Life, Love, Freedom* until early June, yet it was premiered on 12 November 1983, a production time-span of less than six months, this play is a fine achievement.

Certainly the propaganda content, centered around beautiful poetry and coinvincing human tensions, was much more sensitively handled than in *Fervent Hearts*, a play which deals with a living soldier called Zhu Boru. An order of the Central Miliatry Commission, issued on 22 July 1983, "called on the army to learn from Zhu Boru and to work hard to build socialist culture and ethics."[52] Actually to make a play from a current model hero is most unusual in the People's Republic, despite the many singing the praises either of political leaders or other virtuous revolutionaries of the recent past.

The authors of *Fervent Heart*, Wang Peigong, Li Dongcai and Liu Dianchen, faced a problem similar to that of Luo Guoxian in distinguishing between reality and drama. The program tells us that *Fervent Heart* "is a drama, and yet not quite drama; the main character is like Zhu Boru, and yet not completely like Zhu Boru." It goes on to assure its reader that there is not just one CCP member like Liang Ziru, the stage Zhu Boru, but many, and that in the future there should be even more.

Set in 1978 and 1979, the play concerns Liang Ziru's successful attempt to sort out a tangle of problems caused by bad human relations. A young worker subordinate to him, called Liu Zhenzhong, wants to marry Chunhua, who loves him but whose mother demands a gold watch from him. He cannot afford what amounts to a high bride price. Liu is also very sick, and cannot afford the proper treatment he requires. Good CCP member Liang finds him money for decent hospital care and by the strength of his personality and dedication to the people persuades Chunhua's mother to give up her demand. In the end Liu and Chunhua are happily married.

Meanwhile there is a series of subplots, mostly revolving around the issue of conflict between loyalty to family and to society. Liang's wife is very irritated by his continual refusal to give priority to their young son ahead of Liu. The young worker's family bitterly resents the demand for a gold watch and are much slower to forgive than Liu himself or Liang. To them, family sentiment is paramount. However, they are prepared to accede to the iniquitous requirement set by Chunhua's mother, and Liu's brother even steals a watch from Liang Ziru to meet it. Liang's virtues also sort out these frictions. Liu's brother admits to the crime, returns the watch and is forgiven.

There are no class enemies in *Fervent Heart*, nobody is really negative. Yet at the beginning only Liang himself is fully positive but by the end all the main characters have seen the errors of their ways and are willing to live in harmony.

This play is very much a propaganda piece, extolling the leadership of the CCP. Indeed, the education it offers is extremely direct and lacking in subtlety. Its theatrical conventions, scenery, the mannerisms of the performers, music etc., are somewhat stereotyped in the sense of being remarkably similar in style to most other contemporary plays I have seen in China.

Yet *Fervent Heart* is not without interest for the main message it propagates: The failings it airs in society are interesting, including theft even among good people, and the at least isolated effective persistence of bride prices, even in the cities.

Despite the thick propaganda content, *Fervent Heart* has been popular. The performance I attended was completely booked out and seats were said to be difficult to obtain. The audience reacted very favorably. Despite the seriousness of the subject, the play has the great virtue of humor, and raises issues which are of great concern to many people. The continuing strength of traditional thinking in family matters is clearly inimical to modernization, and most people perceive it as such. Unfortunately, this does not mean that in their own lives they do not give ample weight to the interest of their family.

In a Time of Stress a Friend Comes[53] is similar to *Fervent Heart* in treating a family problem, but sharply different in the nature of the issues handled. It revolves around equality between the sexes, in particular in professional and academic circles.

On 21 December 1983, I interviewed the author of *In a Time of Stress*, Bai Fengxi. She is very concerned about the problems of urban Chinese women, especially their freedom and equality with men, both in the family and in their work careers. She believes increasing numbers of women in Chinese cities want a full career and are not prepared merely to play wife to men. If a man can enjoy the advantages of a wife and a career at the same time, why not women? As China has become more prosperous over the last few years, she has seen more and more urban women demanding that their husbands share in domestic chores and allow them a career equal to a man's.

A very specific problem of inequality between married partners is how to cope with tensions which arise when a woman actually surpasses her husband professionally. Bai is herself married to a man successful in the theatre world, but I do not know if there is any rivalry between the two on that score.

The play *In a Time of Stress* concerns Peng Yin'ge, a brilliant young mathematician, who defeats her husband, Cheng Kang, by a narrow margin in an examination to decide who should go to West Germany to write a Ph.D. dissertation. Her mother supports her wish to go, but Cheng's mother thinks she should stand aside and encourage her husband to replace her. When it becomes clear that the married couple are in fact rivals, divorce begins to threaten, even though the marriage is still new. Cheng's mother tries to incite him against Peng Yin'ge and tells him "she has a bad temperament" (*piqi buhao*). She overhears the conversation and tensions mount.

Cheng Kang suggests to her that neither should go abroad. This will overcome the rivalry and avoid a lengthy separation. He thinks he is being magnanimous and compromising, but in reality he is showing that he has no idea of his wife's feelings. She reacts angrily against his suggestion.

The situation is solved by the arrival of Pen Yin'ge's father. He is the "friend" of the title. It turns out that he and Peng's mother had divorced over precisely the same issue: the wife's professional superiority over her husbands. He had never remarried through regret over his failure to understand his wife's legitimate ambitions. He thus supports Peng Yin'ge's wish to go abroad. He succeeds in silencing opposition from her mother-in-law. In the end it is clear that Peng will indeed go to West Germany, but the fate of her marriage is left ambiguous. However, Bai Fengxi told me "I think the problem can be solved" and thus suggested a happy ending to the main thread of the story. On the other hand, there is no hint of reunion between Peng's parents.

The title of the play means literally "a person of old comes during wind and rain" and is drawn from a poem of the Tan dynasty. This gives a sense of romance to the play, especially since the full stanza is quoted in the play. The device of using five characters from a Tang poem to entitle a play has been used before by Bai Fengxi.[56]

One feature which struck me with particular force in the play's content was the total failure to mention the Party. "Intellectuals, and especially intellectual women, must solve their own problems," Bai told me. "They should not rely on others, even the Party, to do it for them." The lack of reference to the Party was quite deliberate.

This is not a completely new feature in Chinese plays, being found, for instance, in the excellent *Juedui xinhao* (Warning Signal), premiered late in 1982 in Beijing. But it is worth noting all the same, because it shows that neither Party consolidation nor the attack on spiritual pollution has prevented the composition and performance of plays which accord no credit to the Party. Bai Fengxi told me that she regarded the male tendency to refuse their wives equal rights to a career as spiritual pollution and thus strongly supported the criticism currently being meted out to that deviation. She was bemused and surprised by my suggestion that recent trends might have inhibited the development of new themes and directions in the theater.

In terms of content this play is experimental in that it exposes problems not previously treated in Chinese plays. However, in terms of production it is rather disappointing. The style of the costumes, stage properties and scenery was typical of Chinese plays, although the setting for the scene taking place in the dwelling of Cheng Kang's mother showed it as more salubrious and better appointed than any Chinese academic's I have ever seen. The rain in the scene when the "friend" appears was portrayed simply by the continuous sound of dripping water and umbrellas used by those meant to be outside, in other words in a rather traditional way.

Whereas the possibility of divorce hovers in the background of *In a Time of Stress*, it is central in *Fifteen Cases of Divorce*, written by Liu Shugang, another play focussing on social and family problems in contemporary China. Here too the Party plays no great role. The piece enquires into the causes of divorce in China, but offers no solutions to the problem. There are no heroes or anti-heroes.

According to a senior official of the Supreme Peole's Court, 370,000 couples were divorced in China in 1982. This is the highest rate in the last three years, but still below the national average since 1949, which is about 400,000 per year.[57]

The main three characters in *Fifteen Cases of Divorce* are Luo Nan, a young man, and two women, Lu Yeping and Panqiu. Lu Yeping is a sociologist writing a dissertation on divorce in China. Luo was formerly in love with her in the country and wanted to marry her, but she wished to study in the city and refused his offer, even though she returned his love and continues to do so in the play.

Luo Nan marries the peasant woman Panqiu and later he leaves for the city. There he takes a job in a law court where he again meets Lu Yeping, who is collecting material for her disseration. Towards the end of the play, Panqiu applies for a divorce, on the grounds that she and Luo Nan no longer have anything in common and are quite unsuited to each other. Luo Nan finds out about her application only when his duties in the law court take place before his eyes. He begs her to reconsider. The ending is inconclusive, but implies that probably she will withdraw her application.

Against the background of the central plot, numerous cases of divorce appear before the court, mostly from younger couples. In one case the man is very oriented towards foreign things; he expects a good career and a wife who will act as a kind of docile domestic slave to him, in the traditional way. She resents his attitude and is not prepared to tolerate it. The male chauvinist who assumes a right to a doormat wife is quite a problem in China today. Ma Yuan lists "masculine authority of husbands" as one of the three most common reasons for divorce in 1982.[58]

On the other side of the coin is the woman who places unfair demands on her husband. One of the "fifteen cases" concerns a young woman who despises her husband as stupid because he is not ambitious for a higher salary.

Despite the serious topic of the play *Fifteen Cases of Divorce* includes a very important comic element. Much of it is also quite poignant. The program tells us that this mixture of tragedy and comedy is designed to make people think about the nature of love, marriage, family and so on. The play offers no formal line on divorce, but does imply clearly the need for a well-structured legal system to cope fairly with the problems marriage breakdown raises.

One feature of *Fifteen Cases of Divorce* which the program describes as "different from usual performance patterns" is "the thousand-face persons," who "change their images on the spot, and converse with the minds of the main male and femals characters." What this means in practice is that one actor and one actress play the roles of most of the divorcees. They also comment on the aims, feelings, and hopes of Luo Nan, Lu Yeping and Panqiu. They are the narrators, commentators, social consciences and also most of the subsidiary characters rolled into two.

This device succeeded in the performance I attended in Beijing in December 1983 given by the Central Experimental Spoken Play Company (*Zhongyang shiyan huaju yuan*) for two main reasons. One was brilliant acting, especially by the two "thousand-face persons," the other was the costuming procedure. On either side of the stage was a clothes rack. When the "thousand-face persons" were about to assume a new role they each took a set of clothes off this rack and donned it quickly on the stage.

There was no scenery and no curtain. The "thousand-face persons" announced the interval and conclusion, woven into the play itself. There are complicated stage priorities which remained unchanged throughout the play and were designed to be able to represent a whole series of scenes. Mime helped to clarify any confusion of precisely where the action was supposed to be taking place. For example, the crossing of a rivulet in the countryside was shown by miming leaps across stepping stones. The flashbacks, which are common in this play, were indicated mainly by changes in the intensity and color of the lighting.

In terms of both of content and production techniques *Fifteen Cases of Divorce* is the most experimental of the four plays under discussion here in the sense of striking out in directions new in the Chinese spoken play. As literature it is possibly inferior to *In a Time of Stress* in that it probes the emotions of the characters less deeply and develops a single important theme in a less concentrated way. But as theater, its variety and novelty makes it the most successful of the four here discussed.

One point common to all four plays is the lack of significance of the Cultural revolution. There are occasional references to it in *Fifteen Cases of Divorce*, but it never dominates. Gone are the days of "wound" plays which focus on the harm caused by the Cultural Revolution. This is not to say that the Chinese or their playwrights have forgiven Mao for that catastrophe, but now that the Sixth Plenum has formally and totally discredited that mass movement, the Chinese prefer to forget it and dwell on other things.

None of these four plays contains anything which could be remotely described as commercialized, or vulgar. It appears to me likely that long and complex plays such as these are going to appeal to urban audiences and be performed more or less exclusively by the state-run fully professional troupes. The emphasis in all cases is on high professional standards and quality.

Though politics is clearly still important, it is currently less all-embracing than it used to be even two years ago. Neither the attacks on "spiritual pollution" nor the partial revival of the Mao cult have prevented the appearance of plays which hardly mention the Party or propose no soltion to social problems. Experimentation may have been stifled by the return to emphasis on Mao's views about literature and art, but as of the end of 1983 the impact appears to have been mainly temporary and rather less than sweeping.

Conclusion

Both in the Chinese countryside and the cities, the quantity and variety of drama is still expanding. This is so especially of "ancient costume drama," but also of pieces on modern themes. At the same time, every effort is being made to raise professional levels. Not only is the state increasing its budgetary allocation to culture[59] but it is encouraging individuals and groups to increase theirs to theatre. In the case of the peasants, it appears that enthusiasm is great enough so that no official support is needed anyway. Organizational reform is certainly aimed at improving standards . The issue is how best to do this, not whether it should be done. At the same time, the pure amateur is declining while the semi-professional is rising rapidly. All these factors in combination constitute a process which may be termed the professionalization of the Chinese theatre. They contrast strongly with the theatre of the Cultural Revolution decade (1966–76), which emphasized the pure amateurs and decried the professionals to the extent of suppressing many of their troupes.[60]

The process of professionalization has resulted in demands by performers of more recognition of their work, including monetary rewards. The authorities' reaction to this has been mixed. On the one hand they have supported it, or at least allowed it. If peasants can demand and receive more material rewards for their work, why not artists? Those in charge of culture have allowed the experimental implementation of a system which could make for greater inequalities than at present and the growth of a larger artistic elite. They have permitted the growth of a large class of rural and urban semi-professional performers who do not depend in any sense on state money nor public organization, and who are in that respect private.

Commercialization is thus hardly surprising. But where precisely lies the distinction between, on the one hand, seeking more material rewards and regarding art products as commodities, both perfectly legitimate in Marxist terms, and, on the other, the commercialization of theatre, which is always used in a bad sense in Chinese documents? There appears to be one main criterion, explained in the words "putting money above everything else" (*yiqie xiang qian kan*). The phrase implies giving profits so high a priority as to affect content, making it "vulgar" or spiritually polluted in some way, or to influence the texture of human relations within troupes, changing their basis from comradeship to money. Commercialization begins when the priority given to money starts to undermine socialist values and replace them with those of capitalists.

The fact is that the border between what is good and what is impermissible commercialization is impossible to define precisely. But it appears to me that the government has allowed to be set in motion processes which it is going to find increasingly difficult to control. That is why the authorities are approaching Zhao Yanxia's experimental organizational system with such care. Probably the revival of the status of Mao Zedong as a revolutionary and the campaign against spiritual pollution indicate similar care in society as a whole, especially those areas which some Marxists term the superstructure.

Two deputy leaders of the Bureau of Culture in Shaoxing told me that they sometimes receive letters from the masses if unhealthy material appears on the stage. They argued that the masses did not like such pollution and were quick to protest against it. The Bureau responded by sending cadres to correct the problem. Together with the insistence the Bureau exercises on approving anything publicly performed, the two believed it was able to curb unhealthy tendencies. They might be right, but where audiences like "vulgar" content nobody is going to report it and performers who are in effect private are quite likely to provide what they believe their audiences want. The problem of control of content, let alone human relations in troupes, is by no means solved and could easily get worse. The fact is that the professionalization of the theatre, as it is operating in China, is to some extent the source of commercialization.

How does the process of professionalization in the theatre relate to modernization? Deng Xiaoping has laid down the lines as follows:

> The common objectives surrounding the implementation of the four
> modernizations, the way of literature and the arts should get broader and
> broader. Under the guidance of correct creative ideology, themes and
> methods of expression in literature and the arts should daily become richer
> and more varied, and daring in creating new things.[61]

Deng is referring here to content and style. If one accepts that theatre influences popular attitudes, and Deng and the Chinese certainly do, then one can argue convincingly that drama can contribute to modernization through its content. Patriotic "ancient costume dramas" encourage patriotism, which may not always help modernization but certainly does so where the Party has declared it the national goal. What is needed is a modern drama showing Monkey conquering all the difficulties an act which typifies his daring spirit, and in which the values essential to the theme of modernization are portrayed. The four plays discussions earlier would fit Deng's categories nicely. They tackle problems such as relationships between the sexes, and between family and social loyalties, which have a substantial ability either to hasten or impeded modernization. A direct propaganda content is desirable, in a context referring either to the past or present. On the other hand variety is essential. New topics and plays which are challenging and provocative can contribute to modernization, even if they do not mention the CCP, provided of course they are healthy and in no way pornographic or otherwise polluted. New ways of producing dramas, new techniques, should also be tried out, including those showing foreign influences, again as long as they contain no unhealthy elements.

But officials with whom I have discussed the matter are rather vague on precisely how the vairous aspects of organization which I have labelled professionalization in this paper help modernization. One offered the suggestion that orgnaizational reform "will contribute to modernization because it will improve levels in the theatre and make it more splendid". He claimed that anything which improved entertainment and recreation for the masses contributed to modernization, whether or not it helped raise the people's cultural and educational level.

These arguments appear valid to me, but only on the assumption that the tensions inherit in the process of professionalization do not get out of hand. In a sense, modernization, as it applies in the theatre, and professionalization are quite close to each other in meaning, and modernization includes professionalization. Certainly the two point in the same direction. Deng's comment about "the guidance of correct creative ideology" shows that in his view of modernization control is essential in the arts. Should the tensions discussed above result in the slackening of control, or what Chinese sources called Party leadership, the resultant theatre could be even more varied than the authorities presently want. It could still be associated with a modernization process, but one based more on private, less on collective or state enterprise than that envisaged by the current Chinese leadership.

Notes

1. Den Xiaoping, "Zai Zhongguo wenxue yishu gongzuiozhe disici daibiao dahui shang de zhuci," *Deng Xiaoping wenxuan (yijuqiwu-jijiubaer nian)* (Renmin chubanshe, Beijing, 1983), p. 180.

2. Kaming, "Fanrong he fazhan xiju chuangzuo de zhizhen," *Juben 8* (28 August 1983), p. 2.

3. "Guanyu sixiang zhanxian shang de wenti de tanhua," *Deng Xiaoping wenxuan*, p. 346.

4. Wo-lap Lam, "Deng *vs.* the Right: The Dangers Ahead," *Asiaweek* IX, 51–52 (23–30 December 1983), p. 20. Lam discusses the strengthening of censorship in the area as a result of the attack on spiritual pollution.

5. "Resolution on Certain Questions in the History of our Party since the Founding of the People's Republic of China," included among many othe places in *Resolution on CPC History (19949*–81) (Foreign Language Press, Beijing, 1981), pp. 1–86.

6. For example, the first point Deng makes in his first suggestion, in March 1980, on the draft of the Sixth Plenum's resolution is "to affirm the historical place of Comrade Mao Zedong." See "Dui qicao 'Guanyu jianguo yilai dangde ruogan lishi wenti de jueyi' de yijian," *Deng Xiaoping wenxuan*, p. 255.

7. "Zai Zhongguo wenxue yishu gongzuozhe," pp. 181, 182.

8. Xiao Xue, "Women de wenyi shuyu renmin," *Wenyi bao* 9 (7 September 1983), p. 15.

9. "Zai Zhongguo wenxue yishu gongzuoxhe," p. 182.

10. See the full text of the Second Planum's resolution, entitled "The Decision of the Central Committee of the Communist Party of China on Party Consolidation," *Beijing Review* XXVI, 42 (17 October 1983), centerfold pp. I–XI.

11. Cao Yu, "Jianchi he fazhan Mao Zedong wenyi sixiang dizhi he qingchu jingshen wuran," *Xiju bao* 12 (18 December 1983), p. 3. *Xiju bao*, which began publication in January 1954, was suspended in 1966 becuase of the Cultural Revolution. In Maych 1976, the journal *Renmin xiju* began publication, but from the beginning of 1983 divided into two periodicals, one of them being the revived *Xiju bao*.

12. *The First Session of the Sixth National People's Congress (Main Documents)* (Foreign Languages Press, Beijing, 1983), p. 51.

13. Cong Shen, "Xiju jie gengyao jingti shangpinhua," *Juben 7* (28 July 1983), pp. 4–5.

14. "Bixu kefu xiju yishu shangpinhua de xingxiang," *Xiju bao 7* (18 July 1983), p. 3.

15. An Zhiguo, "Ideological Contamination Clarified," *Beijing Review* XXVII, 7 (13 February 1984), p. 4.

16. John Fitzgerald, "A New Cultural Revolution: The Commercialization of Culture in China," *The Australian Journal of Chinese Affairs* 11 (1984), p. 11.

17. A good example of a journalistic foreign report taking a very broad view of the situation in the countryside since 1979 is "China," in *Far Eastern Economic*

Review Asia 1983 Yearbook (Far Eastern Economic Review, Hong Kong, 1983), pp. 135-7. For an academic view, see W. Klatt, "The Staff of Life: Living Standards in China, 1977-81," *The China Quarterly* 93 (March 1983), pp. 25-39.

18. Wei Yi, "Wenyi gongzuozhe yao zhan zai gaige de qianlie," *Wenyi bao 3* (7 March 1983), p. 3.

19. "Jianjue er youzhixude gaige xiju tuanti de tizhi," *Xiju bao* 3 (18 March 1983), p. 3.

20. Giichi Yokoyama, "Good-Bye to 'Big Public Pot,'" *Beijing review XXVI*, 14 (4 April 1983), p. 26.

21. Ibid.

22. Zhang Pei and Wang Wenzhang, "Jutuan tizhi gaige shi kaichuang xiqu gongzuo xin jumian de guanjian," *Xiju bao 2* (18 February 1983), p. 6.

23. On this Company see *Zhongguo xiju nianjian 1982* (Zhongguo xiju chubanshe, Beijing, 1983), pp. 479-481.

13. Giichi Yokoyama, "Good-Bye to 'Big Public Pot,'" p. 27.

25. Zhang Pei, Wang Wenzhang, "Jutuan tizhi gaige," p. 6. See further commentary on structural reform in state drama troupes, especilaly outside Beijing, in Fitzgerald, "A New Cultural Revoultion," pp. 6-9.

26. This is laid down by "The Individual Income Tax Law of the People's Republic of China," which was adopted by the Third Session of the Fifth National People's Congress in September 1980. See "National People's Congress Ends Session," *Beijing Review XXIII*, 37 (15 September 1980), p. 6.

27. Three articles on the subject of troupe reform from 1981 are contained in *Zhongguo xiju nianjian 1982*, pp. 237-443.

28. The figure 3,400 is that cited by Zhu. The official statistical yearbook gives 3,460 for the number of "arts performing groups" in 1982 over the whole country, Sichuan being the largest province with 223. See Guojia tongji ju, *Zhongguo tongji nianjian 1983* (Zhongguo tongji chubanshe, Beijing, 1983), p. 533. The highest number since liberation has been 3,533 in 1980. IBid., p. 532.

29. "Restructuring Cultural Institutions," *Beijing Review XXCI*, 3 (17 January 1983), p. 8. *Renmin ribao*, 1 January 1983.

30. "Jianjue er youzhixude gaige," p. 3.

31. Zhang Pei and Wang Wenzhang, "Jutuan tizhi gaige," p. 7.

32. Jianjue er youzhixude gaige," p. 3.

33. E.g. Zimu, "Jiaqiang xuexi qingchu jingshen wuran," *Yewu ziliao huibian tekan* 5 (December 1983), p. 62.

34. E.g. Cao Yu, "Jianchi he fazhan Mao Zedong wenyi sixiang," p. 3.

35. Ren Guilin, "Ye tan xiqu jutuan tizhi gaige," *Xiju bao 3* &18 March 1983), p. 5. See also Jin Yi, "Jutual tizhi gaige de jidian yijian," *Zhongguo xiju nianjian 1982*, p. 438: "to strengthen and improve Party leadership over theatre work is a guarantee of the smooth implementaiton of troupe organizational reform."

36. Zhang Fei, "Gaige yao xiangzhe bayi nongmin," *Xiju bao 4* (18 April 1983), p. 32.

37. In 1981 two performers in Shaanxi received praise for promotion spiritual civilization because they were not interested in profits, but only in serving the people and socialism. See Liu Ming "Zuo yige mingfuqishi de linghun gongschengshi," *Renmin xiju 4* (18 April 1981), pp. 3-5.

38. See also Fitzgerald, "A New Cultural Revolution," p. 4.

39. I have discussed the attacks on professionalization in some other periods in *Amateur Theatre in China 1949*-1966 (Australian Naitonal University Press, Canberra, 1973), pp. 29-34.

40. The letter, by Liu Rexu, is dated 29 March 1983. See *Xiju bao 7* (18 July 1983), p. 63.

41. "Zenyang kaizhan yeyu Jingju tuan de huodong," *Xiju bao 7* (18 July 1983), pp. 63-64.

42. Zhang Fei, "Gaige yao xiangzhe bayi nongmin," p. 32.

43. See the figures given in *Zhongguo xiju nianjian 1982*, pp. 516, 524-526, and 552.

44. Luo Guoxian, "Yishu xingxiang de suzao he lishi zhenshi de lijie – guanyu huaju 'Shengming, aiqing, ziyou' ji qita," *Yewu ziliao huibian tekan 5* (December 1983), p. 24.

45. Luo Guoxian, "Xiangshan yin, fang Yin Fu de guxiang," *Shanghai renmin yishu juyuan juxun* 2 (1983), p. 2.

46. I held a symposium with the author, most main performers and directors, all of these members of the Shanghai People's Arts Company (*Renmin yishu juyuan*), on 30 December 1983.

47. See also Luo Guoxian, "Yishu xingxiang," p. 21.

48. The sex of the baby is not made clear in the play, and the authors told me this was not a relevant factor. However, in the performance I attended the few words uttered offstage by the child were from a female voice.

49. Luo Guoxian told me that Yin Fu's elder brother is in fact still alive in Taiwan.

50. Huang Zuolin, "Guanyu 'Shengming, aiqing, ziyou' de getiao he jige renwu," *Yewu ziliao huibian tekan 5* (December 1983), p. 7.

51. Pei Minxin, in *China Daily*, 2 December 1983.

52. "Emulate Zhu Boru," *Beijing Review* XXVI, 32 (8 August 1983), p. 7.

53. The play has been published in *Shiyue* 5 (September 1983).

54. *China Daily*, 7 March 1983.

55. Quoted from the summary of Kang's speech given in "The Fifth National Women's Congress," *Beijing Review* XXVI, 38 (19 September 1983), p. 6.

56. *Mingyue chu zhaoren (The Bright Moon Just Begins to Shine)*, performed in 1981. See two reviews of it in *Zhongguo xiju nianjian 1982*, pp. 124–127.

57. "Woman Judge Talks about Divorce," *Beijing Review* XXVI, 37 (12 September 1983) pp. 5–6.

58. Ibid., p. 6.

59. Minister of Finance Wang Bingqian claimed in his "Report on the Final State Accounts for 1982," given at the First Session of the Sixth National People's Congress on 7 June 1983, that expenses for culture, education, science ans public health services in 1982 had risen by 2.56 billion *yuan*, an increase of 14.9 per cent over 1981 and constituted 35.9 percent of all additional state expenditure for 1982. *Beijing Review* XXVI, 28 (11 July 1983) centerfold pp. VII–VIII.

60. The number of state-run professional "arts performing groups" in 1965, on the eve of the Cultural Revolution, was 3,458. It fell every year from then to 1971 when it eached a minimum of 2,514. See *Zhongguo tongji nianjian 1983*, p. 532.

61. "Zai Zhongguo wenxue yishu gongzuozhe," p. 183.

Glossary

Bai Fengxi	白峰溪
baoming	报名
Beijing Jingju yuan yituan	北京京剧院一团
Cao Yu	曹雨
Cheng Kang	程康
Chunhua	春花
cuzhilanzao	粗制滥造
daguo fan	大锅饭
Deng Xiaoping	邓小平

diji 低级

dilie 低劣

duanping 短评

Fengyu guren lai 风雨故人来

geju 歌剧

gong ji jin 公积金

gonghui 工会

Gongren yishu tuan 工人艺术团

gu wei jin yong 古为今用

guzhuangxi 古装戏

huaju 话剧

Huanglong zhen 黄龙镇

Huore de xin 火热的心

Jiang Qing 江青

jingshen wuran 精神污染

Juben 剧本

Juedui xinhao 绝对信号

julebu 俱乐部

Kang Keqing 康克清

kuaiban 快板

Li Baofan 李保翻

Li Dongcai 李东才

Li Taicun 李台村

Liang Ziru 梁子如

Liu Dianchen 刘惦晨

Liu Shugang 刘树纲

Liu Zhenzhong 刘振中

Lu Yeping 路野洋

Luo Guoxian 罗国贤

Luo Nan 罗南

Mao Zedong 毛泽东

Mei Lanfang 梅兰芳

Meier	梅儿
Mingyue chu zhaoren	明月初照人
minjian	民间
Panqiu	盼秋
Peng Yin'ge	彭银鸽
Qier	琪儿
quyi	曲艺
Renmin xiju	人民戏剧
Renin yishu juyuan	人民艺术剧院
Shaoxing	绍兴
Shengming, aiqing, ziyou	生命,爱情,自由
Shiwuzhuang lihun an	十五桩离婚案
Shiyue	十月
tie fan wan	铁饭碗
Wang Bingqian	王丙乾
Wang Peigong	王培公
Wenhua ju	文化局
Wenhua ju fujuzhang	文化局副局长
wenhuazhan	文化站
Wenyi bao	文艺报
wenyi gongchang	文艺工厂
xialiu	下流
Xiangshan	象山
xiangsheng	相声
Xiangyang	襄阳
xiaoxing duoyang	小型多样
Xiju bao	戏剧报
Xu Boting	徐柏庭
Xu Zhiqing	徐志卿
xuesheng hui	学生会
yang wei zhong yong	洋为中用
Yanggu	阳谷

Yantai 烟台

Yin Fu 殷夫

yiqie xiang qian kan 一切向钱看

yuan bu 院部

Zhao Chuanying 赵传英

Zhao Yanxia 赵燕侠

Zhao Ziyang 赵紫阳

Zhengdang 整党

Zhongguo qingnian yishu juyuan 中国青年艺术剧院

Zhongguo xijujia xiehue 中国戏剧家协会

Zhongyang geju yuan 中央歌剧院

Zhongyang shiyan huaju yuan 中央实验话剧院

Zhu Boru 朱伯儒

Zhu Muzhi 朱穆之

zhuanyehua 专业化

9. The Darkened Vision:
If I Were For Real *and the Movie*

GILBERT C. F. FONG

In January 1980 the Seminar on Playwriting *(Juben chuangzuo zuotanhui)* was held in Peking to discuss the trend of exposing bureaucratic corruption and abuse of privilege in recent literature.[1] *If I Were For Real (Jiaru woshi zhende)*, written by Sha Yexin, Li Shoucheng, and Yao Mingde,[2] was among the most rigorously debated and criticized. Upon Hu Yaobang's suggestion, the performance of the play was temporarily halted pending revisions.[3] The decision alarmed overseas China observers, suspecting a return to the literary persecution of the Cultural Revolution years. In the same month, the text of the play, which had only been issued in China in a restricted-circulation publication, was published in *The Seventies (Qishi Niandai)*, a Hong Kong magazine. The editor, Lee Yee, who had written various articles supporting the new post-Gang of Four literature, touted the play as one of the prime examples of "New Realism" *(xin xieshizhuyi)*, which focuses on the realities of injustice in the socialist system.[4] The play became a more politically sensitive issue when it was adapted and made into a movie in Taiwan in 1981. Making some predictable changes, the movie turns the satirical comedy into political propaganda which condemns Chinese communism. Probably for political reasons, the movie was given several awards, including the Golden Horse Award as the picture of the year.[5]

The play was inspired by a widely publicized scandal in Shanghai, in which an "educated youth" from the country impersonated the son of Li Da, the Deputy Chief of Staff of the People's Liberation Army. The imposter, as reported in the newspapers, was showered with special treatments by the local cadres, for which they demanded and were promised many favors in return. The scandal caught the attention of the public and raised the question of the dedication and the moral quality of the cadres.[6]

The play was first staged in August 1979 by the Shanghai People's Art Theatre and since then briefly toured a few major cities. The reactions were mixed. Some critics applaud the young playwrights for their daring and penetrating analysis of the symptoms of elitism.[7] But Hu Yaobang, in a talk given at the Seminar on Playwriting, observed that the play offers only a partial and thus "unrealistic" picture of society. Zhang Senior, the positive character, is unconvincing and appears extrinsic to the plot. There is also an inaccurate account of the idealism of the young people, who, as represented in the play by Li Xiaozhang, would use any possible means, including fraud, to acquire a transfer back to the city. And by putting all the blame on the cadres, the play intensifies the unwarranted sympathetic feeling towards the imposter-hero. According to the criterion of "social effects" (*shehui xiaoguo*), that it is the responsibility of literature to unify and educate the people, the play suffers from many serious drawbacks and may lead to undesirable influences on society.[8]

The question of "realism" is a spurious one. The writing of literature inevitably calls for selection, rearrangement, and transformation, and satire, by its inherent quality, requires exaggeration. Due to its concern for the aesthetic, literature is different from real life, presenting either an idealized or a mis-shapen picture of human existence. Lee Yee's labelling of the play as a work of "New Realism" is untenable, as his argument appears to impose the standard that literature should conform to social and political realities. If one finds Gogol's *The Inspector General* "realistic," as Hu Yaobang has suggested, in that it typifies the phenomena of the social abnormalities of Tsarist Russia,[9] then one could consider *If I Were For Real* in a similar manner. The central issue in most of the writings on the play is not literary but political, whether exposure is necessary or tolerable as the mediator between life and art (*ganyu shenghuo*) and to what extent. Other Chinese critics took the hint from Hu Yaobang and criticize even more scathingly the play's distorted view of contemporary China.[10] The controversy soon developed into a debate on artistic freedom and what is permissible in literature, with Sha Yexin arguing that placing the play under "house arrest" (*ruanjin*), is tantamount to disguised literary suppression.

The political issues have obscured the discussion of the play as an effective satirical comedy. In terms of the development of contemporary Chinese drama, *If I Were For Real*, unlike the model plays during the Cultural Revolution, is not aimed at glorification. It breaks new ground in presenting a negative hero who is neither superhumanly virtuous nor heroic, moving itself away from the romanticized stereotypes prescribed by the rule of "the three prominences" (*san tuchu*). On the other hand, the play still retain some features characteristic of its immediate predecessors: a dominant symbol (the fake *maotai* wine), a plot based on "class struggle," and a manadatory happy ending.

The Play: Comedy, Satire, and Didacticism[12]

If I Were For Real is a satire against the abuse of special privileges among the ruling class. As an exposé of official misrule, the play is governed by an awareness of the discrepancy between the real and the apparent, between serving the people and exploiting them. There are two underlying structural principles: (1) the proximity and fusion of the world of the audience and the world of the play, and (2) within the play, the interactions among the real world (of knowledge), the false world (of deception), and the ideal world (of possibilities). These are not substantial but conceptual entities; they exist as points of reference and play an important role in the overall meaning-generating mechanism. The false world produces comedy, its relationship with the real world is characterized by the understanding of the incongruities between the two worlds and the irony which calls attention to the satirical theme. The ideal world uncovers by comparison the inadequacies in the false and real worlds through exposure, and in a positive vein, also emphasizes propriety and correctness in behavior for the edification of the offenders and the general public. Comedy, satire, and didacticism in succession illustrates the progression of the general tonal pattern of the play. Their presences are not exclusive of one another and may be co-existent, but comedy predominates, especially in their juxtaposition and in the transition from one world to the other, when comedic tolerance is maintained to prevent satire and didacticism from becoming invective.

The play has six scenes flanked by a prelude and an epilogue. The prelude, enacted among the audience, is an authentication process which connects the play world with the audience's world. The delay of the performance due to the late arrival of some honored guests has a direct effect on the audience. And when the hero Li Xiaozhang, who is sitting at front row center, is arrested by the "public security officers," the audience is witnessing the action in their midst and is drawn into the play world despite their later realization that the arrest is part of the act. The spatial link developed between what is on and off stage tends to break down the aesthetic barrier pointing to the difference between life and art.

> Plays have their origins in life. And this play of ours also is taken from actual lives as they really occurred. (stage direction, p. 201)

The provisions relating drama to life have already been shown when Director Zhao announces the delay: "Things like this happen frequently; there is nothing unusual about it." (p. 201). As an actress who also directly addresses the audience, she performs a dual role and creates a channel linking the audience with the world of the play.

On the semantic level, the announcement is a sign denoting the satirical target of the abuse of privileges and its wide acceptance. While the audience as the addressees are implicitly admonished for their tacit approval of the delay, they are also victimized by a "make-believe" performance, which of course is inherent in the nature of drama. The scene is thus a "prelude" in the literal sense, affording a glimpse into the world of deception and mistaken identity which the audience are to witness.

In Scene I the action is moved onto the stage. Verisimilitude is pursued in a continual effort to reduce the distance between the audience and the performers. The setting, demands the stage direction, "should resemble as closely as possible the front entrance of the theatre where it [the play] is performed." (p. 203). And the scene where the theatre-goers scramble for tickets is to be executed realistically, "just as though the performers were the spectators themselves or the members of the audience had themselves mounted the stage to perform." (p. 203). The scene does not call for the portrayal of society at large, but instead attempts to reproduce the immediate environment of the theatre. The resultant familiarity provides additional access to the play world, and the grotesque and ridiculous, which are about to occur, are brought close to home and made to appear as normal happenings in real life. In this way, the realistic milieu lends credibility to the escapades of the imposter—hero while permitting the introduction of the main action on a hypothetical level of dramatic pretense.

To Li Xiaozhang, his imposture at first is a joke which has little bearing on reality, a means of escaping from the humdrum of daily life and the frustrations he suffers from a hopeless situation. The motif of his flight from reality is introduced when, for no practical purpose, he misleads the theatre-goers into believing that he has the tickets for the performance of Gogol's *The Inspector General*. Afterwards, he derides one of the theater-goers:

> It was just a joke. So what if I trick people. Putting on plays is tricking people too, isn't it? You people ignore the real drama taking place all around the world and instead have to come here to watch make-believe drama. Don't you think you're being tricked here too? (p. 204)

Li Xiaozhang's derision is also levelled at the numbers of the audience, who are represented by the theater-goers on stage. What the audience is about to witness is a "trick and a make-believe drama," and it is, as Li Xiaozhang says of his own adventure, only a "performance," (p. 203). The declaration of the hypothetical tone has the effect of detaching life from art and runs counter to the verisimilitude pursued in the previous scenes. The result is a paradox, made up of the contrasting yet completmentary relation between real life and drama, questioning the truthfulness of drama yet asserting its relevance to reality. The paradox anticipates the imposter story in the main action, as the existence of the false world depends largely on its perceived indistinguishability from the real.

As soon Li Xiaozhang adopts a new identity, the play is split into the real and false worlds which are related by a series of parallels and contrasts. The false point of view of the cadres belongs to the internal plot which operates in a system of misconceptions: (1) Li Xiaozhang is Zhang Xiaoli, a reliable ally who is the son of a high-level cadre; (2) privileges and influences are the perogatives of the officials; (3) by ingratiating themselves, the cadres could advance their self-serving goals. The cadres are in dead earnest in their undertakings, unaware that they themselves have become the butt of jokes. Their self-delusions are perceivable from the audience's point of view, which also uncovers the concealed rivalry between the hero and the cadres. And with the orientation of the audience's loyalty towards the non-privileged, the incongruities between the real and false worlds are to be interpreted in the context of social inequality.

Director Zhao's invitation of Li Xiaozhang into the VIP lounge of the theater signifies the hero's induction into the false world. From then on, its dominance of the plot is only interrupted by infrequent flashes of the real world threatening to expose the deception scheme. As Li Xiaozhang has adopted a double identity which overlaps the two worlds, his success is dependent upon his ability to isolate them from each other. Comedy arises from his effort to maintain this partition, as he often has to call upon his play-acting to conceal his true identify and to prevent the real world's intrusion. When Director Qian invites him to move into her house, he pretends to telephone the "hotel clerk" to cancel his room.

Zhang [Li]:	Hello. Nanhu Guest House?
Middle-Aged Man:	What? The Nanhu Guest House? No, no, this is a mortuary.
Zhang:	I'm Zhang Xiaoli in Room 102.
Middle-Aged Man:	Wrong number! What is this? Who are you?
Zhang:	Hu Eryu? Listen, Comrade Hu, I won't be back this evening.
Middle-Aged Man:	How come I'm Comrade Hu? Name's Lei Te!
Zhang:	Letters? None from my father? What about a telegram?
Middle-Aged Man:	You're a case!
Zhang:	My case? No, don't you worry about it. I'll come back for my bags in a few days . . . [13]

The Nanhu Guest House is a real entity, but Li Xiaohang shuns the real and misrepresents it as something false, a mortuary, In appearance, a telephone conversation is taking place, but it is in fact a monologue which, through Li Xiaozhang's manipulation, confines the references only to the false world. By presenting just a semblance of reality, he makes certain that the real and false worlds are separated by half-truths.

In this scene, comedy is produced from, though not necessarily confined to, the existent elements and conditions within the false world. The word-plays, malapropisms, and puns generate humor and excite mirth in the audience by a forced combination of incompatibles, thereby creating the comic effect. Putting the Nanhu Guest House in apposition to the mortuary is ironic and ludicrous: what houses the dead is made to misrepresent that which accommodates the living.

The middle-aged man on the other line, as with the cadres, is being used, and Li Xiaozhang is the only character who knows the real context of the non-conversation. While the cadres are oblivious of the absurdity and the inconsistencies, the audience is in a position of knowledge, the superiority of being able to observe and judge the false world. The situation allows the contradictions to co-exist on stage, but also exposes the cadres' gullibility to ridicule. As the juxtaposition of the real and the false undercuts facade, what happens on stage can be assessed for what it really is — an of deception. The jokes which first appear as incidental humor are thus given a moral significance with the perceived connection with the real world of social phenomena.

Li Xiaozhang's scheme is made possible and even encouraged by the cadres, and its success forces an evaluation of their conduct, of what they should do and are actually doing. They are not given names (*ming*) but are described by their capacities, the official titles which define their obligations to the state. The performance of their official duties, however, are deliberately kept off stage, and the audience only see them as fawning bureaucrats, pulling strings and making connections. They never express their concerns for the people's welfare, and as Li Xiaozhang is "taking care of himself." They are also preoccupied with their own selfish pursuits: Director Zhao covets a larger apartment, Bureau Chief Sun wants his son-in-law transferred back from the northeast, and Director Qian solicits support for herself to join an overseas delegation with Secretary Wu.

The cadres are thus characterized by a series of "absences." the non-performance of their duties. The betrayal of the people's trust in them, focusing on the incongruities between reality and appearance, makes their offices a sham, and forces an understanding of their behavior in terms similar to the hero's, that they too have adopted "false identities." Li Xiaozhang reminds Zhang Senior:

> You can't say I'm the only one fooling people, can you? No, everyone is in this game. Aren't the people I was fooling all going around fooling others? They not only provided me with situations and opportunities and helped me

commit my fraud; some of the people I fooled even *taught* me how to fool others. I don't deny that I've used your identity and your position to get what I wanted for myself. But you can't tell me they haven't also tried to use the identity and position I pretended to have in order to achieve even bigger goals for themselves. (p. 244)

As the cadres repeatedly violate the very principles which have been entrusted to them, their exposure leads to the explanation of their transgressions in political terms—"they aren't always as idealistically communist in their hearts as they are with their mouths." (p. 244) The play thus portrays a society infested by deceptions. The main plot and the subplots are in this manner related not only by causality but also by mutual definition. The sharing of the false world's values acts as the common denomination, reinforced by amplification of the ideas of misrepresentation.

From Scene 1 to 4, the stylized mode of behavior of the cadres and their repeated blunders are the source of fun and laughter. Despite the satirical theme, light-heartedness is the pervasive mood, as the main action is realized as a "joke" played on the unknowing by an otherwise benign and harmless rogue. None of the parties, including the victimized cadres, has committed heinous crimes or has been subjected to any serious damage. But a change occurs in Scene 5, where the perniciousness is brought home in the shift from implicit deception to overt practices of fraud and favoritism. This underlines the issue of immorality and forces the satirical meaning over innocuous humor onto the plane of the didactic. Unlike the ignorant and callous cadres, Director Zheng of the state farm is aware of and aggrieved by the dishonesty around him. The farm workers requesting leaves of absence conjure up feigned and ridiculous excuses and disguise them as legitimate reasons. The recurring travesty of truth elucidates the absurdity of the situation, and imposes by juxtaposition in a similarly condemnatory interpretation on Bureau Chief Sun's demand for Li Xiaozhang's transfer. Powerless against the widespread deceptive practices, Director Zheng has to abide by the "rules" and grants permission for all the requests. His feeling of impotence has turned into cynicism:

The higher the rank the more the clout. Right-of-way! Right-of-way! Get the rights, and you've got the ways! This is "truth," according to some, and it *has* passed "the test of practice"! (p. 236)

The prevalence of the false world has rendered the "truth" ironic, for it presupposes the acceptance of false pretenses. Director Zheng, the reluctant collaborator, is tormented by the demands of the two worlds. His knowledge and conscientiousness have become irrelevant to his job as the director of the state farm, and they only inflict on him despair so intense that drinking is his only recourse to escape from reality.

The focus on the judgmental indicates an explicit relationship of the actions to moral precepts by the use of allegory. The ruined state farm is a sad reminder of a society being destroyed by the scandalous receptivity of the "back-door" connections permitted by the privilege system. The moral is clear. It gives warning that the country is in grave danger, and its youth would be corrupted beyond salvation if the immoralities were allowed to run rampant.

The dominance of the world of deceptions reaches its peak in Scene 5, but its imminent collapse is signified by the arrival of Zhang Senior. Transition to the ideal world is provided in Scene 6 by a return to the real world. The complaints of Li Xiaozhang about his unhappy experience and the discovery of Zhou Minghua's pregnancy are the realities of life. He has fervent hope of translating his success in the false world into the real world, and is so obsessed with his new identity that he becomes a believer of the false world and its values. Zhang Senior's intervention, however, brings ruin to his life and shatters all the illusions. What follows is an attempt on his behalf to absolve his guilt by unmasking the real intentions of the cadres. The downright exposure of falsehood denotes a further movement towards didacticism; whereas the judgement had been conveyed by parallels and allegory, now the attack is a direct condemnation. In his defeat, the embittered hero takes on the role of the author's mouthpiece, a witness and protester of injustice.

The epilogue reduplicates the effort to fuse the audience with the world of the play in the early scenes. The stage is transformed into a courtroom, and the audience is to act as the jury sitting in judgement of the hero's crime. They are treated to a moral and emotional appeal of extenuating circumstances by Zhang Senior, now the defense counsel. He points out the corrupted historical and social circumstances and implicates the cadres as the cause and effect of the transgressions, denouncing their "feudalistic, privilege-oriented mentality"'

> You have told the people to make allowances for the difficulties of the nation, to show self-restraint and obedience, to take the "big picture" into consideration, while there you are — grabbing your housing and calculating your own self-interest. You tell everybody else's children to "put down roots on the farm," while you use every means at your disposal to have your own sons and daughters transferred back to the city. And you want the masses to suffer privation and live simply while you yourselves crave a life of even greater luxury! (p. 250)

The tedious grandiloquence of Zhang Senior subjects the epilogue to an ironic interpretation, and the implausibility of a high-level cadre acting as defense counsel for a common criminal (especially one who impersonated his son) could be regarded as an implied criticism of society by wistfully acting out an impossible scenario. It has also been pointed out that the forces combatting the improper elements lack cohesion with the main action, and except in the ending, are only tenuously related to the plot movement.[14] Comedy and satire, however, depend on the perception of incongruities, and Zhang Senior, far from being the *deus ex machina*, is an essential component of the real world with whom the perpetrators are compared and found inadequate, and to whom the imposture, the main action, refers. He is an outsider, the same way Li Xiaozhang is precluded from the cadres' world before he adopts the new identity. The intrusions of both outsiders in fact are the major impetus leading to the theme of exposure. Moreover, the hypothetical tone is maintained throughout the play: the allegorical framework in Scene 5 and the neat array of repetitions of a processional nature reveal a deliberate strategy of dramatic pretense. The epilogue continues this artificiality, maintaining the general illuson to preseve the unity with the previous scenes and to prevent realism from taking over; otherwise the satire would lose its impact by being too "oppressively real."[15] But the play's fantasy also rests on the substructure of verisimilitude (the attempt to fuse the audience with the play world) to provide a creditable setting. In this way, the plot and characters are not so removed from reality that the satirical attack misses its targets.

Despite their exposure at the end, the cadres remain unrepentant and arrogant, still clinging to the misconceived idea of their privileges. Their attitude urges the pressing need for the eradication of the existent short-comings. Li Xiaozhang's impassioned plea is voiced from the standpoint of a victim of the unjust system, and Zhang Senior' call for a new, ideal world speaks for the national interest, the concern for the country's future. The resultant moralistic impulse is so strong and brought forth with such immediacy that they leave little room for any alternative reading.

As the didactic message of the play is carried through negative examples, the positivity generated by the ideal world is not total or without question. The quotation from Gogol's "At the Theatre Entrance" which prefaces the text also acknowledges this framework:

> Cannot positive and negative serve the same end? Cannot comedy and tragedy express the same sublime thought? Is not the dissection of shameless souls of some aid to outlining the images of the virtuous? And cannot all that which violates law and constitutes depravity tell us what the nature of law, duty, and justice should be? (p. 200)

The emphasis on the utilitarian function of the negative is intended to make an example of the immoral and depraved. Zhang Senior insists that Li Xiaozhang's case should go to public trial, trusing it will "educate not only our cadres but — at the same time — our youth." (p. 247). His prescription of justice is a cautionary warning, accompanied by promises, not a definite implementation of the ideal. Conforming with the negative-to-positive direction, the plot follows the progress towards the dominance of the ideal world. As is typical of comedy, the play depicts the restoration of order from disorder, but as satire, the negative becomes primary, for the exposure of inadequacies is necessary in the contrast to the ideal.

The latent negativity which threatens to override the positive feeling in the epilogue is also evident in the hero's sympathetic treatment. Li Xiaozhang is not a deliberate cheat: he only stumbles into a situation which fosters his imposture, learning to adjust his ways as he goes. His passivity is a reflection on the abnormalities of the cadres' world and thus lessens the weight of the moral significance of his actions. His goals are modest: a decent job and a good marriage are reasonable expectations with which the audience can identify. He is on the side of the oppressed, and despite the questionable motives and tactics, the empathy towards him pre-determines the audience's moral and emotional responses. In this manner, the interference of Zhang Senior is perceived as an antagonistic force, even though he stands for justice and righteousness, and Li Xiaozhang's arrest, while legally justified, is morally ambiguous. During the trial, the cadres are verbally condemned and Li Xiaozhang is given a sympathetic hearing. But he still has to face the judgement of law, while the cadres, who have committed more serious wrongs, are protected and can act with impunity. The feeling of injustice is so strong that Zhang Senior's tiresome homily becomes a necessity, a rebuttal to reorient the didactic response.

The cadres as members of a group are assigned the collective traits of belonging to the privileged class. Their elitism is highlighted and defined by those who are less fortunate. During his escapades in the cadres' world, Li Xiaozhang is allowed many opportunities to observe the disparities between the lifestyles of the two classes. In Scene 6 he triumphantly shows off to the dumbstruck Zhou Minghua the luxuries in Secretary Wu's house, which include "electric lights and telephone, steel frame windows, built-in cabinets, carpeting, padded sofa and chairs, television, phonograph, and last but not least, air conditioning." (p. 239). The material comforts, the use of a chauffered limousine, and the tickets to restricted shows are the overt signs of the workings within a closed society of elites. To Zhou Minghua, the luxuries and privileges are what the honest young worker can never obtain and probably never craves. But her fate in contrast to that of her classmate Juanjuan illustrates emphatically that the inequality goes beyond mere life-style. The two young girls share a common goal of having their lovers transferred. Because Juanjuan's father is a bureau chief, the transfer can easily be arranged through personal commections. As Zhou Minghua is only the daughter of an ordinary worker, she has to plead for help at Juanjuan's house, "barefoot and sweating, washing clothes and mopping the floors" (p. 240), but despite humbling herself, she still cannot succeed.

The dividing of the characters into two contrasting classes makes up the social setting but provides little dramatic tension, for the cadres' exploitations are underhanded maneuvers and are accepted as the norm by the non-privileged, who are habitually submissive and indifferent to their own inequalities. The play's conflict is largely created by the rigidly demarcted boundary of social identity and by the invasion of the protected territory of the elites. Except for those who are willing to resort to foul play, such as the delinquent farm workers, the non-privileged are described by disappointment, the non-fulfillment of their goals. Li Xiaozhang is aware of his own presumptuousness in his climb up the social ladder, and he therefore prefers to work inside the system instead of outside it. Taking advantage of that which has caused his frustrations, he adopts for himself a "good father" (*hao baba*), the symbol of power and influence in the network of connections. At the height of his success he proves that "how different life can be when you have a good father." (p. 240). But his feeling of powerlessness to enact change also convinces him to wisely restrict his ambition to success in his own class, not coveting the high living of being "Zhang Xiaoli" but only trying for the transfer to the city as a factory worker.

The absence of an open class war does not totally eradicate the consciousness of class distinction. Li Xiaozhang cannot even realize his modest dream, but as the privileged Zhang Xiaoli, he is given all the good things in life. In this context, his bitter outcry during the trial is especially poignant:

> I was wrong because I was a fake. If I were real, I were really the son of Zhang Senior or another leader, then everything I've done would have been completely legal.[16]

Legality, then, is not the major consideration, as fraud is permissible with the power and influence that come with high position or being its protege. The underlying theme of class discrimination denotes an abnormality that appears irremediable and inherent in the social structure which is perceived to be the protector of privileges and improprieties.[17] The play thus forces society to face the important question of its own nature and viability: in a system which takes pride in egalitarianism there still exists discrimination, and the class stratification is so rigid that mobility from one class to another can only be achieved by means of deception, a denial of one's identity.

The Play and the Movie

The movie underlines the negative impressions by seizing upon the ambiguities in the play's underlying structure. The changes which drastically alter the meaning are mainly executed in the following areas (1) the total dominance of the false world of the cadres, (2) the positive transformation of the character of the hero, and (3) the dark ending.

The false world of immorality is broadened to include a wider spectrum of society, making up a devastating force ready to strike down the hero and his goal. This is accomplished mainly by increasing the number of characters associated with the cadres. Deputy Mayor Wang is an abrasive and domineering braggart who unabashedly flaunts his power and privileges. Compared to the other cadres, he is more excitable and therefore more human and interesting. He is the former comrade-in-arms of Li Da (Zhang Senior in the play) and considers his responsibility to take in Li Xiaozhang under his wings. His enthusiasm, however, belies an ulterior motive — that by ingratiating himself with the leading cadre he may procure a promotion to the central government.

The Deputy Mayor has a weakness for beautiful women. He secretly keeps a mistress, Qiao Hong, a star performer with Director Zhao's drama company. Innocent and kindhearted, the beautiful actress is willing to trade her sexuality for luxury and special favors. In Director Zhao's crooked scheme, she is the tender trap waiting for Li Xiaozhang's surrender to her charms. In contrast to the true love of Li Xiaozhang and Zhou Minghua, it is clear that the cadres are incapable of genuine feelings; there can only exist the pretense of love, for sale for a purpose.

The cadres in the play are acting in accordance with roles defined and accepted by social conventions. Their follies are the result of their ignorance of reality, not only of Li Xiaozhang's true identity but also of their wrongheadedness. As unself-conscious offenders, they are more benign than evil and more laughable than odious. The new characters in the movie, however, call attention to the insidious and scandalous nature of the official world. To further intensify this negative tenor, some original cadres of the play are rehashed with additional unsavory personality traits. Director Zheng, a voice of conscience in the play, has been silenced and has undergone a total metamorphosis into a pathetic figure. Now a clownish, loud-mouthed drunkard with a quaint accent, he readily accepts bribes and bullies his workers. He also secretly listens to Deng Lijun music, and as a sign of his hypocrisy and generally of the world of deception, he hides a picture of the beautiful songstress on the back of Chairman Mao's portrait. While he still retains the despair and cynicism of the original character, he has been deprived of the moral indignation and the sense of duty.

Zhang Senior, who dominates the play's ending, becomes Li Da and is only accorded a minor role in the movie. He is not as treacherous as the other cadres, but he lacks the humanity and warmth of his counterpart in the play. Still the party's representative, he emphatically projects an image of a merciless disciplinarian, cold, aloof, and keen on punishment instead of persuasion. And as he has no desire of reforming the existent social injustices, his capacity as the link with the ideal world is curtailed, and total darkness prevails over the ruling class.

In the play, the party as represented by Zhang Senior is seen as a benevolent and concerned father-figure disassociated from the transgressors. But the movie consistently dehumanizes the Communist bureaucracy by demonizing it. Either by caricature or by portraying the cadres as cold-blooded creatures, the conclusion is that behind their masks lurks a sinister propensity for treachery and oppression. In the absence of any admirable character from the official circle, the party and the cadres are lumped together to make a corruptible regime.

The hero in the play is far from being a blameless character. Some critics even condemn him for his shamelessness and extreme bourgeois individualism.[18] His depressing experience in the state farm has changed him from being "idealistic and clever" (p. 218) to a delinquent who indulges in smoking and drinking. In Scene I he appears nonchalant and mischievous, a roguish vagabond with a satchel slung over his shoulders and a cigarette dangling from his mouth, aimlessly wandering around the city and dreaming of a good life. Always the opportunist, he effortlessly moves from one world to the other. His penchant for joking and role-acting evinces his readiness to escape from his responsibilities and from reality by obliterating its difference with falsehood.

At the beginning of the movie, the hero takes after the original character and to some extent remains influenced by his roguishness. The turning point which renders the imposture of the hero morally ambiguous occurs early in the movie with the disclosure of Zhou Minhua's pregnancy. The emergency provides an incentive for his opportunitism which now becomes a fight for survival of his future family, and he can no longer regard his role-acting as a prank, an extension of the joke he plays on the theater-goers. The accent on the love motif[19] is a constant reminder of his obligation. A devoted lover, he demonstrates his faithfulness in his constant rejections of Qiao Hong's amorous advances. His rivalry with the factory manager's son, who is favored by Zhou Minghua's father, also makes it imperative for him to improve his own prospects.

The movie's modified circumstances thus bestow on the hero the additional qualities of maturity and the sense of responsibility. The emphasis on his human problems has the effect of evoking a sympathetic response among the audience, who are drawn into the dilemma of the hero and are concerned with his well-being. The feeling of empathy in the play is strengthened in the movie's inspiration of emotional identification and moral support. Whereas ambiguity is characteristic of the play's attitude towards the hero, the increased complexity of his crisis in the movie paradoxically simlifies the issues, for the moral viewpoint has already been established — the hero is described as a helpless target being harried by an inhuman system. The environment, which in the play provides the background for comedy, takes on an adversary role, a persecuting force driving the hero to his downfall.

The positive transformation of the hero and the deformation of the cadres has the effect of polarizing the two sides. As the class conflict becomes a confrontation of the good and the evil, of righteousness and turpitude, the cadres can no longer be immune from condemnation. The incongruities between the false and the real are absorbed into the highly moralized and politicized interpretation of the conflict. The moral relativism of the play is thus displaced by absolute values, and the sense of fantasy is dispelled by individualizing the hero's struggle and by the presentation of details that are "oppressingly real," the foreboding milieu of conspiracy and gloom which muffles the comedic tone.

The negative judgement also becomes overpowering in the movie's ending, which is a complete reversal of the optimistic epilogue in the play. The despondent Zhou Minghua is seen wading more and more deeply into water, resolved to drown herself and the baby in her womb. In a dark jail cell, Li Xiaozhang stares fiercelly at himself in a mirror and poses the question: "Do I look like the son of a high-level cadre?" Recognizing the impossibility of the success of his image-making, he smashes up the mirror and cuts his wrists with the broken pieces of glass. Before his death he inscribes with his blood the words "If I Were For Real!" on the dingy cell wall. Close-up of the blood writing. The End.

The movie thus concludes with a pathetic note of protest against the victimizing effects of corruption and inequity. Hopelessness pervades the suicide of Li Xiaozhang, which is portrayed as an execution scene, a violation of innocence and a crime against the very humanity that the hero represents. However, any attempt to bring in pity and fear and to elevate his death to the tragic proportions of martyrdom is thwarted by the despair and sheer darkness of the outcome. There is no displacement of the immoral society, as the movie is unwilling to address the question of remedying the nightmarish and the diabolical. Treacheries, corruptions, and wickedness become unbearably oppressive, the permanent fixtures which stand in the way of the possibility of redruess.

The deletion of the ideal world permits a neater and tighter structure. Whereas the framework of deception of the play operates on the interacting levels of the play operates on the interacting levels of the structural and the semantic, the movie turns its focus on the latter, preferring clarity and directness. In a total disregard of the inherent ambiguities in the play, the movie treats as simplisitc the problem of injustice and special privileges, and in this manner, enables itself to condemn the cruelty and inhumanity of the Communist system in unequivocal terms.

If I Were For Real is characterized by tolerance and restraint. The avoidance of extremities and harsh criticism is comparable in spirit to the prevailing tenor in Gogol's *The Inspector General*, whose story of an imposter provides the inspiration for the Chinese play.[20] *The Inspector General* is pervaded by the atmosphere of light-heartedness, fantasy, and game-playing. The central theme is bribery and the corruptibility of human nature, but the ridiculous and the absurd which make up the satirical elements are less understood in moral terms than in the context of social conventions. There are no positive characters in this comedy of manners, nor are there any villains in urgent need of reform or removal. At the end , the bureaucrats and the townspeople, who have been the butt of jokes, are dumbstruck, "frozen" in a pantomine scene. They have been taught a lesson, but they remain oblivious to their own moral turpitude. Their world is fixed and gives no hint of its reform or displacement. In contrast to the laughable society, the ideal only exists by implication as the moral yardstick.

If I Were For Real is more specific and determinate in its didacticism. Sha Yexin, after the Seminar on Playwriting during which his play was criticized, insists that exposure, along with glorification, is one of the primary functions of drama.[21] The aim of comedy, he argues, is to "instruct through amusement," seeking to educate the people with "ideological entertainment and political education."[22] In the play Zhang Senior, performing the role of the "real" inspector general, carries out the instructive function in unmasking the cadres' abuses. His paternalism finds a counterpart in Sha Yexin's more recent work *Mayor Chen Yi (Chen Yi shizhang)*.[23] A eulogy of Chen Yi, the first mayor of Shanghai after liberation, the play describes how he stands for the moral uprightness of the Communist Party and its concerns for the people's welfare. Setting himself up as the modern version of the traditional "judicious official" (*qingguan*), he undertakes to correct ideological mistakes such as favoritism and selfishness. His humanity touches all classes of people, allaying the fears of the former Kuomintang bureaucrats and industrialists, settling down the intellectuals, and looking after the workers.

Paragons of morality such as Chen Yi and Zhang Senior are conspicuously absent in Gogol's play, for its impact is dependent upon the total
elimination of positive characters.[24] Klestakov, the imposter-hero, is a
study in pure mischievousness. An empty-minded scoundrel, he has no
real motive and merely enjoys his role-acting in having the whole town at
his feet. He is a functional character, a nonentity who has no story of his
own. The satirical targets are his victims, the bureaucrats and the townspeople, who are exposed to ridicule after Klestakov's disappearance. In
contrast, the imposture of Li Xiaozhang and its progress move the plot
forward. He has retained some of Klestakov's roguishness, but his
knowledge of his own wrongfullness also brings with him into the world
of the cadres the moral standard by which their actions are judged, thus
firmly establishing the play on the level of social criticism. The fact that
he is made to face judgement while Klestakov is able to escape unscathed
points to the strong didactic impulse of the Chinese play.

   If I Were For Real aims at the betterment of the social system and the
movie urges the destruction of it. In the absence of the displacement of
the abnormal society, the movie is close to *The Inspector General*, but
while the latter avoids explicit moral judgement, the movie insists on the
standard of moral and especially, political norms in its exclusion of the
ideal. The movie operates on a more personal level, and the hero's suicide
is a scathing judgement of injustice, the inhumanity of victimizing the
good in an evil political system.

   The Chinese versions of *The Inspector General* are structured in a
manner such that social and political interpretations become unavoid-
able. Both are more didactic than the original Russian play: one con-
ceives the imposter story as a social problem, and the other as political
propaganda. As for the two versions of *If I Were For Real*, the play
diagnoses the disease and prescribes possible cures; while the movie
merely flaunts the cancerous symptoms.

Notes

1.   A summary of the opinions expressed during the seminar is published in
Wenyi bao, No. 4, 1980.

2.   The play is collected in Beijingshi Wenlian Yanjiubu, ed. *Zhengming zuopin
xuanbian*, Vol. I, n.p.,n.d. Reprinted in *Qishi niandai*, January 1980 and in Li

Yee, and Bi Hua, ed. *Zhongguo xin xieshizhuyi wenyi zuopin xuan*, Vol. II, Hong Kong: Qishi niandai zazhi she, 1980. Quotations from the Chinese version are made from this edition. There are two translations of the play. One is by Edward M. Gunn, "If I Really Were", in Perry Link, ed., *Stubborn Weeds: Popular and Controversial Chinese Literature After the Cultural Revolution*, London: Blond & Briggs, 1984. Quotations in English are made from this edition. The other translation is collected in Lee Yee, ed., *The New Realism: Writings From China After the Cultural Revolution*, New York: Hippocrene Books, Inc., 1983. The translator of the play is not noted.

3.   Hu Yaobang, "Zai juben chuangzuo zuotanhui shang de jianghua," *Wenyi bao*, No. 1, 1981, p. 15.

4.   Lee Yee, "Introduction: A Reflection of Reality", in *The New Realism*, pp. 3–16.

5.   The movie was directed by Wang Toon (Wang Tong), starring Alan Tam (Tan Yonglin) and Hu Kuan-chen (Hu Guanzhen). It was also released in North America in 1984.

6.   Qi Xin, "Cong Deng Xiaoping guanyu tequan wenti de jianghua tan qi—jian tan huaju 'Jiaru wo shi zhenda' de shehui beijing". *Qishi niandai*, No. 120, January 180, p. 74.

7.   For a positive opinion on the play, see Qu Liuyi, "Yishu shi zhenshanmei de jiejing," *Wenyi bao*, No. 4, 1980; reprinted in *Zhengming zuopin xuanbian*, pp. 312–321. See also Chen Baichen, "'Huiji jiyi' yu jiangjiu 'liaoxiao,'" *Wenyi yanjiu*, No. 2, 1980; reprinted in *Zhengming zuopin xuanbian*, pp. 291–296. And Du Gao, and Chen Gang, "Huaju chuangzuo fanrong xingwang de yinian," *Renmin ribao*, March 19, 1980, p. 5.

8.   Hu Yaobang, p. 14.

9.   Hu Yaobang, p. 14.

10.   See for example Chen Yong, "Cong liangge juben kan wenyi de zhenshixing he qingxiangxing," *Renmin ribao*, March 19, 1980, p. 5; and Shen Minte, "Rang silu xiang shenghuo yiyang kuanguang," *Xiju jie*, No. 4, 1980. Both articles are reprinted in *Zhengming zuopin xuanbian*, pp. 297–306; pp. 285–290.

11.   Sha Yexin, "Che 'tan'," *Wenyui bao*, No. 10, 1980, p. 26.

12.   The definitions of "comedy," "satires," and "didacticism" are taken from M.H. Abrams, *A Glossary of Literary Terms*, fourth edition, New York: Holt, Rinehart, and Winston, 1981. "Satire is the literary art of diminishing a subject by making it ridiculous and evoking towards it attitudes of amusement, contempt, indignation, or scorn. It differs from the comic in that comedy evokes laughter mainly as an end in itself, while satire 'derides'." (p. 167) "A didactic work is one that is designed to expound a branch of theoretical, moral or practical knowl-

edge, or else to substantiate, . . . a moral, religious, or philosophical theme or doctrine." (p. 42).

13.   The Chinese text of this quotation is in *Zhongguo xin xieshi zhuyi wenyi zuopin xuan*, Vol. II, pp. 280-281. The passage contains a lot of word-plays which are untranslatable. Edward Gunn's translation differs somewhat from the original but excels in being able to capture the spirit.

14.   See for example Li Geng, "Dui juben 'Jiaru wo shi zhende' de yijian — zai Juben chuangzuo zuotanhui shang de fayan," *Jenmin xiju*, No. 3, 1980, p. 9.

15.   Northrop Frye, *Anatomy of Criticism*, Princeton, New Jersey: Princeton University Press, 1973 (c. 1957), p. 224.

16.   *Zhongguo xin xieshi zhuyi wenyi zuppin xuan*, Vol. II, p. 300. This is my translation. Edward Gunn renders the passage as: "I was wrong to be a fake. If I really were the son of Zhang Senior or another leader, then everything I've done would be completely legal." (p. 248)

17.   "Juben chuangzuo qingkuang jianshu," in *Zhengming zuopin xuanbian*, p. 323. Originally published in *Wenyi bao*, No. 4, 1980.

18.   Li Geng, p. 7.

19.   Adele Freedman, "An Ill-fated, Great Pretender," *Globe and Mail* (Toronto), May 11, 1984, p. 311. The review of the movie is generally favorable. Adele Freedman considers it "A love story twisted around a political fable . . . The lovers in *If I Were For Real* hardly ever touch . . . Their relationship is presented as a thing of fragile formal beauty; when things turn out badly for them, you can almost hear the sound of cracking crystal." This is perhaps an overstatement, but it demonstrates the stress on the love story in the movie.

20.   See Marian Galik, "In the Footsteps of *The Inspector General*: Two Contemporary Chinese Plays," *Asian and African Studies* (Bratislava), XX, 1984, pp. 49-77. He traces the history of the introduction of *The Inspector General* to Chinese literature and the play's influence on Chinese drama.

21.   Sha Yexin, "Che 'tan'," p. 26.

22.   Sha Yexin, "'Yuehui' chuangzuo ji," in *Xiju*, Changchun: Jilin Renmin Chubanshe, 1981, p. 277.

23.   *Juben*, No. 5, 1980, pp. 2-39.

24.   Vasily Gippius, "*The Inspector General*: Structure and Problems" in Robert A. Maguire, ed., *Gogol from the Twentieth Century*, Princeton, New Jersey: Princeton University Press, 1974, p. 249.

Glossary

Bureau Chief Sun (Sun juzhang) 孙局长

Chen Yi 陈毅

Chen Yi shizhang 陈毅市长

Deng Lijun 邓丽君

Deputy Mayor Wang (Wang fushizhang) 王副市长

Director Qian (Qian chuzhang) 钱处长

ganyu shenghuo 干预生活

hao baba 好爸爸

Hu Yaobang 胡耀邦

Jiaru wo shi zhende 假如我是真的

Juanjuan 娟娟

Juben chuangzuo zuotanhui 剧本创作座谈会

Lee Yee (LI Yi) 李怡

Li Da 李达

Li Shoucheng 李守成

Li Xiaozhang 李小璋

maotai 茅台

ming 名

Qiao Hong 乔虹

qingguan 清官

Qishi niandai 七十年代

ruanjin 软禁

san tuchu 三突出

Secretary Wu (Wu shuji) 吴书记

Sha Yexin 沙叶新

shehui xiaoguo 社会效果

xin xieshizhuyi 新写实主义

Yao Mingde 姚明德

Zhang Senior (Zhang Lao) 张老

Gilbert C. F. Fong

Zhang Xiaoli　　　　　　　張小理
Zhou Minghua　　　　　　　周明华

10. Tensions of Reconciliation: Individualistic Rebels and Social Harmony in Bai Fengxi's Plays

CONSTANTINE TUNG

Invidualism, in a society which demands conformity, is always perceived as rebellious. Individualism is clearly evidenced in many of the post-1976 plays in China.[1] But the expression of individualism is consciously restrained by the playwright who attempts to reconcile the tension between the longing and struggle for independence of the individual and the prevailing standard of social and political behavior. Often, the attempt to reconcile the two causes incoherence in the play. The plays of Bai Fengxi provide some examples of this.

As literature, few plays written after 1949 have given more reading pleasure than those by Bai Fengxi. In her plays language is beautifully employed, the action is under sure control, the characters are complex, and the themes are thought-provoking. Born in 1934, Bai Fengxi had a long theatrical career behind her when she was accepted into the North China People's Revolutionary University in 1949 to learn acting. Half a year later she became a member of the performing arts branch of the Cultural Work Corps (*wengongtuan*) of that university. But her very sophisticated literary taste and knowledge were, according to the playwright, cultivated in the tradition of her family, which can be considered a "book-fragrant family" (*shuxiang mendi*); when she was a child, she could recite many classical poems.[2]

As an actress, Bai Fengxi has played in many major roles such as the heroic young revolutionary martyr Liu Hulan in the play of the same name, the noble and patriotic Princess Wencheng in Tian Han's *Princess Wencheng (Wencheng gongzhu)*, the tragic and lovely bondmaid Mingfeng in Cao Yu's adaptation of Ba Jin's novel *Family*, Chunni, the honest and pure wife of a PLA soldier in *On Guard Beneath Neonlights (Nihongdengxiade shaobing)* by Shen Ximeng, and the mischievious and witty Cherubin in Beaumarchais's *The Marriage of Figaro*. Her acting

career, like that of many other actors and actresses in China, was interrupted during the Cultural Revolution. After the Cultural Revolution
ended with the death of Mao and the fall of the Gang of Four in 1976,
Bai Fengxi returned to theatrical life. Seeing that she had entered middle
age, she attempted to break out in a new direction in her theatrical
career, and she began to write play.[3]

In 1977, Bai Fengxi wrote her first play, "The Lamp in the Cave Brings
Light to Thousands of Families" (*Yaodong denghuo zhao qianjia*), a
one-act play in verse praising the late Premier Zhou Enlai. The play was
favorably received. Bia's second play *Lift Your Veil* (*Liaokai nide miansha*), co-authored with Wang Jingyu, was awarded a second prize in a
drama festival celebrating the 30th anniversary of the People's Republic
of China in 1979. But not until the publications of her two full-length
plays *When the Bright Moon Shines* (*Mingyue chuzhao ren*, 1981) and
An Old Friend Comes at a Stormy Time (*Fengyu guren lai*, 1983) in the
prestigious literary journal, the *October* (*Shiyue*) bi-monthly[4] did Bai
Fengxi establish herself as a playwright in post-1976 China who deserves
our ctritical attention. The two plays were subsequently staged by the
China Youth Art Theatre (*Zhongguo qingnian yishu juyuan*) in Beijing, in
which theater Bai Fengxi is a resident playwright.

When the Bright Moon Shines (hereafter, *The Bright Moon*) aroused
enthusiastic debates. A play of five acts, *The Bright Moon* has two equally
important and mutually complementary plots, but the heroines (there are
no male characters in the play) are Fang Ruoming, the mother and Fang
Wei, Fang Ruoming's elder daughter. Fang Ruoming, who is a chairperson of a women's association in a certain province, is entrusted with
the responsibility of safeguarding women's rights. She has two
daughters; the elder one, Fang Wei, is a graduate student in physics and
the younger, Fang Lin, is an English language teacher, both professions
well-suited to the post-1976 political direction, the Four Modernizations.
The controversy over the play, however, evolved around the life of the
elder daughter, who falls in love with her directing professor who is a
generation older than she. To make the situation more awkward, the
professor was the former boyfriend of Fang Wei's mother some three
decades earlier. The discovery of that fact is a shock to all, as falling in
love with one's own mother's former lover is clearly against accepted
social mores. But after going through a soul-searching struggle, Fang
Wei's determination in love wins her mother's support.

Love, as a drama subject, used to be unusual in contemporary Chinese
drama, and when love does appear in a play, it is often treated disparagingly as a background or an insignificant drop in the sea of human life,

and it has always been viewed by doctrinaire critics as bourgeois. As one Chinese critic wrote recently, "For a long time, this kind of un-Marxist-Leninist leftist restriction [on love as a literary subject] has had a harmful influence on literature. During those times, any work dealing with human sentiments other than political ones was invariably subject to criticism and accusation. . . . and love between a man and a women became a forbidden subject that could not be dealt with . . ."[5] In post-1976 years, however, a playwright's freedom has greatly expanded, and love is no longer a forbidden subject.

In many of the post-1976 plays that have love as a vehicle, there is the commonly shared attitude that love is not the focal point itself. It is subordinated to a higher cause and is ennobled by great idealism. In *The Treasurable Past* (*Zhenxi*, 1983), for instance, a four-act play by Xing Yixun, a young fellow playwright of Bai Fengxi in the same China Youth Art Theater, a woman engineer is assigned to an important construction project far away from home. Before leaving, she asks her husband to take good care of their friend, a female co-worker and former classmate, who has terminal cancer which is kept secret from the patient. The friendship is admirable though not unusual at first. What makes this situation interesting is that this cancer-stricken female co-worker is a former girlfriend of this trusting woman engineer's husband. The husband is hesitant to accept the trust, but his wife says to him smilingly: "You were in love with each other before. You and Youzhen would have married had not Ding Hao come between you two (Ding Hao married Youzhen but abandoned her later. This is another interesting point in the playwright's treatment of love). But that is all in the past (So she is confident that her husband will never fall in love with his former girlfriend!)." (Act I, *Zhenxi*, published in *Juben*, 6, 1986, p. 62). While the woman engineer is away for more than a year, the husband provides good care for his former girlfriend entrusted to him by his wife. Admittedly this is a moving show of a noble human relationship and a trusting friendship. Whether this scene is realistic, naive or simplistic, it reflects the playwright's very idealistic attitude toward love and human relations.

For many Chinese playwrights, authors of such plays as *The Disarming Moonlight* (*Yuese rongrong*, 1983) *The Waltz of Spring* (*Chun zhi yuanwuqu*, 1983), and *Atoms and Love* (*Yuanzi yu aiqing*, 1980), love conquers evil and selfishness, and it raises the lovers to a higher level of moral existence and consequently benefits society and the socialist reconstruction. In Bai Fengxi's plays, love is an individual concern; it is the focus of the individual's value of existence and struggle. It even pits the individual against society. But, in spite of the individualistic overtones, the playwright Bai Fengxi consciously or unconsciously attempts to prevent individualistic rebellion from breaking away from or from being alienated by the social collective.

In _The Bright Moon_, rebellious individualism is shockingly pronounced. In spite of the fact that the play has an all-women cast and that the playwright has stated that, being a woman herself, she has a natural concern for the well-being of women,[6] _The Bright Moon_ consists of a meaning larger than the stated feminist concern. The awareness of individual integrity and independence and the very determined search for one's own well-being in Bai Fengxi's plays are a most striking feature that makes the playwright unique.

Fang Ruoming, the mother of the _The Bright Moon's_ heroine Fang Wei, has a responsibility to look after the welfare of the women in her province. But, in a sense, Fang Ruoming is only an instrument of the Party and she carries out faithfully those Party policies that were determined from above. The playwright tests Fang Ruoming's ability and conscience as a policy executor by placing her in a sitution which involves her personally. Her younger daughter has a boyfriend from the countryside, the son of a poor and "uncultured" peasant family. When she discovers this, she becomes furious and upset, forgetting that her present responsibility is to help a young peasant girl to be freed from a marriage arrangement that she is being forced into against her will. In fact, the girl is in love with a city boy. Fang Ruoming is caught in the conflict between her personal bias and concern for her daughter's future and for "public acceptance," and her own responsibility to fight against injustice imposed on women.

What distinguishes Bai Fengxi as a mature playwright is that she does not attempt to solve Fang Ruoming's inner conflict by ideological argument and persuasion, a practice which has been employed by many other playwrights and which has resulted in more confusion than solutions. Fang Ruoming understands the importance of self-determination for individuals because of her painful experience in the past. She and Pei Guang were schoolmates and were deeply in love thirty years earlier (The time of the play is not given, but since the play was written and published in 1981 and the scene is post-1976, the "thirty-years earlier" is at the time when the People's Republic of China has just been founded). Fang Ruoming abruptly dropped her beloved when the Party became suspicious of Pei Guang's political reliability. Subsequently, for self-protection and public acceptance, she married a "red safety box" (_hongse baoxianxiang_), in the words of her younger daughter. Fang Ruoming did not marry for love, and as expected, her married life was unhappy and brief. Fang Ruoming confesses:

. . . it was indeed my life-long regret. But during those days, it was the only decision I could make. It was the early days of the Liberation, a time of high passion for the Revolution, and I myself was a 'hot blooded' youth. How could I bear it when I heard that my loved one was politically unclean? I truly believed that the time of testing had arrived, and I truly thought I must sacrifice love for revolution, and truly believed that there was a genuine evidence for the Party's suspicion (of Pei Guang), and I must make my own political stand clear, even though I loved him so dearly. . . ." (Act III, p. 185)

Fang Ruoming's confession draws no sympathy from her daughter, who sarcastically responds: "So many 'I truly this' and 'I truly that'." Nevertheless, Fang Ruoming's words reveal a profound sense of regret and disillusionment which are both very personal and political. The political source of Fang Ruoming's regret and disillusionment apparently caused some uneasiness to the political sensitivity of the playwright's colleagues when the play was chosen to be staged. Consequently, the performed version of this episode was altered. The Party did not suspect Pei Guang's political reliability and Fang Ruoming did not leave her loved one for fear of persecution or because of her political loyalty. Instead, the performed version follows a time-worn (at least in China) formula: public interest vs. self-interest. The two lovers separated because Fang Ruoming had decided to give up her studies and to go to the Northwest to join the Revolution.[7] Unfortunately, this version, done in haste, is inconsistent with the subsequent development of the plot. Thus the published version, rather than the performed version, is the accurate and true reflection of the playwright's mind, and it certainly reveals an experience more compelling, more immediate and personal.

The unsympathetic reactions of the two daughters to their mother's revelation of her painful past and regret are a further testimony against unquestioned individual submission to any form of public acceptance, even if the "public" is the Party. Fang Lin, the younger and more vivacious daughter, criticizes her mother's decision to break her relation with Pei Guang for political reasons as an act of vanity which has destroyed the happiness of Fang Ruoming's entire life. What Fang Lin is driving at is that one should be honest to one's true feelings. She asks her mother: "Did you have any of your own ideas?" (Act III, p. 184). And the elder daughter Fang Wei demands, when she is confronting the opposition to her relations with her mother's former lover," . . . Is it right that I must pay for the mistakes and sufferings caused by the previous generation?" (Act V, p. 195) The questions of the two daughters underline a challenge to the accepted views and the authority which is no longer infallible in their minds, and consequently motivate the drive toward individualistic self-determination.

In the final act, the words spoken by the mother to her daughter Fang Wei are in fact an introspective soliloquy that transforms her sense of guilt into understanding. She finally realizes that her fault was that she had lacked ideas of her own. This penetrating self-reflection on her weakness, past mistakes and losses, which is expressed both intuitively and analytically, enlightens Fang Ruoming and gives her a different perspective toward her daughter's love for her professor. Says Fang Ruoming to her daughter: "What your mother didn't suceed in getting, you should get. You are determined to your love!" (Act V, p. 195).

The treatment of the mother-daughter relationship in this scene is uniquely "contemporary Chinese." Eugene O'Neill, for instance, or a majority of the playwrights from the West, would very likely construct the triangular mother (Fang Ruoming)-daughter (Fang Wei)-Pei Guang relationship from a different perspective and delve into a penetrating exploration of the characters' psychological, conscious and unconscious, truths. But Bai Fengxi, who is herself the wife of an actor-director and has a talented actress-daughter, deals with this situation on the sociopolitical level. In Bai Fengxi's perception, the mother's feeling of shock and embarrassment is largely social, for a daughter's falling in love with her mother's former boyfriend is socially unconventional, if not unacceptable. The playwright seems to attempt to avoid any possible mother-daughter competition and jealousy, even though one feels the undertone of such sentiments. The playwright intentionally downplays any possible personal entanglement of this kind. Rather, she turns to a different aspect of human relations, an aspect which is more pressing and relevant to the playwright's own experience and/or longing and at the same time more universally applicable to the conditions of present day China. It is the liberation of the individual self.

The characters in the play repeatedly speak about "*yulun,*" which means "public opinion," and they blame "*yulun*" for not always being fair and just, and because "sometimes it even kills people." (Act III, p. 184). It seems to me that the use of the term "*yulun*" or "public opinion" is not congruous with the experiences of the characters, especially the experience of the mother. "Public opinion" is by and large social, but Fang Ruoming's separation from Pei Guang was political and caused by political pressures and motivations. In this sense, the use of the term "public opinion" in the play indicates the inseparability of what is social and what is political, at least in the pre-1976 years, or it might be the playwright's intention to de-emphasize the political. But, on the other hand, the use of the socially-oriented term "public opinion" does fit the tenor of the play; the assertion of individualism has a significance that goes beyond the political. As the younger daughter Fang Lin says to her mother: "Being afraid of public opinion . . . and worrying a lot are your weakness. I really don't care about public opinions. If I am happy, it doesn't matter what people say, I am still happy . . . If you are not happy, no matter how many people say that you are happy, you still secretly suffer . . . " (Act III, p. 184)

But this philosophy of happiness cannot transform itself into an experience to be shared by the reader/audience. That real experience is still very political, for Fang Lin says: ". . . for many years, who knows how many beautiful unions of love have been broken up and how much life-long regret has been stored in the hearts of the people as results of the ceaseless (political) winds and rains (*fengfeng yuyu*) and of man-made suspicions and doubts." (Act V, p. 192) The very basic cause of unhappiness and regret in life was the political condition of China.

The retrospection of the characters into the by-gone years also serves to verify a difference from the present, the condition of the poast-1976 years, which have become less political and collective, and in which one sees the rise of self-determination, a more rebellious spirit and less regard for social and political authorities. Granted, the Communist Revolution was rebellious, and the Cultural Revolution was rebellious in the extreme, but these rebellious movements were under the control, manipulation and leadership of a higher authority and a well-organized power machine, and they were totally anti-individualistic. Individualism has now emerged in the awareness of the playwright.

In *The Bright Moon* when another mother challenges her daughter to make a choice between mother and lover, the daughter answers: "I . . . I want him." (Act IV, p. 187). The play's heroine Fang Wei says to her mother in a more gentle but no less determined tone: "If you are really opposed to (my relations with Pei Guang), I will have no choice but to go against your wish," and she continues, "This is my business, and it is not necessary for me to convince you and to have your approval!" (Act IV, p. 189). The daughters' rebellious stands against their mothers' wishes imply a new social attitude and behavior held by individuals, to pursue and safeguard their well-being even against society and the authority which, in *The Bright Moon*, is symbolized by the mother. It is interesting to notice that in *The Bright Moon* and *An Old Friend Comes at a Stormy Time*, the mothers are all authoritarian, strong-willed, domineering and, sometimes, oppressive, and it is the mother, not the father, who is facing the younger generation's rebellious challenge.

The search for and pursuit of self-fulfillment of the individual are dealt with in a more complex situation in Bai Fengxi's second major play, *An Old Friend Comes at a Stormy Time* (hereafter, *A Stormy Time*). Artistically, the play demonstrates the playwright's more masterly control of the plot and an increased ability in dramatization. Although the play-wright intended to focus on problems a women often confronts in society (not just in China), it is again a play advocating individualism.

The curtain rises on the wedding day of Cheng Kang, the groom, and Peng Yin'ge, the bride. Both Cheng Kang and Peng Yin'ge are intelligent and ambitious students in mathematics. To enhance the romantic and sometimes melancholic atmosphere, Peng Yin'ge plays the violin, a scene which would be considered very bourgeois and decadent during the Cultural Revolution. As is the custom, the groom's mother, Mo Qin, who was a schoolmate of Peng Yin'ge's mother in a medical school years ago, comes to pay a visit to the bride's family. The two mothers haven't seen each other for quite a few years because they do not get along with each other. When Mo Qin and her son arrive, Peng Yin'ge's mother Xia Zhixian, a medical doctor now, is still in the hospital and has nothing prepared for the expected visit. A very career-oriented woman, Dr. Xia has separated from her husband, Peng Lun, who is also a prominent scientist. By contrast, Mo Qin interrupted her medical studies after get-ting married so that she could devote herself entirely to her family as most women do. In her eyes, Dr. Xia is a *guairen* or an eccentric.

The relationship between the two newlyweds seems to have a solid foundation: mutual respect for each other's academic excellence and career ambitions. But conflicts eventually occur when competition unex-pectedly emerges between them. Peng Yin'ge has not only passed the competitive examination for graduate studies together with her husband (what a joy!), but, because she is placed first, she has been chosen to study in Gottingen University in West Germany for a Ph.D. degree with full scholarhsip! Studying in Germany for a doctorate means not just a four-year long separation from her husband. A full scholarship, advanc-ed study in West Germany, and then a doctoral degree four years later for the wife are an intolerable challenge to a man's pride and the feeling of superiority that a husband has always enjoyed. "When she gets her Ph.D. degree, people will introduce you (on social occasions) like this: 'This is *Dr.* Peng Yin'ge's husband, Comrade Cheng Kang,' What are you compared to your wife? . . . " (Act II, p. 52). The basis of con-flict in well laid.

The husband (male)-wife (female) conflict is exposed as a family feud, and involves everyone in the family. Cheng Kang's mother Mo Qin is a dedicated wife and mother. She sacrificed her own career aspirations in order to provide her husband, now an influential official in the govern-ment, a worriless family life and to raise their son, who is now academ-ically succesful. She believes that a woman's foremost duty is to give sup-port to her family and, therefore she nicknamed her former schoolmate

Dr. Xia Zhixian eccentric. In Mo Qin's eyes, Dr. Xia's behavior and lifestyle are certainly very unwomanly and unconventional. For Xia Zhixian, her separation from Peng Lun was due to her resentment of his insistence that a woman's place is in the kitchen.

Peng Yin'ge is under pressure from her husband and particularly her mother-in-law to withdraw herself from accepting the scholarships which, if she does, will automatically be awarded to the next highest competitor, who happens to be her husband. Disappointed and angry, Peng Yin'ge goes back to her mother's home, hoping that her mother will render support. She protests: "I don't understand why the path of my life has to be determined by other people!" (Act III, p. 54). She sees only the uncompromisable contradiction between a woman's striving for a career and her wish to have a happy family life.

At first Peng Yin'ge did not understand what her mother had often said, that it was impossible for a woman to have both a family and a career; now she argues with her mother and says: "If marriage is a trap, I would rather get out of the trap!" To her surprise, her mother sternly cuts her short and tells her that her wish to get out of the marriage and to free herself for her career is selfish! The mother invokes her daughter's idol, the famous Polish woman scientist Madam Curie, who "shouldered the responsibilities of being a wife, a scientist and a mother, and who had neglected none of the three. She had a strong will and also rich feelings." (Act III, p. 54). The daughter is totally confused by her mother's unexpected change of attitude. This is also a testimony to the playwright's sensible insight into the seemingly illogical and unpredictable nature of human sentiments and thoughts, reacting to complex situations in life. It also demonstrates the playwright's skillful manipulation of dramatic surprises and crises.

Reflective and yet anxious, the mother says to her daughter: "Ai! Sometimes life is really deceptive" . . . (Sincerely) my child, whatever your mother said before are really not life's maxims, neither are they the truth you should believe. Why do life and career have to be so polarized? We should succeed in our careers, but we also should have a happy life. (impatiently) Why do you follow my path? . . ." (Act III, p. 54). Xia Zhixian's words reveal the deep sorrow, regret and longing of a woman who is successful in her career but misses a happy family life. Seeing an old family photo album beside her mother, the daughter suddenly realizes the hidden reason behind her mother's unexpected change: loneliness. The discovery of her mother's loneliness only heightens the conflict between the mother and the daughter. Now Peng Yen'ge, who has hoped for her mother's support, realizes that they are now standing on opposite ground. Angry, anxious, disappointed and in great pain, Peng

Yin'ge accuses her mother: "You are the one who is really selfish!" (Act III, p. 55).

Defending herself against her daugher's accusation, Xia Zhixian reveals her past to her daughter. It is a past in which a wife and her husband could not reach a compromise between their individual aspirations for careers and the sacrifice demanded on the part of the wife for the family. Consequently she made the Ibsenian choice and left her husband. Years later, however, Xia Zhixian, seeing her daughter about to take the same path, advises her to compromise and to make sacrifices. The mother's confession only reminds the daughter of her own childhood, when she had been sent away to the country to live with her grandmother so that her parents could be free to make their own life and to pursue their own careers. She feels that her existence was a burden to her parents.

With the exception of Cao Yu, China's most accomplished playwright, seldom has a modern or a contemporary Chinese dramatist been able to sense and to explore the deeply buried complex sentiments of guilt, hatred, love, admiration, and an urge for revenge that are harbored consciously and unconsciously. Bai Fengxi's characters are given psychological depth and complexity. Retorts Peng Yin'ge to her mother with a rebellious and retaliatory air: "To tell you the truth, I won't listen to you; I will take my father's advice." (Act III, p. 55).

Why take her father's advice? Does the daughter's rebellion or protest still need the support of an authority? The rebel Peng Yin'ge in Bai Fengxi's play is quite different from the rebellious Miss Tian in Hu Shi's "A Great Event in Life" (*Zhongshen dashi*) in the May 4th era. Miss Tian rebels against both her father and mother. It was Peng Yin'ge's father's chauvinist insistence that broke up the family, and Mo Qin, her mother-in-law, is enlisting her father's support to press her to give up her scholarship, to stay home and to let her husband go to Germany instead. But there is one more of Bai Fengxi's surprise! In a long-distance phone call to her father, Peng Yin'ge found her father on her side. Her father told her: ". . . on the path to career success, a woman will confront more conflicts and meet more resistance than a man will. You must have courage and persistence, and don't remind yourself that you're being a woman." And he gave an example: "Isn't it true that your mother has succeeded?" (Act III, p. 55). Her father and her mother have reversed their respective positions completely! Xia Zhixian, who was an Ibsenian Nora, now advises her daughter to compromise and even to give up her career aspirations for the sake of her family; her father Peng Lun, whose male chauvanism had driven his wife away, now encourages her daughter to fight for her independence and career and speaks with respect of his ex-wife. Why such changes?

Retrospection into past mistakes, which still bring agony to the present, is a major motif in Bai Fengxi's plays, and it is the key to the solution of the present conflict. In *The Bright Moon* guilt and regret for past wrongdoings convince Fang Ruoming that she has no right to prevent her daughter from pursuing her love simply because it is against "public opinion." Perhaps in an attempt to redeem herself from her "sin," Fang Ruoming not only consents but even supports her daughter's love for the professor. The same retrospection of past agony is the determining factor that changes the stands of Peng Yin'ge's parents when they are asked for advice by their daughter.

The playwright has so far displayed her profound psychological insight into the very complex inner world of Xia Zhixian, who is a mother, a divorced woman, and a devoted and successful medical doctor. The playwright demonstrates the strength and weakness in the mother's concern for her daughter's future, which for a while blurred her vision of the values upheld all her life. In her conversation with her old friend and arch-rival, the conservatives Mo Qin, Xia Zhixian pours out a moving and yet pathetic admission of her dilemma:

> You know very well how Peng Lun and I separated. . . .We lacked the mutual understanding and forgiveness, and we both were stubborn in pursuing our own careers. As a result, family life became a burden . . . I have succeeded in my career, but I have also missed the happiness of family life. Do you think that I don't feel miserable? Do you think it is a proof of my strength? Of course not! Therefore, I am worrying and anxious when my daughter faces the same dilemma, and I am afraid that she will repeat my mistake. Do you know what I advised her just now? . . . I even asked her to make some sacrifice . . . (Act III, p. 59)

Xia Zhixian's dilemma is overcome eventually by her strong conviction of the integrity of women as independent human beings, as she says to her daughter: "A woman is not a moon; she doesn't need to borrow (depend on) other people's light to glow." (Act III, p. 59). Her daughter echoes: "To have self-respect, one cannot allow one's own destiny to be dominated by others." (Act III, p. 58). Therefore, in spite of her sorrow for not having enjoyed family life as other women do, Xia Zhixian is totally opposed to conservative Mo Qin's ideal of women which, as Xia Zhixian points out, can be summarized in one old Chinese saying: "A woman without talent is a virtuous one" (*nüzi wucai bianshi de*). Being strongly committed to defending women's rights and independence, Xia Zhixian leaves the worry about her daughter's family happiness behind, and encourages her daughter to "radiate with her own light!" This is another dramatic surprise, in which Xia Zhixian turns away from her motherly concern for the daughter's personal happiness to a stand as a determined bulwark for the ideal she has lived up to all her life. The curtain falls with Mo Qin's angry accusation: "Xia Zhixian, you broke up your own family and ruined your husband and now you are breaking up another's family and ruining my son's life. You are an eccentric, a real eccentric!" (Act III, p. 59).

Bai Fengxi's dramaturgical virtuosity begins to strain in the final act. It may be the playwright's attempt to find a positive solution that fits the formula usually required in socialist realist literature, or it may be the playwright's conviction that creates a subtle inconsistency in the play's final act with the preceding three acts. In other words, it is a problem resulting from tensions between the intrinsic dramatic essentials derived from the playwright's keen observation and experience and the extrinsic socio-political considerations and/or the philosophical conviction of the playwright.

One obvious problem is the playwright's dramatization of Peng Yin'ge's struggle and dilemma in her striving for self-fulfillment and the social magnitude of the struggle set by the playwright. Peng Yin'ge's mother, Dr. Xia Zhixian, because she chose her career rather than her family, is viewed by people, notably her old friend Mo Qin, as an eccentric, which is a clear indication that Dr. Xia's choice is a behavior outside the socially and traditionally accepted norm. In this sense Peng Yin'ge's dilemma in choosing between career and family is given a social meaning: a quest for individual fulfillment versus social convention.

In the final act, Peng Yin'ge's father Peng Lun enters and takes part in the conflict. He was called in by Mo Qin as a supporter of Mo Qin's attempt to prevent Peng Yin'ge from going to West Germany; she expects that Peng Lun's own experience of having lost his wife will make him a dependable ally against "feminist" trends. But as I have pointed out earlier, the painful experience of Peng Lun only changes his view and turns him into an advocate of his daughter's cause, though not necessarily the feminist cause. He lends his support to his daughter. At the same time poor Mo Qin, while arguing her case with Peng Lun, gets a call from her husband. On the phone Mo Qin's husband "very sternly" tells his wife that he "is strongly opposed" to her attitude and supports Peng Yin'ge's determination to study abroad. This is another example of human unpredictability the playwright presents to us. Mo Qin's husband has been enjoying a comfortable and possibly happy family life which is made possible by his wife's sacrifice of her own career and adherence to the traditional social values assigned to married women: staying home and taking care of husband and children. She angrily reminds her husband: "Don't forget! It was because of you, I sacrificed my career. Now you are talking lofty ideals. (Tearfully) I understand now, people respect Xia Zhixian because of her accomplishments; they respect me because I am your wife. . . ." (Act IV. p. 68) Mo Qin's anger and sorrow reveal the dilemma and burden of a woman in modern times.

Now Mo Qin is completely isolated. But her isolation in the play makes Peng Yin'ge's struggle less dramatic and meaningful. Mo Qin nicknames Xia Zhixian eccentric, which implies the counter-social nature of Xia's life-style, and that her own stand represents the accepted view about a woman's role in society. Thus, throughout the play until the last act, the playwright pitted Peng Yin'ge, even though supported by her mother, against the force that is deeply rooted in tradition. In the final act, however, the roles of the antagonistic forces are reversed. It is the desperate heroine who gains the suport of the majority and is rescured by her father and father-in-law. The nature of Peng Yin'ge's dubious victory changes the signficance of her heretofore lone and determined struggle against social prejudice and traditional values. It is Mo Qin who turns out to be the lone conservative and appears to be an anarchronistic female Qixote without any comic effect.

On the other hand, Peng Yin'ge, the feminist fighter of the China of the 1970s and 1980s, is obviously not the Nora whom Ibsen created a hundred years before nor is she the very radical Miss Tian in Dr. Hu Shi's "The Great Event in Life" written more than half a century before. Whereas Nora fights single-handed for integrity and independence, and Miss Tian chooses her own mate against her traditionalist father and superstitious mother, Peng Yin'ge's determined fight for similar causes is presented in the last act as only following the prevailing social trend that has already made her opponent's position obsolete and vulnerable. She is not a vanguard of a new social movement; she merely fights the remnants of the conservative force. Consequently, Peng Yin'ge's struggle is mellowed and her heroic image which has been so successfully sharpened in the previous acts is also compromised in the final act. If my criticism of the final act is valide and my high opinion of the playwright allowed to stand, a question must be answered then: why the playwright has failed in the final act, or has created an inconsistence between the final act and the rest of the play.

There could be several possible reasons for this inconsistency. The unexpected intervention of Mo Qin's husband on behalf of the beleaguered heroine falls in line with the post-1949 dramatic convention in that the final solution to a dramatic situation always depends on the intervention from the highest authority. Being a veteran communist revolutionary and in a high position in the government, Mo Qin's husband, who never appears on stage, is a personification of authority who bestows justice to all even though, ironically, his successful career and happy family life are largely the result of his wife's sacrifice and adherence to the traditional role assigned to women. Furthermore, Mo Qin's husband is invested with the air of "husbandly" authority so that he can speak "sternly" to his wife. Without the support of her father and father-in-law who are the highest authority in the family, one may wonder whether the courageous heroine could ever have won the battle against the antagonistic force represented by her husband and her mother-in-law.

Realistically, the answer could be a "yes," and Peng Yin'ge could succeed in her fight. But Bai Fengxi did not structure her play in such a manner as to permit success to one who fights single-handed. In *When the Bright Moon Shines* and *An Old Friend Comes at a Stormy Time*, there is a similar conclusion for inter-personal conflicts between the struggling characters and between the protagonist and the society. In both plays, as they end, the antagonistic forces diminish, and the rebellious individuals enter a harmonious relationship with society.

In *The Bright Moon* Fang Ruoming not only consents to her daughter's love for the old professor, she even resolutely tells her daughter, when the professor has suddenly left, that she must find him! In *Stormy Time* Peng Yin'ge discovers that she has the support of all except her mother-in-law. The Chinese struggle in the 1980s is quite different from the struggle Ibsen presented in *A Doll's House* as Nora decided to leave her husband and children. For Ibsen, the society and the individual are irreconcilable. Nora declares that she has duty to herself and says to her husband Helmer:

> I don't believe that anymore. I believe that before all else, I am a human being, just as you are — or at least that I should try and become one . . . I can no longer be satisfied with what most people say — or what they write in books. I must think things out for myself — get clear about them. (Act III, p. 77).

And she continues: "I want to find out which one of us is right — *society or I* (italics are mine) (Act III, p. 78)[8]

In *The Bright Moon* the heroine Fang Wei is closest to the determined rebellion and individualism of an Ibsenian heroine. But, again, neither Fang Wei nor Peng Yin'ge has become a Chinese Nora or a Miss Tian of the 1980s. The playwright did not permit her struggling heroines to break away from their families and society. If Bai Fengxi were a Chinese Ibsen or a Hu Shi of the 1980s, she would be likely to have Fang Wei marry the professor or to end the girl's uncompromisable stand tragically. But she did neither one. The sudden disappearance of the professor at the very last moment prevents either a tragic ending or a clear-cut victorious finale for the heroine, but it is also a scheme the playwright used to save herself from taking a stand on such a social and moral dilemma. The playwright has created a very radical dramatic situation and her heroine is truly iconoclastic, individualist and rebellious, but Bai Fengxi stopped, hesitated and finally compromised at the very last moment of the play.

In *The Bright Moon* the social mores and customs were challenged but not violated by the playwright; yet the dramatic situation aroused wide controversy, especially regarding the relationship between Fang Wei and her mother's former friend. The play was premiered in Beijing by the China Youth Art Theater in October 1981. The play's director, Chen Yong, spoke of her opinion of the play: "As time progresses, changes of certain concepts have already penetrated into every corner of our daily life and they are difficult to detect. People are searching for the ideals (*lixiang*), love (*qingcao*) and morality (*daode*) of the new age. One must be creative to be happy, and one must be brave to be creative . . . [9] Chen Yong's words echo the individualistic persuasions and searches of the characters in *The Bright Moon*.

No sooner had the play been staged than controversies erupted. On November 5, the editorial board of *Zuopin yu Zhengming*, a monthly published by the Institute for the Study of Contemporary Chinese Literature, called a meeting with more than fifty invited participants from literary and academic circles and journalism to discuss problems of love as a literary subject.[10] On November 26, the *Guangming Daily* in Beijing devoted its entire page 3 to the problems of love in literature. Of the three long essays published on the page, two are on *The Bright Moon*. The editor of the special issue explains: "In recent years the practice of literary writings has clearly indicated that how to deal with love in literature has become a problem related to the healthy development of our socialist literature, a problem which deserves our attention. . . . "[11] At the same time, the Board of Editors of the *Juben*, a monthly published by the Chinese Dramatists Association, also called a meeting, in which Bai Fengxi was invited to participate, on "How to Correctly Present Love In Dramatic Works" (*Xiju zuopin ruhe miaoxie aiqing*).[12] Numerous essays on the subject also appeared in other periodicals and newspapers.

Though the focus of the controversy was on the proper treatment of love in drama and literature, the real point in question was on an individual's relations with society. *The Bright Moon's* stage director Chen Yong had already disclosed the play's individualistic implications; love, as the subject of the play, is in fact a vehicle of the individualistic striving for a life according to one's own perception and belief. People who are critical of *The Bright Moon* are particularly alarmed by the play's anti-traditional and anti-establishment messages.

In repudiating a proponent of *The Bright Moon*, who cited Engels'
words to support his stand on more freedom for love[13] Du Gao, a func-
tionary of the Chinese Dramatists Association, argues: "Engels explained
the lack of freedom of marriage caused by the economic relationship in
capitalism from the viewpoint of historical materialism, but he never
claimed that after the end of the capitalist production relationship, there
would emerge a kind of absolute freedom of marriage that subjects itself
to no restrictions of social relations and social morality." And Mr. Du
Gao continues:

> Today, to propagate absolute freedom of love regardless of the demands of
> social morality, . . . to abstractly promote the destruction of all restrictions
> upon love imposed by the mother-daughter relationship, by the family
> structure, by our national tradition, and by public opinion, and to en-
> courage people "to take one's own path" can only create chaos in
> thinking. . . .These will bring harmful influences upon the minds of the
> vast majority of young audiences.

By quoting Hu Yaobang's speech at the February 1980 meeting on
writing plays, in which Hu said that "generally speaking, problems of
love cannot be separated from society," Du Gao demands that the playwright "correctly reflect the real life of society and correctly represent the
moral and ethical ideals of society in dealing with love themes. These will
be helpful to the reconstruction of the socialist spiritual civilization of
our people. Seen from this point-of-view, the mother-daughter love entanglement in *The Bright Moon* presents the playwright's false ideal, pro-
claiming that love can break all social restraints. This is not a kind of new
thought."[14]
Some supporters and sympathizers of *The Bright Moon* indeed expressed their view in the individualistic and rebellious strain. Said one:
"Marriage should be a union of love. If sentiments of love were developed between two people in the midst of their common careers, and if
they loved each other truthfully, then social status, wealth, age, work,
public opinion and criticism should not become obstacles to their love.
To enjoy real love is a person's most basic right. If it does not violate the
social moral norms and the law, other people should not and have no
right to intervene."[15] There were others who praised the playwright's
courage for challenging the traditional and socially accepted concept.[16]
Tian Fen, another noted woman playwright and a colleague of Bai
Fengxi in the China Youth Art Theater, was outspoken and straightfor-
ward in defending the play: "Let bygones be bygones, the creation of a
future will depend on people's use of new ideals, new concepts, new
morality and customs. If love does not cause harm to others and is good
for the careers of the two persons and can give strength to both of them,
it deserves our support."[17]

A Stormy Time deals with the dilemma of choosing between family and career, and on a higher level, conflict between individual self-determination and society's demands for conformity. Bai Fengxi solves this universal conflict and dilemma not by an either/or choice but by a compromise so that one can have both a career and a family. Since the ideal situation cannot be actualized, the playwright takes a philosophical approach. Peng Lun, the heroine's father, who has grown wise, advises the young couple: "Success in careers can only add more glow (happiness) to married life!" (Act IV, p. 69)

The father's advice is not really convincing, since the parents' own career successes were made by sacrificing the family, and Mo Qin's happy family life has resulted from her giving up her career goals. Peng Lun's advice is in fact the voice of the playwright who believes and hopes that a woman's pursuit of a career can be in harmony with her instinctive and social need for a happy family (social) life. Being a woman herself, Bai Fengxi has an intuitive understanding and sympathy for the difficulties and dilemmas a woman faces.

An influential factor which affected Bai Fengxi's concluding *A Stormy Time* with a compromise could be Bai Fengxi's own personal experience. With a successful acting career behind her, and having begun a new but already outstanding undertaking in playwriting, Bai Fengxi has given me the impression that she has a contented family life. In terms of fame, that of Bain Fengxi seems to have exceeded her husband's and yet her family's togetherness remains intact. From her own experience, Bai Fengxi may have found it possible for a career-accomplished wife to live compatibly with her husband. Yet, Bai's own fortunate experience does not seem to enable her to offer concrete advice to the less fortunate ones such as Pen Yin'ge and Cheng Kang in the play; obviously one's own experiences may not provide one with analytical perceptions of the problems of others. Thus, Bai Fengxi has set forth thought-provoking problems but has been hesitant to let the drama, the plot of the play, develop according to its own course and to make Peng Yin'ge's struggle more significant dramatically. Her artistic objectivity is overcome by her personal wishes, and consequently weakens the play's dramatic impact.

Peng Yin'ge's victory, if it is real victory, is ambiguous. Her father supports her wish to go to study in West Germany, but this does not guarantee that her husband or her domineering mother-in-law would accept this decision. And she hesitates. Her father promises confidently: "Him, . . . I will be responsible for convincing him. (To Yin'ge) Your father will do his best to make you two understand each other profoundly." (Act IV, p. 69). But one doubts the young couple can achieve the vital mutual understanding that would enable the husband to stay home willingly and allow his wife to study abroad and eventually to surpass him in the profession he shares with her. The father, actually the playwright herself, finds no better solution and can only comfort the heroine wishfully: "To forgive and to understand (*liangjie*)! Forgiveness and understanding can create miracles . . . "(p. 69) Again, one would question further: on what basis can forgiveness and understanding be achieved? The conflict remains unsolved. The playwright ends it with a philosophical comfort that gives an unassured truce to an eternal conflict.

Bei Fengxi's two plays have challenged the traditions and moral codes of a stubborn society. Although the two plays end with moderation, the heroines' moral convictions and courageous struggles are the manifestations of the daring quests of individualism that have begun to flourish in post-Mao China.

Notes

1. I have an essay discussing some aspects of individualism in post-Mao China in "From *The Loyal Hearts* to *By the Gold Water Bridge*: The Changing Political Perception of the Chinese Playwright in post-Mao China," published in *The Journal of Chinese Studies*, (September 1984), I, 3, 313-324.

2. Letter from Bai Fengxi, April 21, 1984.

3. Letter from Bai Fengxi, December 21, 1983.

4. My discussions of the two plays are based on the following versions: *Mingyue Chuzhao Ren* (When the Bright Moon Shines), in *Shiyue*, 1981, no. 4, pp. 170-196. *Fengyu Guren Lai* (An Old Friend Comes at a Stormy Time), *Shiyue*, No. 1, pp. 38-69.

5. Tang Zhi, "Wenxuezhongde Renxing yu Rendaozhuyide Wenti — Du Hu Qiaomu Tongzhi 'Guanyu Rendaozhuyi he Yihua Wenti' Biji" (Problems of Human Nature and Humanitarianism in Literature: Notes on Reading Comrade Hu Qiaomu's 'Problems Concerning Humanitarianism and Alienation.'" *Wenyi Bao*, 1984, No. 4, pp. 32-33.

6. Letter from Bai Fengxi, December 21, 1983.

7. Comments on the performed version of *Mingyue Chuzhao Ren*, See Liu Zhengxin, "*Mingyue Chuzhao Ren Faren Shensi' (When the Bright Moon Shines* Inspires People to Think), *Juben*, (December 1982) No. 12, pp. 43-44.

8. *A Doll's House*, in *Six Plays by Henrik Ibsen*, translated by Eva Le Gallienne, The Modern Library, 1957.

9. "Daoyande Hua" (The Director's Words), *Mingyue Chuzhao Ren* (The Bright Moon Playbill) Zhongguo Qingnian Yishu Juyuan, October 1981.

10, *Guangming Ribao (The Guangmind Daily)*, November 26, 1981, p. 3.

11. Ibid.

12. *Juben*, (December 1981) No. 12, pp. 32–44.

13. Wang Chunyuan, "Ba Mei Daido Shenghuozhong Qu" (Bring Beauty to Life), *Renmin Xiju*, (November 1981) No. 11, p. 8.

14. Du Gao, "Ping *Mingyue Chuzhao Rende* Munü Aiqing Jiuge" (Commenting on the Mother-Daughter Love Entanglement in *The Bright Moon*), *Renmin Xiju* (December 1981) No. 12, p. 19.

15. Liu Zhengxin, op. cit., p. 43.

16. Lin Yuxi, "Jiaojiao Mingyue; Genggeng Danxin – Tan *Mingyue Chuzhao Ren* zhong Fang Ruomingde Xingxiang Suzao" (The Clear Moon; the Unforsaken Faithful Hearts – A Discussion on the Making of the Image of Fang Ruoming), *Guangming Ribao*, November 26, 1981, p. 3.

17. Ai Ye (Tian Fen), "Mingyue Chuzhao Ren Gei Wode Meigan he Sikao" (The Beautiful Feeling and Thought Given to Me by *The Bright Moon*), *Shiyue* (January 1982) I, p. 256.

Glossary

Bai Fengxi	白峰溪
Cao Yu	曹禺
Chen Yong	陈颙
Cheng Kang	程康
Chun zhi yuanwuqu	春之圆舞曲
Chunni	春妮
daode	道德
Ding Hao	丁浩
Du Gao	杜高
Fang Lin	方琳
Fang Ruoming	方若明
Fang Wei	方玮

fengfeng yuyu	风风雨雨
Fengyu guren lai	风雨故人来
hongse baoxianxiang	红色保险箱
Hu Shi	胡适
Hu Yaobang	胡耀邦
Juben	剧本
lixiang	理想
Liaokai nide miansha	撩开你的面纱
liangjie	谅解
Liu Hulan	刘胡兰
Mingyue chuzhao ren	明月初照人
Mo Qin	莫瑾
Nihongdengxiade shaobing	霓虹灯下的哨兵
nüzi wucai bianshi de	女子无才便是德
Pei Guang	裴光
Peng Yin'ge	彭银鸽
Peng Lun	彭卷
qingcao	情操
Shen Ximeng	沈西蒙
Shiyue	十月
shuxiang mendi	书香门第
Shuangren langmanqu	双人浪漫曲
Tian Fen	田芬
Wang Jingyu	王景愚
Wencheng gongzhu	文成公主
wengongtuan	文工团
Xia Zhixian	夏之娴
Xiju zuopin ruhe miaoxie aiqing	戏剧作品如何描写爱情
Xing Yixun	邢益勋
Yaodong denghuo zhao qianjia	窑洞灯火照千家
Yuanzi yu aiqing	原子与爱情
Youzhen	尤真

yulun	輿論
Yuese rongrong	月色溶溶
Zhenxi	珍惜
Zhongguo qingnian yishu juyuan	中国青年艺术剧院
Zhongshen dashi	终身大事
Zhou Enlai	周恩来
Zuopin yu zhengming	作品与争鸣

11. *The Drama* Tragic Song of Our Time (Shidai de beige): *Functions of Literature in the Eighties and its Socio-Political Limitations*

HELMUT MARTIN

Tragic Song of our Time *and Ke Yunlu's Novel*

Lu Ye and his Drama Tragic Song

The writer and former rightist Lu Ye finished a play in 1980–81 which he first entitled *The Poet Who Died Before Dawn*, then renamed *Tragic Song of Our Time*. In his youth, Lu studied abroad for many years and in 1981 served as vice-chairman of a provincial league of writers and artists (*wenlian*). The text of Lu's *huaju*-drama was circulated and the play was staged and produced by his wife, Shu Hua, who headed a provincial drama troupe. It was first performed in March 1981.

Tragic Song of Our Time[1] is a restrained but unambiguous attack on the personality cult of Mao and its most pernicious manifestation, the Cultural Revolution. The idea of his *huaju* is to show how thirty years of government intrustion have utterly destroyed Chinese culture and how the Chinese tragedy—the miserable treatment of the intellectuals by the rulers—has not improved at all for 2,000 years.

The drama has distinctly autobiographical traits. The author creates a gloomy atmosphere by comparing himself and the main protagonist with the ancient "patriot" Qu Yuan. This can be viewed as a summary of the experiences of Lu Ye's own life and, to a certain extent, of the intellectuals of his generation. *Tragic Song of Our Time* was immediately seen by the authorities as a veiled but full-scale attack on Mao Zedong's ideology and politics. It conveyed—on an emotional level—dissatisfaction with the system and alienation from the leader and the Party. Lu in fact denies the role of the Party in matters of art and considers his responsibility to be to the "people," not to the censorious propaganda apparatus.

Lu Ye's play was given an enthusiastic reception, especially by the younger members of the audience and by "dissidents" — so called by certain opponents in the literary controversy developing around the play. It was hailed by some literary critics as an "epoch-making" (*hua shidai*) work of art. *Tragic Song*, however, was in danger of being banned immediately by the political authorities. Performances were resumed after formal revisions had been made, but again the waves of protest rose high. Indeed, the clash of opinions over *Tragic Song* was no longer restrained to the field of art; it became a perilous political affair. The authorities finally strangled the play by imposing three demands: No more performances, open criticism of the play, and a self-criticism by the author.

Fiction Within Fiction

As one may already have guessed, the author Lu Ye (whose name might be translated "his road is dangerously wild") is not a real person, just as his *huaju* drama *Tragic Song of Our Time* is fictitious. The Lu Ye Affair serves as the point of departure in an 85,000 character novel (*zhongpian*) that portrays the simmering conflict between the political and cultural leadership and an outspoken writer who has behind him a large amorphous group of followers and sympathizers. The political struggle as to how to handle a controversial drama in a situation such as that in 1982 is part of the novel *History Will Decide*[2] which was first published in spring 1983 by the imaginative and daring Canton Journal *Huacheng*.

The novel appears to have been circulated quite widely and, as a result, was reprinted and extensively discussed in the Journal *Works and Criticism* at the end of the year (1983). The authors Ke Yunlu and Xue Ke opted for the *baogao wenxue* reportage style to treat the general problems of the relationship between literature and politics under prevailing conditions in the PRC. Ke Yunlu is otherwise known in China for his industry novel *Thirty Million* (*Sanqianwan*)[3] which deals with efficient economizing while building a factory.

The drama *Tragic Song of Our Time* is thus another example of those phantom literary and intellectual products which have recently figured prominently in major works on controversial subjects relating to China's swiftly changing society in the eighties. In much the same way as *Tragic Song* is embedded in the novel *History Will Decide*, Zhang Jie's novel *Heavy Wings* (Chenzhongde chibang) integrates the hotly disputed reportage (*baogan wenxue*) by the journalist Ye Zhiqiu while portraying an efficient and reform-minded manager in her *zhongpian* novel *Ark* (*Fangzhou*),[4] in which she includes the censored film of Liang Qian. One may also recall the rehabilitated rightist He Jingfu, prototype of the modern alienated intellectual, and his manuscript *Marxism and Humanism*, which figures in Dai Houying's sharply attacked *Mankind!* (*Ren a ren*). Another example is *Endless Flows the Huanghe*, the poetry manuscript of the poet Yu Ziqi, in Dai's autobiographical *Death of a Poet* (*shiren zhi si*). This manuscript is actually a portrait of the author's former lover Wen Jie, the party poet who committed suicide in 1972, and is thus a direct reference to his partially lost *Flames of Revenge* (*Fuchoude huoyan*) which recounts aspects of the history of Xinjiang and Chinese settlement there. Works of this kind are thus either transfigurations of key intellectual ideas or are conceptions of China's fate and the future of the individual author. They are put into the mouth of the protagonist as symbolic and condensed "truths" (and/or plans for action) — but they also serve as political safety devices. Then again, they are, more directly, actual literary products, sometimes thinly veiled under new titles, in *romans à clef*, as in Dai Houying's *Death of a Poet*.

Lu Ye's drama *Tragic Song* also fits this category: it is a disguised replica of Bai Hua's film script *Bitter Love* (*Kulian*),[5] an affair which irritated China's literary and intellectual circles and was consequently very much analyzed outside of China.

The Novel History Will Decide

After the drama *Tragic Song* has been performed, criticized, slightly revised, again widely performed and heavily attacked for a second time, a special conference in the rooms of the provincial assembly discusses the play, with the author and his wife attending. First Secretary Fang, just returned from abroad, familiarizes himself with the drama, the arguments surrounding it, and the rapidly widening affair. After a new internal performance of the play, student activities from the local university lobby for a final decision in favor of "democracy" (*minzhu*) in literature, putting an end to the pressures on Lu Ye. Mouthpiece of these activities is the students' newspaper (Fang's daughter is editor-in chief!). The students distribute more than a thousand leaflets calling for a discussion of the case on the university campus. The provincial party committee and the school authorities try to block the meeting and *gong'an ju*, the Public Security Bureau, intervenes. Lu Ye declines the students' invitation to join, because their views are too radical for him. Secretary Fang reduces the tension by allowing the meeting to take place, and attends and speaks personally to the audience, with television relaying his speech to the whole region. Only then are the angry and eventually hesitant students given the floor. Fang declares: There are to be no further performances, ideological "help" is to be given by the propaganda department of the provincial party committee, and pressures are to resume on the author to give in and recant.

The novel provides us with the details of a heated discussion between Fang and his daughter, symbolizing the conflict between the authorities and the young generation. It describes Fang's prudent maneuvering and analyzing of the basic problem. The affair is now closely watched by the Central Committee, after having been further discussed in universities and cultural centers throughout the country.

Fang mildly criticizes the errors of his leftist propaganda cadres and especially those of the editor-in-chief of the provincial newspaper, Liang Feng, for "criticizing errors with erroneous methods." He demands appropriate self-criticism. As a kind of summary of the affair, secretary Fang, who is presented as a "theoretical authority" and "philosopher," writes an article which eventually becomes part of the large-scale official propaganda effort to defuse and terminate the affair. Such combined pressure isolates the author Lu Ye. In a way not very convincing for the reader, he suddenly wavers after Fang's intervention and begins to understand his mistakes (without recanting on the play, however). A foreign journalist succeeds in interviewing Lu Ye — after an internal row about the advisability of letting him do so. Lu Ye is eventually allowed to prepare for a European lecture tour that he has been invited to, on the 'History of Modern Chinese Literature.' The party, in short, has asserted the principle of guidance in the literary field but has also shown previously unknown forethought and tolerance. The author tries to convince us that the foreign journalist drops his suspicions about the suppression of intellectuals in China:

"All I have seen is true, everything is convincing. You certainly have problems, but there is also hope for the future."[6]

Even from this short summary, the close parallels between the novel *History* and the *Kulian* affair are obvious. Bai Hua's film script was published in 1979. The attacks on the script began in April 1981, were renewed during August and abated at the end of the year with Bai Hua's self-criticism.[7] *Tragic Song* was, as we have seen, first performed in March 1981, and the main action takes place two months later.

The transfer of action to the provincial level is simply a technical device: it gives the author more personal alternatives and unwanted parallels on the central level can be avoided. The national importance of the 'provincial' *Song* affair remains and is explained on several occasions in the novel *History*.

The author Lu Ye is, like Bai Hua, characterized as a former rightist who has only recently been rehabilitated and who succeeds in integrating aspects of his own life experience into his *huaju* drama. Even the title *History Will Decide* is an indirect allusion to an article by Bai Hua in which he defends his script, maintaining that only "after a lapse of some time"[2] may judgement of a writer's person and work be possible.

The intervention of the provincial propaganda head and the two-time suppression of the *huaju* in the novel is analogous to the internal CCP instructions given in February and March 1981, restricting criticism and banning "the portrayal of the dark sides of life"[9] by so-called scar literature.

At an army conference in January 1981 senior cadres asked for Bai Hua to be re-labled a rightist and expelled from the army and the party. In the novel, the cadres of the army and the propaganda department demand the same punishment for Lu Ye.

Following the parallels further, a second interpretation alongside the *Kulian* re-enaction can be given to the play: Secretary Fang Zhiyuan, now sixty, is an idealized portrait of Mao's heir Hu Yaobang, the liberally inclined representative of the active reformers in the Chinese government and the CCP. This puts the novel among the many literary glorifications of revolutionary leaders, written in response to the demands of an official cultural policy designed to consolidate the present leadership and to rebuild "revolutionary traditions."

Fang is new to his position as provincial secretary, just as Hu Yaobang[10] was when he took over as party chairman in June of 1981, after having been responsible for literature and arts policy in his capacity as head of the party's propaganda department.

Fang has to fight on two fronts: against the "leftists," who tend towards harsh measures and the use of methods mostly borrowed from the ultra-leftist years, on the one hand, and against Lu Ye on the other, who, with his grave indirect accusations, was incriminating the party and advocates of "democracy in literature and the arts" among the young generation. This conflict closely resembles the situation both Hu and Zhou Yang[11] were maneuvered into by the hawks in the army.

As a final parallel, we might mention the open protests at Peking University and Fudan University in Shanghai in favor of Bai Hua, corresponding to the unruly protest of the provincial university students[12] in Ke's novel.

This chain of parallels could be prolonged at random. More important, however, are the arguments of the groups involved. The novel reenacts the argumentation of the conflict in the PRC during 1981, either through direct dispute between advocates of the various viewpoints or by a stream-of-consciousness detailing of the reflections and though processes of the main figures.

Here I will try to evaluate the relevance of the novel on the *huaju* affair and the facets of its message.

The authors present themselves as loyal and 'elightened' followers of the basically moderate cultural policies of the present leadership. No critical, independent judgement is formulated in this 'argumentative' novel—unlike Li Tuo[13] in his comments about the dwindling importance of 'realism' as well as the impact of foreign literature on the contemporary Chinese literary scene, or Gao Xingjian[14] in his didactically simplified integration of Chinese fiction into the context of world literature. There is none of the ideological pugnacity which the sharply criticized Zhang Xinxin[15] demonstrates in her polemics against a patronizing writer of the Literary Institute of the Academy of Social Sciences. We do not find traces of the evasion tactics adopted by Bei Dao[16] in his exploration of new techniques in fiction, or Gu Cheng and others[17] in their search for a new and acceptable anesthetic, for a new and satisfactory code of "beauty" in the arts, or those other "modernists" such as Feng Jicai[18] who attempt to establish more flexible forms of independent literary judgement.

It is, above all, Ke Yunlu's answer to the expected and theoretically sanctioned literary exaltation of "contemporary" heroes and his sensitive and convincing portrayal and interpretation of the party's general secretary Hu Yaobang which reveal the main function of his novel: the legitimization of current policies.

Psychologically, this sanctioning of a moderate leadership and its cautious measures to attract voluntary loyalty, published in early 1983, have also become an involuntary commentary on the confused campaign "to eliminate spiritual pollution," which was launched in the fall of 1983 and graudally petered out by the spring of 1984.

The novel's function of legitimizing seems partially responsible for the tendency to embellish situations and persons, to display a sort of "utopian harmony." However, the depicted leadership techniques, the use of political flexibility and experience in handling complex controversies in the cultural field, cannot gloss over the fact that the basic problem remains unresolved. The party's aim to 'guide literature' on the one hand and the aspiration of serious authors to tackle topics relevant to contemporary Chinese society on the other, will continue to produce the same conflict in an alternation of new "affairs" and uneasy compromises, much the way literary policies[19] in the Soviet Union have during the last three decades.

Broader Relevance of the Lu Ye Case

The treatise on enlightened party leadership, as exercised in the handling of the affair over Lu Ye's drama *Tragic Song*, is meant to be applied on a much broader scale, transcending the 'problem-drama' (*wenti huaju*) and the entire *huaju* field. This holds equally well for other genres.

In a complex linking of reality and fiction, almost all art genres are involved in some way. In his film script *Bitter Love*,[20] the army writer Bai Hua deplores the fate of the talented painter and Chinese patriot, Ling Chenguang. The script, which was originally entitled *Sun and Man* (Taiyang he ren), is an expansion of the lengthy epic poem *Starting Out on an Unending Road* (*Lu zai tade jiaoxia yanshen*). Bai Hua, too, is an accomplished poet who compares himself to the semi-legendary Qu Yuan, claiming to have the same fate, as does the fictitious Lu Ye. It has been considered that Ling is in fact a partial portrait of the well-known painter Huang Yongyu.[21] The author Bai Hua and the fate of his film *Kulian* became the model for Lu Ye and his drama *Tragic Song of Our Time*. Ke Yunlu has sought to provide a solution to scar literature like *Bitter Love* in his short novel *History Will Decide*. The exposure of *baogao wenxue* is also implicitly involved, with Liu Binyan[22] stating that if the severe attacks in the Bai Hua affair had continued, the next target of the campaign against "bourgeois liberalization" would have been his own reportage literature.

In short, we find writers linking works of art from the fields of painting, film, drama, fiction and lyric. Ke's novel, in which he discusses the legitimacy of the harsh official criticism of contemporary Chinese artists and their writings, thus relates to literature and the arts in general. The perspective of the young novelist Ke, however, is even broader than this. The artist figures only as the spearhead of the Chinese "intellectuals." What he is, in fact, dealing with are the contradictions and the relations between the Party and these intellectuals in general. The artist represents the intellectuals. In a broader sense, we might thus include in our perspective even the natural sciences.

The novel actually attempts to refute the harsh criticism that a European journalist (and professor of history) brings up and discusses in detail with the Party secretary Fang Zhiyuan:

> Not since Lenin's October Revolution was victorious sixty years ago has a Communist power managed to maintain harmonious collaboration with the intellectuals for any length of time. Stalin failed in this endeavor, Mao Zedong likewise had no success; not one of the socialist governments in power today has been able to accomplish this. History will prove that the conflicts between the intellectuals and the Communist parties in power cannot be resolved by any leader of a Communist government.[23]

Functions and Limitations

Chinese literature has developed rapidly since 1978–1979 and serious writers have come more and more to see themselves in a new role. Literature has taken over, on a symbolic level, functions of social criticism which remain comparatively difficult to formulate in other areas such as journalism, the legal sphere, or the Peoples' Congress and the Political Consultative Conference on both the central and local levels. The active response of the audiences addressing "their" writers in thousands of letters and the insatiable demand for literary journals underline the new functions. Social criticism is expressed by these authors in a number of different forms.

New Functions of Literature

A. – Autobiographical confessions, often directly inspired by Rousseau, were one of the most natural forms the authors used to cope with their dark experiences during the campaigns. Yu Luojin's *Wintertale* and *Springtale*[24] might be referred to here. On a more articulate and reflective level, again Dai Houying's depressing document about the relations of a young radical and an elderly party writer in Shanghai, *Death of a Poet*[25] or her better known *Mankind!* might be discussed.

B. – While these confessions bear a more subjective introspection into the past, other authors have opted to more directly become the real historians of their generation and of their time, some even looking further back to the fifties. Shu Ting has very emotionally stated:

> At that time I swore, I would write a classic like Ai Wu's *Journey to the South*, to bear witness for a whole, an entire generation that has been Victimized.[26]

C. – A more journalistic approach denouncing the dark sides of society, inhuman bureaucratism, ultra-leftist vestiges and corruption, has been chosen by writers like Liu Binyan. Authors of reportage literature are easily trapped in the conflict between the official doctrine of emphasizing impressive progress and their own conviction that exposure is a crucial function of contemporary literature:

> And the consequences of a wrong political line have not disappeared . . . they continue to make a lasting and powerful impression on peoples' minds. They soil our sun and pollute our air; they create further tragedies, they even threaten and endanger the successes we have meanwhile achieved.[27]

D. – Politically less dangerous and controversial is the author's discussion of China's modernization process. This, after all, is a task the party has explicitly called on writers to fulfill. Jiang Zilong's novels or other authors' fiction in this category, such as Zhang Jie's *Heavy Wings*,[28] certainly cannot be called simplistic propaganda pictures of a new leap. In a critical and detached way, these authors treat the complex problems of introducting new management methods, especially on all levels in industry, and the human dimensions of this process.

One precondition for all serious writing has been formulated and reiterated, recalling discussions that took place two decades earlier in Soviet literary debate: what China needs, several writers have emphasized, is a literature of truth, not "half-true half-false" prose. Ba Jin, in his admirable memories in essay form, has probably given this demand its most authoritative form, making even him the target of hidden attacks from many quarters.

Literature's new functions have created considerable tension with "orthodox" political cadres educated in the leftist Maoist spirit; the more daring and outspoken writers have periodically felt the brunt of this, as our novel *History Will Decide* makes clear.

Strategies of Evasion

It might be helpful towards an understanding of the contemporary situation in the PRC to consider some specific examples of how authors have countered increasing pressure from the government to glorify the present and to obliviate the past. They have conceived strategies which take them onto more remote levels of discourse, thereby avoiding head-on collisions with the policy-making level.

Escape Into History

Historical themes have figured prominently both in recent drama and in fiction. While historical fiction[30] seems not to be a hotly debated subject, historical *huaju* drama certainly is. Plays written to take the audience back into some aspect of China's storehouse of annals, or dramas that choose their plot from recent history in order to glorify leaders[1] or events, are not what we are looking for at the moment.

Historical themes set during the last dynasties, during the Republican period, or after 1949, have been used as a "coded" comment on or evaluation of contemporary events. Indeed, this method of "oblique hitting" (*yingshe*) has been so common that it might even be called the main tradition of the Chinese stage. It is a convention we might label the "indirect way of being direct." The most evident case in recent history is Wu Hang's Hai Rui drama[32] in which he treats Peng Dehuai's opposition to Mao Zedong's radical policies.

During a conference on historical drama in Shanghai in 1983, playwrights and stage directors admitted that post-1949 historical drama has used history in a "way too direct and childish . . . to serve current policies."[33] Many participants have drawn their own conclusions and see current conditions in China as being ideal for making the historical drama "educational." For them, the "task of the historical drama is to rediscover history." At the same time, however, "oblique hitting" remains accepted, especially to those who choose to rely on the playwright Guo Moruo: Guo has used *huaju* as a "weapon" and "established the fighting tradition of serving the current revolutionary struggle." To be more specific, his drama *Qu Yuan*, written in January 1942, was intended, in Guo's own words, as an "attack on the darkest period under the Guomindang reactionaries"; it was to "revive the wrath of the time in Qu Yuan's time"[34] Thus, a skeptic quips, even foreigners,[35] before watching a drama in China nowadays, must first inquire as to who and what might be hinted at in a given play.

Due to the strict regimentation, playwrights and producers run into problems the moment they treat contemporary themes and controversies; satire[36] on the stage brings even more restriction. Theater people from the progressive People's Art Theater[37] have complained how difficult it was to stage *Who is Strong?*, a play that castigates corruption, or the existentialist *Absolute Signal* by the French oriented Gao Xingjian, about a young criminal and an unemployed *zhiqing* (educated youth) who attempted to rob a train. The experience of this theater's resident crew of playwrights is that authors of *huaju* easily become disillusioned and eventually abandon contemporary subjects, escaping into historical themes. Some authors do not stand up to the pressures, they "bury themselves in heaps of dusty paper" to concentrate on "historical style or traditional drama." The experts of the Art Theater regret that, because of the difficulties, "Some authors in our society don't care to write drama any more, while others switch to writing fiction."[38]

China's contemporary drama audience is thus confronted with "oblique hitting," a "rediscovery of history," and in many cases an "escape into history."

The Foreign Theme

Another way of expressing social criticism is through using carefully selected foreign settings. Generally speaking, the 'foreign theme' in modern Chinese literature already has a quite successful history. The late Qing novel, for example, satirically treats the machinations between foreigners and the Chinese.[39] The thousands of knowledge- and progress-seeking Chinese in Japan at the turn of the century were an especially convenient topic for many Shanghai authors. Scarcely heeded up to now, such "international settings" appear to have acquired a special significance, considering the similarities between the present modernization effort and China's large-scale, but only partially successful, attempt at change some eight decades ago.

The period of the Republic has produced many authors well-versed in a foreign culture; this influence is reflected in their writings. We might refer, for example, to the fiction writer and versatile journalist Xiao Qian[40], to mention just one of an impressive number. On Taiwan, thousands of intellectuals have been exposed to the U.S.A. since the fifties, with such contacts abundantly documented in the literary field as we see in Chen Ruoxi's novel about Chinese in the U.S.A., *Yuanjian*.[41]

PRC literature, however, bears the traces of years of isolation from the outside world, and in post-1979 writing, we find only the first, shaky steps toward "international themes" (*guoji ticai*). Science fiction set in Hong Kong, for example, a city the author Ye Yonglie did not see before the time of writing, has a rather unconvincing and pale effect. The increasingly popular travelogs, like Feng Jicai's report on England or Jiang Zilong's *Diary of Crossing the Ocean* about the United States[42] to mention only two, likewise fail to convince.

Liu Xinwu patronizingly counsels a "literary youth" (*wenxue gingnian*), who attempts an entire novel on people and events abroad — writing on countries about which he has not the faintest knowledge. Furthermore, in a climate with eruptions of latent anti-bourgeois and anti-foreign sentiment, as the anti-pollution campaign has shown, considerable courage is needed to tackle "international themes" in an acceptable way. Feng Jicai, for one, has experimented with his "foreign area." I do not refer here to the fashionable titles of his short stories "Italian Violin" or the partly autobiographical "Hungarian Bicycle," which has as its theme the eternal power of music and the dangerous adventures of a writer during the Cultural Revolution. Rather, a good example of a disguised criticism in a foreign setting in his story "Old Qiuli and Feifei"[43] about a clear-sighted hack and a dog. Through the dialogue between the cautious old horse and the arrogant dog who anticipates every whim of his master, the author castigates those who practice diastrous servility towards superiors and shows the awakening of a fool who has been used. For reasons of safety, the "master" is Russian — not a Soviet citizen but a landowner. Feudal Russia serves Feng Jicai as a convenient and extra-safe scapegoat for Chinese society. Significantly, this story was first drafted as early as 1972.

Forms of evasion such as those using the "foreign theme" are reminiscent of earlier techniques employing foreign literature as a decoy. In order to escape possible criticism, some younger authors camouflaged their writings during the Cultural Revolution and the late leftist period as "translations" from "safe" works of foreign literature. It is only a small step from the foreign theme to other realms of fantasy.

Science Fiction

Science fiction (*kehuan*) seems at first to be a very innocuous new genre, borrowing heavily from foreign prototypes, as Ye Yonglie,[44] the well-known science fiction author concedes. Science fiction was officially much in favor and was deemed a convenient vehicle for promoting an understanding of the mysteries of a technical world among a young audience.

However, during the campaign against spiritual pollution of 1983–84, at a special conference[45] on this genre, critics detected previously unforeseen dangers propagated by irresponsible *kehuan* authors. Some, to summarize, had spread corrupt bourgeois thinking, doubts about the socialist system and the leadership of the party, hostile views on mankind, and pessimism about the future of the world. They used robots and men from space as mouthpieces in debates on social questions relating to real circumstances and to satirize Chinese society. In one particular novel, a study group discussed all kinds of systems of thought, from Confucius and Aristotle to Hegel, but pointedly omitted Marx and Engels. Another controversial story, "The Eyes; Mysterious Pupils,"[46] has an old cadre using a newly invented type of spectacles, only to find that nobody around him is trustworthy, the whole of society being in chaos; this discovery eventually drives him to madness.

The criticism expressed at the conference was from the director of the Chinese Society for the Popularization of Scientific Literature. One of the editors of the official *Literary Gazette* made a self-criticism of the journal during the conference for having thoughtlessly overlooked the dangers of the science fiction genre. Thus, the campaign brought a warning to insubordinate science fiction writers. Considering the rapid expansion of the genre (over 400 works between 1978 and 1980)[47] and its additional popularizaiton by millions of *lianhuan* cartoon booklets, this form of camouflaged social criticism will remain difficult to control.

Dreams and Symbols

A fourth method of evading direct attacks, while at the same time expressing one's own feelings and doubts, is to take refuge in a world of enigmatical dreams, symbols, tales, aesopian parables, and allegories, which characterize either an entire work of fiction or major segments of it.

Zhang Xinxin, in her novel *Crazy Orchid* (1983),[40] portrays a town in its wild pursuit of these flowers, the inhabitants of whom are eventually all turned into orchids themselves. The story symbolizes China's recent craving for money and material goods.

A short story by Zhang Zhongguang[49] from the same year explores the deplorable meanness of a group of apes in their cage. At a famous restaurant specializing in ape's brains, this customer makes his choice of ape, and the dish is prepared for him. A brutal guard suggests parallels to the *niupeng* during the Cultural Revolution and to other concentration camps. Zhang Kangkang's short novel *Northern Lights*[50] presents multifaceted symbols of the quest for pertnership. Zhang uses fairy tales in her novel which take on a quasi-ideological ironical function.

Official criticism of such 'hiding away' during the *fanwuran* months is aimed at the pessimistic and nihilistic mood of Zhang Kangkang's fiction. Her picture of the estrangement of man from society betrays an affinity to Kafka's beetle or Ionesco's rhinoceros. Zhang's ape society is criticized above all for the depressing comparison between humans and apes, for the exposure of the cruel lust for power over others, and for the morose view of the world in general.

As in evaluating *baogao* exposure literature, the assumed influence of a tainted society on the audience apparently weighs more heavily and negatively with the orthodox political critic than does the impulse from such fiction to see things as they are: a warning as a plea for change.

Transient Words

A further outlet seems to be the transient spoken word, a method of evasion that is per se confined to the *huaju* drama and to the stage in general. Su Shuyang's play *Neighbors*,[51] treating the rapidly changing situation amongst members of a small community living in a Peking courtyard (*siheyuan*) since 1976, has been a considerable success. The written text has been adapted several times to the volatile political situation and has been substantially "tamed." Reading the printed version of the play, I found it quite different from the staged version I saw in Peking in 1980: the spoken dialogue had been saturated with disrespectful illusions and political puns — if I remember correctly. Similar forms of witty "transience" which do not figure in the printed text, seem to be common in this genre. In February 1984 I saw in Shanghai a play[52] using local dialect, produced by one of many amateur worker troups on its experimental stage. The play was about a housewife who considered the products of the pharmaceutical company for which she worked to be the "property of the people," reselling medicine to relatives and friends in the countryside. But the plot was really only a convenient framework for poking fun at official catchwords and empty political phrases. Every pun and creative misuse was met with vigorous applause. Again, I doubt whether the scripts of such amateur plays are available in printed versions. Such social criticism is confined to "transient words."

Withdrawing

An unconventional way has been chosen by a number of writers who appear to have lost interest in the tedious official discussions. They avoid participation in organized debates on recent topics such as the fight against "bourgeois liberalization," "humanism," "alienation," or "spiritual pollution." Authors like Li Tuo, Feng Jicai, Liu Xinwu et. al. have founded their own more flexible platform for discussing literature by publishing open letters[53] to each other. In an informal way, they argue particularly about questions of form. On matters of content, there is a seemingly silent accord among people with the same experiences and similar options. Thus, a kind of new literary criticism has emerged alongside the official evaluations reflected in the annual selection of prize-winning fiction. Feng is currently preparing a book[54] that will contain a more systematic survey of the most successful Chinese works as seen from the view of this informal group of "modernists."

Obscurity

Finally, a group of critical young writers has created a very personal poetry which is beyond the reach of the proponents of docile political verse-writers. At least this is the criticism levelled at them during the *fan-wuran* campaign. This is not the place for a discussion of their so-called "obscure" poetry,[55] in our context, only the purported or real aspects of hiding away and expressing their inner world as a kind of resistance against an unacceptable social reality are relevant. The theorists Xie Mian and especially Xu Jingya in his brilliant thesis *A Group of suddenly Emerging Poets: Modern Trends of China's New Poetry*[56] have pointed out that this kind of poetry, originating in the turmoil of the Cultural Revolution and in the underground literary circles of the seventies, reflects the estrangement of the young intelligentsia during that decade. The poets protested against conventions which "alienated poetry into prostitution." Their poetry is the result of "deep thought" and "bitterness." Discarding Lei Feng-style poetic heroism, they have opted for subjective introspection and a very personal psychology. What their critics attack as "obscure" or "strange" (*menglong, guguai*) is, in fact, very appropriately a "mood of complexity" common to this "awakened" generation. "Obscure" poets like Bei Duo, Gu Cheng, Yang Lian, Shu Ting, and Xu, who was himself forced to recant in March 1984,[57] consider themselves to be the "mainstream," formulating a new attitude toward history and the nation.

The motives of older established poets like Ai Qing and Zang Kejia for joining the *fanwuran* campaign and for criticizing their younger colleagues are rather complex. They saw a "serious crisis," castigating the youth for their "blind admiration of the West," for "lacking faith in socialism" and for their "unhealthy mood," etc. "Obscure," "strange and difficult to understand," they were "hiding in the narrow realms of their souls." They propagated "absolute humanism" and at the same time, "nihilism."

Very soon thereafter, these poets of the older generation had misgivings about their accusations. It was questionable indeed as to who had "turned his back from reality and his face to his inner self."[58]

The two aspects that have probably led the obscure poets to their distinctive poetic language are the quest for purity and truth, for a new aesthetic system, and the desire to seek refuge and avoid direct political involvement. In any case, the feud over these poets' art has ironically given their poetry much wider recognition than could ever have been hoped for.

Such subtle strategies of evasion have, of course, been received with much disdain by certain more conservative cadres of the "whatever type"[59] responsible for cultural policies. It appears to be quite another matter, however, to effectively counter such tendencies. No one can easily be attacked for using the dimensions of history, scenes abroad, science fiction or Aesopian symbolism for such evasive purposes; neither an evasive move into the transitory spoken word, a retreat into small circles nor the hiding behind "incomprehensible" poetry written for a tiny intellectual minority is an easily punishable offense.

Some cadres acquiesce with helpless threats: No matter how carefully the writers' real intentions might be disguised, they will be detected eventually and punished in due course.[60]

Fears and Compromise

Some writers have indeed given way under the pressure and constant fear that sooner or later their "serious" writing might lead them to face some kind of difficulties. They are also not convinced that even the most sophisticated strategies of evasion will protect them from the wrath of the doctrinaires.

Adjusting under such circumstances means making far-reaching compromises. It is possible to write the kind of "half-true, half false" (*banzhen banjia*) literature that Yu Luojin[61] has criticized. The authors' reactions are clearly demonstrated in the *huaju* scene of the early eighties: a revealing article in the official *Literary Gazette* (*Wenyi bao*)[62] in 1983 states that the favorite topics of the more cautious writers along with the general public are crime, detective stories, and love entanglements. A pouplar variation to using the evasion pattern is to take the action to Hong Kong, Taiwan, and to other foreign settings, attracting the audience with "low taste outlandish styles, abnormal clothes, hairstyles, and ways of life." Indeed, "low taste" (*yongsuhua*) and the tendency to "avoid real struggle" (*huibi xianshi douzheng*) characterize the new plays, which are produced in quite amazing numbers. In 1981 alone, for instance, some 4,200 of these plays[63] were published. In the final analysis, only a handful of these thousands of new plays find national, let alone international acclaim.

Other writers have found an effective way of ensuring the "safety" of a new play. They simply look around for fiction which has been applauded or at least sanctioned by the official critics.[64] As a result, such novels and short stories are transformed into new *huaju* dramas in a dozen versions.

The only kind of conflicts permitted in plays are "trifles" (*xiaoshi xiaofei*); real problems find their unconvincing solutions *deus ex machina*-style — through the sudden intervention of senior cadres.

Some playwrights proceed from the concept "You are good, I am good, he is good." A contradiction between "good" and "better" unfolds: a Chinese critic comments in despair, "we really are faced with a bunch of idealized heavenly kingdoms." He concludes that the memories of the former ultraleftist "theory of no conflict" (*wu chongtu lun*) appear to be still very much alive.[65]

This is how the same literary critic has characterized the complex situation with which the playwright very often has to cope:

> A number of creative writers have all kinds of misgivings in the ideological field. They are afraid and stand in fear. Some say: 'The trends in politics are constantly changing, writing plays on contemporary themes is really dangerous.' Certain comrades who have been criticized in the past fear that 'sooner or later the waves will close over their heads.' The mood is sullen, they feel restless the whole day. Even their families and friends urge them: 'a chicken that doesn't lay still finds food to eat, why do you have to keep on writing at all costs? This atmosphere has greatly curbed the spontaneity of our creative writers. . . .'[66]

It is all too easy for both the Chinese critic and the outside observer to make sweeping condemnations when judging those writers who have mended their ways by sticking to shallow and "safe" themes.

Liu Xinwu, who, as a former teacher, takes a special interest in children's literature and in the youngest end of the audience[67] as well as in the quanderies of young aspiring writers, commented in a very convincing way on the dangers of placing excessive demands on the contemporary Chinese author. Liu warns writers against following the current politial line too closely, against relying upon official documents and editorials when looking for inspiration and for suitable topics for their own writing. Such an orientation reveals only that the author lacks "depth," that he is incapable of "thinking for himself."

Liu Xinwu is despondent over the constant demand for the writer to "express his opinion" (*biaotai*) on the "most important problems in our social life," to be politically "the more daring the better": "I feel that literature and the arts cannot carry such an historical obligation for any length of time."[68]

Quoting Wang Meng, who has argued in his same vein, Liu Xinwu expresses doubt that the foremost function of literature is to help other people give vent to their anger, to oppose the darker sides of society, bureaucratism, and corruption.

Liu, however, by no means gives his blessing to the superficial writings of "low taste." Rather, literature has for him first and foremost an aesthetic and moral function. It should "reconstruct the soul" (*xinling jianshe*) and "produce confidence in life." Literature should radiate a "humanistic, all-embracing love." Apart from its obligations towards contemporary society, literature must explore the dimensions of history and of the future of mankind. Liu refers to Zhang Jie and Cong Weixi as writers with similar convictions: Zheng Jie explores the realm of morality and ethics, and Cong Weixi,[69] who writes on prison life and wrongly condemned persons, manages to portray suffering protagonists full of Christian-like humility.

It is Liu Xinwu's belief that purely political issues should be resolved through political activities, activities quite outside the literary sphere.

The new social functions of contemporary Chinese literature have resulted in smaller or heavier waves of political pressure, which have in turn led the writers to adopt strategies of evasion. But they have also forced some less resilient writers into compromises of varyingly grave consequences. In his novel, Ke Yunlu has tried to offer his solution to the constantly flaring struggle, and therefore, it seems only appropriate to return for a last time to his perspective on reconciling the conflict between literary autonomy and the government's quest for loyal compliance.

What Does History Decide?

Only "History will decide" who has right on his side in this conflict; the "orthodox (*zhengtong*) but not dogmatic Marxist" Fang or the stubborn playwright Lu Ye, who refuses to deliver the required self-criticism. Ke Yunlu and his co-author leave no doubt as to how they understand the title of their novel. Lu Ye is isolated in the end and regrets,[70] rather unexpectedly, his enthusiasm for "spiritual liberation," the "policy of opening up" (*kaifang zhengce*). He has qualms about falling into the traps of "bourgeois liberalization," of "exposing scars" and is concerned over his not averting the "crisis of confidence."

The "high level of democracy" (*gaodu minzhu*) in Fang's leadership, we are told, wins the final victory in this controversy.

Yet it is precisely here that the weakness of the drama-novel lies. The author himself has actually provided the argument against his own conclusion. Lu Ye's wife formulates this conclusion at a forum of the provincial party committee on the *Tragic Song* affair where she speaks in defense of her husband's play:

> Works are often rejected by those in power during the lifetime of the author, but after his death they withstand the test of time. Thus, history proves them to be immortal writings. Nowadays, we still have some "Big Sticks," who love to criticize one thing today and another tomorrow. But history has proven that with their critical reviews they will be quickly thrown aside. What remains are precisely those works they today criticize.[71]

Chinese critics of the novel have pointed to this weakness in the concept from another perspective. They seem dissatisfied because the work does not arrive at a decision on and an evaluation[72] of the play *Tragic Song of Our Time*. Such vagueness in dealing with a fundamental question may have been subconsciously tolerated by the author, but leaves a door open for the above conclusion of Lu Ye's wife (this would and does, in fact, affect the credibility, even the *raison d'etre* of the entire novel).

Fang's remark to the editor-in-chief of the provincial newspaper that had slammed Lu Ye's play underlines this weakness in plot development. Fang grumbles: "This affair goes against your wishes—but your criticism, quite to the contrary, has made a hero out of comrade Lu Ye!"[73]

We may thus conclude, in shifting from the poor ending of this novel to the actual confrontation, that similar conflicts in Chinese society will probably drag on for quite some time, flaring up and being settled as they threaten to become virulent.

Writers who have opted to express the "truth" as they see it are strongly opposed to the party's "guidelines," which advise them to take an optimistic view of the world and to look forward to a "brighter future" (*xiangqian kan*). This opposition is voiced in the angry comment of the octogenarian Ba Jin: He reprehends narrow-minded politicians who ignore "freedom for scientific research, for literary and art creation, and for other cultural activities as guaranteed in the constitution":

> . . . in the minds of these people, the constitution simply does not exist, they have abundant experience of handling our first and our second constitution, they are only awaiting a convenient opportunity . . . the situation is now excellent. But as to the significance of this adjective "excellent," there are quite definite opinions and distinct explanations. On the other hand, we are healing our wounds, on the other, we are fighting forward . . . By no means can we afford to become intoxicated with ourselves — again to forget yesterday. Many will be the times we shall have to pour ointment on our wounds.

Ba Jin then ends with a piece of advice for those writers who have become prone to compromise:

> Those who have been bitten by a snake and who get irritated the moment they see a rope, for them it might be better not to indulge in creative literary work any longer.[74]

While the Western critics will certainly agree with Ba Jin and back his verdict, taking into consideration the recent development of Soviet or East German literature, we have to evaluate Ke Yunlu's attempt on another scale. The 1947-born Ke, who published his first novel only in 1980, on the industrial reform situation, has — as a representative of the "skeptical generation" (*sikaode yidai*) — shown courage in choosing another risky but highly topical subject. He has, moreover, treated it in an intelligent and differentiated way.

Baogao-style novels like *History Will Decide* help us to understand the complex situation of the Chinese literary scene: even more important, they stimulate the Chinese reader into rethinking major conflicts over the new function of intellectuals and artists in society. Thus, the discussion about Lu Ye's drama *Tragic Song of Our Time* seems to me neither a superficial triviality nor a ritual phantom debate. It is a viable form of coming to terms with Chinese social reality of the eighties — as far as literature can provide critical comment or more symbolic elucidation.

Notes

Abbreviations

ZZ: *Zuopin yu Zhengming*
WYB: *Wenyi Bao*
RMRB: *Renmin Ribao*

1. *Shidaide beige*, originally *Shiren zai liming qian siqu*.

2. Cp. *Lishi jiang zhengming*, in *Huacheng*, 1983, No. 2: republished in ZZ, 1983, Nos. 11 and 12, with several critical articles on this novel.

3. On the author cp. Jiang Zilong's essay "Xiaoshuo zatan," in *Jiang Zilong xuanji*, (Tianjin: Renmin, 1983), pp. 379–80.

4. Zhang Jie, *Chenzhongde chibang*, (Peking: Renmin Wenxue, Dec. 1981), s. p. 240–241. The consecutive printings of the novel have been rewritten or considerably changed by the author. Dai Houying, *Ren a ren*, (Guangzhou, Huanchens: May 1983). For a representative article resulting from the heated discussion surrounding this novel see Zhang Jiong, in WYB., 1984, No. 1, pp. 35–38. His manuscript is entitled "Makesi zhuyi yu rendao zhuyi." "Endless flows the Huanghe (Bujin changjiang gungun liu)," is treated in Dai's *shiren zhi si*, (Fuzhou Fujian, 1982), see also Wei Junyi's commentary in WYB, 1981, No. 5, p. 141. Cp. Wen Jie's *Fuchoude huoyan*, (Peking, 1983), the text as far as preserved. On Wen, see the informative *Wen Jie zhuanji*, (Fuzhou, 1982).

5. The *Kulian* script was written in April 1979 in Guangzhou and revised during May of the same year. My edition is Bai Hua, *Kulian*, reprinted Taibei, New York, Yuanliu chubanshe, New York.

6. *Lishi jiang Zhengming*, chapter 7, p. 66.

7. For the following comparison, I have mainly used Anna Dolezalova's article, "Two waves of criticism of the filmstrip *Bitter Love* of the writer Bai Hua in 1981," in *Asian and African Studies*, XIX, Bratislava, 1983, London, pp. 27–54.

8. Bai's article in RMRB, Sept. 3, 1980.

9. Dolezalova, p. 30.

10. Dolezalova, p. 36.

11. Dolezalova, p. 34.

12. Dolezalova, p. 37.

13. Cp. Li Tuo, "Lun 'geshi geyang' di xiaoshuo," *Shiyue*, 1982, No. 6, pp. 238–246. The article was finished on June 23, 1982.

14. I refer to Gao Xingjian's widely discussed *Xiandai xiaoshuo jiqiao chutan*, (Canton, Huacheng chubanshe, 1982).

15.   See Zhang Xinxin's "Biyaode huida," (A Necessary Answer), WYB., 1983, No. 6, pp. 76–78; an attack on Wang Chunyuan's criticism of Zhang in WYB., 1983, No. 2, pp. 7–13. Cp. also ZZ, 1983, No. 8, pp. 62–64. A general report on Zhang is in WYB., 1984, No. 2, pp. 12–26.

16.   On Bei Dao see: Bonnie McDougall ed. and transl., *Notes from the City of the Sun: Poems by Bei Dao*, (Ithaca, Cornell University Press, 1983). On the author's fiction, see: Wolfgang Kubin, "A Liberary Manifestation of the Peking Spring-time: Shi Mo's The Stranger's Homecoming (1979)" in *The Hunt for the Tiger, Six Approaches to Modern Chinese Literature* (Bochum: Brokmeyer, 1984), pp. 161–181.

17.   I refer to "Gu Cheng's Poetry, and Criticism Concerning his Work" (Chinese Manuscript).

18.   On Feng Jicai, cp. note 53.

19.   S. Karl Eimermacher, "Literaturpolitik in der USSR," in the *Encyclopedia Sowjetsystem und demokratische Gesellschaft*, Munich, 1970.

20.   Cp. note 5 and Anna Dolezalova, op. cit.

21.   *Zhonggong yanjiu*, 1981, 14, 4; pp. 79–80 on Huang Yongyu.

22.   Liu Binyan mentions this in his interview with Li Yi, *Qishi niandai*, 1982, No. 12, pp. 64–76. I am currently preparing a German translation of this interview for publication.

23.   *Lishi jiang zhengming*, p. 2.

24.   Yu Luojin, "Yige dongtian de tonghua," *Dangdai*, 1980, No. 3, pp. 58–107. *Chuntiande tonghua*, (repr. Hong Kong, Yuanfang chubanshe, 1983).

25.   Dai Houying, "Shiren zhi si and Ren-a-ren," See Note 4.

26.   Shu Ting in *Zou xiang wenxue zhi lu* (Hereafter *Lu*), Changsha, Hunan renmin, 1983, p. 283.

27.   Liu Binyan in *Lu*, p. 54., Cp. note 26. See his collections *Jiannan de qifei*, (Changsha: Hunan renmin, 1982) and *Liu Binyan baogao wenxue xuan*, (Chengdu, Sichuan renmin, 1980). On *baogao wenxue* in general, see e.g. *Baogaowenxue zonghengtan*, (Chengdu, Sichuan renmin, 1983). A huge collection has been published as *Zhongguo baogao wenxue congshu*, Peking: Renmin, 1982) in several volumes.

28.   *Jiang Zilong xuanji*, (Tianjin: Renmin, 1982–83), vols. 1–3. Cp. also *All the Colors of the Rainbow*, Peking, Panda, 1983. On Zhang Jie's novel see note 4. A German translation of this novel has been published in a translation by Michael Kahn-Ackermann: *Zhang Jie Schwere Flügel* (Munich, 1985).

29.   See note 19 for the general background and personal information by Prof. Eimermacher, Bochum. Ba Jin's memoires have been printed as *Suixianglu* (I),

(Hong Kong, Sanlian, 1980), *Tansuoji* (II), (Hong Kong, Sanlian, 1983), *Zhen huaji* (III), (Hong Kong, Sanlian, 1982). See also *Chuangzuo huiyilu,* (Hong Kong, Sanlian, 1981) and *Tansuo yu huiyi,* (Chengdu, Sichuan renmin, 1982).

30. Wu Xiuming has written interesting surveys of contemporary historical fiction and edited selections. See his *Duanpian lishi xiaoshuo xuan,* (Changsha, Hunan renmin, 1983) and *Zhongpian lishi xiaoshuo xuan,* (Changsha, Hunan renmin, 1983). Feng Jicai has, to quote one example, written the first part of a novel on the female group of Boxers during 1900 in his hometown Tianjin, partly a parallel to the Red Guards Movement duing the Cultural Revolution, *Shendeng qianzhuan,* (Peking, Renmin, 1981); but he temporarily abandoned this novel for other, more urgent subjects.

31. Recent plays on party leaders include Sha Yexin's *Mayor Chen Yi*; 1981 saw the performance of the *huaju General Zhu De, Weiwei Kunlun* about Mao, and other dramas about He Long, Ye Ting, etc.; also two plays on Sun Yatsen. Works of fiction include *Shangdang zhi zhan* (1983), portraying Liu Bocheng and Deng Xiaoping, or the reportage *xiaoshuo* about an alleged "will" of premier Zhou Enlai, used as a literary form of protest in early 1976 (ZZ, 1983, No. 6, pp. 48–59).

32. On Peng Dehuai and Wu Han, see Jurgen Domes, *Peng Dehuai,* (Wiesbaden, Harrassowita, 1982) and Clive Ansley, *The Heresy of Wu Han,* (Toronto: University of Toronto Press, 1971).

33. WYB., 1983, No. 11, p. 63.

34. WYB., 1983, No. 6, pp. 64–70, esp. p. 67.

35. WYB., 1983, No. 11, pp. 61–64, esp. p. 63.

36. Cp. Yao Mingde, co-author of Sha Yexin's *Jiaru wo shi zhende,* on difficulties of satire in the PRC, *Juben,* 1983, No. 8, pp. 56–68; "Even though we may be restricted by life, we do not accept restrictions in our life," p. 58.

37. On Beijing *renmin yishu juyan* see: Wyb. 1983, No. 1, pp. 64–66; Gao Xingjian's play is reprinted and discussed in Gao Xingjian, Liu Huiyuan, *Juedui Xinhao,* repr. in ZZ, 1983, No. 3, pp. 17–36 with following critical articles.

38. See WYB., 1983, No. 5, pp. 42, 43, and 46.

39. See Marius Jansen, "Japan and the Chinese Revolution of 1911," in *The Cambridge History of China,* Vol. 11 (Late Ch'ing 1800–1911, part 2) (London, 198]), pp. 339–374, and A'Ying, *Wanqing xiaoshuoshi,* repr. (Taibei, 1968), passim.

40. See: *Xiao Qian xuanji,* (Chengdu, Sichuan renmin, 1983), vols. 1 and 2, especially his reportage literature in vol. 2. See also the autobiographical parts in his *Yiben tuisede xiangce,* (Hong Kong, Sanlian, 1981).

41. Cp. Chen Ruoxi's novel *Tuwei,* (Hong Kong, Sanlian, 1983), depicting the life of a famous Chinese-born literary historian in the U.S.A., or Chen's new

Yuanjian, (Hong Kong, Sanlian, 1984), on the society of American-Chinese in San Francisco; see: *The Nineties*, 1984, No. 8, pp. 98–100. In the PRC, Taiwanese literature with foreign themes and otherwise is beginning to become better known, cp. the anthologies *Taiwan zuojia xiaoshuo xuanji*, (Peking Guangbo, 1981–82), vols. 1–8, and other publications by Fukian-People's Publishing House such as *Taiwan xiaoshuo xinxuan*, (Fuzhou, Fujian renmin, 1982), 2 vols., and the information from Feng Zusheng, *Taiwan xiaoshuo zhuyao liupai chutan*, (Fuzhou, Fujian renmin, 1983) and *Taiwan yu haiwai huaren zuojia xiaozhuan*, (Fuxhou, Fujian renmin, 1983), or *Taiwan Xianggang wenxue lunwenxuan*, (Fuzhou, Fujian renmin, 1983).

42.   See: Ye Yonglie's "Hei chi hei" in his selection of stories and essays *Leng ruo bingxiang*, (Fuzhou, Fujian yenmin, 1982), pp. 74–98, a murder story about gold in Hong Koing. Feng's report (with interesting sidelines on comparative drama) is *Wuli kan Lundun*. (Tianjin, Renmin, 1982). Rather simplistic and too general is Jiang Zilong's "*Nansilafu jianwen*", pp. 5–64, on Yugoslavia and *Guohai riji*, pp. 67-263, on the U.S.A., in *Jiang Zilong xuanji*, op. cit.

43.   "Yidali xiaotiqin" (Italian Violin) and "xiongyali jiaotache" (*Hungarian Bicycle*) are included in the selection *Yidali xiaotiqin*, (Tainjin, Renmin, 1982). For the autobiographical report connected with the bicycle cp. *Lu*, pp. 82–87. The story "Lao Qiuli he Feifei" is also included in this collection, pp. 150–57.

44.   See the essays and interviews and a survey of science fiction by Ye Yonglie in *Leng ruo bingxiang*, op. cit., pp. 137–175, especially pp. 161–167. On the genre cp. Rudolf G. Wagner, "The Real Future in the Passing Present, Science Fiction in the PRC," a paper presented to the conference on Contemporary Chinese Literature, St. John's University, New York, May 1982; and Charlotte Dunsing, "Science Fiction in the People's Republic of China," postscript to a selection of translations by Wilhelm Goldmann publishers, Munich, under the same title presented at the Cologne Workshop, to be published by Voice of Germany (Deutsche Welle), Cologne, 1985; see note 50.

45.   For earlier positive evaluations of the official journal cp., e.g., WYB, 1981, No. 15, pp. 25–27. The conference was held on November 22, 1983; WYB., 1984, No. 1, pp. 16–21. A series of more than 900 Chinese science fiction stories have been published: *Zhongguo kehuan xiaoshuo daguan*, (Peking, Renmin, 1983).

46.   Wei Yahua, "Shenqide tongkong," ZZ, 1983, No. 10, pp. 50–64.

47.   Wyb., 9184, No. 1, p. 17.

48.   Zhang Xinxin, "Fengkuangde junzilan," in *Wenhui*, 1983, No. 9. A critical article can be found in ZZ (1984), No. 2, pp. 70–72.

49.   Zhang Zhongguang, "Muxi bimanwen," a synopsis in ZZ, 1984, No. 2, p. 78. For the text see *Qingnian zuojia*, 1983, No. 10.

50.   Zhang Kangkang, *Bei jiguang*, (Tianjin, 1981), cp. Wolfgang Kubin, "Die Unruhe des Traums": Zhang Kangkangs Roman das Nordlicht," paper presented

at the Cologne Worshop on post-1979 contemporary Chinese Literature, April 1984. Cp. WYB., 1982, No. 1, p. 69.

51. A German translation of *Zuolin youshe* by Roswitha Brinkman has been published 1984 in the series Chinathemen, Bochum, vol. 19: Su Shuyang: *Nechbarn (1979-80) Zuolin youshe. Ein chinesisches Familiendrama uber die Periode des Umbruchs*, transl. by Roswitha Brinkmann, Bochum Brockmeyer, 1984. An analysis of different versions of the play is contained in Roswitha Brinkmann, "Politisches Theater im heutigen China: Vergleich zweier Versionen des Stuckes 'Nachbarn' von Su Shuyang (1979-80)." (Gottingen, 1983), unpublished MA thesis.

52. These amateur theaters seem to be a cradle for new talented playwrights.

53. See the letters of Feng Jicai, Li Tuo and Liu Xinwu in *Shanghai wenxue*, 1982, No. 8, pp. 88-96. Involved in the discussion were Gao Xingjian and Wang Meng. Cp. Thomas Harnisch, "Gedanken zur Diskussion uber literarische Schulen der westlichen Moderne und die Entwicklungsrichtung der chinesischen Literatur," presented at Cologne Workshop, see note 50.

54. Interview with Feng Jicai, 17 March 1984.

55. A convenient collection is Bi Hua, *Jueqide shiqun, Zhongguo dangdai menglongshi yu shilun xuanji*, (Hong Koing, 1984). From Hong Kong sources, I have obtained two manuscript collections of poetry by Gu cheng and Bei Dao as well as a collection of articles of the PRC press on both authors. A thorough treatment is given by B. McDougall, see note 16.

56. Xu Jingya, "Jueqi de shiqun — ping woguo xinshi de xiandai qingxiang," in Bi Hua, *Jueqi*, op. cit., pp. 97-129 (written January 1981).

57. Xu Jingya's self-criticism, much detested by his fellow poets, was published in RMRB, March 5, 1984.

58. Ai Qing and Zang Kejia's statements in Bi Hua, *Jueqi*, op. cit., pp. 171-72.

59. On the original "whatever" *(fanshipai)* group see Helmut Martin, "Cult & Canon, The Origins and Development of State Maoism," *Armonk*, (New York, Sharpe 1982), pp. 81-82.

60. On fear of authors see WYB., 1981, No. 12, pp. 34-35; on the deplorable consequences of criticism by name see ZZ, 1983, No. 6, pp. 72-73.

61. Yu Luojin, *Chuntiande tonghua*, p. 112.

62. WYB., 1983, No. 5, pp. 42-47.

63. WYB., 1983, No. 5, p. 42.

64. WYB., 1983, No. 5, p. 43.

65. WYB., 1983, No. 5, pp. 43, 45.

66. WYB., 1983, No. 5, p. 46.

67. Liu Xinwu, *Tong wenxue qingnian duihua*, (Peking, Gongren 1983), pp. 174-177 and interview with Liu Xinwu, March 24, 1984.

68. Ibid., p. 174.

69. On Zhang Jie's work cp. note 4. and *Zhang Jie xiaoshuo juben xuan*, (Peking, Renmin, 1980). On Cong cp. the four collections *Cong Weixi zhongpian xiaoshuo ji*, (Peking, Renmin, 1980), *Ranshao de jiyi*, (Peking, Renmin, 1983), *Yuanqude baifan*, (Chengdu, Sichuan renmin, 1983), and *Yiluo zai haitande jiaoyin*, (Guangzhou, Huacheng, 1982).

70. *Lishi jiang zhengming*, pp. 63-64.

71. Ibid., p. 5.

72. ZZ, 1983, No. 12, pp. 69-70.

73. *Lishi jiang zhengming*, p. 60.

74. Ba Jin, *Suixianglu*, op. cit., pp. 150-52 (essay No. 27); see also note 35.

Glossary

A Ying	阿英
Ai Qing	艾青
Ai Wu	艾芜
Ba Jin	巴金
Bai Hua	白桦
baogao Wenxue	报告文学
banzhen banjia	半真半假
Bei Dao	北島
Bujin changjiang gungunliu	不尽长江滚滚流
Chen Ruoxi	陈若曦
Chen Yi shizhang	陈毅市长
Chenzhong de chibang	沉重的翅膀
Cong Weixi	从维熙
Dai Houying	戴厚英
fanwuran	反污染

Fang Zhiyuan 方志远

Fangzhou 方舟

Feng Jicai 冯骥才

Feng Zucheng 封祖盛

Fuchou de huoyan 复仇的火焰

Gao Xingjian 高行健

gaodu minzhu 高度民主

gonganju 公安局

Gu Cheng 顾城

guoji ticai 国际题材

Huacheng 花城

He Jingfu 何荆夫

He Jingzhi 贺敬之

Hei chi hei 黑吃黑

Hu Yicheng 胡义成

Hua shidai 划时代

Huang Yongyu 黄永玉

huibi xianshi douzheng 迴避现实斗争

Jiang Zilong 蒋子龙

Kaifang zhengce 开放政策

Ke Yunlu 柯云路

Kehuan 科幻

Kulian 苦恋

Lao She 老舍

Lishi jiang zhengming 历史将证明

Li Tuo 李陀

Li Yi 李怡

lianhuan 连环

Liang Qian 梁倩

Ling Chenguang 凌晨光

Liu Binyan 刘宾雁

Liu Xinwu 刘

Lu Ye 路野

Lu zai tade jiaoxia yanshen 路在他的脚下延伸

Lun geshi geyangde xiaoshuo 论各式各样的小说

menglong guguai 朦胧古怪

Muxi bima wen 木樨弼马温

Nanxingji 南行记

niupeng 牛棚

pianzi 骗子

Ren a ren 人啊人

Sanqianwan 三千万

Sha Yexin 沙叶新

Shidai de beige 时代的悲歌

Shiren zai limingqian siqu 诗人在黎明前死去

Shiren zhi si 诗人之死

sikao de yidai 思考的一代

Shu Hua 舒华

Shu Ting 舒婷

Su Shuyang 苏叔阳

Taiyang he ren 太阳和人

Wang Chunyuan 王春元

Wang Meng 王蒙

Wei Junyi 韦君宜

Wei Yahua 魏雅华

Wen Jie 闻捷

Wenti huaju 问题话剧

Wenxue qingnian 文学青年

Wenyi bao 文艺报

wu chongtu lun 无冲突论

Wu Xiuming 吴秀明

Xiwang Chang'an 西望长安

Xiao Qian 萧乾

xiaoshi xiaofei	小是小非
Xie Mian	谢冕
xinling jianshe	心灵建设
Xu Jingya	徐敬亚
Xue Ke	雪柯
Yang Lian	杨炼
Yao Mingde	姚朋德
Ye Yonglie	叶永烈
Ye Zhiqiu	叶知秋
Yige dongtiande tonghua	一个冬天的童话
Yiluo zai haitande jiaoyin	遗落在海滩的脚印
yingshe	影射
yongsuhua	庸俗化
Yu Luojin	遇罗锦
Yu Ziqi	余子期
Yuanjian	远见
Zang Kejia	臧克家
Zhang Jie	张洁
Zhang Jiong	张炯
Zhang Kangkang	张抗抗
Zhang Xinxin	张辛欣
Zhang Zhongguang	张重光
Zhengtong	正统
Zhiqing	知青
Zhongpian	中篇
Zuopin yu zhengming	作品与争鸣

Part Four

Foreign Theaters in China: Two Case Studies

12. Austrian Musical Theater and Music in China

GERD KAMINSKI and ELSE UNTERRIEDER

The Period up to the 1930s

The first personalities from 'Old Austria' who made an impact on musical life in China were Jesuit fathers. One of them, Karl Slawiczek, in his report on his inaugural visit in 1717 to the emperor Kang Xi tells us of the vivid interest which the emperor of China took in European music. After a deliberation of the arts of mathematics and surveying, says the report, the emperor eagerly changed the subject to questions of music.

> . . . following which he sang to me the ut, re, mi, fa, ordered me to repeat after him, played on the clavicord, inquired about the various musical keys and, with abundant manifestations of his grace and benevolence, made himself heard playing voluminous *oeuvres*. . . .[1]

Florian Bahr, of Silesian descent and likewise a Habsburg subject, is described in contemporary reports as a master composer of organ music.[2] Jointly with the Bohemian Johann Walter and Theodorico Pedrini he set up a European-style orchestra recruited from young noblemen at the imperial court of China.

Letters written by Jesuits at the court of Peking provide information on another two topics: Firstly, that the Jesuits also introduced vocal music to the imperial court of China, which in all likelihood included samples taken from contemporary Austrian musical theater; and secondly, that the emperor of China took great pleasure in this kind of singing and playing music.[3] The exit of the Jesuits from China deprived Austrian music and musical theater of any chance to gain a wider sphere of recognition under the patronage of the highest level of authority.

New beginnings in the 19th century were not made under imperial support; on the contrary, they followed in the trail blazed by the forcible opening of China against the will of the emperor. In the Treaty of Nerchinsk signed in 1689 China had excluded the Russians from all territories in the Amur and Ussuri river basins. In the 19th century China no

284

longer possessed the strength to hinder the stride of the Russian bear. Chinese territories had partly to be ceded, partly to be leased to the Zarist empire. Russian subjects flocked into Chinese cities. In the places where they pursued their trading interests, they did not want to be deprived of European music. Again, it was mainly Bohemian subjects of the Austrian emperor who took the lead in meeting the demand. Their innate gift for music, together with the affinity of their native language with the Russian language smoothed their way as they speedily advanced. Soon there were so many Austrian subjects residing in Harbin that from the beginning of this century until the outbreak of war with China in 1917 the Austrian consular court in Tianjin had to travel to Harbin at least once a year to adjudicate acts of physical violence among the easily aroused artists. At that time, tunes from Austrian operettas resounded in many of Harbin's establishments.[4]

But during the late decades of the 19th century Austrian marches and operetta melodies spread even farther south. The municipal authorities of Shanghai were glad to hire Austrian military band leaders; the detachments of the Austrian (imperial and royal) navy stationed in Beijing and Tianjin since 1901 had their own music bands; and the vessels of the Austrian navy cruising in East Asian waters made their won contributions of Austrian music through musicians among their crews.

The First World War considerably increased the potential for Austrian music in China. Many prisoners of war escaped from camps in Siberia and made their way into Chinese territory. Quite a few of them had received musical education. Music bands manned by Austrian ex-soldiers were organized to provide background music of high quality for the silent films that were shown in Chinese cinemas.[5]

Since cinema going quickly gained popularity among the Chinese population, to the detriment of the less costly forms of traditional Chinese entertainment such as shadow plays and puppet plays, this 'Austrian monopoly' on cinema background music vastly contributed to the spread of Austrian operetta music. This influence weakened, however, with the advent of the sound film. But there were enough music bands who gladly hired Austrian musicians. Cities like Tianjin, or the fashionable beach resort Beidaihe, or Shanghai provided a surrounding in which visual effects and culinary accompaniments effectively complemented the offerings of Austrian music. Austrian-run establishments offered specialities of Austrian cuisine in the settings of Austrian-style decor.

The most famous of these was Kiessling and Bader, with branch establishments in Beijing, Nanjing, Tianjin, Beidaihe and Shanghai. It came into Austrian ownership in 1928 when Robert Toebich, an ex-member of the Austrian vessel *Kaiserin Elisabeth* (which had once been positioned in Far-Eastern waters), married into the business and saw to it that in his establishments Austrian music of adequate standards was expertly played by his Austrian countrymen.

In this respect Austrian residents in China distinguished themselves from German residents. The German community concentrated on cultivating the language-based stage play. Proof of this can be found in the special issue of *Bühnenspiegel in Fernen Osten* (Stage Mirror in the Far East) published by the Deutscher Theaterverein (German Theater Society) in 1929–1930.

Naturally enough, spoken stage plays in the German language were hardly suitable material for building cultural bridges to the majority of the Chinese poupulation. Probably they were not even intended to build such bridges. It was to be theater by Germans for Germans.[7] This may be concluded on the one hand from the haughty lines dedicated by Vinzenz von Hundhausen to the *State Mirror in the Far East*,[8] and on the other hand from the fact that the only Chinese mentioned in the special issue is the stage carpenter Ah Yuen.[9] The Austrian community did not want to be deprived of their operettas. G.F. Gmehling, the famour Austrian painter who was an antiques dealer by profession, directed with great success amateur performances of Viennese operettas. Here the universal appeal of the sound of music came into play, reaching out to Chinese audiences to whom the sound of the German language was incomprehensible.[10]

The presence of the Viennese operetta in China was soon receive a powerful impetus from the beginning immigration of renowned professionals of the Austrian musical theater. At that time, the reputation of Austrian music was already well established in China even beyond the boundaries of the operetta. In the early Thirties the president of Nanjing Central University, Zhu Jiahua, insisted on addressing to Austria a request for the delegation of a professor of music, overruling thereby the opposition of the head of the department of music, who had received *his* musical education in France.[11]

Guest performances by Austrian musicians, such as the violin virtuoso Robert Pollak in 1934, attracted considerable attention in China.[12] Such contacts were not limited to a one-way movement. In the Thirties Chinese students came to Vienna to study music. Among them was one Ma Weizhi[13] but most notably Li Weining, who came from the Shanghi conservatory. At the Vienna Conservatory he studied composition with professors Josef Marx and Karl Weigl. Li won the first prize in the state examination. Austrian radio broadcast samples of his works: songs based on ancient Chinese poems ('The Fisherman' by Zhang Zhihe, 'Complaint on Life in Imprisonment' by Li Yu) as well as the song of the fisherman from 'Wilhelm Tell' (as rendered by Guo Moruo) and the piano piece 'Variations on Composer's Own Theme and Fugue.' Between 1942 and 1945 Li Weining was director of the Shanghai conservatory.[14]

The Influence of Austrian Immigrant Musicians, Musical Theorists and Singers

The enforced immigration of top Austrian artists into China, especially into Shanghai, resulted in a "great leap forward," starting with the influx of the precious antique instruments those Austrian musicians brought with them. Nothing similar had been seen or heard before in Chinese orchestras.[15] Added to the exquisiteness of the instruments was the mastery of the musicians. In addition, substantial quantities of valuable musical scores were moved from Austria to China.[16] The immigrant musicians from Austria not only created the conditions necessary for a better interpretation of the works of Austrian composers, but also laid the foundations for the professional training evolved by Austrian musical theorists based on the theories evolved by Austrian musical creators. Between 1941 and 1947, Wolfgang Fraenkel taught composition theory at the Shanghai conservatory. He was a pupil of Schoenberg and used the latter's *Theory of Harmony* and his *Fundamentals of Musical Composition* as his main textbooks. He also used the *Theories on Form and Harmony* by Richard Stohr, a well-known Austrian musical theorist, as supplementary teaching material. In 1947 a pupil of Alban Berg, J. Schloss, succeeded Fraenkel at the Shanghai conservatory. Thus a direct link was established with the 20th-Century School of Vienna:

> Berg's "Wozzek" not only served as study material in his [Schloss's] teaching, he even handed the piano score over to his students . . . . Although this influence did not reach very far, it was after all the earliest reception in China of music produced by the 20th Century School of Vienna.[17]

Such works did not fail to make their mark on the Chinese students of music of the period. Zhou Jingqing (also known by the name of *Sang Tong*), who later was appointed deputy-director of the department of composition at the Shanghai Conservatory, wrote under the influence of Schoenberg's early works ("Pierot Lunaire," pieces for piano op. 11, 19, and others) free atonal compositions such as his opus for violin "Nocturnal Scenes." Its performances in Shanghai was well received. Subsequently, when Zhou studied with J. Schloss, he composed a piece for piano 'In those far away distances' based on a Chinese folk tune. In this piece he had given up atonality, but the harmony for the folk tune still contained many half-tones and dissonances. After its first performance in Shanghai the composition was very positively reviewed.[18]

Concurrently, Austrian operetta music in Shanghai received essential support from the presence of Austrian immigrant musicians, although operetta was aiming at an audience outside the circles of students of music at the Shanghai Conservatory. "At this time, we were very serious young people," remembered Li Delun, the famous conductor, in April 1984 when touching on this subject.[19]

In general the inhabitants of Shanghai had a very positive attitude towards the Vienna operetta. Pieces and tunes from this form of Austrian musical theater were presented to them in a variety of settings, for example in establishments frequented by Chinese and European patrons. The Fiaker on the Rue Joffre, to name but one, had been founded jointly by the former theater secretary Hans Jabloner and the former actor Fritz Strehlen. The Fiaker not only offered Viennese operetta flavor in its menu, but the outstnading pianist Professor Anton Zilzer saw to it that the sound of Viennese operetta melodies never stopped ringing in the ears of their patrons.

Some establishments, such as the White Horse, the Delikat or the Cafe Barcelona were located in the district of Hongkou. In Hongkou the Jewish aid organizations for immigrants were able to rent cheaper accommodations than elsewhere in Shanghai. It was in that district of Hongkou where the Japanese set up a kind of ghetto for the Jewish refugees, under the name of "designated area," on February 18, 1943.[20] Customers were for the most part immigrants, interspersed with a few isolated Chinese. On Sunday afternoons the Cafe Barcelona was often used as the venue for artistic programs. Smaller establishments provided similar attractions for smaller purses.[21]

Operettas were also presented by congregations at Jewish cultural and religious centers. Here, of course, attendance by the Chinese public was at a minimum. The school organized parents' days where programs such as scenes from the "Dreimaderlhaus" were performed on April 27, 1940 on the occasion of the anniversary celebration of the Chaoufoong-Road home.[23]

Music and English texts might have served well as bridge-builders, but the overall context of such celebrations, religious congregations and festivities of a typically Western style, such as Mothers Day gatherings, must of necessity have put narrow limits on their influence on their Chinese environment. But we do know of instances when persons from outside the Jewish community were invited to attend such programs as guests. Such was the case at the Mothers Day matinee at the Eastern Theater which incorporated a musical frame that spilled over in the afternoon to nine different establishments throughout Hongkou. These arrangements had on purpose been made with a view to other segments of the population, as the Shanghai Jewish Chronicle put it, ". . . more convincingly to disprove racist anti-semitic allegations of the subversive, all-destroying activities of the Jews."[24] Certain items of the program, however, were strictly aimed at the Austro-Jewish audience. Their purpose was neither to build bridges nor to evoke goodwill for the cause of the refugees, but to strengthen the spirit of resistance among the immigrants themselves. To quote an eye-witness:

Lippen schweigen
'sflüstern Geigen
In Shanghai
Ew' ge Operettentöne
In Shanghai.
Mitten im Theater
Bin ich aufgewacht,
Leider uns'res Lebens
Klingen durch die Nacht . . .

(Lips are silent,
Violins whisper
In Shanghai.
Immortal operetta tunes
In Shanghai.
In the middle of the theater
I woke up,
Songs of our Life
resounding through the night . . .)

That was sweet old Lehar, clad in new verses. There were not a few who had tears in their eyes, and it must be admitted that men cried even more bitterly than women. They were startled in the middle of the performance, but did not find themselves in the stalls at the *Merry Widow*, rather amidst the stage settings of the world theater where they had to act and live as supernumeraries until they would be swept off the stage like rejected puppets. But then, Franzi Berger's voice rose, hard and indomitable:

Und während wir noch leiden,
Erklingt von fern ein Lied . . .

(But while we here still suffer,
A song rings far away . . .)

In spite of Jewish Gestapo informants and Japanese plain-clothesmen this stout little woman dared to laugh in the face of Hirohito and his rascals. This was the Austrian version of "There will always be an England." This was the Viennese diction of "In Tyrannos!"[25]

Operettas were also performed by professional singers under the direction of professionally trained producers provided much-welcomed entertainment for the immigrant patrons and at the same time important visual education for the Chinese audience. It happened for the first time that Vienna operettas were staged in China with a cast of professional artists. In collaboration with the Shanghai Dramatic Association, operettas were played at the Lyceum Theater near the French Club. Among them were *Die Fledermaus*, (The Bat), *Der Graf von Luxemburg*, (The Count of Luxemburg) and *Die Lustige Witwe*, (The Merry Widow).[26] Occasionally cinema halls were hired for the staging of operettas.[27]

In 1940 even a Viennese Operetta Theater was founded, which for six years running presented an Austrian theater season. Fritz Frieser was the stage director. The composer Leo Schonbach, who later died in Shanghai, was in charge of the musical direction. The repertory featured masterpieces of the Viennese operetta such as *Grafin Mariza* (Countess Mariza). According to a former member of the cast, Leopold Brodmann, performances were always sold out. Once even a new Shanghai operetta was launched, named "Sag, bist du mir treu?" ("Say, are you faithful to me?") The music was by the composer Sonnenschein and we are told that it was a smashing success.[28] Performances were abundantly and with great dedication rehearsed. In 1940 Professor Wilhelm Deman, the former head of a translation bureau in Vienna, who had started a kind of adult education center in Shanghai, put his school premises at the disposal of the operetta company for their rehearsals:

> As no suitable location could be found within the designated area, we agreed to the suggestion of a Mr. Breuer, husband of the singer Carla Thalheimer, to make our lecture hall available to them for several hours a week for the rehearsal of operettas . . . [29]

It was only after the end of World War II that this excellent ensemble dispersed, after having staged Lehar's *'Wo die Lerche Singt'* ("Where the Lark Sings").[30] Farewell thanks were given to the Allied Forces and to the city of Shanghai, but first and foremost to its Chinese inhabitants, in a way that was both Viennese and musical. Under this motto the European Jewish Artist Society gave a gala performance of Johann Strauss's *Fledermaus* or *The Bat* on April 29, 1946. Early in May 1946 Martin Hausdorff published in the *China Daily Tribune* a concluding survey of the works performed by the Austrian operetta ensemble in Shanghai.[31] Altogether twenty-two operettas were performed, including works by such composers as Lehar, Kalman, Milloecker, Strauss, Gramichstaedten, Eysler, Fall and Benatzky.

For the sake of completeness it should be added that American-produced film versions of Austrian operettas and radio broadcasts also had their share in acquainting Chinese audiences with this Austrian art form. Just as an example, Lehar's *Lustige Witge*, or The Merry Widow, remade into an American film, was a big success in Shanghai cinemas.[32] Many of the thirty or so broadcasting studios active in Shanghai at the time transmitted operetta programs of a rich variety; in particular the French broadcasting studio favored Austrian composers.[33]

Summing up the evidence on hand, the conclusion may be justified that pieces of Austrian music, both serious and light, and of Austrian musical theater had met with a lively response in the China of the Thirties and Forties, particularly in Shanghai.

The Period of the People's Republic of China

At the Time of the Founding of the PRC

At the time of the founding of the PRC, it was by no means an un-propitious omen that a fair share of the radio programs broadcast under the new government consisted of Austrian operetta and dance music.[34] In Nanjing, the Austrian ambassador Stumvoll did his best to keep Chinese interesat in Austrian music alive even during the period of political transition. Only a few months prior to the taking of Nanjing by the PLA, Stumvoll had set up a Sino-Austrian Cultural Association (SACA). Such associations were also in existence in Beijing and Shanghai. The Austrian ambassador, anticipating the victory of the Chinese communists, took care that these associations did not take a stand on issues of Chinese politics but pursued "purely cultural and economic aims."[35] In doing so, Stumvoll's attitude was in accordance with the attitude taken by other Western diplomatic representatives. In a secret meeting on April 22, 1949, which Stumvoll also attended, the Western diplomats agreed not to follow the retreat of the KMT government but rather to play for time and to establish contacts with the communist authorities after the fall of Nanjing.[36] On the evening of the same day Stumvoll staged an Austro-Chinese cultural *soiree* regardless of the artillery duels that took place in the vicinity of the city. After a recitation from works by Austrian and German writers, the Austrian ambassador personally sat at the piano, playing music by Hayden, Mozart, Beethoven and Schubert. As he reports, there were no more KMT dignitaries present at this social gathering, but "only liberal-minded Chinese."[37] On May 7 Stumvoll cabled to Vienna via the British Foreign Office: ". . . Informal contacts with Foreign residents Affairs Commission Nanking established today."[38]

In Vienna Stumvoll used his power of persuasion to the full in advocating the continuation of the Austrian mission in China and an early assumption of diplomatic relations. He was convinced that it would be a worthwhile task to further promote Austrian culture in the New China. He pointed to the potential latent in the Sino-Austrian cultural associations in Nanjing, Shanghai and Beijing, which could be put to good use as there were indeed many affinities between the Chinese and Austrian world outlooks. Viennese melodies, he said, could be heard all over the north and south of China.[39] Indeed, initially the representatives of the new Chinese leadership openly displayed their interest in Austrian musical culture. As early as June 4, 1949 Stumvoll, acting on behalf of SACA in Nanjing, gave a musical entertainment featuring Chinese and Austrian songs, mostly songs by Franz Schubert. Stumvoll succeeded in welcoming 140 guests, part of them caders in uniform from the City's Department of Education. They had previously attended another function but did not want to miss at least the final stages of the Austrian gathering.[40]

Another social event was held under the patronage of Stumvoll on September 9, 1949, attended by 150 guests, among them 100 Chinese university teachers and 50 diplomats. The musical program was executed by the businessman and amateur musician Herbert Ruff, who played the piano, and his son Bernhard, a professional violinist. The audience particularly acclaimed pieces by Shubert, Mozart, the Strauss brothers and Lehar.[41]

The communist authorities were interested to such an extent in a widespread popularization of Austrian culture that they agreed to the reactivation of the Sino-Austrian Cultural Association in Shanghai, the city where Austrian musical culture had struck its deepest roots. On August 8, 1949, Stumvoll wrote on the subject to the Austrian physician Dr. Leo Kandel who acted as Austria's unofficial representative in Beijing:

> On the subject of SACA, I am glad to advise that in spite of enormous difficulties I managed to establish SACA in Shanghai on August 3, 1949. I have no doubt that SACA Shanghai will soon be able to fulfill its function effectively. Considering the prevailing situation, owing to which foreign associations in Shanghai and other big cities in China were forced to close down, the case of SACA Shanghai is unique.[42]

In this context Stumvoll was able to report to his superiors another success, namely, that among the 40 Chinese and 15 Austrian participants in the first meeting of the SACA there were Li Tiancai, the former secretary to Marshall Zhang Xueliang, and Sun Qian, a legal advisor to the Shanghai City government. Li Tiancai assumed the function of president, and the two municipal councillors Chuang Chen and Meng Qianshu constituted the supervisory board. Stumvoll himself was elected honorary president.[43]

Regrettably, due to the four-power occupation of Austria, the foreign ministry in Vienna was unable to act on Stumvoll's urgent advice to recognize the Beijing government. All Vienna could do was to devise an "Austrian way": It came to mind that Stumvoll had already overstepped the official age of retirement, so the government retired him from active service and left his position unfilled for the time being. Regretfully, Stumvoll wrote to his superiors on June 30, 1950:

I am sorry to say that without official Austrian backing the sympathies
which Austria has always enjoyed in China are no longer able to manifest
themselves. Up to the closing of this embassy the Austrian position in
China was the most advantageous it could possibly have been thanks to the
absence of any political leanings. In the present circumstances nothing of
what I have initiated and nurtured in two years of intense efforts, the remains of which I am still trying to keep alive against all odds, can be made
useful or realized . . .[44]

One cannot but agree with Stumvoll's view that an Austrian diplomatic mission and a Sino-Austrian cultural association closely collaborating with that mission would have provided an ideal platform for the promotion of Austrian and European musical culture. Without such official backing, any Chinese person wishing to explore this domain found himself politically at risk. In the early Fifties, when Soviet models were introduced in all spheres of China's activities, music and musical theater were equally brought into line.[45] Soviet music theorists tried to cut any links Chinese composers had formed with Western music by denouncing them as "unhealthy passion." A new cycle of piano pieces which appeared in Shanghai in the autumn of 1951 was commented on by G. Schneerson in the following terms:

This music has nothing in common with national Chinese culture, nor with
the aspirations of the new Chinese school. It is reminiscence of the anemic
creations of the late French impressionists. The composer imitates the long
since bankrupt mannerism of the formalistic West European school . . . We
don't know when these pieces were composed, but it does seem to us that
their publication in 1951, at a time when the great majority of Chinese
composers were ardently striving for a kind of realistic music on a high

ideological level which was both close to the people and needed by the people, was a grave error by Ma Si-tsung.[46]

The quarrels going on among Chinese musical experts and composers were not restricted to adherents of musical theories evolved in Austria. In volume 11/1949 of the periodical *Soviet Music* the Chinese musicologist Zhao Feng accused the composers of "bowing before the bourgeois European musical culture" in pursuit of their ambition to become a "yellow-faced Schoenberg."[47]

Notwithstanding these counter-currents, contemporary Austrian musical theory was able temporarily to maintain its influence. Professor Zhou Jingqing, deputy head of the department of composition at the Shanghai conservatory, could not be deterred from using Schoenberg's *Theory of Harmony* as one of the most essential works of reference in his courses.[48] The Austrian classical composers too could successfully maintain their important positions notwithstanding the lack of diplomatic relations between Austria and China.

> The 200th anniversary of the birth of Mozart was commemorated in Beijing, Shanghai and other cities by memorial concerts, lectures, and the publication of scholarly articles in the newspapers on the life and work of Mozart.[49]

A concert in commemoration of Mozart was held, conducted by the Austrian composer Alfred Uhl, to which a semi-official Austrian trade delegation was also invited.[50] That the "leaning to one side," that is to the side of the Soviet Union, could not suppress sympathies for Austrian musical culture even among the top leadership of China is proved by the fact that prime minister Zhou Enlai personally requested the head of the delegation, F.J. Haslinger, to lend a hand in bringing about a visiting tour to China by a leading Austrian orchestra.[51] Haslinger promised to get in touch with the Vienna Philharmonic Orchestra. Regrettably, their first appearance in Beijing had to wait until 1973, mainly due to radical phases in Chinese politics and their effect on cultural policies.

The Periods of Restricted Tolerance of Foreign Art in the PRC

Following the withering of the 'Hundred Flowers' in the late summer of 1957, numerous personalities in China who had more outspokenly advocated the reception of foreign culture were severely persecuted. After a period of relative calm during the early Sixties even more severe setbacks were brought about by the Cultural Revolution, particularly between 1966 and 1968. Records of Mozart and other composers were smashed by the Red Guards, musical scores and books were burned, teachers and students of conservatories of music were sent to the countryside. Chinese singers could only secretly practice pieces by Austrian or other foreign composers. When they were caught in the act, they were accused of "worshipping things foreign," severely criticized and often enough physically maltreated. There was the case of one male singer in Shanghai whose larynx the Red Guards tried to crush in an attempt to silence once and for all the apostle of European musical culture.

After the Cultural Revolution had passed its peak, occasional intervals of calm prevailed between 1970 and 1976 during which the susteined preference for Austrian music by the Chinese public had a sweeping chance to reassert itself. For example, the foreign diplomats attending the first reception given by the Austrian ambassador in Beijing in 1972 to mark the Austrian National Day were greatly astonished when a Chinese military band intonated with visible delight Mozart's "Kleine Nachtmusik," the "Donauwalzer" by Johann Strauss and Schubert's overture to "Rosamunde."[52]

Shortly thereafter an enlarged Chinese audience was given the opportunity to appreciate samples of Austrian musical culture in the interpretation of the Vienna Philharmonic Orchestra. In the spring of 1972, the then Chinese foreign minister Ji Pengfei had agreed to a program of cultural exchanges comprising an exhibition of Chinese archeological relics in Vienna, to be reciprocated by a visting tour to Beijing by the Vienna Philharmonic Orchestra. The Chinese government wanted to avail itself of this opportunity to present the Austrian musicians to the largest possible audience. The wish was therefore expressed that in addition to three concert hall performances a concert should be arranged to be attended by 18,000 representatives of the peasants, workers and soldiers. On the point of program, music by Mozart and Strauss was expressly requested. The then Austrian ambassador in Beijing, Dr. Hans Thalberg, remembers:

> I was particularly struck when at the announcement of the "Blue Danube" waltz the entire audience of 18,000, all attired in green and blue, broke out in thundering applause. Clearly, the fame of this waltz, so dear to our ears, had even spread to the factories and military barracks in and around Beijing.[53]

Professor Hubner, at the time director of the orchestra, reported similarly.[54]

At another concert given by the Vienna Philharmonic Orchestra in Beijing the Chinese pianist Yin Chengzhong played the piano part in the piano concerto "Yellow River." Yin had made a name for himself through performance in the style of the Cultural Revolution. At this Philharmonic concert he had the courage play as an encore, "as a token of friendship for the Austrian musicians," the Impromptu in G Flat Major by Schubert,[54] who at that time was not yet fully accepted in China.[55]

Thus, the impressions left by the Vienna Philharmonic Orchestra acting as Austria' musical messengers were profound and manifold.[56] They were also durable in spite of the criticism of European composers which soon afterwards made headlines in Chinese and European newspapers. A total of 21,000 people had attended the four concerts, and an audience many times larger had watched them on television. Reportedly Deng Xiaoping, then China's deputy prime minister, gave expression to the feelings of many Chinese when he said that Austrian music was a tonic and that it would be wonderful if such achievements could be matched by Chinese artists. Deng also persisted in his high regard for Beethoven, Mozart and Schubert at a time when their music was publicly condemned in China. This attitude may have added fuel to the hatred displayed by the Gang of Four towards Deng.[57] A widely-ready Austrian paper even carried the headline: "Philharmonics overturned Mao's crown-prince."[58]

Music was also abused as a source of argument in the battle for power waged by the Gang of Four against Deng, Zhou, and others. However, the radicals never succeeded in stirring up a genuine counter-current against the works of those Austrian composers among the Chinese public in general. The secretary general of the Austro-Chinese friendship society could satisfy himself on this point when he was in charge of a delegation of Chinese archeologists visiting Austria in 1974, at a time when the criticism of Beethoven and other Western composers was at its peak in China. To spare the feelings of the Chinese visitors, the Austrian host offered them a visit to Humperdinck's *Hansel und Gretel* at the Vienna Volksoper, but the delegation insisted unanimously on seeing a performance of the *Zauberflote* (Magic Flute) at the State Opera. During the interval the members of the delegation held friendly conversations with members of the Philharmonic Orchestra. Such attitudes were by no means limited to scholars belonging to a social group of middle-aged intellectuals. They could likewise be observed when the Chinese national football team visited Austria in 1978. On extended coach tours the sportsmen shouted in chorus: "Strauss, Strauss, Strauss!," and after the first waltzes had resounded, the head of the delegation said with brightly shining eyes: "This kind of music is much beloved by our masses."[59]

Even Jiang Qing, who fervently opposed Western culture, was sometimes willing to compromise. Austrian musicians and composers were among the beneficiaries of such occasional inconsistencies. When in the Seventies the Chinese national ballet in Beijing underwent preparations for touring abroad, Jiang Qing requested that musical films from Austria or American films on Austrian musical themes (the Trapp family) be shown to the members of the ballet, albeit to give the dancers the opportunity to acquaint themselves with these artistic productions.[60]

When an ensemble of the Chinese national ballet toured Austria and West Germany in the late summer of 1976 with performances of *The Red Detachment of Women* and *The White-haired Girl*, the program was supplemented by stage appearances of Chinese singers whose presentations included Austrian operetta melodies. However, a full-scale revival of the study of music and musical theater from Austria became possible only after the fall of the Gang in the autumn of 1976.

The Period of Renewed Opening

In 1978 the official Chinese news agency for the first time dedicated an extensive report to the Salzburg Festival.[61] This was followed shortly afterwards, in November 1978, by prominent public events to commemorate the 150th anniversary of the death of Schubert. The head of the department for musical research at the Shanghai Conservatory, professor Qian Renkang, produced a television serial in four parts, each lasting 40 minutes, on "The Life and Work of Franz Schubert," including music and a large amount of visual background material.[62] Early in 1979 a Chinese youth orchestra named Red Scarf performed Schubert's "Unfinished Symphone" and a piano concerto by Mozart in memoriam of Franz Schubert.[63]

In February and March 1980 Chinese encounters with Austrian musical culture were continued on Austrian soil. An ensemble of five of China's best vocal and instrumental soloists, under the care of the two writers of this contribution, gave fifteen concerts in Austria. The pianists Li Qi (at present deputy director of the Guangdong Philharmonic) and Cui Shiguang as well as the tenor Shi Hong'e, teacher at the Shanghai conservatory, and the soprano Deng Yun proved by their interpretation of the works of Austrian composers that the presence of Austrian musical culture in China had enjoyed an uninterrupted continuity.

Towards the end of March 1980 the Austrian piano teacher and professor at the Vienna conservatory Walter Fleischmann went to Shanghai to take up a teaching assignment at the Shanghai conservatory. Starting from June 1980 he was assisted by his wife, Wang Gin, herself a teacher at the Vienna conservatory. A letter by the Shanghai conservatory on the subject of this teaching project states:

> He possesses rich experience and masters the works of all the different styles. Most of all he excelled in the teaching of works of the Viennese

classical and romantic periods. The result was outstanding. He has won the appreciation of teachers and students of our conservatory . . .

In May 1981 one of Professor Fleischmann's students took part in the Beethoven competition in Vienna. This link was followed up over the next few years by concert tours, combined with teaching, by professors Paul Badura-Skoda and Hans Kann. Beginning in the early Eighties, students of piano, horn, trumpet and cello from the PRC have been studying at the Vienna conservatory. In 1982 a chamber music ensemble of the Vienna Philharmonic, directed by Professor Wilhelm Hubner, gave a guest performance in Beijing. The works by Mozart, Haydn and Schubert performed at those concerts were so enthusiastically received that a third concert had to be added.

Valuable contacts could also be established in the field of the musical theater. Although a touring performance of operettas by the Vienna Volkstheater planned for 1982 fell victim to financial considerations, the Austro-Chinese Friendship Society was able to secure the permission of the Ministry of Culture in Beijing for Shi Hong'e, China's best-known tenor, to pursue his studies in Vienna. During his stay, from February to October 1982, he was given extensive opportunities to study numerous productions of the Vienna State Opera and to establish contacts with singer colleagues, teachers of vocal music, and stage designers. In the summer of the following year Shi Hong'e sang the part of Alfredo in *La Traviata* conducted by the American conductor Sarah Caldwell from Boston.[64] In 1984 he tried to realize a production of *The Marriage of Figaro* in Shanghai, with support from Austria. This project could not be realized because the Beijing conservatory anticipated it by staging a studio production in 1983. Another obstacle may have been the campaign against ideological pollution launched by the Ministry of Propaganda in the autumn of 1983. But meanwhile approval was given for the performance of European operas and operettas both in Beijing and Shanghai.

This international recognition, which at the same time serves to enhance the prestige of the Chinese government, is one of the main assets Austrian Music and Austrian musical theater can rely on as a support of their continued influence on the musical life of the PRC. Auspicious factors for this continuity are:

1.　Vienna has successfully reestablished in China its high reputation as a musical center. Chinese successes scored in Vienna have double value and are emphasized accordingly by the political leadership as well as the Chinese mass media. It is by no means accidentally that the Deputy-Minister of Culture Zhou Weizhi compared the successful performances of the two Chinese prize winners at the 1984 Vienna opera song competition with China's triumphs at the Los Angeles Olympic Games (NCNA, August 16, 1984). Nowadays, Vienna is referred to by many members of the Chinese political leadership as "the capital of music."

2.   The decision in principle by the Chinese leadership to re-admit the cultivation of foreign musical theater in China. As recently as 1981, when at the Austrian embassy in Beijing a Chinese singer performed opera arias in honor of the visiting Austrian vice-chancellor, there was one prominent Chinese guest who conspicuously refrained from applauding. However, since the faltering of the campaign against spiritual pollution, opinion has shifted in favor of the admission of European music and European musical theater. The following facts may be called to mind in support of this statement: (a) The participation of the tenor Zhang Jianyi and the mezzo-soprano Zhang Manhaua, both winners at the Vienna competition, at the great Beijing theater festival commemorating the 35th anniversary of the founding of the PRC, and the explicit underscoring of this fact in the Chinese media (NCNA, September 17, 1984); (b) the recent visit to Beijing of the Bavarian State Opera with performances of Mozart's *Marriage of Figaro* and *The Magic Flute*, in which members of the Vienna State Opera were essentially involved, and which was enthusiastically welcomed by the Chinese public and press: "The world-famous Bavarian State Opera gave Mozart's wonderful music a lively and expressive interpretation. The Chinese audience requited this artistic enjoyment with enthusiastic applause." (China i Bild 1/1985); (c) the fact that the Chinese ambassador in Vienna, Wang Shu, continuously publishes articles on Austrian musical theater in Chinese publications and is at present preparing a voluminous book on the same subject.

3.   The manifold endorsements by leading Chinese politicians of the two policies of "opening to the outside world" and "let a hundred flowers blossom" may be seen as a necessary precondition and safeguard for the cultivation of foreign musical theater in China. Were it not for these official policies, there might still be Chinese opera houses here and there managed by officials who may claim a past military career, but who have not rubbed shoulders with European musical theater. This has occasionally produced awkward suggestions, such as the suggestion to drop orchestra rehearsals for the staging of a new opera and instead simply to use the music from a previously performed opera—so to speak, to use the music from *Butterfly* for a performance of *Figaro*. At present, however, the experts are in charge, and the Chinese officials responsible for the cultivation of European musical theater in China are well aware of the fact: in her speech, Professor Zhou Xiaoyan, who led the Chinese singers' group to Vienna, at-

tributed the major reason for the success in arts to China's present "Let one hundred flowers blossom" policy. The offical recognition of European musical theater, and in particular of Austrian musical theater, has by now spread to circles as remote from the musical scene as, say, experts on foreign politics who at conferences dealing with the subject of political neutrality adorn their speeches with references to the composer Mozart.

There is no doubt that in the process of reception of Austrian musical theater the peculiarity of indigenous Chinese musical culture will constitute an important element.

. . . the music of China had undoubted merits of its own and . . . its distinctive merits and the distinctive qualities of the art should be maintained even though much of the more advanced phases of Western technique will be incorporated.[65]

The ballet version of *Leiyu* or *Thunderstorm* given by the Shanghai ballet ensemble in Beijing and Shanghai in June 1981 showed excellent standards of dancing, but a modest level of musical inspiration. Strauss waltzes could be spotted almost without modification. Hopefully, better results will be achieved with Nestroy's *Talisman*, a farce with songs, the production of which in 1985 in Beijing is planned jointly by the Austrian theater specialist Michael Gissenwehrer and a lecturer of the Central Drama Institute in Beijing.

But the Vienna operetta, whatever its reception may be at any given time, is sure to continue as a permanent feature of musical life in China. Its enthusiastic welcome by the masses is confirmed over and over again at each appearance of touring Austrian ensembles.[66] Leaving behind a sinister interval of its past, China is again moving towards new horizons. This new, happier period finds its equivalent expression in the mood of the Vienna operetta. This is how Li Delun, conductor of the Beijing Philharmonic, put it in a conversation with the authors: "In the past, I disliked anything light. At the time of China's oppression I wanted to cry, not laugh. Today, it's quite different!"

Notes

1.   Slawiczek's letter to Julius Zwicker, written in Beijing on March 19, 1977; in: Weltbott No. 156, pp. 20 f.

2. Anton Huonder, *Deutsche Jesuitenmissionare des 17. und 18. Jahrhunderts,* (Freiburg, 1899), p. 184; Joseph Dehergne, *Repertoire des Jesuites de Chine de 1552 à 1800,* (Rome-Paris, 1973) p. 22.

3. Letter from Beijing written on the 19th of the winter month 1743; in: Weltbott No. 680, p. 68.

4. Information obtained from Friedrich Mitura, who participated in those negotiations as a consular secretary and was in charge of keeping records.

5. Information obtained from Ottokar Schubert, the son of Otto Schubert, an Austrian musicain who lived in China.

6. *Bühnenspiegel im Fernen Osten* (1929–30) pp. 34 f.

7. Ibid., p. 51.

8. Ibid., p. 50:

> "Theater is being played here in the distant East,
> German theater, not the flimsy stuff of movie dens.
> Where we, accompanied by fiddles out of tune,
> May sample and digest absurdities!
> The right chaps have come to the fore.
> They bring the shimmer of true art, still hesitant,
> To the tumult of gluttons, traders, trimmers,
> And works of poets grown on German soil
> Our puzzled eyes can now perceive on stage.
> Good luck to artists who have dared to dare!
> Good luck the journal that has smoothed their way
> And woes and battles for the German stage—
> A battle seldom waged these days!
> Good luck the patrons who in cheerful mood
> Through smoke and noise proceed to the *musion,*
> Patrons whose uncorrupted hearts
> Beat faster when their native art unfolds its wings."

9. Ibid., p. 48.

10. Information obtained from Lise Schiff, widow of Friedrich Schiff, a formerly prominent Austrian painter in Shanghai.

11. Dr. Rudolf Muck, (then advisor to the Nanjing government on police affairs) to Federal Chancellor Schober on October 1, 1931. *Haus-Hof-und Staatsarchiv (hereafter HHSta), Neues Pol. Arch.* 1605.

12. Report on the concert given by professor Robert Pollak on March 24, 1934 in Shanghai; consul Ockermuller to the federal chancellery, Department of Foreign Affairs, on April 23, 1934; *HHStA, Neues Pol. Arch./*606.

13. Ma Weizhi, son of the famous university founder in Guangxi, studies musical history in Vienna between 1934 and 1936. The operetta impressed him even more than the opera. From 1939 to 1953 Ma taught at the Academy of Arts in Guangxi. Subsequently he taught musical history and piano at the Zhongnan Music School at Wuhan. Since 1971 he has been in charge of the German Depart-

302   *Gerd Kaminski and Else Unterrieder*

ment of Wuhan University. The operettas he most clearly remembers are *Dreimaderlhaus* and *Das Land des Lächelns'*. Informations obtained from professor Ma Weizhi in May, 1983.

14. Liao Naixiong, 'Im Reich der Tune fliessen Jantse und Donau zusammer," in *China-Report* No. 60/1981, pp. 31 f. Also, information obtained from Wu Zuqiang and Situ Huacheng, the former director, the latter professor of musical theory and violin at the Central Conservatory in Beijing, in April 1984.

15. Information obtained from Li Delun, conductor of the Beijing Central Philharmonic, in April 1984.

16. Information obtained from Leonore Kovacs, who at that time was a violinist in Shanghai.

17. Liao Naixiong, op. cit., p. 36.

18. Ibid.

19. Also compare Schneerson's opinion on the Linksradikala Chinese composer Nie Er: ". . . After the magazine where he worked ceased publication, he was for a time jobless. Then he received the very timely offer by Li Djing-gue, director of the popular song and dance ensemble 'Minyua' and himself a composer of light music, to join as a violinist Li's small mixed European-Chinese orchestra which accompanied that ensemble. Li Djing-gue in his own creations as well as in his artistic work with the collective directed by him was guided by the taste of the bourgeois Chinese public and of the European residents in Shanghai. The 'Minyua' troupe produced itself with sentimental, decadent little songs and ballads bare of any social relevance in which the native Chinese exterior only served as an erotic element tingling the nerves of patrons frequenting the more elegant cabarets along Nanking Road. Niä Or (Nie Er) worked for about one year with the 'Minyuä' troupe. Naturally enough, work in an establishment of this type could not satisfy the young musician . . . " G. Schneerson, *Die Musikkultur Chinas*, (Leipzig, Friedrich Holmeister, 1955) pp. 122 f. Also cf. Bernd Eberstein, *Das chinesische Theater im 20. Jahrhundert*, (Wiesbaden, Harrussowitz, 1983) p. 156.

20. Gerd Kaminski and Else Unterrieder, *"Von Österreichern und Chinesen,"* (Viennal-Munich-Zurich: Europa Publishing House, 1980) pp. 787–783.

21. Alfred W. Kneucker, "Shanghai, die Stadt uber dem Meere," unpublished typescript, pp. 345 ff.

22. Ernst Pollak, "Elterntag Veranstaltung der S.J.Y.A. Schule," *Shanghai Jewwish Chronicle*, May 13, 1941, quoted from William Deman, 'Ein verlorenes Jahrzehnt – Shanghai 1939-49, Tageblatter eines Heimatvertriebenen,' unpublished typescript, p. 120.

23. William Deman, *Ein verlorenes Jahrzehnt*, 21F/97.

24. *Shanghai Jewish Chronicle*, May 20, 1940.

25. Alfred W. Kneucker, *Shanghai, die Stadt uber dem Meere*, p. 501.

26. Information obtained from Hans Jabloner, former emigrant and owner of the 'Fiaker.'

27. Information obtained from the actress and singer Jenny Rausnitz; also from Mary Steinhauser and Vivien Pick.

28. Maurice Hirschmann, "Sechs Jahre Wiener Operette in China," *Welt am Montaq*, No. 90, p. 8.

29. William Deman, *Ein verlorenes Jahrzehnt*, p. 162.

30. Maurice Hirschmann, "Sechs Jahre Wiener Operette in China," *Welt am Montaq*, No. 90. p. 8.

31. Newspaper clippings in the possession of Jenny Rausnitz.

32. Information obtained from his Excellency Wang Shu, ambassador of the PRC in Vienna. There were still other American films with a strong Austrian scent and songs from Austrian operettas which have been very opular among the Chinese: Ernst Lubitsch's "Love Parade" (1939), Victor Scherzinger's "The Smiling Lieutenant," "With One Hour With You" by Oskar Straus, and "The Great Waltz" (Luise Rainer) which included "Blue Danube" and "Tales of the Vienna Woods," which had an especially enthusiastic Chinese audience. Information obtained from C. T. Hsia.

33. Information obtained from Li Delun in April 1984.

34. Information obtained from Georges Wachter.

35. Stumvoll to the Federal Chancellery, Department of Foreign Affairs, on January 10, 1949; *HHStA*, GZ 81.022, China K/80075; *HHStA* 1949, GZ 87.448, China K/80.075; *HHStA* 1949, GZ 88.527, China 3/80.109.

36. Stumboll to foreign minister Gruber on April 22, 1949; *HHStA*, GX 85.123, China 3/80.109.

37. Andante con variazioni in F-minor (Haydn), phantasy in D-minor (Mozart), the minuet in G-Major from the sonata op. 45/2 (Beethoven), 'Fur Elise' (Beethoven), and a selection from Schubert. Stumvoll to the Federal Chancellory on April 27, 1949; *HHStA*, GZ 85.260, China K/80.075.

38. *HHStA*, GZ 86.814, China 30/80.109.

39. Stumvoll to Gruber on October 6, 1949; *HHStA, GZ* 88.527, China 3/80.109.

40. Stumvoll to the Federal Chancellery on June 6, 1949, *HHStA*, GZ. 87.855, China K/80.075.

41. Stumvoll to the Federal Chancellery on September 10, 1949, *HHStA*, GZ, 87.855, China K/80.075.

42. The letter is preserved in the archives of the Ludwig Boltzmann Institut fur China- und Sudostasienforschung.

43. Stumvoll to the Federal Chancellery on June 30, 1950; *HHStA*, GZ 87.856, China K/80.075.

44. Stumvoll to the Federal Chancellery on June 30, 1950; *HHStA*, GZ 125.866, China 2/120.866, China 2/120.203.

45. Cf. Liao Naixiong, Im Reiche der Tone fliessen Jangtse und Donau Zusammen, p. 30: "After liberation until the early Sixties Russian and Soviet musical theories were in the ascendant."

46. G. Schneerson, *Die Musikkultur Chinas*, pp. 185 f.

47. Freely quoted from Schneerson, op. cit., p. 130.

48. Liao, op. cit., p. 30.

49. Liao, op. cit., p. 32.

50. F. J. Haslinger, "lecture on a China trip" (lecture typescript by Haslinger, who personally headed the delegation in 1956), p. 5.

51. Interview with F. J. Haslinger, 1977; report by the head of delegation of industrialists visiting Beijing (undated typescript), p. 9.

52. *China-Report* 7/8 1972, p. 34.

53. Hans Thalberg, "Als erster osterreichischer Botschafter in der VR China; *China-Report* 41/1978, pp. 12 f.

54. Ibid., p. 13.

55. Gu Wen, "Music of Friendship — Vienna Philharmonic Orchestra visits China" *China Features*, 1973.

56. Kaminski and Unterrieder, *Von Österreichern und Chinesen*; op. cit., pp. 1001 f.

57. Ibid., pp. 1001 ff.

58. *Kronenzeitung* June 22, 1976.

59. Kaminski and Unterrieder, *Von Österreicher und Chinesen*, pp. 1002 f.

60. Information obtained from Lin Ping and Bai Xiufeng, formerly masters of ballet at the ensemble.

61. *China-Report* 42/43 1978, p. 77.

62. *Liao Naixiong*, op. cit., p. 32.

63. *Die Presse*, January 24, 1979.

64. Else Unterrieder, "Traviata Premiere in Peking," *China-Report* 60/1981, p. 33.

65.   John Hazedel Levis, *Foundations of Chinese Musical Art*, (Beiping, Henry Vetch, 1936), p. 209.

66.   Cf. among others, the report by the Chinese news agency Xinhua on the tour of the 'Veldener Doppelsextett': ". . . The concert was climaxed by the last three scheduled songs composed by world-famous musicians Mozart, Schubert, Strauss. Clapping hands rhythmically, the Beijing music lovers brought back an encore of their favorite 'The Blue Danube.'" *China-Report* 71/1983, p. 43.

Since the biggest part of this article is based on materials in German and English it is in most cases impossible to trace the Chinese characters for names which have been transmitted only phonetically. Therefore, a list of Chinese characters has been ommitted.

13. Performances of Ibsen in China After 1949

ELISABETH EIDE

To my knowledge Ibsen has been staged on three occasions in the People's Republic of China since 1949. My main concern in this article will be with the 1956 performance of *A Doll's House* and the 1983 performance of *Peer Gynt*, both in Peking. Both of these theater productions involved cooperation between Norwegian and Chinese expertise, and can to some extent be regarded as bilateral productions. They may thus serve to illustrate interaction and influence between a Western and a Chinese theater. Since the two plays mentioned are very different, both in content and in structure, they can also illustrate various reasons given by the Chinese for producing Western plays. By comparing information on these performances with what is known of other performances before 1949 I also hope to be able to say something about possible developments in dramatic ideals and conceptions in China since 1949.

The reasons for producing a play may differ from country to country, but certainly high on any list for both producer and audience must be the desire for good entertainment. The financial aspect of a production must not be forgotten; even state-owned companies must pay some consideration to public taste when deciding upon a repertoire. Practical reasons may play their part in the selection of plays; a technically complicated play with elaborate stage changes may be impossible to put up on some stages, or it may be too costly.

One play may be selected because of its artistic qualities, another because of its controversial theme or because of its actuality at a given moment. Practical reasons must have been in the forefront when the numerous amateur groups that existed in China before 1949 decided upon their repertoire. Plays with elaborate stage shifts would imply a serious technical problem for the traditional Chinese stage. One-act plays must also have appeared to be preferable to an amateur group because it would simplify the production. Another relevant practical consideration for Chinese productions was availability of texts in translation. A substantial number of one-act plays were written in Chinese, but it took some time before complete dramas by Chinese dramatists were available.

Spoken drama gained in importance when the war with Japan grew nearer and the Chinese plays written during that time offered a simple emotional outlet for national and patriotic feelings. After 1949 the state gained control over the repertoire, and financial security almost disappeared as a motive for producing a play. Political acceptability became of prime importance and any controversial play must be justified by its didactic content, even more so before 1966 than after 1978. This point will be illustrated by examining the two plays mentioned before. It seems to me that the didactic reasons given for producing *A Doll's House* in 1956 were stronger than the reasons given for putting up *Peer Gynt* in 1983, although both plays are mentioned as morally acceptable.

I have gathered information of about 25 productions of Ibsen's plays in China before 1949.[1] Of most performances only the roughest details are known, such as when it was played, where, and who played the leading parts. Most of the performances were *A Doll's House*, three or four were *An Enemy of the People*. *Ghosts* was put up at least twice, and *The Wild Duck* once. One or two of the performances were in English, put up by the students in the foreign languages departments.

Performances since 1949

As mentioned earlier, there have been three Chinese productions of Ibsen's plays since 1949. First *A Doll's House* was produced in Peking in 1956, and then the same play was staged in Shanghai in 1962, put up by the final classes of the Shanghai Drama Institute (*Shanghai xiju xueyuan*) as their "show-piece" of the year. Not very much is known of this performance, and it did not have any impact outside of the school. In 1978–80 *A Doll's House* in a Norwegian, dubbed version was shown on Chinese television and it created such a stir that it was shown two more times. A debate in the newspapers and journals followed, and Cao Yu was interviewed on radio about his impressions of Ibsen. Then the first Ibsen play to be staged after the Cultural Revolution as a Chinese production was *Peer Gynt*.

Concerning the 1956 production of *A Doll's House*, I have been in the fortunate position to have been able to interview both the Norwegian co-instructor and the Chinese Nora. Since the event did not go unnoticed in the papers, it has been possible to gather a fairly accurate impression of it. Unfortunately, I have not seen the performance myself. As for *Peer Gynt*, I have seen a video version of the play, and I have had several talks with the Chinese translator, Xiao Qian. I have also talked with some of the Norwegian assistants called in to help with the play. I also base my impression on debates following the performances, both in Chinese and in Norwegian media.

The 1956 Performance of A Doll's House

A Doll's House is a drama about a marriage based upon illusions. Seemingly happily married to a man who shelters her from the harsh realities of life, Nora is content in the knowledge that she has once made a real sacrifice to save her husband's life. He is unaware of this, and she fears if he knew, it would dint his manly image. When he was seriously ill several years ago, she raised money for them to go to Italy by forging a cheque. She believes that if her husband, Helmer, was told of this, he would take all blame and responsibility on his shoulders. This belief she keeps as a gold nugget to comfort her while at the same time being determined that she would rather take her own life than let him make this sacrifice. But when the forgery is disclosed, her husband is seen to have feet of clay. He is only concerned with his public image and would not dream of sacrificing his honor to protect her. In the final debacle Nora leaves her husband and children to go out into the world and discover for herself what laws a society is governed by, what constitutes a real marriage and what duties she owes to herself.

This play is no doubt one of Ibsen's most famous, and it certainly is well established in China. When the Chinese decided to put up *A Doll's House* in 1956 to commemorate the 50th anniversary of Ibsen's death, they asked Mrs. Gerda Ring to be a co-instructor to the play. She had directed *A Doll's House* in Copenhagen in 1955, and her version had met with universal acclaim. The Chinese instructor, Mr. Wu Xue, was sent to Norway in the spring of 1956 to learn what he could about Ibsen and Norway. He visited all the places where Ibsen had grown up, and he watched all the Ibsen-performances that were put up in Norway to celebrate Ibsen. That year there was a super-abundance of plays, bad and excellent productions, and Wu Xue watched them all.

Mr. Wu Xue visited Gerda Ring several times and they had long talks about the play.[2] He brought three interpreters with him to each session, and the play was gone through in detail. He also received a lot of photographs of the performance of *A Doll's House* in Copenhagen; to some extent the stage decor from Copenhagen was copied into his Chinese Ibsen production.

Wu Xue was himself both an actor and a director. While she was in China, Gerda Ring saw him in a Chekov play, wherer he played in a completely Western style. He was a director of the China Youth Art Theater

(*Zhongguo Qingnian Yishu Juyuan*), at that time China's largest theater, with premises on Chang'an Street.

When Gerda Ring arrived in China, the auditions were finished, and the actors had been rehearsing for five weeks. They already knew the play by heart, and rehearsed without prompters. This was the rule all over China, and it was also the rule not to use prompters even during performances. The rehearsals took place on a smaller stage; they moved into the new, grand and completely renovated stage on the Chang'an Street just before the play opened. The atmosphere at the rehearsals was very like that of a Western one, the only difference being that the actors were dressed in white, the men in white trousers while the women wore long white dresses.

Having watched the first rehearsal Gerda Ring's thought was: "what on earth will be my job here." In acting, they had adopted an understated manner of playing that was also common in Norway at that time. This manner of playing had been introduced to Norway in the 1930s, and had been predominant since then. No grand gestures and demonstrations were to be found in their acting. Certain details remained to be discussed, though. Gerda Ring wanted to make one change in the cast. Dr. Rank was originally selected to convey the idea of an old medico, but to her conception of the play he was first and foremost a lover, not an elderly doctor. He walks in and out of Nora's house like a grey cat, consumed with love for her. Gerda Ring did not want to suggest a new actor, but she mentioned to Wu Xue that they had to work on making his image different. The very next day this "miscast" had been exchanged for a "lover-type" who, according to Gerda Ring, was exellent. He was tall and almost fair, with some extraordinary eyes that he used to watch Nora with, not obtrusively, but in the same understated manner that hinted at his passion and made the audience aware that he kept himself on a tight leash. The most difficult image of Dr. Rank to convey to the cast however, was his *fin-de-siecle* mentality, which the actors found difficult to understand.

Nora had also been selected before Gerda Ring arrived in China. Her name was Ji Shuping and she had played in *A Doll's House* before 1949. She loved the play so much that although she had tuberculosis, she refrained from telling people about it for fear of losing the part. Gerda Ring could remember her always being wet on the back, but not knowing the reason for this extreme perspiration. Ji Shuping had the greatest trouble with the final discussion, or debacle, scene. When they began rehearsing, she came to that scene with ready-made conclusions. After some time she learned to express the gradual development Nora goes through before reaching a new perception during the final scene with

Helmer. There was no need to explain or cut out Western effects in the play. When Dr. Rank receives his "death sentence" and sends out a little black cross, this was immediately understood by the actors and by the audience.

In all Gerda Ring's discussions of the play with Wu Xue, the political implications of play were only hinted at once. Wu Xue suggested that Helmer's attitude to Nora stemmed from his petty-bourgeois attitudes. Gerda Ring maintained that *A Doll's House* was first and foremost a play about a marriage, centering around the inner conflicts of Nora and Helmer. All other implications must be subordinate to that central theme. In the subsequent enacting of the play, Gerda Ring noticed no such political implications. She admitted that since she knew no Chinese, she may have misunderstood some of the finer points of the acting, but she claimed to know the play so well that she could follow every gesture and intonation in the story. If an actor made a wrong interpretation, it originated from the individual actor's temperament, and not from any deliberate interpretation on the part of the actor.

Gerda Ring also watched other Western productions while in Peking, among them one Russian (Chekov) and the Shaw commemorative selection. In her opinion, both performances would have benefited from the use of the understated manner of playing. There were too many exaggerated effects, too much stressing of points and too much overacting, which displeased her instructor's mind. Instead of conducting a dialogue with a fellow actor on stage, they were giving monologues to the audience. They all seemed overeager to emphasize any educational value a play might have, and this gave Mrs. Ring the impression that the actors wanted first and foremost that the audience should leave the theater with an elevated mind. She claimed that she had managed to instruct *A Doll's House* so that this element was not too prominent in her and Wu Xue's production.

As she summed up the Peking experience, she claimed that it had been very instructive to work within her own field with part of her own cultural heritage in a foreign environment. It gave a new dimension to her impression of Ibsen.

On July 26, 1956, a banquet to commemorate the 50th anniversary of Ibsen's death and the 100th anniversary of G. B. Shaw's birth was held. Mao Dun, the president for this arrangement, gave a speech. Tian Han, as the chairman of the Chinese Dramatists Association, spoke. An Englishman talked about Shaw, and Gerda Ring talked about Ibsen. Then one act from Shaw's play *The Apple Cart* and two acts from *Mrs. Warren's Profession* were shown.

The next day *A Doll's House* had its opening night, watched by an audience of two to three thousand people. An exhibition on Ibsen was opened at The National Library, and a special celebration meeting was held at Peking's largest assembly hall. There Wu Xue gave a long speech, Gerda Ring gave a short one and a Norwegian specialist gave a long exposé of Ibsen's dramatic art. The Norwegian Embassy reported home that it was amazing how the political emphasis on Ibsen was toned down during the festival.

The festival lasted for four days, from July 27th to the 31st, 1956. According to Ji Shuping, who played Nora, all the tickets to the first four performances were sold out one hour after the box-office opened. The intention had been to play *A Doll's House* only for a short time, but it turned out to be such a success that it was staged much longer. In Peking, the first halt in the playing came on August 7th, when Ji Shuping had to go to hospital for her tuberculosis. She then wrote a very moving letter to Gerda Ring, claiming her as her spiritual instructor-mother. Every time she stood before the audience she remembered her instructions, and she still strove to come further into "the soul quality and inner sight of Nora." Since the play met with such success, a parallel version with a new cast was planned, so that the two casts could alternate. As far as I have been able to ascertain, the alternation of two casts never happened, because every time Ji Shuping got out of hospital, she acted as Nora. The play was revived both in 1957, and one Westerner I met claimed to have seen it in Peking in 1959. It was also sent on a tour around China, and everywhere they had a full house. Selected parts of the play were made into a film, and distributed to various towns and districts as part of a commemorative film about Ibsen.

But, although the Norwegian Embassy noted that the emphasis on Ibsen as a social reformer had been toned down, it seems to me that the Chinese "authorities" — cultural people — in their speeches only draw attention to the ideas in Ibsen's plays, and hold them up against their ideology. Thus Mao Dun said in his speech:

> . . . the works of Shaw and Ibsen inspire a love for peace and freedom. As early as May 4th, Ibsen's ideas and sentiments expresed in his plays — that people must seek freedom and liberation — exercised a profound influence on the new literary movement in China.

Then Mao Dun mentioned Shaw as the great anti-imperialist, who placed himself firmly on the side of the socialist countries, and continued with Ibsen who:

> was concerned about the progress of mankind, and wrote plays connected with the society of his day. The Chinese commemorate him becausae his works encourage mankind to strive for freedom and liberation. The characters in his plays are pure-hearted, noble individuals.[3]

Tian Han continued in the same vein. Although the growth of modern Chinese drama owes much to China's own traditional heritage, it also owes Ibsen and Shaw a great debt. Ibsen especially deserves mention because, claimed Tian Hun, he:

> launched a vigorous struggle against hypocrisy and callousness in society, and for the emancipation of the individual. He voiced the people's strong demand for democracy, freedom, peace, and happiness, he resolutely exposed the evils of the capitalist society and the ugliness of the bourgeois philistines. Even though his aim was not always clear, he was able to call for a spiritual revolt against all outworn conventions.[4]

Ibsen is placed in a political frame, and Tian Han concludes that Ibsen could not overcome his petty-bourgeois conventions.

Wu Xue, in a long exposition on Ibsen, also becomes clearly political. He begins by telling what he experienced in Norway, all the places related to Ibsen that he saw with his own eyes etc. He sat through seven Ibsen performances in Norway, and watched a film of *A Doll's House*. When he finally gets down to the play, he takes as his starting point for discussion that Ibsen himself said that he did not have emancipation of women in his mind when he wrote *A Doll's House*. This Wu takes to imply that Nora:

> carries a much broader sense of importance than the mere emancipation of women and the struggle for women's suffrage. Ibsen was fighting against the unreasonable and progress-blocking social morality and social laws of the times, and against the trivial selfishness of ordinary citizens.[5]

And he continues in an article in *Renmin Ribao* on July 28th:

> Has not *Nora* (Chinese title for *A Doll's House*) still its sense of realism? For the theme of *Nora* had not only broached the problem of women's suffrage, it, through the life of Dr. Rank, the affairs of Krogstad and Mrs. Linde and especially the characterization of Nora's husband, Helmer, also unveiled the hypocritical civilization of the whole capitalist class and the inhuman customs and standards of morality.

Wu Xue thus endorses the official Chinese doctrine which claims that *A Doll's House* is a petty-bourgeois play that still may teach the Chinese something. But since they have achieved more in actual and real liberation than any capitalist country, where the seemingly great liberation hides a suppression of people, the message of *A Doll's House* is to a large extent a negative one. It can serve as a warning to older women who:

> like Nora, prior to her running away, concentrate their whole attention on the individual's affairs of odds and ends lacking the flight of imagination in occupation and life. And there are still husbands like Helmer, selfish and hypocritical.

There seems to be little difference between the political interpretation of *A Doll's House* before and after 1949. One reason for this is, of course, that the play was regarded as iconoclastic before 1949, and would thus be selected for performance by the same people who later came into power. From a desire to reform the whole world, the emphasis switched after 1949 to a desire to preserve the revolutionary fervor. A paraphrase of the contents of all the articles and discussions that appeared in connection with the performance of *A Doll's House* in 1956 runs as follows: Well, now we have had our revolution, we do not really need Nora because our society has advanced beyond these problems. But the drama should be staged to remind us of how hopeless a capitalist husband can be, and to show that some women chose the individualistic approach like Nora, and think only of themselves. A revolutionary girl will break out to reform society, she will not forego her obligations to improve herself only—such a limited outlook went overboard once the revolution arrived.[6]

After the Cultural Revolution came some halycone days, and things slowly began to move again. In 1978–1980, a dubbed Norwegian version of *A Doll's House* was shown on Chinese television. The debates following these showings had less emphasis on the ideological aspect than in 1956. Apart from the inevitable introductions to Ibsen, either by the old guard who grew up with him, or by the new who discovered him in 1978, there was more emphasis on his innovative role as a dramatist. His importance in the development of the Chinese *huaju* was stressed, and it was admitted that many Chinese men, and for that matter, Chinese women still needed to reform their minds. People were still not certain what the revolution was all about. The political message was still negative, but less so than in 1956, and there was a greater attempt to place China in a world context. The Norwegian version of *A Doll's House* was certainly not a production along didactic lines, and one gathers the impression that the social message was sufficiently blurred to make the debates more open.

The 1983–1984 Production of Peer Gynt

On the surface *Peer Gynt* is a drama about a young man who flees from his mother and his beloved. He leaves the small, rural village where he has grown up, goes abroad and makes a fortune. He loses the fortune and returns home, an old, destitute man. At home he finds that his beloved has waited faithfully for him all these years.

It is a drama in rhymed prose, full of humor, paradoxes and whims. It was primarily meant to be a drama to read, and Ibsen once mentioned

that he felt *Peer Gynt* would never be understood and appreciated outside of Scandinavia. But as the play moves from Norway to Africa and
back, so the production of it has moved around the world. It created a
stir in Japan, and the latest performance in the East is the Chinese one.

A few more words need to be said about the play and its main
character, Peer Gynt. He dominates the five acts and 38 scenes in the
play, living out his life both in reality and in his own imagination. he constantly flees reality, avoids difficulties and problems and eschews the
fundamental question — what is it to be oneself? This question is
predominant in the play, and is given several definitions, the most well-
known being the one that is given in the second act. Peer finds himself in
the palace of a trolling, (a troll is a kind of mountain monster, who may
have more than one head and usually has a tail, apart from that he is
often portrayed as none too bright) who the English version calls the
Dovre-master. His definition, when asked by Peer what the difference
between a human being and a troll is, is:

> Out there, under the radiant sky,
> They say "To thine own self be true."
> But here, in the world of trolls, we say
> "To thine own self be — all-sufficient!"

In the fourth act Peer finds himself in a madhouse in Cairo where he is
appointed king of the madhouse. Peer claims to have been himself all his
life, and the director accepts this with enthusiasm, saying that all the inhabitants in the madhouse are also true to themselves in a manner that
can be called all-sufficient.

In the last act Peer is confronted with a buttonmoulder who wants to
melt him down in order to create something new out of the raw material.
The buttonmoulder economizes thus with everybody who has not been
true to himself. Peer claims that he has been himself all his life, and asks
for time to prove it. He also asks the buttonmoulder what is meant by being oneself. The answer is: "To be one's self is to kill one's self." Peer
finds nobody who is willing to testify that he has been true to himself and
has almost given up hope when he is approached by the buttonmoulder
for the last time. As a last resort he asks his beloved, Solveig, who has
waited faithfully for him all her life, whether he has been himself. Her
reply gives him a respite from the buttonmoulder when she answers
Peer's question: "Where was I myself, the entire, true man? . . ." with:
"In my faith, in my hope, and in my love." One interpretation of this is
that it is possible to be oneself in the creativity of others, and that Peer,
who has never been true to himself, in the end must accept Solveig's
poetic vision of him as being true — in her hopes, her faith, and her love.

The merit of making it possible to make a production of *Peer Gynt* in China lies with Xiao Qian, author, essayist and translator. He had seen *Peer Gynt* on the London stage during the war, and been thoroughly fascinated by it. While watching it, the air-alarm went off, but the audience was so riveted by the play that they almost unanimously decided to remain, and not seek shelter. Xiao Qian himself tells that he was enraptured by the play. He also heard it twice on the wireless while in England and formed the ambitious decision to translate the play into Chinese. He brought back with him to China four different English versions of the play, but decided in the end that the translation was too demanding a task for him. He persuaded Pan Jiaxun, the most established Ibsen translator in the People's Republic, to have a try, and handed all his material over to Pan. Xio Qian was sent to the countryside in 1957, and heard nothing more about *Peer Gynt* before he returned to the intellectual scene in the mid-seventies. He then received a parcel from Pan Jiaxun, containing the four English versions of the play, and a letter of excuse. Pan had found himself unable to do it, and in 1976 he was also very ill.

In 1976 Xiao Qian was approached by the editor of *Shijie wenxue* and asked to contribute to the periodical. The only thing he could think of at the time was to have a try at *Peer Gynt*. He had only the four different English versions of the play and a small dictionary to help him along, and he had to work at the kitchen table. Having translated the first and the fifth acts, he delivered them to the editor, who vacillated for a long time before printing them. By that time Xiao Qian was so caught up with the play that he decided to translate the whole. By that time I had made contact with him, and was able to send him some material needed for a fuller comprehension of *Peer Gynt*.

The whole translation was subsequently published in *Waiguo xiju*, and professor Xu Xiaozhong of the Directing Department of the Central Academy of Dramatic Arts (*Zhongyang xiju xueyuan*) became so fascinated with it that he decided to try his hand at directing it. He sought Xiao Qian out (he was at that time in hospital) and asked leave to produce it. Since this had been one of Xiao's life ambitions, he was naturally very happy to say yes to this request.

The decision to stage the play having been made, the Norwegian Embassy was roped in to assist on questions of scenery, historical background, etc. A Norwegian student in China, formerly a student of drama history, was asked to help on occasions.

At the first meeting she attended, the three Chinese instructors, the translator and two or three other people from the Norwegian Embassy were present. The dramatic outline of the play was discussed, but it soon became evident that the Chinese had fixed ideas on how they wanted the performance to be. The Norwegian advisors tried as best as they could to argue against making it into a "Norwegian play," they feared that pseudo-Norwegian scenery, costumes and music would ruin the effects of the play, and draw attention from the dramatic tensions of *Peer Gynt*. The Chinese, on the other hand, were determined to make it as Norwegian as possible; one reason being that with a setting very different from China, they could take more political liberties. They could refer all the daring parts to "Norwegian-ness," and thus exempt themselves from criticism of being brazen. The Norwegian advisers received the strong impression that both setting and contents of the stage version of the play had been settled before their help was called upon. What the Chinese wanted from their Norwegian aides was assistance with national costumes, landscape, stage decor, etc. They were, as it were, technical assistants without any real influence on the production. As an example, the Norwegian girl mentioned that she had argued against the use of yellow wigs, but to no avail. She also mentioned that at the auditions and rehearsals where she had been present she felt as if she were in a classroom with strict discipline. None of the actors ever asked her a question, and she never knew what the actors made of the play.

When the Norwegian advisers asked why *Peer Gynt* was chosen, the answer was that there were political implications and lessons to be drawn from it. Parallels to the Gang of Four were constantly mentioned. The trolls and all that was negative in the play were taken as symbolic references to the Gang of Four. Another reason given was that Ibsen's name was so well-known that people would want to watch anything by him. It was only later, after having rehearsed for a long time, that the actors discovered that the play also could be great fun, and have entertainment value.

I do not know if the Norwegian advisers were asked about the music by Greig which is associated with *Peer Gynt* (and written for the play). They were, however, consulted about other suitable Norwegian folk-music, and settled upon a kind of accordian waltz that to my mind suggests dancing in the village harbor. This music was then contrasted to the decadent music of old-fashioned disco, thus utilizing good and bad music to underline the didactic lessons of the play. Disco music is used for effect both in the scene of the troll-king and in the mad-house scene in Cairo. My Norwegian informants admit that if one discarded one's own national conventions, this enhanced the dramatic value of the play.

A lot of dancing took place in the play. Folk-dancing was used to link one act with the other, and during practice the dancers used string around their long skirts so as not to stumble. The dancing itself had little to do with traditional movement in a classical opera, but it struck one of the Norwegian spectators (who has a liking for opera) when he finally watched the play in real performance, with the actors all dressed up in costumes and with make-up rather heavily laid on, and it gave him an impression of unreality almost as strong as a Peking opera. This same Norwegian had several discussions with the directors of the play, and he had argued against the heavy makeup and yellow wigs because he felt that the combination of yellow wig, national costume and heavy make-up gave a ludicrous effect. But the instructors maintained that the Chinese tradition of heavy make-up and the agility (or plasticity) of the actors added dimension to what he had seen of European performances. The Chinese instructors also claimed that one intention of the play was to give the students a deeper impression and understanding of Ibsen's dramatic art. The play could teach Chinese youths not to lose control and be utterly selfish whilst young.

Xiao Qian's exposition of how the play was transferred from a reading piece into a stage-play is in some respects more revealing about the Chinese ideas of the play. According to him, he first sat down with the instructors and cut the play down to an ordinary three hour performance. (This procedure all instructors have to go through, because a version of *Peer Gynt* without cuts would take about 8 hours.)

According to Xiao Qian, the following principles for cutting the play were laid down:

1. The play may be abridged, but as a great classic, it may not be changed.

2. Only the subordinate or minor episodes may be abridged, whereas the main thread or contour may not be damaged.

3. The long soliloquies may be shortened or taken out without impairing the message of the play.

4. All must be done to preserve the most famous or characteristic episodes.

5. The parts that are too obscure or ambiguous for a Chinese audience may be taken out.

Thus 38 scenes were cut down to 22. This resulted in the Chinese version placing a rather heavy emphasis on the young Peer, to the detriment of the middle-aged and old Peer. The young Peer appears in the first three acts; in the fourth act Peer is shown as a middle-aged man, successful as a businessman, idling away his time among sycophants, having nightmares on the beach, fighting with monkeys, finding a white horse and being seduced by an Arab girl, Anitra, who hails him as a prophet and steals his worldly goods. When she has galloped away on his white horse and left him in the desert, he finds himself in a madhouse in Cairo where he is proclaimed emperor. The Chinese kept only the Cairo madhouse scene thereby drawing attention to the parallel between the trolls and the madhouse. But they might as easily have drawn attention to the corrupt capitalist way of living or drawn a moral from the seductiveness of bad women.

The fifth act shows an old Peer returning to his native country. Not quite poor in the opening glimpses, he soon loses the rest of his wealth in a shipwreck. Gradually both his wealth, his illusions and ideas about himself are peeled away like the onion he himself peels to see if he can find a kernel in the end. The only place where he has been true to himself – through no effort of his own – is in the idea Solveig has of him in her own mind. In other words, his own kernel exists only in another's mind. This act, the most philosophical one, is also reduced by several scenes. One of the most famous scenes, and one most important to the main thread of the play, that of a priest giving a sermon over a deceased man who has his whole life been true to himself though never receiving praise or riches for that, was cut out. Presumably the idea of a sermon given by a priest would be too foreign for the Chinese, but from a philosophical point of view the play loses in dramatic impact.

The same subjection can be raised to the exclusion of the Boyg – a symbol of all that Peer avoids. Every difficulty Peer encounters, he avoids. He never cuts through any business, he prefers to bend with the wind and hope for the best. But this image is perhaps more difficult to convey to a not-too sophisticated audience.

The sermon of the priest is usually not left out of a Western production because of the parallel it offers to Peer's own life. It may be said, however, that the life of Solveig offers an equally interesting parallel because she too remains true to her own self and her own ideals. The Chinese actors had difficulties understanding how a good girl like Solveig could fall in love with and remain faithful to a good-for-nothing like Peer. In the performance the girl playing Solveig resembled any other bashful, simpering and stilted girl seen on the Chinese screen, except that her hair was yellow. She acted as a stereotype, and had she been any more stereotyped one could have thought that she was trying to give an example of the disengagement of emotions that Brecht wanted actors to display.

The alluring Anitra is also kept in Western performances, presumably because it adds to the vivacity of the play. But it might be argued that the seductiveness shown by the woman in green in the Chinese production of *Peer Gynt* had had a few parallels on the Chinese stage after 1949. To a

Chinese audience she must have appeared both daring and alluring, though the fact that she also wore a pig's mask somewhat reduced the allurement. But all in all, I found it an excellent example of innovation mixed with Chinese traditions, and it would be wrong to assume that the cuts made in the play were for purely political reasons.

The instructors clearly believed in the "Stanislavski mode of production." Before starting on the rehearsals, the actors discussed the play for more than two months, going in and out of explanations, intentions, interpretations and ramifications of the play. Similarities to the Cultural Revolution were mentioned; the scenes at the troll-king's palace and in the Cairo madhouse where everything is topsy-turvy, they thought were especially pertinent to those years. All the actors maintained that they had both a little of a troll, and a little of Peer in themselves. As they mention in their collective preface to the play's programme:

> "Everywhere man is confronted with: What is the true worth of man? What is man's aim in life? How should man live to avoid the dangers life confronts him with? Although Ibsen does not provide us with the ideal answer, he makes us think about these problems in his play."

To me it was of special interest to note what attempts the Chinese had made at portraying a Norwegian drama, and to what extent they had blended traditional Chinese drama with the modern production. In the stage decor one could say that the ideal of simplicity of the classical opera was wedded to a few obviously foreign stage props such as a Norwegian lofted hut and a huge sphinx. There were never many items on the stage, as a rule it was kept bare and open. Suggestions of landscape and mood were given by sifting light of varying color through some gauze at the back of the stage, and snow and wood effects were achieved in the same manner. Some of the symbolic gestures also bore a strong resemblance to traditional Chinese acting, such as a pig's dance in the manner and style of the lion dance, and certain acrobatic features related to fighting scenes. The idea of portraying a troll — or a mountain monster as a pig is certainly very foreign to a Norwegian,[8] but nevertheless very effective. As a summing up, one might say that the suggestive scenery and the bare necessity of the stage-props in the production of *Peer Gynt* represents a turning away from the realistic setting towards the abstract stage of the classical opera.

Xiao Qian also drew my attention to the change of color on the face of the buttonmoulder, who in the last act wants to recast Peer into a new form. Sichuan opera uses change of face color to create a sense of terror in the audience, and the same effect was used in *Peer Gynt* with great result.

Both the Chinese audience and the Europeans who saw the play agree that Peer carried the day. He acted with such vigor and exuberance that he became ill after a few days. People were impressed, both with his vitality and with his creditable transformation into an old man. It would also be mentioned that in all the acting sentimentality was kept down to a degree remarkable to a Chinese performance. Although the disco music that was played during the scenes in the troll king's hall and in the madhouse did not convey the same feeling of decadence to a European as it perhaps did to a Chinese, it was certainly an effective accompaniment to the scenes.

As a production, *Peer Gynt* was not given the same official atention as the 1956 production of *A Doll's House*. It was put up by the fourth-year students at the Central Academy of Dramatic Arts, and less of the official paraphernalia that surrounded *A Doll's House* was visible. But the production did stir up some attention, both in Norway and in Chinese drama circles. For a real comparison of Western-Chinese co-productions it might have been more appropriate to look at *A Doll's House* in 1956 and *Death of a Salesman* which Arthur Miller directed to a Chinese cast in Peking in 1983.[9] But to my mind it is clearly possible to draw some implications from the production of *A Doll's House* in 1956 and that of *Peer Gynt* in 1983. Both involved cooperation between two countries and two theatrical traditions. But the interaction between the two and the influence from the Western tradition is markedly less in the *Peer Gynt* production.

No box-office was connected with the staging of *A Doll's House*; it was all done under official auspices. But due to the fame of Nora, the play might even have been a financial success. Nora was after all a cardboard model for Chinese youth in the 1920s and 1930s. After 1949 she somehow lost most of her glamour, but a lingering attraction remained. She acquired no new facets to her personality, and in the comments on the 1956 performances she is a one-dimensional, abstract person.

Peer Gynt had no official backing but owed its appearance more to private initiative. The decision to stage it was unofficial and taken for purely theatrical reasons. Since it was put up as a student performance, the box-office was not taken into consideration. The instructor did claim, however, that he hoped to trade a little on the fame of Ibsen in China.

A Dolls' House is an easy play to stage and the Chinese might have drawn heavily on their own *huaju* traditions when they decided to perform it. But the production was intended as a showpiece for the new cultural policies where the overriding ambition appears to have been to show accuracy in every stage-prop detail. This involved close cooperation between China and Norway, with the result that the Western interpretation of the play was superimposed upon the more simplistic and ideological Chinese *huaju* tradition. I use the word superimposed because in their articles neither the Chinese instructor nor other Chinese commentators show any awareness of the inner conflicts of Nora, or mention that *A Doll's House* may be interpreted as a play about a marriage.

A little facetiously it might be said that the Chinese reflections on *A Doll's House* were as simple as the outer appearance of the play. It is a chamber play with only one setting, few actors and a lucid story. The evaluations of the play in China tend to run along the same lines. The possible depths of the actual performance were provided by the Western instructor, whilst her Chinese counterpart, at least in public, made biographical and ideological interpretations along traditional Communist lines. The interaction with a Western instructor may, however, have given impetus to Chinses actors' attempts for declamation. Through the Cultural Revolution, however, most of the actors active before 1966 lost some of their best years. Ji Shuping, who played Nora in 1956, admitted that she would no longer be able to play Nora again, and to her that was a bitter thought.

The Norwegian, dubbed version of *A Doll's House* shown on the Chinese television in 1978–1979, represented high Western culture and must, to most of the audience, have appeared as a refined problem drama dwelling on inner middle class life in the city. But the debates in Chinese journals show a greater perception of some aspects of the play. Ibsen has been promoted from a Nineteenth Century iconoclast, limited by his class and time, to a serious playwright whose drama could still be of interest even in socialist China. Instead of being a self-centered individualist, Nora is now seen as a common denominator for female emancipation even within a socialist country. But even in 1978–1979 there is still no discussion of Nora as the pleasure-bringing creature, spontaneous like a child in her happiness and with a capacity for transforming her love to the highest level. Her visionary idea of a marriage where "the wonderful" might happen might have been contrasted with her total disregard for social obligations and rules within society, thereby providing an interesting starting point for a discussion of ways and means for revolutionary women.

But both in 1956 and in 1978–79 the debates about *A Doll's House* rely on the play as a clear-cut topical play on the cruder issues of female emancipation. Nora is an individual but the Chinese perceive her more as an abstract model. *Peer Gynt*, however, becomes more real through his purely theatrical appeal, and is viewed as both more individualistic and more human than Nora.

Peer Gynt is certainly no drawing-room comedy. It breaks every rule there is for drama, except that of being entertaining, and it demands a lot both technically and in the acting. It is almost as if the complexity and imaginativeness of the drama itself infected the Chinese instructors and critics. The blending of Western and Chinese traditions and the artistic subtleties of the play were decided purely by the Chinese, with little assistance from outside. Scenes and items that might appeal to the didactically-minded Chinese as well as scenes made purely for entertainment were decided upon more from an artistic consideration than from ideological motives.

The instructor Xu Xiaozhong, in articles about the play, compares it with traditional opera.[10] *Peer Gynt* is episodic in its structure like most song-dance dramas of China, and it demands as much from the audience's imagination. When Peer rides his white horse in the desert the pantomine element can be compared with what a Chinese actor performs in a traditional play. In his instructions Xu attempted to give the essence of what Ibsen had meant with the play. The lack of logic in the play Xu feels is intentional from Ibsen's hand. It emphasizes that Peer himself is without logic and system in his search for his true self. The conflict of the outer appearance and the inner essence is what the instructor must strive to convey to the audience.

Xu does not mention specifically that he wanted to draw parallels to the Chinese tradition of a lover caught between one passive and good woman and one aggressive and passionate. But he wanted the audience to "step outside" of the play when he portrayed The Woman in Green, and he thus emphasized her unrealistic character. Opposed to her is Solveig, who is both good and loyal. She is absent from the play for a long time, and in order to keep her in the mind of the audience he had Solveig's song played in an intermission. When she makes her reappearance in the final scene of the play, she certainly epitomizes the Chinese ideal of a docile, passive and good woman.

The critic's evaluation of *Peer Gynt* are also more complex than was the case with *A Doll's House*, even in 1978–79. Admittedly they draw attention to the main message of the play, that of the troll philosophy versus the human ideals, but they are also struck with the similarity in the relationship between Peer and his mother and an ordinary Chinese mother-son relationship, with its ups and downs. As a whole the audience shows sympathy with Peer because of his many weaknesses and feels compassion with the ambiguity within his character. Thus a complex adventurer becomes more of an individual and less of a didactical example than Nora.

According to eye witnesses, the audience viewing *A Doll's House* in 1956 was comprised of intellectuals and the urban middle-class. However, the play was sent out to tour the countryside, where the audience presumably also included workers and peasants. Through television the play reached larger audiences in 1978–79, but the impact appears to have been on the urban intelligentsia.

The translator of *Peer Gynt*, Xiao Qian, was extremely pleased to note that the audience watching the play comprised many levels of society. He had watched the play several times, and every time took care to interview some of the audience about their impressions. He had talked to both young and old, workers and intellectuals, and the play seemed to have a universal appeal. This is of course a highly subjective impression of the audience, but it may well be that *Peer Gynt*, staged as it were as a mixture of Chinese and Western theater, held an attraction for a wider audience than *A Doll's House*. Some of the younger people in the audience had also read the play and voiced the opinion that the instructor had oversimplified the message of the play and distracted attention from the subtler elements of it. Some had also argued that the instructor had atempted to dazzle the audience with technical gimmicks.

One may conclude that there has been a progression in theatrical possibilities in China from 1956 to 1983, and this may be exemplified through the "career" of Ibsen. From being merely a social innovator he has become a dramatist in his own right, and several facets have been added to his dramatic art. In her summing up of the situation of the performing arts in China after 1949, Bonnie McDougall makes the following statement:

> In the 1950's and early 1960's, the co-existence of modern drama and traditional opera epitomized the tendency toward cultural diversity that undermined the national goal of a unitary mass culture. On the one hand was opera, a traditional form highly popular at different audience levels but highly resistant to revolutary modernization . . . On the other hand was the drama, a modernized form patronized almost exclusively by the urban intelligentsia and obviously designed to transmit a modern revolutionary content."[12]

Perhaps the dream of a unitary (and uniform) mass culture has faded and an idea of diversity within a cultural life has come to the forefront. And perhaps a greater assurance, both within China's traditional drama and in relation to Westernized *huaju* will open up for a successful blending of Western and Chinese dramatic styles. The complexities in both the instruction and in the acting of *Peer Gynt* may have started a trend of theatrical innovation with appeal to both the intellectuals and to other elements within society. If artistic considerations will be allowed to take precedence over didactic purposes, the new theater form may have a hope of surviving in China.

Notes

1. Elisabeth Eide: "*Huaju* performances of Ibsen in China," *Acta Orientalia*, Cph., 44, 1983. pp. 95–112.

2. Interviews with Gerda Ring in 1972 and 1982.

3. Programme to the commemorative performance of H. Ibsen, Peking, 1956.

4. Ibid.

5. *Renmin ribao*, 27.7.1956.

6. It may be of some interest to note here that in 1956, the Chinese society of the University of Hong Kong put up *A Doll's House*. It was played in Cantonese; the actors basing their performance on a translation of *A Doll's House* by a man who styled himself "Only Me" or "Alone With Myself." The actors admitted that they had taken liberties with both the text and the translation in order to make the play sound "real," they had also abridged it somewhat. But in their programme one finds hardly a trace of didactic purpose, nor do any political overtones mar the introduction. The ideal, model housewife of Nora in the first act is compared with the traditional Chinese concept of how a model wife should behave. Any model wife would have falsified a cheque in order to save her husband, but no model wife would on any account have left her husband and children. The example of Nora offers a new ideal image and gives her Chinese counterpart the possibility of opting out if she feels her true identity to be endangered by marriage. A marriage that suppresses the woman and leaves her no room for self-realization can take Nora as a model. Here edificatory purposes shine through, but still on a smaller and more subdued scale than in Peking.

7. Interviews with Xiao Qian in 1982 and 1984. During his visit to Norway in 84, Xiao gave a talk on *Peer Gynt* in China. I have used parts of this unpublished talk in my paper.

8. In the play, however, the greenclad girl rides on a pig.

9. See: Miller, Arthur: *Salesman in Beijing*, (N.Y.: Viking Press, 1984).

10. See: Xu Xiaozhong in his two articles: "*Peini Jinte*" de daoyan gousi," *Xiju suexi*, 4, 1983 and "Zai xian Ibusheng," *Xiju bao*, 8, 83.

11.   For another subjective impression see: McDougall, Bonnie, "Writers and Performers, Their Works, and Their Audiences in the First Three Decades." pp. 269-304. In: McDougall, Bonnie (ed), *Popular Chinese Literature and Performing Arts in the People's Republic of China, 1949-1979.* (Berkley, University of California press, 1984) p. 287.

12.   Ibid., p. 291.

Glossary

Ji Shuping	冀淑平
Mao Dun	茅盾
Pan Jiaxun	潘家洵
Shanghai xiju xueyuan	上海戏剧学院
Shijie wenxue	世界文学
Tian Han	田汉
Waiguo Xiju	外国戏剧
Wu Xue	吴雪
Xiao Qian	萧乾
Xu Xiaozhong	徐晓钟
Zhongguo qingnian yishu juyuan	中国青年艺术剧院
Zhongyang xiju xueyuan	中央戏剧学院

14. Conclusion

COLIN MACKERRAS

The period of the Peoples Republic has seen far-reaching changes in China, not only when one measures it against earlier eras but also when one compares particular years or sets of years with others within the period itself. China is a highly integrated society, and consequently changes in society as a whole have affected, and been reflected in, Chinese drama. The papers in the present book highlight many of these changes, because all the decades since 1949 are represented and covered in them. The drama of the Cultural Revolution period, and its theory, are utterly different from the counterparts of either the 1950s or the 1980s.

So it is that the arrangement of this volume, although mainly thematic, is also chronological as well. Part One, which concerns drama on historical themes, takes more examples from the pre-Cultural Revolution years than any other. Part Two on theory includes more material on the Cultural Revolution years than either before or after them. Part Three is specifically chronological, dealing entirely with the eight years separating the fall of the Gang of Four in October 1976 from the Conference on which the volume is based, which took place in October 1984. In fact, the great bulk of the material in Part Three concerns the early 1980s rather than the late 1970s.

The introduction by Constantine Tung quite properly gives the theme prominence by tracing how it has operated through the various different periods. It emerges strongly in more or less every paper in the book. It is true that in some periods of the PRC this relationship has functioned more oppressively or constrained creativity more tightly than in others. The pictures that emeges from Ellen Judd's paper on dramatic theory during the Cultural Revolution shows a vastly more controlled drama than those from Constantine Tung's on Bai Fengxi or Daniel Yang's on theater activities in general in the 1980s. Yet politics is never irrelevant in the Chinese theater. There is not a single play or drama discussed in the present book which can really be called apolitical.

326

It has been said that "he who controls the present, controls the past." This aphorism is nowhere more true than in China, where in all ages the current victor has been able and willing to write history according to its own political and ideological predilections. Since drama is, and has long been, a good way of imparting a notion of the national history to the people, it follows that dramas reflecting history are likely to feel the weight of the current line.

A section of this book has been quite properly devoted to the theme of dramas on historical themes. Wu Han's *The Dismissal of Hai Rui*, the item considered by Lin Chen, attained great fame becausae unrelenting criticism of it introduced the Cultural Revolution. Lin Chen's focus is on the play as the expression of opposition to Mao in the late 1950s. He considers that Wu Han's stature as a true historian lies precisely in his ability to look beyond his own interest as a person or member of a group. Wu Han's play is set in the past, but it is the present that is really under review. Wu Han criticized that present and paid the price for doing so.

Guo Moruo, discussed in Bruce Doar's paper, took precisely the opposite approach. His concern was to revise historical judgments not in order to criticize the current political order but to defend it. In particular, he presented the Empress Wu in a far more favorable light than had been done traditionally in order to show that a woman could indeed hold a ruling position and do so well. In a very real sense Guo Moruo thus defends women's rights and upholds a doctrine espoused by the Chinese Communist Party.

Part Two of the book deals with theoretical problems relating to drama. Judd's and Denton's papers focus on the "model dramas" of 1966 to 1976, though from different perspectives. Judd takes an anthropological view but does not consider any of the "model dramas" in particular. She criticizes this "prescriptive" theory, in particular because it bases itself on class conflict yet always brings resolution as the drama's result, but she certainly does not dismiss it out of hand. Denton's paper takes a semiotic look at one particular sample of the "model dramas": *Taking Tiger Mountain by Strategy*. His analysis of the function of this drama as myth concludes that it "creates a world which denies the 'complexities of human acts' and the dialectics of human history. It imposes a simple world of blissful clarity." This is consistent with Judd's conclusion.

Sun Huizhu looks at theory from a much wider perspective, one which spans not ten years but the whole of Chinese history. He traces three "systems" of drama, Mei Lanfang's being in effect the Chinese tradition, Stanislavsky's the Western innovative modern realism, and Brecht's a partial return to the traditional theater and rejection of realism. "The purpose of rejuvenating the old forms was to help modern men see the deeper meaning of life through distorted images." Sun sees the future of Chinese theater in the Brechtian system. It has been gaining ground since 1978, he believes, and will grow much stronger in the course of time.

Adrian Hsia deals with the ideas of a single Chinese theater director, Huang Zuoling of the Shanghai People's Art Theater. Since Huang is renowned as the most influential follower of Brecht in China, this paper nicely embellishes Sun's treatment of the three systems and sets one of them in deeper context. Hsia inevitably addresses the interrelationship between Chinese and Western theaters. He argues that although Huang is not using Brecht's foreign theory to explain Chinese drama, he is indeed relying on Brecht more or less to prove that Chinese traditional drama is a superior art form. "If anything is regrettable," he states, "then it sould be the fact that Huang needed Brecht to prove this to the Chinese."

Part Three of the book deals with drama since the death of Mao and the fall of the Gang of Four in 1976. This has been a short period but one of great development and interest. One can pinpoint two main landmark events from a political and policy point of view, namely the Third and Sixth Plenary Sessions of the Eleventh Central Committee which took place, respectively, in December 1978 and June 1981. The first gave full emphasis to modernization and opened the lid on criticism of the Cultural Revolution, while the second condemned that phenomenon officially and more or less totally. Social change in the direction of private enterprise, liberalism and individualism has gathered momentum in the 1980s in a way which would have been barely predictable or imaginable during the Mao years.

Part Three considers how the many different changes are reflected in the world of theater. Two papers, Daniel Yang's and my own, attempt general surveys, but from very different aspects. Yang's focus is on the dramas themselves, while mine gives most space to considering the reforms in the organization of theater troupes, the function of the semi-professional in the theater, and the issue of how modernization and the theater relate to and affect each other.

Several papers in this section consider individual spoken plays or playwrights. These include *If I Were For Real* (1979), to which Gilbert Fong's paper is devoted, and two plays by the female dramatist Bai Fengxi, *When the Bright Moon Shines* (1981) and *An Old Friend Comes at a Stormy Time* (1983), both discussed in Constantine Tung's paper and the latter also in mine. In addition, one paper, that of Helmut Martin, deals with a fictional drama called *Tragic Song of our Time*, the production of which is part of the plot of a novel first published in 1983.

These plays all reflect the period when they were written and illustrate the increased liberalism and individualism, though still within constraints, of the years since the Third Plenum. *Tragic Song of our Time* denounces the Cultural Revolution and is in this respect like not only many other dramas but also the Sixth Plenum. Despite its being fictional, this drama raises the same issues as authentic theater. It is a case study of the examination of reality in fiction and consequently of relevance to this book. Martin interprets the play to extrapolate the role of the author and intellectual as social critics. They become the dissidents, the protestors of society, often in opposition to the Party.

The two plays of Bai Fengxi break away from concerns posed by the Cultural Revolution and address the social problems of women; as Tung puts it, they challenge "the traditions and moral codes of a stubborn society." Their heroines' moral convictions and courageous struggles are the manifestations of daring quests of individualism. Politics and individualism are not necessarily mutually exclusive, although certain types of political control can stifle individualism. During the Cultural Revolution the Party tried consciously to eliminate individualism, which it considered to be counter-revolutionary and harmful. The milder climate of the 1980s has removed this constraint and Tung has shown the influence of individualism on a major playwright of the 1980s.

The central interest of *If I Were for Real* is that its focus is a full-scale attack on corruption among senior cadres, not in the past or during the Cultural Revolution, but in the here and now. Although the ending paints a reasonably optimistic view of society, the thrust of the play is critical. The central character who is most unusual in Chinese drama of any period in being a negative hero, can say "I was wrong because I was a fake. . . If I were real, . . . then everything I've done would have been completely legal." Fong points out that there is a strong feeling of class discrimination in the play, but it is the cadres who are guilty, the masses who suffer. The notion of class conflict survives, but in a form utterly different from that of the Cultural Revolution, when the Party and the masses took a united class stand against reactionaries such as the Japanese invaders or the Guomindang.

The last section of the book takes up another important aspect of Chinese drama, namely the role of foreign theater. This was substantial in the 1950s, mainly from the countries of Eastern Europe and those espousing neutralism. During the Cultural Revolution foreign influence was more or less suppressed altogether, and in 1974 a formal campaign denounced even Beethoven. However, since 1976 admiration for things foreign, including Western, has grown enormously and is producing a notable impact on Chinese theater. Two papers address this aspect, both concerning Western theater. One is about the music theater of a nation,

Austria, the other a particular progressive and important dramatist, Ibsen.

Eide writes that Ibsen "has been promoted from a nineteenth-century iconoclast, limited by his class and time, to a serious playwright whose drama could still be of interest even in socialist China." Ibsen's work raises political and social issues which are highly relevant to China today and Eide points them out through a detailed analysis of the 1956 production of *A Doll's House* and the 1983 performance of *Peer Gynt* in China. Austria has produced a theater as fine as any in the world, as names like Mozart will testify, but despite its popularity in certain times among particular classes in China, as demonstrated by Kaminski's and Unterrieder's paper, Austrian theater has never really entered the mainstream of Chinese drama development. Unlike Ibsen's plays, the main Austrian contribution to drama does not bear directly on social and political issues of relevance and concern to theater audiences in China.

Part Four on foreign theater brings to mind the vitally important issues of Western influence on Chinese spoken drama and of the emergence of a national spoken drama. In the case of the traditional music-drama, China had, and has, a unique form of theater which is instantly identifiable as Chinese. But the spoken play was introduced originally into China from the West through Japan. Playwrights, performers, directors and others must wrestle with the problem of how effectively to sinicize an initially foreign form. The issue becomes more acute in the 1980s because of the substantial and probably increasing foreign, especially Western, cultural influence in China since the late 1970s. Almost all Chinese spoken dramas are set in China and deal with Chinese problems; they use the Chinese language. But that is hardly enough to claim a "national' spoken drama. Issues of style, technique, absorption of qualities like pathos, tragedy, freedom, psychological tension, become important. Few would still argue against foreign influence altogether, but how does one distinguish between those strands which assist the development of "national" spoken drama and those which impede it? What are the criteria that help those in the Chinese theater to know when a foreign importation has blended well enough with Chinese elements to enter the mainstream of any effective "national" theater?

Most of the plays discussed in this book cast judgments on society or on particular groups within it. The great majority take sides. The historical plays put forward a definite and clear view not only about the past personages with whom they deal but also about those of the present. The dramas of the Cultural Revolution were explicit in praising revolutionaries but blaming the class enemy or the traitor. Plays of the 1980s likewise cast their value judgments, more subtly no doubt but clearly all the same. The majority, it is true, reserve their harshest barbs for anti-social phenomena like conventions discriminating against women. When they attack what the Party has done they usually refer to the period of the Cultural Revolution. A drama such as *If I Were for Real* is definitely exceptional and it is not surprising that it should have come up against official censure.

If the plays themselves cast judgments, it is as well to remember that so do the critics of the plays, including the various authors of the papers in this book. Just as the dramas put forward observations about society, we as authors are reacting not only to the plays but also to the society which produced them. This is not a bad thing, since scholarship is quite entitled, indeed ought, to draw judgments from analysis.

The assumptions and priorities from which the authors begin obviously affect the judgments which they reach. Thus it is that some authors are harshly critical of Chinese society and see playwrights as straining for freedom within its tight restrictions. Others are more sympathetic to the aims which underpin Chinese society, while still admiring the playwrights and the works they produce. There is an overall sense of enthusiasm for Chinese theater in the People's Republic in the papers of this book, and that is to be expected, since few people are prepared to take trouble over studying what they dislike. Nevertheless, there is quite clearly political and aesthetic cleavage among the authors, a diversity which adds both variety and interest to their commentaries.

Another source of divesity which emerges strongly from the papers in this book is the interdisciplinary nature of drama in general and Chinese drama in particular. The overriding theme of the political nature of drama emphasizes the value of drama to the political scientist. The literary nature of drama is also vital, as seen in many of the papers. One aspect of critical importance which comes forward in Sun's and Denton's papers is drama as performance. Judd's and Denton's papers identify philosophy as a discipline relevant to drama, Lin's and Doar's history, and my own shows the drama's relationships with society and the economy. The discipline of international relations bears on the papers of Else Unterrieder and Gerd Kaminski and Elisabeth Eide. The comparatively new study of semiotics is the focus of Denton's paper. And this listing is not exhaustive. Moreover, the possibility of including some papers under several headings shows the integration of the disciplines in the study of drama.

It is thus obvious both that the tools of many disciplines can assist in the study of drama and that Chinese theater can tell us an enormous amount a whole range of aspects of China. In some areas drama may be no more than a supplementary source, but in others it could be more central. Thus, nobody would treat a drama seriously as a record of a political event, because drama is not history and makes no pretense to be. But what characters in a set of dramas *say* about a political event, their *reaction* to it, might tell us an enormous amount, not only about the author's views but even about popular feeling, and such attitudes and opinions might be very difficult indeed to find out through other sources. Moreover, this observation is valid whether the dramas in question are set in the present, the recent or the distant past. Drama is in a real sense an important source of knowledge and understanding about the PRC, and especially in the 1980s, when the variety of subjects covered, the range of emotions expressed, has expanded to an unprecedented extent.

It follows that the theater of the PRC is an important subject. It is well worth study for its own aesthetic and literary value and for its bearing on other topics associated with contemporary China. It is both fortunate and not surprising to find it a growing field of research both in China and the West.

The present contribution to this research does not pretend to be comprehensive. The focus selected is the relationship with politics. Although quite a few other approaches quite rightly intrude into so broad and important an overall theme, there are many which are more or less or entirely neglected. Thus, there is not very much coverage of the vast repertoire of purely traditional music drama, or the several hundred regional styles in which it still not only exists but thrives in China today. The livelihood and social status of the author, actor, actress, theater-manager or the whole range of people who make performance possible are touched upon only marginally. Music has always played a central role in most forms of Chinese drama and even to this day it is a rare spoken play which gives it no place at all. Yet there are only isolated references to this topic.

Two important aspects of the Chinese spoken play which deserve further research are language and stagecraft. Both receive some attention here, but rarely are they the focus of attention. The discussions of dramatic ideal and theory give some material on styles of acting and attitudes towards stagecraft, certainly enough to emphasize their significance. But issues such as how language, methods of performance, makeup, costuming, scenery, stage properties and so on are handled in the Chinese spoken play and what changes have taken place over the last few years in these areas are still understood only imperfectly. How does the operation of such techniques affect the political and social content of the spoken play in China?

Another approach to drama worthy of much more research is its function in communication. It is mentioned here separately and specially because of its relevance to politics and thus to the dominant theme of this book. In any society, people tend to derive their images of good or bad from fictional characters, and in China drama still reaches the masses much more extensively than novels. It cannot fail to influence the way they think. Although the study of semiotics can help illustrate and clarify how this happens, further research is necessary to compare the differing communicative impact of the various forms of drama and the influence which they exercise on particular class, age, occupation and gender groups, and so on. It is only very recently that the ideas of a social survey has taken root as desirable in China, and the way may soon be open to undertake systematic research on drama as communication.

According to the policy of the current Chinese government, supported by most counterparts around the world, the future of China lies in economic and social modernization. Much of what happens in the theater can be interpreted as an attempt to make drama part of this process. A richer and more varied cultural life, higher technical standards, can be construed as part of a better standard of living, which is part of modernization. The increasing cultural and ideological freedom is considered by many to be a "fifth modernization," but it remains limited.

Since the beginning of this century, Chinese dramatists and the performing profession have wrestled with the problem of combining modern forms of various kinds with their own tradition. The liberation of China by the CCP gave the problem new dimensions but did not solve it. The Cultural Revolution offered one way out, but it failed to gain support and proved ephemeral. The post-Mao years have seen an explosion in the debate on just how one integrates new, foreign and good ideas on theater with a magnificent tradition which nobody wants to sacrifice. How does one select and absorb foreign influences in such a way as to promote a truly traditional theater? Will modernization, which everybody also wants, help or hinder traditional art-forms, and how does one preserve the best of both worlds? Sun Huizhu's paper presents an optimistic framework for answering these questions. But, even if he is right, it should surprise nobody if, in a century's time, Chinese dramatists are still exploring how best to integrate modernization and tradition in the theater.

Notes on Contributors

Lin Chen, Ph.D., University of Chicago, is associate professor of political science at Furman University, South Carolina.

Kirk A. Denton is a doctoral candidate in Chinese literature at the University of Toronto, Canada. He is currently at work on his doctoral dissertation, a study of the fiction of the modern Chinese writer Lu Ling.

Bruce Gordon Doar has studied at Sydney University, Australia and Beijing University. He has completed a doctoral dissertation on developments in drama and dramatic criticism in the late-Qing and early Republic periods. He is currently at Macquarie University, Sydney, Australia.

Elisabeth Eide is a doctoral candidate in philosophy with a major in Chinese at the University of Oslo, Norway, and is Librarian at the Royal Library, Oslo, in charge of the Chinese Department since 1973.

Gilbert C. F. Fong received his Ph.D. from the University of Toronto, and now teaches Chinese literature at York University, Canada.

Adrian Hsia studied German literature in Cologne and West Berlin where he received his doctorate, and now is on the faculty of the German Department, McGill University, Canada since 1968. He is the author of *Hermann Hesse and China* and a book on the Cultural Revolution; he is also editor of *Goethe and China* and *German Philosophers on China*.

Ellen R. Judd is a social anthropologist specializing in the study of symbolic production in China. She studied and did research in China from 1974 to 1977, including a year (1975–1976) studying literature and drama at Fudan University, Shanghai. She currently teaches anthropology at the University of Western Ontario, Canada.

Gerd Kaminski received his Doctoral degree of Dr. Habil from the University of Vienna. He is a dozen at the University of Vienna, director of the Ludwig Boltzmann Institute for Research on China and Southeast Asia, Vienna and adjunct professor of Chinese at the State University of New York at Buffalo. His publications include *China Gemalt-Chinesische Zeitgeschichte In Bildern Friederich Schiffs* (Vienna, 1983) and *Austrians and Chinese: A History of Austrian-Chinese Relations* (Vienna, -Munich-Zurich, 1980, in German).

Colin Mackerras has been Foundation Professor in the School of Modern Asian Studies, Griffith University, Australia since 1974 and was School Chairman from 1979 to 1985. He has written widely about Chinese theater and history. His main publications include *The Rise of the Peking Opera* (Oxford, 1972), *The Performing Arts in Contemporary China* (London, 1981), and *Modern China: A Chronology* (London, 1982).

Helmut Martin is Dean of the Faculty of East Asian Studies and Professor of Chinese Language and Literature, Ruhr-University Bochum, Federal Republic of Germany. He has edited since 1984 for the German publishers Diederichs Verlag a series of translations from contemporary Chinese literature, and is the author of many works on Chinese literature and politics.

William Huizhu Sun a playwright and critic, received his M.A. from Shanghai Drama Institute and M.A. from the Department of Theater and Dance, State University of New York at Buffalo. Currently he is pursuing a doctoral degree in theater in the United States.

Constantine Tung received his Ph.D. from the Claremont Graduate School, California and is on the faculty of State University of New York at Buffalo, teaching Chinese language and literature. He has published numerous studies on modern and contemporary Chinese literature and drama.

Else Unterrieder is deputy director of the Ludwig Boltzmann Institute for Research on China and Southeast Asia, Austria. She has published works on Chinese folk arts.

Daniel S. P. Yang is professor of Theater at the Department of Theater and Dance, University of Colorado, Boulder. He is also Producing Director of the Colorado Shakespeare Festival. Dr. Yang is author of a book, five translated plays and many scholarly articles on traditional Chinese theater and on Shakespeare, published in the U.S., China, Taiwan and Hong Kong.

Index

339